Charles Ludwig's

MOTHER
OF AN
ARMY

CHAMPION
OF
FREEDOM

Two books in one special volume

Charles Ludwig's

MOTHER OF AN ARMY

CHAMPION OF FREEDOM

Bethany House Publishers
Minneapolis, Minnesota 55438
A Division of Bethany Fellowship, Inc.

Published by Bethany House Publishers
A Division of Bethany Fellowship, Inc.
6820 Auto Club Road, Minneapolis, Minnesota 55438

Printed in the United States of America
First Combined Edition for Christian Herald
Family Bookshelf: 1988

Library of Congress Cataloging-in-Publication Data

Ludwig, Charles, 1918–
    Mother of an Army.

    Bibliography: p.
    1. Booth, Catherine Mumford, 1829–1890—Fiction.
2. Salvation Army—History—Fiction.   I. Title.
PS3523.U43M6   1987   813'.52   86–33439
ISBN   0–87123–924–8

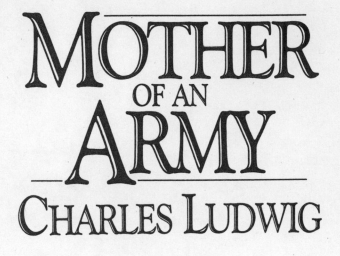

MOTHER
OF AN
ARMY

CHARLES LUDWIG

BETHANY HOUSE PUBLISHERS
MINNEAPOLIS, MINNESOTA 55438
A Division of Bethany Fellowship, Inc.

Published by Bethany House Publishers
A Division of Bethany Fellowship, Inc.
6820 Auto Club Road, Minneapolis, Minnesota 55438

Printed in the United States of America

Library of Congress Cataloging-in-Publication Data

Ludwig, Charles, 1918–
    Mother of an army.

    Bibliography: p.
    1. Booth, Catherine Mumford, 1829–1890—Fiction.
2. Salvation Army—History—Fiction.   I. Title.
PS3523.U434M6   1987   813'.52   86–33439
ISBN 0–87123–924–8

In memory of another
indomitable woman—
Twyla Innes Ludwig,
distinguished missionary to
Kenya. Mother was born in
1890, the year Catherine
Booth was promoted to glory.

Author Charles Ludwig grew up on the mission field in Kenya. He brings to his second historical novel with BHP an impressive writing experience, having more than forty books already published, several of which have been read or dramatized on worldwide radio. Ludwig also has a rich pastoral and evangelistic ministry, having preached across Europe and in many other countries. He and his wife make their home in Tucson, Arizona.

Acknowledgments

As on previous occasions, I found The Salvation Army to be extremely cooperative. I especially want to extend my appreciation to the following for their special help:

Lt. Colonel Henry Gariepy, Editor in Chief in the United States, answered all my letters and directed me to those who had the information I needed. The late Commissioner Richard E. Holz (R) forwarded anecdotes about Army music; Major Jenty Fairbank, Archivist from International Headquarters in London, was prompt in answering several questions. Lt. Colonel Houston Ellis, of the Atlanta Supplies and Purchasing Department, sent me many valuable books and bulletins. And Commissioner John D. Waldron (R), Archivist in the United States, answered my queries, read the manuscript, offered valuable suggestions, and saved me from numerous errors.

In addition to the above, I want to extend sincere thanks to my publishers, Bethany House in Minneapolis.

I alone am responsible for the mistakes all of us have tried to avoid.

Preface

THE crowd that marched by refused to be hurried. Its mood was expressed by a tottering old woman who insisted on taking her time. "No, no! Let others move on," she whispered to the crisply dressed officer as she studied the pale face in the casket before her. "I've a right to stop. I've come sixty miles to see her again. She was the means of saving my two sons."

Altogether, fifty thousand streamed by to pay their last respect. And additional thousands attended the funeral. Her death was an occasion the city of London did not wish to forget. Catherine Booth, mother of The Salvation Army, had at last finished her course.

Few women of any generation have been as much used by the Lord as Kate—the affectionate name her husband employed. Though tormented by painful disease from childhood, she had learned the secret of making her sickbed a Mount Pisgah and then claiming, and possessing, the land below.

As a result of tuberculosis and curvature of the spine, Catherine completed only two years of formal education. Before she entered the classroom, however, she was well taught. Because the school system in some areas of England was deplorable, Catherine was educated at home. Her mother supplied her with enough books to keep her busy. By the time she was twelve, she had read the entire Bible through eight times. Moreover, she knew the classics and loved theology.

Catherine lived in a difficult age—1829–1890. There was no cure for tuberculosis; and such diseases as smallpox, cholera, and whooping cough infected almost every family. A child's chance of attaining the age of ten was 27.7 percent, and that of reaching seventy a mere 5.9 percent.

In spite of these facts, all eight of her children became adults. All were earnest Christians, and all became officers—two of them generals—in The Salvation Army.

Catherine was surrounded by impossibilities. In addition to her illnesses, lack of education, and days of poverty, her father was an alcoholic. But the word *impossible* was not in her vocabulary. She agreed with Tertullian: "It is certain because it is impossible!"

Although she filled the largest auditoriums, wrote books, and became known as the mother of The Salvation Army, she never lost the common touch. She both sewed and mended all of her children's clothes. She even loved their pets.

During the days of her fame, she said to some cart-boys: "If I were you, I should like to feel that I had done my very best by my donkey. I would like to know that I had been kind to it and had given it the best food I could afford—in fact, that it had had just as jolly a day as though I had been the donkey and the donkey *me*."

This book is about Catherine Booth, one of the most remarkable women who ever lived. In several places I have invented scenes. But I only did this when it was extremely probable that such a scene might have taken place. An example is Catherine's visit to St. Paul's and later to Bunhill Cemetery. I have no documentation for this. But, being a devout Wesleyan, she certainly would have visited the church John Wesley attended and where he had a remarkable urging from the Lord. Also, I have invented conversations. Otherwise, the book is as factual as I could make it.

Charles Ludwig
Tucson, Arizona

Contents

1

Invisible Fingers

Alarmed by her four-year-old's frantic sobs, Sarah Mumford rushed up to her daughter's room. Holding a candle close to her little girl's face, she stared at her and questioned, "Are—are you ill, child?"

"N-no, Mama, I'm not i-ill," sobbed the brokenhearted Catherine.

"Then, what's the matter? I could hear you downstairs in the parlor."

Throwing her arms around her mother's neck, a new flood of tears streamed down her face. As Catherine gained control, she confessed, "Mama, I t-told you a l-lie. I-I did tear the page in the Bible. B-but I didn't do it on purpose. I'm sorry." The tears that once again flowed freely, slowly began to cease as Sarah rocked and cuddled her little girl.

Assured that she had been forgiven, Catherine was soon asleep with Martha, her favorite doll, lying on the tear-dampened pillow next to her curly black hair.

Having lost three infant sons, Sarah Mumford was extremely protective when it concerned her only daughter Catherine. Born on January 17, 1829, Catherine was considered a special gift by her mother. She was a lively, observant child. Without being taught, she quickly learned her "letters" and could read by the age of three. It was the Bible that really drew her attention with all its exciting stories to feed her active imagination. By the time she was twelve, she had read it straight through eight times.

Catherine had an extremely tender conscience. During chapel services she listened to every word of the sermon, and only on extremely rare occasions peeked through her fingers while the congregation knelt in prayer. Her religious concerns extended to her dolls.

She not only fed and tenderly clothed each one, but also prayed with them. Once as she had them kneeling at her mourner's bench, made out of an old shoe box, she instructed, "Now, Tom, Martha, and Peter, I want you all to agree in prayer that God will show me what I'm to do with my life when I'm grown-up like Mama."

In 1833 the Mumfords moved from Ashbourne in Derbyshire, where Catherine had been born, to Boston in Lincolnshire—her father's native town. In this fishing village where the Pilgrim Fathers had been imprisoned, John Mumford continued his trade as a coachbuilder. The family attended the nearby Wesleyan Chapel, a squarish, double-towered building with Greek pillars ornamenting the front and surrounded by a high metal fence.

When she was nine, Catherine was so intrigued by the way Samuel thought Eli had summoned him that she sought out her mother. "After the second call," Catherine explained, "Eli said to Samuel, 'Go, lie down: and it shall be, if he calls thee, that thou shalt say, Speak, Lord; for thy servant heareth!' Samuel then returned to his room. Soon he heard the voice the third time. Samuel replied just as Eli had told him to reply. Instantly, the Lord gave him a message . . ."

"That's a wonderful story. What is it you don't understand?"

"What I'd like to know is this: Did the Lord ever speak in such a way to a little girl like me?" Her dark brown eyes glistened and her mouth dropped slightly as she awaited an answer.

Pausing with her knitting, Catherine's mother smiled. "Yes, there was an occasion when the Lord did just that—"

"Tell me about it!" Catherine eagerly lifted her head.

"The story's in 2 Kings 5:1–14. That part of history tells us that Naaman, the head of the Syrian army, suffered from the dreadful disease of leprosy. Naaman's wife had a Jewish slave girl. This little maid was impressed by the Lord to tell her mistress that her husband could be healed if he would go to the prophet Elisha, and follow his instructions. Eventually, Naaman obeyed—"

"And what did Elisha tell him?" Catherine interrupted, leaning forward.

"He told him that he would have to wash seven times in the Jordan River."

"Did he do that?"

"Eventually. And when he came out of the water, the Bible says that his 'flesh came again like the flesh of a little child, and he was clean.' "

Thoughtfully Catherine looked at her own clear skin. "C-could God work through another little girl in our time?"

"Of course."

"Even a little girl like me?"

"Yes, even a little girl like you. You see, Catherine, God never changes. Malachi, in 3:16, quoted Him as saying, 'For I am the Lord, I change not.' And the author of the Book of Hebrews wrote in the last chapter, 'Jesus Christ the same yesterday, and today and forever.' "

One Friday afternoon while her mother was making a cake, Catherine stood by the kitchen table to watch. As her mother broke the eggs into the bowl, she asked, "Mama, tell me when you and Papa got married."

"That's a very interesting story. Now, step back a little so you won't get flour on your dress. My mother died when I was quite young, so my aunt came to live with us. She was a very harsh person, and I remember being unhappy many times. But she was a help to us. Papa made a good living, so we had everything we needed. Your grandfather Milward was a hard worker too, and saved his money.

"Then when I was in my early teens I fell in love with a man who had a high position and was very wealthy. All my friends liked him—even Papa, and he agreed that we could get married, so we set a wedding date.

"But just before we were to be married, I discovered that he was a very wicked man—"

"What had he done?"

"It isn't really important now. All I wish to say is that he was a very wicked man—"

"And so what did you do?"

"The day before the wedding I called it off."

"The day before?" Catherine's eyes widened.

"Yes, the day before. Marriage is for life, and I could not live with an unbeliever, especially a wicked unbeliever, for life!" She measured a cup of the sifted flour and after pouring it into the bowl and stirring for a moment, continued. "The next day he came to see me. But I was so terrified I wouldn't let him into the house—"

"Why not?"

"Because I was afraid he might persuade me to change my mind."

"And so what happened?"

"Well, of course he was very upset. He abruptly got on his horse and rode the animal so hard and fast that it finally dropped dead. When they found him, he had gone insane and the next day was confined to an asylum." Deep in thought, she poured some sugar into the bowl and worked it into the batter.

After a long pause she began again. "When I learned that he had lost his mind, I became so ill with guilt that I had to go to bed. I stayed in bed for many weeks. After a while I felt so condemned about it that I believed even hell was too good a place for me. Many times, especially during the long hours of the night, I wished I were dead."

"Why?"

"Because I felt that I was the one who had caused him to go insane."

"What happened after that, Mama?"

"We attended the Anglican Church in those days, so I went to my Prayer Book. There I came to the words, '*I believe in the forgiveness of sin.*' I held my finger on that sentence and reread it many times. But, Catherine, I could not be sure that I had been forgiven of all my sins. And each sin that I could remember seemed as big as a mountain. Then a curious thing took place. Some time before all this happened, the Methodists moved to our town, and as their congregation increased, they decided to build a chapel. Since your grandfather Milward had an extra lot, he sold it to them and soon their building was filled. Many of the people who knelt at their mourner's bench got up from their knees feeling assured that all their sins had been forgiven.

"When I learned that several of my friends were certain that all their sins had been completely forgiven, I longed to go to the chapel and find out about this doctrine of instant forgiveness. But, Catherine, you know, that was impossible because I still couldn't get out of bed—"

"And so what did you do?" Catherine asked eagerly.

"I explained my problem to Grandfather Milward and he arranged for one of their preachers to come to see me. When that preacher came, he explained that all I had to do was to tell the Lord I was deeply sorry for my sins, sincerely believe that Jesus had paid the price for my sins on the cross, and to thank Him for saving me."

"Then what happened?" Catherine leaned forward, hanging on her every word.

"At first the idea seemed so marvelous and yet so simple, I couldn't believe it. But when I did follow his instructions, I was not only forgiven, I was also healed!"

"Healed?"

"Yes, healed! I was immediately able to get out of bed and go to the chapel services. I was so happy I felt as if I were already in heaven." She poured two cups of milk into the batter and stirred until the ingredients were smooth. Next, she turned to the stove and put more wood in and pumped air on the small flame with a bellows until the fire was burning satisfactorily. She then continued with her story. "I really enjoyed going to the chapel. And sometimes I persuaded Father and even Auntie to go with me.

"Your grandfather didn't have much sympathy with all the shouting and loud amens. He also frowned at the plain clothes the people wore. Still, he said that the services were entertaining . . . He especially liked the preachers who waved their arms about as if they were fighting bees." She laughed. "On the way home he mimicked them. Then one Sunday morning John Mumford preached. That was a time I will never forget!" She picked up the baking powder and then set it down.

"As he paced back and forth in his long black coat with the Bible in his hand, I thought he was the best preacher I had ever heard." Her eyes glistened at the recollection. "I was also glad I was sitting near the front. When he spoke, his deep-set eyes made every word come to life; and his black, trimmed beard gave him the appearance of a modern prophet. After his sermon, he gave an invitation, and the mourner's bench was crowded with seekers. I was tempted to go forward myself just to get a better look at him." She laughed and gave the batter an extra stir.

"After that day, I made certain I was there every Sunday he preached, and I always sat as close to the front as possible.

"One Sunday when Papa didn't go with me, Mumford asked if he could walk me home and soon we were going for many long walks together. We shared so many things that I realized I was beginning to like him more and more. After a few months we became engaged. But before we set a wedding date, I insisted that John ask Papa for my hand.

"I'll never forget when he came over to speak to my father. Auntie had gone shopping, so the three of us were alone in the parlor." As Sarah recalled the past, a distant look filled her eyes. And while her mind was reliving her courtship days, she picked up the bowl and absent-mindedly started to pour the batter into a pan.

"Mama!" shouted Catherine. "You've forgotten to put in the baking powder!"

"Oh, my! If that isn't the cat's whiskers! So I did. I also forgot to pour in the chocolate syrup." She shook her head, smiling. "When I think of those days, my mind always gets muddled." She sprinkled in the powder with a little flour and then added the syrup. After vigorously working the forgotten items into the batter, she filled the cake pan and slipped it into the oven. "While it's baking, I'll finish telling you what happened.

"When John asked my father for my hand, he all but exploded. 'No!' he shouted. 'No worthless Methodist preacher is going to marry my only daughter. Do you think I want her to starve?' "

" 'But,' explained John, 'I'm also a carriage-maker. And I-I p-promise that Sarah will be w-well—' "

" 'Out! Out! Out! Get out of my house at once!' he yelled.

"And after Papa had hurried him out with a push between his shoulders, he slammed the door so hard my best pewter mug fell on the floor. Then he bolted the door and turned on me and shouted, 'I don't want you to ever, ever speak to that man again!' "

"What did you do?" Catherine was breathless.

"I was brokenhearted. But the more I hoped Papa would change his mind, the stronger his views became. When he learned that I was determined to marry John anyway, he ordered me out of the house without a penny. I didn't even have a change of clothing!" She put some more wood on the fire and continued. "Fortunately, I had a friend who had a spare room.

"While I was away from home, I continued to pray that God would either change my father's mind or convince me that I should not marry John. My prayers were finally answered. Father did change his mind, and a few months later John and I were married with Papa's consent. He even attended the wedding." She paused, thinking of the wonder of God's ways.

"After we had been married nearly a year, my father became very ill. Knowing that he was about to die, one of our relatives said, 'Let us pray for you.'

" 'No,' my father said, 'I don't want any of *you* to pray for me. Call John Mumford! I have confidence in *his* prayers.' Your father then went to Grandfather's room and led him to Christ just before he died."

"Does all of this mean that God answers prayer?"

"It does."

"But Papa doesn't preach anymore . . ."

"Yes, I know; and we must pray for him. He's a good man and he's working hard in the Temperance Movement." She peeked into the oven. "I think we'll need some more wood," she said.

After Catherine had returned with a fresh supply of wood, she asked one question: "Mama, will the Lord answer *my* prayers?"

"Of course. Why do you ask?"

"Because there are so many things in this world that are wrong. There are children who have to go to bed without having had anything to eat all day." Her dark brown eyes glistened. "Think, Mama, how simply dreadful it must be to go to bed hungry!" She wiped her eyes and shook her head. "I almost wish I could give my portion of the cake to a poor family I know."

Catherine was extremely close to her father, and if he would have continued in his spiritual life, no doubt the father-and-daughter relationship would have been strong. However, when Catherine was twelve, the happy relationship they did have changed dramatically.

Catherine had a dog named Waterford and the two were almost inseparable, partly because she had so few playmates. In later years she wrote in her diary:

Wherever I went the dog would follow me about as my

self-constituted protector; in fact we were inseparable companions. One day Waterford had accompanied me on a message to my father's house of business. I closed the door, leaving the dog outside. When I happened to strike my foot against something and cried out in sudden pain, Waterford heard me, and without a moment's hesitation came crashing through the large glass window to my rescue. My father was so vexed at the damage done that he caused the dog to be immediately shot. For months I suffered intolerably, especially in realizing it was in an effort to alleviate my suffering that the beautiful creature had lost its life. Days passed before I could speak to my father, although he afterward greatly regretted his hasty action, and strove to console me as best he could.

The school system in many parts of England at this time was deplorable. But not all teachers were as corrupt as Wackford Squeers, as Charles Dickens caricatured him in his novel, *Nicholas Nickleby*. In spite of that, anyone, regardless of previous failures, incompetence, or corruption, was free to open a school anywhere. A license was not required. Because of this freedom, Sarah Mumford decided that her Catherine could receive a much better education at home.

Since Catherine loved to read, her mother supplied her with enough books to keep her eyes busy. During those years John Mumford subscribed to several *Total Abstinence* publications and Catherine read them all. Thus, overflowing with information, she liked to join the visitors who often surrounded the Mumford table in order to discuss the evils of drink. On each occasion, Catherine joined in the conversation, and always had something worthwhile to say; her presence was a welcome pleasure to those around her.

Intrigued by the articles in her father's magazines, she frequently wrote letters to the editors in secrecy behind closed doors under an assumed name. At the age of twelve Catherine was elected secretary of the Juvenile Temperance Society, a position that kept her busy preparing meetings, raising money, and publishing bulletins.

At the end of a busy week while she was relaxing by

thumping a hoop down a cobbled street, she had barely passed a throng of hoodlums when a policeman darted out of an alley and seized the barefoot man just in front of her. As the officer was dragging his prisoner off to jail, a mob of hoodlums followed.

"They finally caught you!" mocked the hatless man who had just emerged from a tavern.

"Hope they lose the key," taunted another friend of alcohol.

The taunts and jeers were like cinders in Catherine's eyes. She longed to rebuke the crowd for their heartless insults. But in her heart she knew that such a reaction would inspire the smelly hoodlums to be even more vicious. At that moment "a hot spring of indignation" rose within her that would remain throughout her life—a readiness to stand up in the midst of injustice. Without thinking, she found herself walking by the side of the prisoner. She continued by his side until they reached the police station.

Catherine's impulsive act silenced the mob, and she stayed with the prisoner until he was pushed into the outer office. When she finally left, the tall, haggard man directed a smile of appreciation at her. That smile warmed her heart in a way never before experienced.

Shortly after relating this incident to her mother, Mrs. Mumford said, "Catherine, your father and I have decided that you should go to school."

"When?" Catherine asked eagerly.

"Right away. Mrs. Tate, who attends the same chapel we do, has talked with your father and me. She is a wonderful Christian and the principal of a girls' school she would like you to attend."

"Oh, I really would like to go!"

"Well, I feel it's time for you to begin associating with other girls your age."

"Oh, Mama, I'm so excited!" Catherine hugged and kissed her mother. Then suddenly her mood changed. "But I'll need some new clothes . . ." Her voice dropped.

Taking Catherine by the hand, she led the way into her room and pointed to several packages on the bed. "We've already thought of that. Papa and I bought you two new dresses."

A few minutes later Catherine stood in a new dress, studying herself in the tall mirror. The black, ankle-length garment was a mere shade darker than her hair, which was carefully parted in the middle. Ample sleeves reached to her hands where they funneled into white cuffs. The long V of the dress showed a ruffled white blouse snugly encircling her neck.

As Catherine viewed herself, twisting this way and that, she noticed her dainty lips, a well-formed nose, firm chin, and heavy, nearly perfect eyebrows. Yes, she was an attractive girl. There was no doubt about that! Later, lying awake that night, she wondered what the Lord had in store for her. Memories of various experiences came before her mind's eye like the pages of an illustrated book.

Her earliest memory was at the age of two when her weeping mother showed her the lifeless form of her newly born brother. She could still visualize the redness of his face, his clenched fists, tiny feet. The vision of her brother's still form impressed in her mind that death was an unforgettable fact in her world. She once remarked, "I am sure many parents enormously underestimate the capacity of children to retain impressions made upon them in early days."

A more vivid recollection was centered on the occasion when she had confessed telling her first lie and the intense relief she had felt after her mother had assured her she had been forgiven.

And, of course, she could not forget the tragic circumstances surrounding the death of her dog Waterford.

But the drama that etched itself most clearly in her mind was when she accompanied the prisoner who was being dragged off to jail. She especially remembered the arrested man's thankful smile and her intense satisfaction at the experience.

As these memories presented themselves, she wondered why they were more vivid than others. Suddenly she had an inspiration. *Could it be that some memories were more intense than others because God was directing them with His invisible fingers in order to shape her life?*

Pondering this possibility, she fell asleep.

2

Turmoil

Catherine Mumford was a little nervous when she took her seat in the first school she ever attended. Many of her classmates had already spent several years in school. Yet Catherine did not show herself at an educational disadvantage, but happily applied herself to her schoolwork. In many ways, she was the most advanced student in the class.

Even though she often responded with bursts of temper when teased to an excess, her teacher, Mrs. Tate, developed so much confidence in Catherine that she appointed her class monitor.

Geography and history were favorite subjects, and helped to lay deep foundations in her character. "Napoleon," she recalled, "I disliked with all my heart, because he seemed to be the embodiment of selfish ambition. I could discover no evidence that he had attempted to confer any benefit upon his own nation, much less on any of the nations he had conquered. . . .

"I could not help but contrast him with Caesar, who, though by no means an attractive character . . . appeared desirious of benefiting the people whom he conquered. His efforts for their civilization, together with the laws and public works he introduced on their behalf, seemed to palliate the merciless slaughter of his wars."

Joan of Arc was a character with whom she eagerly identified. While in her early teens, Joan had become convinced that God had called her to liberate France from the English armies and thus make it possible for the Dauphin (eldest son of the king) to be crowned Charles VII, King of France.

Daydreaming about Joan, Catherine all but saw the sixteen-year-old in full armor, mounted on a horse, and leading the 10,000 who eventually lifted the siege of Orléans. She even imagined herself riding with the newly titled *Maid of Orléans* as she won additional victories against the English. In Joan's high moment of triumph, Catherine visualized her standing by the Dauphin in the Great Reims cathedral as he was crowned Charles VII, King of France.

Later, Catherine's mind transported her to Rouen where the nineteen-year-old maid was burned at the stake. That May 30, 1431, a crowd of 10,000 watched her die. When two English soldiers laughed as the smoke twisted upward, a secretary to the English king groaned, "We are undone, we've burned a saint." Many wept.

This tapestry of history seared four major facts into the very being of Catherine Mumford: (1) Fifteen years after Joan's death she was officially proclaimed innocent of the accusations that had condemned her. (2) Although it was through her efforts that the Dauphin was crowned, the new king refused to make the slightest effort to save her. (3) With eyes lifted to the sky, that saint died courageously. (4) After her death, May 30 became a feast day throughout France, and shrines in honor of the martyred girl were erected in several prominent places. Better yet, her positive influence spread around the world. She proved that truth has a way of surviving.

Catherine's love for geography led her to investigate another fabric of history that became a lighthouse to her. That chapter was dramatized by some ancient prison cells in Boston.

Curious about the story, Catherine visited the prison cells, questioned all who had knowledge of the event that had made them famous, and read every book she could find on the subject. Her studies pointed to Scrooby, a tiny village sixty miles northwest of Boston. During the rule of King James (1603–1625), a congregation of Separatists began to meet in Scrooby.

Catherine chuckled as she uncovered a few of the radical dogmas held by these zealots. They were opposed to schools for girls, Sunday dinners, and attendance at Shakespeare's plays. Wedding rings were taboo and were described as "ye diabolical circle for ye devil to dance in." They were even unhappy about the clock Pastor Robinson had on his desk. Clocks, they insisted, were utterly satanic.

Since the Anglican Church forbade the reading of the Scriptures, Separatists were forced to hide their Bibles. Some were hidden behind loose bricks, others in the dough-trough. Many who were caught reading the Bible had their noses disfigured, or one, and often two, of their ears sliced off. Others were branded on their foreheads with a large B, which marked them as Bible worshipers.

By the summer of 1608, harassed Separatists had decided that if they were to continue worshiping in their own way, they'd have to flee to Holland. They sold their possessions and commissioned Elder Brewster to go to Boston and secure passage on a ship.

Brewster made a solemn agreement with a captain.

While members rested after their bone-weary trek from Scrooby, Brewster shouted, "Awake! We're about to sail!"

After the last Separatist had stepped on deck, there was a sudden scream of terror: "Soldiers! They're coming after us!"

The unnamed captain had betrayed them!

Although it was after midnight, crowds gathered in the public square to watch the fun. As the Separatists were herded into the prison, they were humiliated by shouts:

"Serves you right, you stiff-necked, hypocritical blasphemers. We hope you and all the other swine who leave the blessed Anglican Church rot in jail."

Since there wasn't room for all the prisoners to lie down in the cells, they took turns sleeping. Catherine sadly shook her head as she studied the reports. Then the words of an unknown prisoner leaped at her.

Fighting tears, Catherine reread the statement several times: "Don't water the roots of your hope with tears. Where they fall, nothing will grow, nor bloom, nor bear fruit. Take your portion of happiness, however small, without pushing, planning, striving, and enlarge upon it. Don't let the hardness of these bricks, the dampness of the straw, nor the discomfort detract you from your joy. Open your eyes wide. Look through the bars of yon tiny window. If you can't see the sun, look at the colors in the sky and take the glow as your portion of the happiness of the day."*

After a month all but seven of the prisoners were released. The winter that year was bitter; and since the Separatists had sold their possessions, they faced empty cupboards. Adding to their difficulties was the attitude of King James. He decreed that all who attended Separatist meetings were to be considered heretics, mockers, criminals. Like a rat each "was to be trapped and tossed away."

The next spring Brewster found a Dutch captain who agreed to take them to Holland. But incredible trials followed.

Armed guards swooped down on them as they boarded the ship. The captain pulled up the anchor, unfurled his sails, and departed. Almost hysterically, the Separatists watched as their loved ones on shore were rounded up by soldiers. Families were separated. Essentials were left behind.

Hours later a violent storm hit them, with huge waves swooping over the decks. The storm expanded into a hurri-

---

*Preceding The Mayflower, by James P. Leynse, pp. 76–77, Fountainhead Publishers, Inc., 1972.

cane. The compass became useless, leaving the officers with no sense of directions. By the seventh day desperate sailors cried, "We're sinking! We're lost!"

In response, Separatists on the deck formed a circle and got on their knees to pray. The sea calmed. Land appeared. But alas, the land was Norway! They were 400 miles off course! "Take us to Holland," insisted the Separatists.

While those on the ship faced perils, those left behind also faced perils. In humiliation, not knowing what lay ahead, they were marched in front of jeering crowds to the Boston jail. But this time there were too many to be wedged into the cells. However, the frustrated authorities tried to confine them in various homes. The people refused to accept them. In addition, it was impossible to find a judge who would convict the Separatists, for, according to English law, they were not criminals. Following more trials, they were eventually united with their families in Holland. From Holland, they reached America.

Descendants of these courageous people had spoken in chapel. With glowing words, they related how God's providence had inspired their ancestors. One woman boasted, "We have over a dozen places in America named Providence!"

Considering these events, Catherine returned to the Boston jail. As she relived the drama, she thought of the person who said, "Open your eyes, look through the bars." While climbing the steps to the courtroom where Brewster was tried, she repeated the entire passage.

The owner of that voice was indeed an important and useful person. His words had become a part of her very being.

As Catherine reread the eleventh chapter of Hebrews, she identified herself with each of the sixteen characters and became aware that only two of them had been women. Even worse, both heroines had doubtful areas in their lives. Rahab had been a harlot. And Sarah had so doubted God's promise to Abraham that she had laughed and then lied about it by saying, "I laughed not."

Pondering the way men had been used more than women, Catherine's heart sank. Were women second class? And, if so, could she make her life worthwhile?

While praying, she recalled Deborah. That woman had not only judged Israel, but had also inspired Barak to defeat Sisera even though he had 900 iron chariots. It was because of this victory that Barak became number twelve in the Faith Gallery. Had it not been for Deborah, few would have heard of him.

Yes, women were important!

Catherine had many thoughts about Esther, Deborah, Ruth, Naomi, and Mary the mother of Jesus when she was summoned to the evening meal.

On Monday, January 17, 1842, Catherine celebrated her thirteenth birthday. So far, her health, although delicate, had permitted her to attend both chapel and school regularly. Determined to maximize her benefits, she took full notes and frequently outlined the pastor's sermon. Then she was stricken with curvature of the spine. The brief school days came to an end as Catherine was confined to bed.

Being confined to her bedroom was heartbreaking. In addition to the pain, she pondered how she could ever make her life count. As she prayed about it, she decided to be creative with her disadvantages. Having read most of the books in their home, she asked friends to supply more books. "And what kind of a book do you want this time?" inquired a neighbor.

"Get me something on theology," she replied.

"Theology!" exclaimed the visitor.

"Yes, theology. Theology is about God, and what could be more important than to study the nature and purpose of God?"

Catherine was especially intrigued by Bishop Butler's *Analogy of Religion.* Finding her absorbed in that heavy work, her father said, "Since you hate arithmetic, I can't understand how you can enjoy such difficult reading." He shook his head.

"It *is* hard," admitted Catherine. "But it's thorough. It proves that God's Word is true by analogy. It did more to discredit deism than any other work in the eighteenth century. It—"

"I'm going to leave now before you get beyond me." Her father chuckled as he stepped out the door.

Another author Catherine loved was the American preacher Charles G. Finney. Although he was the choir leader and attended prayer meeting regularly, Finney made no profession of being a Christian. When a concerned person asked if he would like the congregation to pray for him, he replied with his usual courtesy, "I suppose that I need to be prayed for . . . but I do not see that it would do any good for you to pray for me; for you are continually asking, but you do not receive."

Finney had an argument for all who approached him. Nonetheless, he continued to search the Bible while hidden away in his office. Since on a certain Monday and Tuesday he didn't have much legal business, he plugged the keyholes with paper so that no one could see him as he studied the Bible. He recalled, "My convictions increased, but it still seemed as if my heart grew harder. I could not shed a tear; I could not pray . . . By Tuesday night I had become very nervous; and in the night a strange feeling came over me as if I were about to die. I knew that if I did I should sink down into hell."

At dawn on Wednesday, while busy with a law book, an inner voice spoke: "What are you waiting for? . . . Are you endeavoring to work out a righteousness of your own?" The voice persisted, "Will you accept it now, today?"

"Yes, I will accept it today or die in the attempt," he agreed. Still not satisfied, he went into the woods. "I . . . found a place where some large trees had fallen over each other, leaving an opening between . . . I crept into this place and knelt down for prayer."

At first it seemed that he was pleading to a stone-deaf jury. He wrote, "I found I could not give my heart to God. My inner soul hung back . . . I began to feel that it was too late . . . that I was past hope . . ."

As he faced despair, scripture began to hammer his mind. He remembered, "The Spirit seemed to lay stress upon the idea in the text, 'And ye shall seek me, and find me, when ye shall search for me with all your heart' (Jer. 29:13). I told the Lord that I would take Him at His word."

After praying from morning until noon, he became conscious that "all sense of sin, all consciousness of present sin or guilt had departed from me . . . The repose of my mind was unspeakably great . . . and the most profound tranquillity had taken full possession of me."

That evening after his law partner had departed, Finney felt impelled to return to his office. While praying, he was baptized by the Spirit. In his own words, this is what happened: "There was . . . no light in the room; nevertheless it appeared to me as if it were perfectly light . . . It seemed as if I had met the Lord face to face . . . He said nothing, but looked at me in such a manner as to break me right down to His feet . . . I wept like a child . . . I bathed His feet with my tears. But as I turned and was about to take a seat by the fire, I received a mighty baptism of the Holy Ghost. Without expecting it . . . the Holy Spirit descended upon me in a manner that seemed to go through my body and soul. I could feel the impression like a wave of electricity going through and through me. Indeed it seemed to come in waves and waves of liquid love . . . Like the very breath of God . . . it seemed to fan me with immense wings.

"No words can express the wonderful love that was shed abroad in my heart. I wept aloud with joy and love; and . . . I bellowed out the unutterable gushings of my heart. These waves came over me and over me and over me one after another until I recollect I cried out, 'I shall die if these waves continue to pass over me . . . Lord, I cannot bear any more . . .' I could now see and understand what was meant by the passage, 'Therefore being justified by faith, we have peace with God through our Lord Jesus Christ' (Rom. 5:1)."

Catherine reread the story of Finney's conversion many times. Likewise, she studied reports about the thousands who were being won to Christ through his ministry. Her copy of his *Revival Lectures* became dog-eared.

But Finney's story created a vacuum in her heart, for she became convinced that she had never been converted. Longing for that experience, she sifted the works of Wesley, Fletcher, Mosheim, Neander and others. Books on prophecy did not interest her.

"Another book I studied was [Benjamin Wills] Newton's on prophecy," she wrote. "After noting the various interpretations, each supported by . . . chapter and verse, I . . . remember deciding, that since so many learned and able people differed regarding the matter, it would be unwise for me to spend time . . . to come to any clearer conclusion. I believed I could better please God by devoting my attention to preparing people for Christ's coming than by fixing a date when it was to take place."

In spite of her studies, however, she failed to achieve a conversion experience that she considered genuine. Even so, during this bedridden period, her spinal condition gradually improved enough for her to attend services.

Then, at the age of fifteen, she fell in love.

3
Rebirth

Concerned for Catherine's health and the many hours she spent reading and analyzing, Sarah Mumford took it upon herself to arrange some sort of distraction for her daughter. She sent an invitation to cousins in Derby to come to Boston for a visit. It had been many years since Catherine had seen any of these relatives, and she looked forward to it with anticipation. But now that she had flowered into a young woman, she began to especially notice one of them.

This young man was a fine-looking man of talent and quick intelligence. Now seeing her at fifteen, he found her a young beauty quite appealing, and very soon he had fallen completely in love with her. Hand in hand, their walks became longer. But from the beginning, Catherine realized that he was reluctant to discuss spiritual things. He was far more interested in her attention than in the Wesleys, John Fletcher or Charles G. Finney.

Disappointed about his coldness to spiritual matters, she still hoped he would become attracted to the more vibrant type of Christianity. One Sunday after the preacher had delivered a fiery sermon, he placed a large open Bible in the exit door, then exhorted: "Think twice before you step over the Word of God!"

Although somewhat shocked by what the pastor had done, Catherine watched her boyfriend out of the corner of her eye and silently prayed that he would respond. But he stepped over the Bible with as little concern as if he were stepping over a puddle of water.

Inwardly, Catherine made excuses for him: The only religious services he had ever attended were in the High Anglican Church. The informality of the Wesleyan Church was shocking to him. Moreover, he was a stranger in a strange city.

A few Sundays later, however, when he began to scratch pictures on the pew in order to divert her attention from the sermon, she knew she had reached a breaking point in their relationship. After many tears and long sessions of prayer, she took a stand on 2 Cor. 6:14: "Be ye not unequally yoked together with unbelievers: for what fellowship hath righteousness with unrighteousness?"

Referring to this occasion, Catherine commented: "It cost me considerable effort at the time. I have far from regretted the step I decided upon, and have lived to see that the whole course of my life might have been altered had I chosen to follow the inclinations and fancies of my own heart rather than the express command of God."

Catherine was almost sixteen now, and shortly after her cousin left, she and her family moved to London. There they settled into a substantial home in Brixton—one of the better areas just south of the Thames. This was a good move, and her father's business began to prosper. Shortly after their arrival, the Mumfords went in a carriage to visit some friends who lived in a village about six miles away. On their return the horse bolted.

"Whoa! Whoa!" Mr. Mumford shouted, pulling on the reins. But the maddened horse responded by running faster than ever. Terrified, Catherine leapt to the ground. Unsteady and quite shaken when she got back on her feet, she watched the horse rearing into the air while her father desperately held on to the reins, struggling to calm the animal. Realizing help was needed, Catherine quickly ran back to the home of their host. She had just reached his driveway when she stumbled onto the soft section of grass. Brushing the hair away from her face, Catherine breathlessly explained to their friends that she needed help immediately.

Back on the road, they discovered, much to their relief, that neither her parents nor her younger brother John had been hurt. They had been saved by the fact that the carriage had run into a ditch, slowing the horse.

On their way home with the now-calmed horse, Mumford said, "Catherine, you amaze me. You had to drop out of school because of your spine. Now you can run like a wild animal." Stroking his goatee he asked, "How did you do it?"

"The Lord helped me so that when I fell, I landed in a soft place." She smiled with new assurance.

Although Catherine continued to study the Bible, read Christian books, and pray, she remained convinced that she had never been truly converted. At least she had never been converted in the manner in which Charles G. Finney or John Wesley had been converted. She remembered that period of her life during her sixteenth year.

"I passed through a great controversy of soul. Although I was conscious of having given myself up fully to God from my earliest years, and although I was anxious to serve Him, and often had deep enjoyment in prayer, nevertheless I had not the positive assurance that my sins were forgiven, and that I had experienced the actual change of heart about which I had read and heard so much . . . For six weeks I prayed and struggled on. Still, I obtained no satisfaction. True, my past life had been outwardly blameless . . .

"I was terribly afraid of being self-deceived. I remembered, too, the occasional outbursts of temper when I was . . . at school. Neither could I call to mind any particular place or time when I had definitely stepped out on the promises and had claimed the immediate forgiveness of my sins, receiving the witness of the Holy Spirit that I had become a child of God and an heir to heaven.

"It seemed unreasonable to me to suppose that I could be saved and not know it."

In seeking assurance of her salvation, Catherine read and reread the manner in which some of her heroes, men like Charles G. Finney and John and Charles Wesley, had received their assurance. Since the areas in London where the Wesleys had experienced their breakthroughs were now evangelical landmarks, she often visited those places in hopes that they would somehow help her to experience a spiritual breakthrough.

Entering St. Paul's Cathedral, Catherine took a seat near the front and reviewed the events that had assured John Wesley of his salvation and inflamed him for his later ministry. A little over a century before, the thirty-five-year-old graduate of Oxford had been sitting in this place when a mysterious revelation, begun in the morning, continued to open his eyes. Having studied and underlined this event in Wesley's *Journal*, Catherine was familiar with each detail. The date was Wednesday, May 24, 1738.

At about five o'clock that morning, John had opened his Greek New Testament to 2 Pet. 1:4. There he read: "Whereby are given unto us exceeding great and precious promises: that by these ye might be partakers of the divine nature."

Then as he left the house, he opened the same Greek New Testament again. This time he read: "Thou art not far from the kingdom of God" (Mark 12:34).

That afternoon, this fifteenth child of Susanna Wesley entered the rebuilt cathedral where Catherine was sitting. The anthem on that now historic day was, "Out of the deep have I called unto thee, O Lord: Lord, hear my voice." The music and the words fit Wesley's needs as a glove fits a hand.

As she meditated on the events of that day which had helped change the world, Catherine considered the way in which both John and Charles had been raised in the Epworth rectory of Samuel and Susanna Wesley. Few ministers were more devout than Samuel. And the energetic Susanna had taught each of her children at the age of five the entire alphabet in one day. Both brothers had Oxford master's degrees, were legally ordained, and had served as missionaries to Georgia.

Catherine recalled the manner in which the brothers had received new light from the Moravians on the real meaning of salvation; and how, because of their new enthusiasm, the pulpits in England had been closed against them.

John Wesley's record of what happened after the services in St. Paul's had burned itself into Catherine's heart. Now, as she lingered, she recalled the words in the *Journal*:

"In the evening I went very unwillingly to a society in Aldersgate Street, where one was reading Luther's preface to the Epistle to the Romans. About a quarter before nine, while he was describing the change which God works in the heart through faith in Christ, I felt my heart strangely warmed. I felt I did trust in Christ, Christ alone, for salvation. And an assurance was given me that He had taken away *my* sins, even mine, and had saved me from the law of sin and death."

Did Catherine walk the few blocks north from St. Paul's to Aldersgate Street and visit the traditional place where John Wesley's heart was strangely warmed? No one knows.

Nonetheless, Catherine's heart was not "strangely warmed" until after a long struggle. She often shared the difficulties she had experienced:

"I can never forget the agony I passed through. I used to pace my room until two o'clock in the morning, and when, utterly exhausted, I lay down at length to sleep, I would place my Bible and hymnbook under my pillow, praying that I might wake up with the assurance of salvation. One morning as I opened my hymnbook, my eyes fell upon the words:

My God, I am Thine!
What a comfort Divine—
What a blessing to know that my Jesus is mine.

"Scores of times I had read and sung those words, but now they came home to my inmost soul with a force and illumination they had never before possessed. It was as impossible for me to doubt as it had been . . . to exercise faith.

Previously, not all the promises in the Bible could induce me to believe; now, not all the devils in hell could persuade me to doubt. I now no longer hoped I was saved. I was certain of it! . . . I jumped out of bed, and, without waiting to dress, ran into my mother's room and told her what had happened . . .

"For the next six months I was so happy that I felt as if I were walking on air."

Certain that she had truly been converted, Catherine eagerly joined the Brixton Methodist Church where she and her mother had been attending. There, she was certain the Lord would inform her why she had been spared; and, better yet, what she was to do with her life. Even though she often lingered on her knees at the communion rail, she never became aware of any divine directions.

This lack of special direction from the Lord was alarming. Immediately after Charles G. Finney's conversion, he had been called to preach. And, although the church doors had been bolted against John Wesley, opportunities for service had opened for him within days after his Aldersgate experience. Indeed, he had almost instantly started to preach to thousands.

True, she was not quite seventeen. But Joan of Arc claimed to have received her special divine assignments when she was only fourteen! Unhappy that she had not received a special directive from the Lord, Catherine soon lost her ecstatic joy.

Many able preachers, including Luke Tyerman, author of the three volume *Life of John Wesley*, preached at the chapel. None of them impressed either Catherine or her mother. To them, the class meetings were dull and they were horrified at the worldly clothes worn by the members. Catherine reminisced:

"At this very time I can remember leaving the chapel burdened at heart that more had not been accomplished of a practical character. I could often see that a powerful impression had been made upon the people, that their consciences

had been awakened and their judgment enlightened. Many
. . . were on the verge of decision. Then, when it seemed every
power should be summoned to help them . . . to give their
hearts to God, the prayer meeting was either dispensed . . . ,
or conducted in such a pointless and half-hearted style . . .
the opportunity was lost and the people streamed out."

During this unhappy period, two additional blows troubled and almost destroyed Catherine. Having given up
preaching, her father had devoted himself to the cause of
temperance. He both wrote and spoke against the use of alcohol. Now, he himself had started to drink. Confessing
heartbreak, Catherine confided to her diary:

"Oh, my Lord, answer my prayer and bring him back to
thyself. Never let that tongue, which once delighted in prais-
ing Thee and showing others Thy willingness to save, be engaged in uttering the lamentations of the lost! Save, oh, save
him in any way Thou seest best, though it be ever so painful.
If by removing me Thou canst do this, cut short Thy work
and take me Home."

The next blow was that she came down with tuberculosis
in September 1846—a nearly incurable disease at the time.
On June 13, 1847, she wrote in her diary:

"I went to chapel in the morning, but felt very poorly with
faintness and palpitation, so that I spent the afternoon in
bed and contemplation. At evening I went again and stopped
to receive the sacrament, but was so ill I could scarcely walk
up to the communion rail, and was forced to hold to it to keep
from sinking. Mr. Heady, the minister, saw I was ill, and held
up the cup for me. I afterward came home, supported between Mr. Wells and another gentleman. The pain was so
violent I had to keep stopping in the street. Cold sweat stood
on my forehead. But amidst all the pain and confusion there
was calm, peace, and joy."

When a toothache became unbearable, she went to her
dentist.

"It needs to be extracted," he announced after a brief examination. "But before I do that, I think I must take your

pulse." Having taken it, he frowned. "It's much too slow," he murmured. "I must not endanger your life . . . Come back when you're feeling better."

Frightened by his daughter's health, John Mumford arranged for her to take a prolonged rest with an aunt at Brighton, a seaside resort some fifty miles due south of London. "The sea and breezes will do you good," he said.

Catherine loved this resort, made famous by the extravagant *Pavilion* built by George IV and William Thackery's *Vanity Fair*, which had just been running as a serial. In the oldest available letter of hers, Catherine wrote about the resort and her reaction to it:

"I have just returned from the beach . . . The sea looks sublime . . . I wish I could see you, though I should be sorry to come home just yet. The change is most agreeable. It is like a new world to me. I was heartily sick of looking at brick and mortar . . .

"Brighton is very full of company. Many a poor invalid is here strolling about in search of that pearl of great price— health . . . If I find not health of body, I hope my soul will be strengthened . . . I should like to spend another week or two here."

Snatches from her letters and diary indicate her thoughts, troubles, and hopes for the future:

"This day I have sometimes seemed on the verge of the good land. Oh, for mighty faith! I believe the Lord is willing and able to save me to the uttermost. I believe the blood of Jesus Christ cleanses from all sin. And yet there seems something in the way to prevent me from fully entering in. But today, I believe at times I have tasted perfect love . . ."

"In the morning I had much liberty in prayer. This afternoon, for the first time in my life, I visited the sick and endeavored to lead one poor young girl to Jesus. *I think if I'm spared, this will be a duty I shall greatly delight in, but Thy will be done!*" (Italics mine.)

Toward the beginning of her nineteenth year, she attempted a new system designed to deepen her spiritual life:

"I have been writing a few daily rules . . . which I hope will prove a blessing to me by the grace of God . . . May the Lord help me to adhere to them. But above all I am determined to search the Scriptures more attentively, for in them I have eternal life. I have read my Bible through twice in sixteen months, but I must read it with more prayer for light and understanding . . . May I meditate on it day and night . . . I feel I want more faith. I want to walk more by faith and not feeling."

A month later, she noted in her diary a resolution she hoped would help keep her in tune with God:

". . . I believe if I got to the means oftener, my soul would prosper better; still I know I might be blessed more at home if I lived in the spirit of prayer . . . I live too much by feelings instead of by faith, for *it is faith that conquers all spiritual enemies*. I want constantly to look to Jesus . . ."

When too weak to leave her room, Catherine spent many hours in prayer, reading the Bible, and writing letters. Her diary indicates this obsession:

"One of my dear cousins is very ill . . . She has three little children. But the Lord graciously supports her, and often fills her with His love. I frequently write long letters to her on spiritual subjects, and the Lord owns my weak endeavors by blessing them to her good."

During the last several years a strong agitation had been stirring among the Methodists. Catherine had been following the conflict with deep interest. The eye of the problem was church government.

In the beginning John Wesley had been the revered leader in the Methodist Church. His word was law, and all of his followers complied without objection. Then in 1783 he drew up the official *Deed Poll* that established the "Legal Hundred." This group of ministers was appointed for life; and, especially after Wesley's death in 1791, they ruled the entire church.

Gradually, however, democratic ideas began to filter into Methodism. Then, an anonymous pamphlet, entitled "Fly Sheets," was circulated. This critical document claimed to have been issued "by order of the Corresponding Committee for detecting, exposing and correcting abuses."

Gradually the conflict between the *Reformers* and the *Conservatives* grew. The Reformers published the *Wesleyan Times*. The Conservatives retaliated with the *Watchman*. Each paper hurled accusations at the other group. As Catherine sat up late reading the rival papers, she was heartsick. Her sympathies were with the Reformers. She longed to go back to the revival era of John Wesley, for she knew the increasing division was devastating the work of Christ.

With this concern in her heart, Catherine prepared to return to Brixton. But before leaving she revisited the Pavilion. Facing the English Channel, its minarets, cupalas and Oriental motifs seemed to her to represent the ultimate in wasted extravagance. As she viewed it, she wondered what would have happened if the price of its construction had been spent on the spreading of the good news of Jesus Christ.

4

Sparks

The tiny glow of health Catherine had experienced while she was relaxing in Brighton disappeared after her return to Brixton. Frequently, she could not get out of bed. But on Sundays, if she had sufficient strength, she attended the Wesleyan Chapel. Mrs. Keay, the class leader, was delighted to have her back.

With warm approval, she often asked Catherine to lead in prayer while the class knelt. Frequently she was so weak the class had to wait quite some time before she gathered enough strength to begin. When Catherine explained her problem, Mrs. Keay replied, "Do not let that hinder you. You will be of use by and by. Catherine, you will have to overcome your timidity and employ your gifts. If you don't, you won't."

As Catherine fought for health, her younger sixteen-year-old brother John immigrated to America. This meant that she and her mother were pushed even closer to one another. As she fervently continued to study and ask the Lord what she was to do with her life, she was disturbed by the deepening conflict between the Reformers and the Conservatives. Three years after the Fly Sheets had first been issued, the Legal Hundred issued a document in which all ministers in the Connection were required to answer with a definite yes or no as to whether they had had any part in the divisive publication.

Seventy ministers refused to sign the "popish document."

Eventually, three were expelled on strong suspicion that they were guilty. Additional scores were reprimanded. But instead of curing the problem, this action spread the fire. The Reformers gathered thousands of followers.

Catherine wholly supported the radicals, and she never hesitated to say so—even in class meetings. Believing that each congregation had a right to make its own decisions, she openly declared that she was for the congregational type of church government.

According to John Wesley's policy, all persons who attended a class meeting were required to have a ticket. Tickets were renewed each quarter. In 1852, the officers in her class decided that her ticket should not be renewed. This decision meant that Catherine Mumford had been expelled from the Methodist Church!

Sharing her grief with her mother, Catherine wailed, "Mama, I don't understand it. I'm twenty-two years of age. I love the Lord with all my heart, and yet I can't find out what the Lord wants me to do. And now I've been excommunicated!" She wiped her eyes.

Taking a seat in one of the high-backed dining room chairs, Sarah spoke. "While you curl my hair let's talk."

As Catherine combed out her mother's graying hair and began to make a long curl that would hang just below her temple, she murmured, "Sometimes I think the Lord doesn't even love me—"

"Why?" asked her mother, a curious tone in her voice.

Combing out a wide strip of hair, brushing it, then dampening it, she explained, "Every door of usefulness in God's work has been bolted against me. Every one!" The tears began to pool as she started to wrap the hair around a strip of cloth. "Because of curvature of the spine, I've had only two years of education. After that disease I developed tuberculosis. And now I'm not even allowed to attend Mrs. Keay's class." Wiping her eyes and blowing her nose, she continued. "I try to do right. I've read the Bible through twelve times. I pray. And I'm not aware of any outward sin. What am I to do, Mama?" Her eyes again swelled with tears.

"God works in mysterious ways," soothed Mrs. Mumford. "Paul had a marvelous experience with the Lord on the way to Damascus, and yet many years went by before he was recognized as a true minister of the gospel—"

"I've studied Paul," interrupted Catherine as she worked on another curl. "He was converted in A.D. 34 and didn't go on his first missionary journey until A.D. 47. But, Mama, I'm not Paul. I'm only a girl and I want to work for the Lord *now*!"

"Maybe the Lord is preparing you—"

"Preparing me? How could curvature of the spine and tuberculosis prepare me to be useful?"

"I don't know. But the Lord does delight in using handicapped people. William Wilberforce was sick all his life and yet the Lord used him to free the slaves. Likewise, John Wesley was not always a well man. He was once certain that—" Stopping, she pointed at the bookcase. "Get Wesley's *Journal* for November 1753." After skimming the page, she said, "Now read his notation for Monday, November 26."

Laying down her brush and facing her mother, Catherine read:

> Dr. F—told me plain, I must not stay in town a day longer, adding, "If any thing does thee good, it must be the country air, with rest, asses' milk, and riding daily." So (not being able to sit an horse) about noon I took coach for Lewisham.
>
> In the evening (not knowing how it might please God to dispose of me), to prevent vile panegyric, I wrote as follows:

Here lieth the Body
of
JOHN WESLEY

A brand plucked out of the burning:
Who died of consumption in the fifty-first
year of his age,
Not leaving, after his debts are paid,
Ten pounds behind him:
Praying,
God be merciful to me, an unprofitable servant!

"And John Wesley lived nearly thirty-seven years after he wrote his own epitaph," concluded Sarah Mumford. "So . . ."

"Yes, I guess that's true," admitted Catherine. "But remember, Mama, John Wesley had talent . . ."

"And who said you don't have talent? Your passionate love for animals and the oppressed is a real talent—"

"My love for animals is a talent?" She leaned forward and stared.

"Of course. Anyone who can be upset because someone is hurting a donkey as you were is a very special person! It requires talent to be upset over something like that!"

"What do you mean?" Catherine frowned.

"Remember when you were only eleven and you saw a boy with a hammer hitting a donkey that was pulling his wagon? You were so upset you shouted to our driver to stop the coach. When he ignored you, you leaped to the ground, ran up to the wagon, seized the donkey's reins, and held them until they finally stopped. Then you lectured the boy and made him promise that he would never beat his donkey again. You even wrote down his name and address. You became so excited you fainted away and we had to take you home in that condition."

"Ah, yes . . . I remember that occasion very well," reminisced Catherine as she smoothed another strip of hair. "We were still living in Boston. I can still see the wound on the donkey's back. It was so bad it really needed salve." Shuddering, she continued. "Mama, there are people who are just too cruel to live! If the Lord was concerned with sparrows, we ought to be concerned with donkeys." As she spoke, her dark brown eyes sparkled with intense enthusiasm.

Mrs. Mumford laughed. "When you jumped from the coach, your dress caught on the step and tore. If it hadn't torn you would have been pulled under the wheels and killed. You know, Catherine, God saved your life for a purpose."

"You mean, He saved my life in order that I might befriend donkeys? If I spent my life doing that, my epitaph could read: 'Here lies a woman who loved donkeys.' "

They both laughed.

Later on that day, Mrs. Mumford had a faraway look as she and Catherine were finishing their lunch. Eventually she said, "Catherine, let's go by the Wesley Chapel and visit the Bunhill Cemetery across the street."

"Visit the cemetery!" exclaimed Catherine. "Do you think I'm about to die?"

"No. No. I don't think you're about to die," chuckled her mother. "But maybe some of those dead people will inspire your life."

Catherine managed to keep still.

After a long trip on an omnibus, they got out at the nearest stop to the cemetery and walked over to the main gate. As they were viewing the vast area crowded with tombs and upright slabs, a one-eyed man tottered over to them. "Used to be called Bonehill," he wheezed. "There are 123,000 restin' here. Last burial was in 1832. That's 'bout twenty years ago."

"Why aren't there any crosses on the markers or monuments?" asked Catherine, her eyes on the tomb of John Bunyan.

"Because this is where the Dissenters were buried. They were against crosses. Thousands who died in the Puritan war between Cromwell and Charles I ended here, and so did thousands who died in the plague of 1665."

After handing the old man a tip, Mrs. Mumford said, "Thanks for all your trouble. Now we'd like to be alone for a while."

"I understand." The man bowed away. "Lots of people come here to meditate. It's a wonderful place. Some of these people helped change the world."

Pausing before John Bunyan's tomb, Sarah Mumford murmured, "His *Pilgrim's Progress* has been translated into over one hundred languages. He wrote it while he was locked in the Bedford jail. Catherine, did you know he had a daughter who was blind?" Silently, Catherine shook her head.

Next, they approached the nearby monument of Daniel DeFoe. As they viewed the tall shaft, Sarah exclaimed, "I wish I could have known him! Other than the Bible, his book *Rob-*

inson Crusoe is my favorite; and, as you know, I don't waste my time reading novels—especially French novels. Poor DeFoe! He had more trouble than a beekeeper. Until he was sixty, everything he did ended in disaster. He was imprisoned in Newgate. Queen Anne humiliated him by making him stand in a separate pillory each day for three days. The Queen hoped the crowds would pelt him with garbage and rotten eggs." Sarah laughed. "Instead, they honored him with garlands of flowers. He also went bankrupt. Nonetheless, he influenced the world . . ."

Mrs. Mumford, with Catherine close behind, continued her search until she found the grave of Isaac Watts. As she studied the faded inscription indicating that he was born in 1674 and died in 1748, she pointed out, "I don't know what we'd do without his hymns. I especially like his hymn *When I Survey the Wondrous Cross*. But like all the others, he had his troubles. And his troubles began even before he was born!

"His father, Catherine, was a very determined man. Being a Dissenter, the King kept him locked in prison; and so when his mother went to visit him, she often nursed little Isaac while she discussed family problems through the prison bars . . ." She shook her head.

"When Isaac was a mere lad he got into the habit of speaking in rhymes. Tired of it, his father demanded that he stop. But Isaac couldn't break the habit. And so, being a stern-faced Dissenter, he bent him over his knee. Between each licking Isaac begged: 'O Father, do some mercy take, And I will no more verses make.' "

While they were both laughing, they wandered around other graves. "When Isaac, who was extremely brilliant, was sixteen," continued Mrs. Mumford, "he was ready for the university. As a child he studied Latin at four, Greek at nine, French at ten, and Hebrew at thirteen. A local doctor offered to pay for his schooling, but since he was a Dissenter and refused to join the Church of England, he was barred from both Oxford and Cambridge."

"And so what did he do?" asked Catherine.

"He enrolled at Stoke Newington, a school near here which had been established by Dissenters. But being kept out of the universities was not his worst trouble. Having read his poetry, a young woman named Elizabeth Singer fell in love with him, and they began corresponding. Since she hadn't met him, she imagined that he was a healthy, square-shouldered man with a glowing personality. But when she visited him, she found a sickly man, barely five feet tall, with a head too large for his body, and a wig too large for his head. Elizabeth Singer was horrified."

"And so what happened?"

"He proposed, but she wasn't interested. It was reported that she said, 'Mr. Watts, I only wish I could admire the casket as much as I admire the jewel.' "

Disgusted, Catherine said, "That was a pretty cruel statement. After all, it's the jewel that's important! Some of our greatest geniuses have had very poor bodies. Alexander Pope was a twisted hunchback, yet he's quoted more than any of our poets, except Shakespeare."

"Cruel, it was," agreed her mother; "and, as a result, Isaac Watts remained a bachelor the rest of his life."

"And yet his life wasn't wasted!" added Catherine with enthusiasm. Her voice had gained a new vibrancy. "John Wesley loved his hymns, and just before he died, he broke out singing one of them."

Although she couldn't carry a tune, she sang the song:

> I'll praise my Maker while I've breath
> And when my voice is closed in death
> Praise shall employ my nobler power:
> My days of praise shall ne're be past,
> While life, and thought, and being last,
> Or immortality endures.

"But, Mama, let's go over to Susanna Wesley's grave. I've read every book I could find about her. Not only did she have nineteen children, but she was number twenty-five!"

As they lingered before the upright slab that marked Susanna's resting place, Mrs. Mumford glanced at her watch and then exclaimed, "We'd better hurry. It's getting late and Father said he'd be home early."

From her seat next to the window in the omnibus, Catherine rambled on, "Of Susanna's children, only eight survived her. She had two sets of twins and all died as infants. One set wasn't even named. Charles was number eighteen. He came two months early and didn't open his eyes for another two months. Hardly anyone thought he'd live, yet he wrote nearly seven thousand hymns."

Neither Catherine nor her mother uttered another word until they were crossing the Thames. Then, lifting her eyes from an anchored ship in the river, Catherine questioned, "Mama, why do you suppose God uses so many handicapped people?"

"I suppose it's because when a person is handicapped, he depends more on the Lord than on his own strength. Paul said in 1 Cor. 1:27: 'But God hath chosen the foolish things of the world to confound the wise; and God hath chosen the weak things of the world to confound the things which are mighty.' "

Catherine sighed as she pondered this perplexity and after several minutes commented, "You are probably right. After Paul had given up asking for the removal of his 'thorn in the flesh,' the Lord said to him: 'My grace is sufficient for thee: for my strength is made perfect in weakness' (2 Cor. 12:9)."

"But, Mama, one thing still bothers me—"

"And what's that?"

"I have enough troubles. But I have no talent. None!"

"We've talked about this before. But, Catherine, did you ever consider that God delights in giving His children spiritual gifts?"

Frowning she asked, "What do you mean?" She cocked her head to one side to avoid the noise of the wheels as they thumped over a stretch of bumpy road.

"Paul also said, 'But every man hath his proper gift of God, one after this manner, and another after that' (1 Cor. 7:7)."

"That *is* something to think about," replied Catherine, nodding her head.

"Of course it is! If God has called you to work for Him, He will supply the necessary gifts. He's not a monster." She studied her daughter's face. "Do you feel He has called you?"

"I'm confident that He wants me to do something. My problem is: What does He want me to do, and when? I'm getting older and I feel I'm wasting my time. You see—" A sudden knifelike pain interrupted her. "Oh! Oh!" she groaned. Sucking in her breath she cried, "It's getting worse—"

"Sit still now; we've almost reached our stop. I'll help you home," replied her mother as she placed an arm around her daughter's waist.

Catherine kept groaning as the two walked the several blocks toward their home. Stopping suddenly, she exclaimed, "Mama, look at that horse over there!"

"What about him?"

"He's so thin his ribs are showing. He's not getting enough to eat!"

"You're probably right. I know the owner. He's been out of work for several months—"

"Then we must send some feed over to that horse. We can't let him starve. Look at his eyes."

"But he's not *our* horse—"

"That doesn't matter, Mama. He's starving! Let's hurry."

"I thought you were sick."

"I was. But I'm all right now. Mama, we must hurry. That poor horse is about to drop."

Catherine quickly set a fast pace for home, her mind only on one thing: the poor beast they had just seen. Her mother strode beside her, breathless but with a gleam in her eye and a playful smile on her face.

5
Providence!

After being denied her quarterly ticket at the Wesleyan Chapel, Catherine joined the Reformers. Since this group, which demanded more democracy and a return to the emphases of John Wesley, was meeting in nearby Binfield Chapel, Catherine and her mother attended their services.

Soon Catherine became the leader of the senior girls' Bible class. It was made up of girls from the age of sixteen to nineteen. Catherine put her heart into the work. Each Sunday after the services were dismissed, she continued with a special prayer meeting for her girls. As a result, several of the class members were converted. Catherine recalls:

"I used to have some wonderful times with my class. I made them pray, and I'm sure anybody coming into one of those meetings would have seen what a Salvation Army consecration meeting is now. Often I went on until I lost my voice, not regaining it for a day or two after . . .

"However, I was greatly disappointed with the Reformers. I had hoped that we were on the eve of a great spiritual revival. Instead . . . everything was conducted . . . in the ordinary style, and I soon became heartily sick of the spirit of debate and controversy which prevailed."

The usual sermons were dull, insipid, lifeless. But on a

memorable Sunday in 1851, Catherine found herself leaning forward from the edge of her pew as the guest preacher expounded the text (John 4:42): "This is indeed the Christ, the Saviour of the world." The tall young speaker, who had arrived at the chapel clothed in a long black coat and wearing a stovepipe hat, moved from one drama to another.

In spite of his spellbinding delivery, Catherine noticed his wide collar, full beard, dark eyes, dark hair, clean-shaven upper lip—and slightly hooked nose. As she followed his sermon, she wondered if he might have a slight touch of Jewish blood. At the conclusion of the service, she approached a friend.

"What's his name?" she asked.

"William Booth."

"Do you know where he came from?"

"I don't know. Mr. Rabbits arranged for him to speak to us."

"I hope Mr. Rabbits sends for him again. A few more sermons like the one we just heard might get a revival going around here, and the Lord knows that we desperately need a revival."

Edward Harris Rabbits, an ardent Reformer, was a well-to-do boot manufacturer. Starting with a borrowed half crown, he had accumulated a fortune of 60,000 pounds. The great passion of his life was to promote Wesleyan-type chapels. Noisy services and loud amens were especially appealing to him. And he was drawn to preachers who loved the Bible.

During the week after Booth had preached at the Binfield Chapel, Catherine met Mr. Rabbits on the street. After motioning her to a quiet place near a bakery, he asked, "What did you think of our guest preacher's sermon?"

"It was the best sermon I've heard in our chapel!" she replied with enthusiasm.

"I'm glad to hear you say that. I've known him for several months. He used to be a pawnbroker. The first time I heard him was at Walworth Road Wesleyan Chapel. I was so impressed I took him out to dinner. While we were eating I asked him why he didn't become a minister. He replied that that was exactly what he wanted to become, but that he was hindered by several problems.

"As I recall, one problem was that he had to support his widowed mother, and another was that he'd been expelled from the Wesleyan Church."

Catherine's eyes widened. "Expelled?"

"Yes. They suspected that he was a Reformer in Wesleyan clothing and so they refused to renew his quarterly class ticket."

Catherine laughed. "That's exactly what happened to me. And so what did he do?"

"He joined the Reformers!"

"And so did I!" Trying to sound casual, she asked, "When are you going to invite him back?"

"As soon as I can. I think he has real quality."

"And so do I."

Unknown to Catherine, William Booth had written a letter to Rabbits from Kennington Row, Kennington, where he had last worked as a pawnbroker. In that undated letter he bared his heart:

> Before your solemn convictions are registered on high, will you as a Christian, as a friend of the friendless, which to me you have ever proved, hear me?
>
> In my present position I am unsettled—unhappy—my occupation is so contrary to my views that I am constantly desiring something different. I feel it in my heart—on my soul from day to day—that I should be a missionary of God. I wish to visit the dying and tell them of Him who is life; the prisoners, and point to Him who is freedom; the wanderer, and tell of Him whose arms and house and heart are open; the great congregation, and speak of that love which is boundless, that salvation which is free, and that mercy which is infinite and eternal. And the opportunity presents itself but I cannot accept it. Souls want reclaiming; Christ wants preaching; backsliders want reclaiming. But a difficulty offers or I would without hesitation go: I want bread

and water—can I have it?*

About two weeks after her conversation with Rabbits on the street, Catherine received an invitation from him to bring her mother to his house for afternoon tea. He was providing the tea, he explained, in order to promote unity and zeal among the Reformers in his district.

The living room in the bootmaker's home was crowded with guests when Catherine and her mother stepped in. Soon after they were seated, William Booth entered and nervously found a place across the room from them. Upon seeing him, Rabbits exclaimed, "We are fortunate indeed to have a former pawnbroker with us! And now, even before we have refreshments, I'm going to ask William Booth to stand and quote *The Grogseller's Dream*."

Looking around, Booth noticed a number of Reformers whom he knew to be moderate drinkers. Flabbergasted, he said, "I'm sorry, Mr. Rabbits, b-but I can't possible repeat it here."

"Nonsense! I've heard you quote it before and you can quote it again . . ."

"B-but I don't want to embarrass anyone."

"Ladies and gentlemen," replied Rabbits, lifting his voice, "we are privileged to have a brilliant new man among us. William Booth will now, at my request, repeat *The Grogseller's Dream*."

Booth's legs felt rubbery as he faced the guests. His only relief was his knowledge that Rabbits was also an occasional drinker, and thus the other tipplers could not blame him for rubbing chimney soot in their eyes. Standing behind his chair, he paused dramatically until every eye was on him. Then, speaking in a low voice in the manner of a trained actor, he began:

> A grogseller sat by his barroom fire,

---

*From *General Evangeline Booth*, by P. W. Wilson, p. 12. The original of this letter was preserved by Evangeline Booth.

> His feet as high as his head and higher,
> Watching the smoke as he puffed it out,
> Which in spiral columns curved about . . .

As he got into the body of the poem, he lifted his voice and skillfully articulated for maximum effect. Catherine listened with increasing fascination. At the same time, she studied the effect on the listeners, especially those whom she knew to be moderate drinkers. All seemed pleased with the opening part, but fifteen lines later their mood began to change, especially when, with a smug look, he continued:

> "The fools have guzzled my brandy and wine!
> Much good may it do them! The cash is *mine!*"
> And he winked again with a knowing look,
> As from his cigar the ashes he shook . . .

Those lines splashed shadows on a number of faces; and they deepened when he continued:

> "There's Gibson has murdered his child, they say—
> He was drunk as a beast here the other day!
> I gave him a hint, as I went to fill
> His jug, but the brute *would* have his will.
> Then folks blame me! Why, bless their souls,
> If I did not serve him he'd go to Coles'!"

At this point, Catherine noticed that some of the guests were beginning to squirm in their chairs. Nonetheless, Booth went on:

> "I've a mortgage too on Tomkinson's lot—
> What a fool he *was* to become a sot!
> But it's luck to me! In a month or so,
> I shall foreclose! Then the scamp must go!
> Oh, won't his wife have a taking on
> When she hears that his farm and his lot are gone!
> How she will blubber and sob and sigh!
> But business is business, and what care I?"

The crude poetry jingled on and on with gut-wrenching descriptions of the horror of drink, including the quatrain:

> "The arm that shielded a wife from ill
> In its drunken rage shall be raised to kill!
> Where'er it rolls, that fiery flood,

'Tis swollen with tears, 'tis stained with blood."

Then, after a total of one hundred and seven lines, it ended with a surprising twist:

With a stifled sob and a half-formed scream
The grogseller woke! It was all a dream.
Solemn and thoughtful his bed he sought,
And long on that midnight vision he thought!

Following a long, awkward pause after Booth had sat down, an incensed Reformer stood up and defended moderate drinking. "Didn't Brother Paul say, 'Use a little wine for thy stomach's sake and thine often infirmities' (1 Tim. 5:23)?"

Another Reformer, sitting next to Booth, all but shouted, "The Bible permits it—"

This last statement jerked Catherine to her feet. "I've not so read and interpreted *my* Bible!" she erupted. Her voice was loud and clear. "At a first superficial glance it might appear to be so. But if you read with care, you will observe that there are two kinds of wine referred to in the Bible, one intoxicating and the other not. The former is generally spoken of as 'strong drink,' or some equivalent term, and is invariably coupled with language of condemnation never used in connection with the other—"

"Maybe so, but you can't get rid of liquor by an Act of Parliament," cut in a belligerent voice.

"I'm not sure about that," she countered firmly. "By shutting the dens you can minimize the evil . . . It has been done in some places with the best possible results. In the villages and districts where it is prohibited, drunkenness is comparatively unknown . . ."

"But what would become of the revenue?" demanded another Reformer.

"Revenue!" she exclaimed. Her voice was now edged with impatience. "What would become of a man if he were to suck his own blood and eat his own flesh?" Out of the corner of an eye, she noticed that Booth's eyes were glistening with admiration. Thus encouraged, she took a deep breath and, shaking her finger, concluded, "How can a kingdom flourish that lives upon the destruction of its subjects? All of us are agreed that we need revival. But, as Charles G. Finney has said, 'It would be as easy to get up a revival in hell as in a church whose members support the traffic!' "

The discussion was interrupted by Rabbits. Lifting his hand, he said, "Ladies and gentlemen, refreshment time." Being eager to be as generous a host as a manufacturer of fine quality boots should be, his lavishly decorated tables were loaded with a large variety of pastries: jelly rolls, English rolled wafers, scones, cakes, fingercookies, and other items that help people gain weight. There were also cold cuts of meat, fruits of all sorts, numerous puddings—and several bottles of expensive French and Italian wines.

But, strangely, none of the guests touched any of the wines—even those whose red noses indicated their taste for alcoholic beverages.

As Catherine and her mother were leaving after the meeting, Booth took Catherine's hand. "Miss Mumford," he said, "I think you must have helped reform the Reformers; and, as God knows, the Reformers need to be reformed!" They both laughed.

"I did my best," replied Catherine.

Later, on Good Friday, April 10, 1852, Rabbits was on his way to a meeting being conducted by the Reformers on Cowper Street, City Road, when he saw William Booth. After stopping his coach, he waved him over. "Why don't you come with me to a special meeting?" he asked.

"I'm on my way to my cousin's place," replied Booth.

"Nonsense! Come with me."

"Oh, all right. I guess I can visit my cousin some other time."

As his carefully groomed white horse clip-clopped down the street, Rabbits questioned, "When are you going to enter the ministry?"

"The moment I find an opening. I quit my job yesterday—"

"You mean you're no longer a pawnbroker?" Rabbits studied him curiously. After a long pause, he asked, "Do you have another job?"

"No. I'm looking for a pulpit. I've been thinking of going to Australia on a convict ship. Those outcasts need a chaplain. I—"

"Mmm. You can't live without some kind of income."

"Yes, I know. That's the reason I was going to spend the night with my cousin . . . Did you receive my letter?"

"Yes, I received your letter; and I've been praying about the matter . . ." He remained silent until he turned on City Road. Then after quite some time he began again. "Catherine Mumford said that the sermon you preached at our chapel was the best sermon she had ever heard from the pulpit."

"Did she really?" He held his breath. His eyes brightened.

"Yes, she did, and that's quite a compliment; for Catherine is a very fine girl. But you'd better pray for her father—"

"Why?"

"He's been drinking too much."

After Rabbits had turned off City Road to Cowper Street, he fixed his eyes on Booth and asked, "How much money would you need in order to live?"

"Oh, about twelve shillings a week will keep me in bread and cheese—"

"That's not enough! Dickens' Bob Cratchit got fifteen shillings a week, and even with that he couldn't buy an overcoat!" Chuckling he added, "I'm no Scrooge. I'll pay you twenty shillings a week for three months."

"A pound a week!" exclaimed Booth. "That's wonderful and I thank you, Mr. Rabbits. But where will I preach?"

"At Binfield Chapel on Binfield Road in Clapham. They've been looking for a preacher, and I'll recommend that they give you a try."

Booth stared. "I—is that where Catherine Mumford and her mother attend?"

"It is."

That afternoon as Catherine was listening to the Good Friday sermon, she found that it was impossible to keep her eyes away from William Booth and Edward Rabbits, who were sitting across the aisle from her and her mother.

Booth also had difficulty in keeping his eyes away from the Mumfords—especially Catherine. In addition, he had another problem. It was too late to go to his cousin's home; moreover, he was short of cash. He considered asking Rabbits for an advance. But his better judgment indicated that this would be the wrong thing to do. Snagged on the horns of a dilemma, he bowed his head and prayed. God's providence had been good to him on this 10th day of April. Not only was it the anniversary of the day that Christ died for him; but it was also his twenty-third birthday, and his first day of employment as a full-time minister of the gospel.

As he stood with the congregation for the benediction, he felt a confident assurance that God's providence would continue to direct him—and to supply his needs. How this would be done, he did not know. Then, as he noticed the Mumfords leaving their pew, he felt an overwhelming inspiration. Responding to this urge, he walked over to them and extended his hand.

"Let me take you to Brixton," he suggested.

"Oh, thank you very much," replied Mrs. Mumford. "That is indeed very kind of you."

Leading them to the nearest stop, Booth secretly counted the coins in his left coat pocket with the tips of his fingers. Was there enough to pay all three fares? He wasn't quite certain. As he was considering what he would do if he didn't have sufficient money, the horse-drawn vehicle pulled up in front of them.

6

Romance!

As Booth courteously waited for Catherine and her mother to step into the carriage, his breath came in short puffs and he nervously licked his lips. *What would he say if he didn't have enough change to pay their fares?* The question formed a hollow place in the pit of his stomach. Providence again came to his aid.

As Mrs. Mumford counted out the fares, she said, "Since you and Catherine are about the same age, you ought to sit together." She pointed to an empty seat on the left side. "I'll sit behind you."

After a few minutes of silence, Booth found his tongue. "From the time of my conversion, I've especially enjoyed Good Friday services—"

"And when were you converted?" broke in Catherine.

"In 1845 when I was fifteen—"

"Who was the minister, and where were you converted?"

"Oh, there was no minister present. I was alone in the streets of Nottingham and it was eleven o'clock at night. I had—"

"You were alone? I, too, was alone. But I was sixteen. Please tell me about it." Her eyes widened as she studied his face.

"It's a long story."

"That's all right. I want to hear every word."

"When I was a lad playing on the streets of Nottingham, an elderly couple passed me. They had only gone a short distance when they turned around for a second look. This made me uncomfortable and I began to wonder if I had done something wrong. I had almost forgotten the incident when later they stopped and approached me.

" ' 'ow are you getting along in school?' asked the white-haired gentleman.

" 'Oh, just fine,' I replied.

" 'We're interested in you because you resemble our son who just died,' said the lady. Tears filled her eyes as she spoke. Shortly after that they invited me to their home. They were Wesleyans and quite frequently they took me to the Wesleyan Chapel.

"When I was twelve my father lost everything he had, so he had me taken from school and apprenticed to a pawnbroker. My father felt there was money in it. The place where I worked was in the poorest section of Nottingham." Shuddering he continued. "Whenever I think about it, I cringe . . .

"When it was announced that Isaac Marsden was conducting revival meetings in the Wesleyan Chapel, I went with two of my friends to hear him. We got there at dusk, toward the end of the service, and sat as far in the back as we could get. We didn't stay to the end, but just as we were leaving, I heard Marsden say, 'A soul dies every minute . . .'

"Those haunting words made me wonder when I was going to die and when I was going to prepare myself to meet my Maker . . .

"I didn't go near him again, but I heard a lot about him." He chuckled. "One day the old boy noticed a woman hanging out her wash. After glancing down the line of fluttering shirts, he said, 'I say, missus, if your 'eart is not washed cleaner than those clothes, you'll never get to 'eaven.' "

After all three had stopped laughing, Catherine remarked, "Marsden's theology wasn't very good. Although our bodies

die, our souls live forever. And I don't think he was very diplomatic. Jesus said, 'Be ye therefore wise as serpents, and
harmless as doves' (Matt. 10:16). Still, I wish I could have
known him." Studying him carefully, she continued. "Mr.
Booth, tell me how you got saved."

"In September 1842, my father became extremely ill. Up
until that time he had thought only about making money.
But as he neared his death, he asked for us to call the minister. The minister served him communion and then all of us
who were surrounding his bed sang *Rock of Ages*. I'll never
forget the moment Papa accepted Christ and the great sense
of peace that settled on him. His was a deathbed repentance.
He then committed Mama and us four children to the Lord.
At that time I longed to make peace with the Lord, but I kept
putting it off. You see I had a problem that no one knew
about.

"Since Mama didn't have much money, she opened a little
shop in Goose Gate. That was an even more wretched place
than where I worked."

"What did she sell?"

"She sold needles, toys, cotton, tape and other things. We
nearly starved, and since I didn't earn much in the pawn-
broking business, we had a very hard time. We—"

"I'm really anxious to hear how you were saved," interrupted Mrs. Mumford, "but we've almost reached our stop.
I've been wondering, Mr. Booth, where are you going to spend
the night?"

"I really don't know. This has been a most unusual day.
You see, it's my birthday; I quit my job yesterday, and Mr.
Rabbits engaged me to be your pastor for the next three
months—"

"Do you mean you'll be preaching for us until the middle
of July?" asked Catherine after she had counted the Sundays
on her fingers.

"I guess so."

"Oh, that's wonderful!" she exclaimed.

"That means, Pastor Booth, that you will be spending the

night with us. We'd be highly honored," concluded her mother.

After Booth had seated himself on the sofa across from Catherine, Mrs. Mumford said, "You must be hungry. I'll go into the kitchen and prepare something to eat." Wagging her finger at him she instructed, "But don't tell Catherine how you were saved until I get back."

Catherine broke the silence. "And what will you be doing tomorrow?"

"Tomorrow will be a busy day. I'll have to find some lodging and prepare sermons for Sunday."

"I have a lot of books I could lend you. I really love the Bible and have a large collection of religious books. I—" She was interrupted by the sudden opening of the front door.

A moment later, her father stumbled into the room.

"Oh, Papa," she blushed, "I-I want you to meet our new pastor, William Booth."

Holding out a shaky hand, Catherine's father studied Booth for a painful moment, then exploded, "You don't let grass grow under your feet, do you? Name is John Mumford."

"What do you mean, sir?" Booth stared as he grasped his hand.

"You haven't preached your first sermon as pastor and yet you've already come to see my daughter!" Swaying a little, he reached for the back of a chair. "But that's all right . . . Ushed to be a pulpit-pounder just like you. 'Twas then I called on Sarah Milward, and do you know what her old man did?"

"Wot did he do?" Booth was so confused he forgot to void the Nottingham dialect of his youth.

"What did he do? He threw me out of the house. Bam! That's what he did. But don't worry. I'm too drunk to do that tonight. You'll have to wait 'til I'm sober . . ." He nodded his head and blinked his eye.

"Oh, Papa, don't talk like that," begged Catherine as she gently led him toward his bedroom door.

His hand on the knob, Mumford asked, "The names B-B-Booth, you say?"

"That's right. Booth, William Booth."

"Any relation to the gin-making Booths?" He winked.

"I don't think so."

"That's good. I like their gin too much! See ya' in the mornin'." As he turned he grinned and nodded his head.

Catherine's face was crimson when she returned. "Please excuse Papa," she said. "He's really a fine, hard-working man and used to be a powerful preacher. When he's sober he's a model of perfection . . ."

"Oh, it's all right," replied Booth with understanding. "Both my older sister Ann and her husband drink. They also ridicule Christianity. Once when I was really desperate, they threw me out of their house and slammed the door."

"Papa never makes fun of Christianity," replied Catherine. "But," speaking in a more confident tone, "alcohol—" She shuddered. "But alcohol has him by the throat. We even labored hard together in the temperance movement! In those days he really denounced it. We must keep praying for him." She shook her head. "It would mean everything to Mama and me if he'd come back to the Lord. Maybe you can help him—"

"Supper's ready," broke in Mrs. Mumford as she untied her apron.

After joining hands and singing a prayer of thanksgiving, Mrs. Mumford said, "Now, Pastor Booth, please tell us how you got saved."

"As I told you," he said as he cut a section of cold ham, "I had been under conviction for several years. But I had a problem in a trading affair with my friends. I made a nice profit while I was making them believe that the whole transaction was done out of pure generosity. Utterly deceived, those friends gave me a silver pencil case in order to express their gratitude. That little deception haunted me for a long time. Inward light convinced me that I not only must renounce everything I knew to be sinful; but, in addition, I must make restitution. Then, while pacing the streets of Nottingham at eleven o'clock one night, I made up my mind that I would confess my sin and make restitution. That was a very difficult decision, like having a tooth drawn." He thoughtfully cut another slice of meat.

"At that moment a profound change came over me. My heart, like John Wesley's heart at Aldersgate, was 'strangely warmed.' " A look of deep satisfaction covered his face as he spoke. Silently he fought the tears. In a lower tone of voice he slowly continued. "I wish now that I had the flagstone on which I was standing when I experienced that transformation. It would be to me as important as the dry stones in the Jordan River were to the Israelites who had just crossed over them into the Promised Land dry-shod." He wiped his eyes.

After supper, Sarah Mumford shooed them into the parlor, where each sat at the opposite end of the couch, nervously wondering what to say. Finally Catherine broke the silence. "Mr. Booth, tell me about your ancestors."

Laughing, Booth began. "To start with, Miss Mumford, I'm not the first William Booth in our family. You see, my father was born in 1775—the year before the Americans signed their Declaration of Independence—and he married Sarah Lockitt in 1797—"

"That means they were married when he was . . . twenty-two," commented Catherine while she figured the numbers on her fingers.

"Correct," he said, leaning toward her. "He and Sarah Lockitt became the parents of a son whom they named William. Sarah died in 1819. Father remained single for five years. That was a difficult time for him. Although he could neither read nor write, he kept busy building and selling houses. His one comfort was my half-brother William. Then William married Catherine Edwards in 1822. But less than two years later he died—"

"Does that mean it's fatal for a William Booth to marry a Catherine?" she asked in mock seriousness as she moved slightly toward the center of the couch.

"Certainly not!" he replied emphatically, not daring to

look at her. "William died of turberculosis. Soon Papa became so lonely he started to seriously look for a wife. While he was at Ashby-de-le-Zouch—he had gone there to drink the mineral waters for his rheumatism—he met Mary Moss. She was thirty-three and he was close to fifty. Now, that didn't matter to him because he needed a wife! She turned him down.

"Papa was disappointed. Still he couldn't forget Mary, so he returned to Ashby-de-le-Zouch and kept pestering her until she finally said yes. They were married in Ashby-de-le-Zouch at the parish church by Reverend MacDouall on November 2, 1824. Papa signed the marriage certificate by making his mark."

"Then what happened?" she asked eagerly, moving still closer.

"As usual, they started a family. Their first child was Henry. He died in his first year. Then came Ann, myself, Emma, and finally Mary. Emma has been an invalid all her life."

"And all of this started at Ashby-de-le-Zouch?" asked Catherine.

"Yes," agreed William. "And it all started because Papa wanted to drink some mineral waters for his rheumatism—"

"And here is some tea to help keep you awake," interrupted Mrs. Mumford as she entered the parlor door. She placed a tray loaded with tea and pastries before them. Sitting down in her favorite Queen Anne chair, she picked up her knitting. Both Catherine and William had taken advantage of the opportunity and innocently slipped closer to the center of the settee.

After taking a sup of tea and a bite or two from a cookie, Catherine had another question. "Mr. Booth, when were you born?"

"Catherine!" scolded Mrs. Mumford. "Where are your manners? William Booth is our pastor. He's not a suspected criminal!" Her dark eyes snapped.

"Oh, that's all right," replied Booth. "And please call me William. I was born in Nottingham, April 10, 1829—"

"Yes, I remember now. You said that today was your birthday. That means you are twenty-three. Correct?"

"Yes."

"And I was born on January 17, 1829." Calculating on her fingers again she commented, "And that means, Pastor William Booth, that I lack only one week of being three months older than you. And because of that I have the right to tell you that it's time for you to have another cup of tea and another slice of cake." She laughed.

The longer they visited, the more their inhibitions faded. By now it seemed quite natural to sit closer together. As the evening progressed, Booth became so relaxed he relapsed into his Nottingham dialect. By 10 o'clock a horse had become a *'orse*, here had been shortened to *'ere*, stranger had changed to *strynger*, pay was turned into *py*, won't you exploded as *won'tcher*, other was pronounced as *hother*, and house as *'ouse*.

Catherine was enchanted.

By the time the hands of the clock had almost reached eleven, William and Catherine were sitting less than a foot apart. He had just started to explain to her the great ambitions of his life when Mrs. Mumford said, "It's getting late." She smothered a wide yawn with her palm. "Maybe we'd all better go to bed. Pastor Booth mentioned having a busy day tomorrow." Pointing to the guest room, she added, "There is your room. Breakfast's at seven."

Catherine found it difficult to get to sleep. Each event of the day continued to flash in her mind. Booth's tall figure, raven hair, gray eyes, shaved upper lip and energetic ways kept coming before her. She smiled, remembering his Nottingham accent. She loved it! It had been fascinating to hear a house called an *'ouse* and the way he said *'ere* for here. She inwardly chuckled at his accent. *What a fascinating man,* she thought. Then, as she savored each moment, she began to ask herself if she was in love. That question opened the door to several other questions.

*If she was in love, was she worthy of him? And even if
she was worthy of him, did she have the strength to be a
pastor's wife?* Next she became realistic: *Could he make a
living?* After all, he didn't have much education and he
wasn't nearly as well-read as she. She also wondered about
his attitude toward women. Did he consider them second-
class citizens as so many of the clergy did? And what was his
attitude toward liquor? Her father had been a preacher, had
lectured against intemperance, and yet was now a confirmed
drinker.

Suddenly, she remembered she had forgotten to pray.
Kneeling by the side of her bed, she pled with the Lord for
guidance.

While they were eating their sausages and eggs at breakfast, John Mumford turned toward Booth. "I'm not anti-Sem-
itic," he said as he nervously stroked his goatee, "but I've been
wondering if you have just a wee touch of Jewish blood."

Catherine inwardly squirmed and unconsciously held her
breath as she awaited the answer.

Undisturbed, Booth replied, "You're not the first one to
ask that question. Being a pawnbroker did make me a sus-
pect." He shrugged. "But I really don't know. My mother's
name was Moss and I've been told that is a Jewish name.
Also, my nose makes me look like a son of Abraham. But I
haven't the slightest idea where I got it," he chuckled.

"Then you haven't made a study of your family tree?"

"No. I've been too busy with other things."

Mumford smiled. "The reason I inquired is because of a
man I heard about a few weeks ago. When asked if he could
trace his line back to William the Conqueror, he replied, 'Further than that.'

" 'Perhaps you could go back to Noah's Ark?' pressed the
man.

" 'Noah's Ark?' he scoffed. 'My ancestors go back much
further than that. My ancestors had their own boat!' "

After the laughter had subsided, Mumford continued. "All

the Booths I know are honorable people. Even the gin-makers had some good points. They financed the Ross expedition to the North Pole in 1829; and, as the result of that expedition, one of the peninsulas up there is named the *Boothia Felix Peninsula.* Later, on June 1, 1831, James Ross discovered the North Magnetic Pole."

"I'm glad to know that my name is so famous," replied Booth. "But as far as I'm concerned, my most important relative is Jesus Christ! Brother Paul tells us that we are 'joint-heirs with Christ' (Rom. 8:17)."

"You are right," replied Mumford, stroking his beard. Then, flashing a smile, he stated, "Since you will be looking for lodging close to the church, I'll let you use my horse and carriage. Catherine and my wife will show you around."

"That will be wonderful, and I do thank you," replied Booth warmly.

"Are you ready to go?" asked Catherine. "I think I know a place which you would like. But we must get there before someone else rents it," she said, stepping toward the door.

7

Labyrinthine Ways

Mrs. Mumford settled herself in the backseat of the carriage and tucked her knitting as well as her favorite book close by. She could almost imagine what was going through her daughter's mind.

With William by her side and the reins in his hand, Catherine's heart fluttered in a strange new way as they headed down the street in search of a suitable lodging for their new pastor.

While passing row after row of trim brick houses, many with manicured patches of flowers in front, Booth remarked, "This district is a paradise compared to the district in which I was raised in Nottingham—"

Taken back by his frankness, Catherine interjected, "Tell me about Nottingham. All I know are the tales about Robin Hood, Sherwood Forest, and that dreadful Sheriff of Nottingham." William laughed and turned to the left on a side street.

Clearing his throat, he proceeded. "Nottingham is one of the poorest cities in the United Kingdom. The place is like a blacksmith's vise. The wealthy live in luxury on each of the opened jaws. The poor, and there are about fifty thousand of them, are squeezed together between the jaws into about twelve thousand houses.

"Seven thousand of these 'ouses, as we say in Nottingham, are crowded back to back and side to side. Some alleys are only a yard wide and many are as dark as tunnels. Children have no place to play. Rats and insects are everywhere.

"Entire sections use a common privy," he mentioned as he touched his nose. "The privies are supposed to be emptied at night and their products hauled to the farmers. But those who empty them are not very efficient. Because of the overflowing filth, Nottingham has one of the highest mortality rates in England; therefore grave-diggers are always busy. During my childhood alone, we had two outbreaks of cholera."

"What do people do for a living?" asked Mrs. Mumford solomnly from behind them.

"Most are stockingers—"

"*Stockingers?*"

"They make stockings and other knitted wear. Top wage is seven shillings a week. And to earn that, the entire family has to work together. I've visited garrets that are only fifteen feet square in which fifteen to twenty children are forced to work fifteen hours a day, six days a week.

"The miseries I've seen in Nottingham, Catherine, have been seared into my heart. I can never forget them. Never!"

Catherine motioned for Booth to stop the horse in front of a house that displayed a TO LET sign in the window. As they approached the front door, she said, "If Dante had known the horrors of Nottingham, he would have described them in his *Divine Comedy.*"

"Dante? Divine Comedy? What do you mean?"

"Dante was an Italian poet and the *Divine Comedy* is his poem about how the Roman poet Virgil led him through purgatory and hell. It's a great poem. . . I've read it several times. You should—" She was interrupted by the red-cheeked landlady who opened the door even before they knocked.

"This is our new minister and he needs a room," explained Catherine.

"Sorry. I've just rented it."

The rooms at the next three stops were also full. Then they stopped in the Walworth district. Here, they found two vacant rooms, both together for five shillings a week.

After looking them over, Booth said, "I'll take them. But you'll have to wait until the end of next week for the money."

"I'm a widow," replied the white-headed woman. "I—"

"William Booth is our new minister," broke in Catherine. "Edward Rabbits is paying his salary."

"Mmm. And who are you?"

"I'm the daughter of John Mumford. In the carriage over there is my mother, Sarah Mumford."

"Then it's all right." The lady's wide grin revealed the complete lack of upper teeth. "Me old man used to work for Rabbits, and I've heard of your father. Builds coaches, eh?"

"You are right."

Booth frowned. "I've another problem. I'll need chairs and a bed."

"No problem," replied the widow. "There's a used furniture store 'round the corner. Tell the man Mrs. Boatman sent you. He'll give you credit."

Within an hour William, Catherine, and Mrs. Mumford had selected a bed, two chairs, a table, and some cooking utensils. After they'd been delivered and the ladies had helped arrange them, Booth said, "Now, I've another problem. How am I to get to church tomorrow?"

Turning to the landlady, Catherine mentioned the address of the chapel. "Ain't over two miles from here." She aimed her finger down the street. "You cawnt miss it."

"Two miles!" exclaimed Catherine. "We'll pick you up."

Booth laughed. "Two miles isn't far. I'll walk."

"Are you sure?" Catherine looked doubtful.

"Of course I'm sure. You see, I used to work right here in Walworth. That's when I was a pawnbroker. The owner of the business was a hardhearted soul. I had to work almost all the time; and, sometimes in order to get home before the door was locked at ten o'clock, I had to run most of the way. I guess that's the reason the Lord equipped me with such long legs." A faint smile crept across his face.

"Then I'll see you in church tomorrow?" asked Catherine.

"Aye. And please pray that the Lord will help me preach a good sermon."

Just as Mrs. Mumford and Catherine started to leave, he opened his wallet and took out a folded piece of paper. "After I was saved," he explained, "I wrote this out as a sort of guide for my life. Take it home, Catherine, and study it. It will show you what kind of a man I am and what I hope to be."

Catherine placed the worn piece of parchment in her purse. She started to leave again and then hesitated. "I want you to know that I really enjoyed the way you quoted *The Grogseller's Dream*," she said. "You must have a wonderful memory."

"Thank you."

"But why did you hesitate to quote it?"

"Because I knew that some of the people there were moderate drinkers. Even Mr. Rabbits takes a drink now and then."

"How about you, are you a teetotaller?"

"W-well, not completely. You see, I believe like Paul that a little wine is sometimes good for an upset stomach. On occasion, I've even taken a glass or two of brandy."

"On that point you and I differ," Catherine said. "I'm a complete teetotaller! I've never tasted a drop of alcohol, and I never will—even though my stomach gets tied in knots. But I think I'd better leave. I'll see you in church tomorrow."

Back at home, as Catherine was reminiscing over the day's events, she remembered the oblong bit of parchment Booth had given her. Spreading it out on the table, she read it out loud to her mother.

December 6, 1849

I do promise—my God helping—

First: That I will rise every morning sufficiently early (say 20 minutes before seven o'clock) to wash, dress, and have a few minutes, not less than 5, in private prayer.

Second: That I will as much as possible avoid all that babbling and idle talking in which I have lately so sinfully indulged.

Third: That I will endeavor in my conduct and deportment before the world, and my fellow-servants especially, to conduct myself as a humble, meek, and zealous follower of the bleeding Lamb, and by serious conversation and warning endeavor to lead them to think of their immortal souls.

Fourth: That I will read no less than 4 chapters in God's word every day.

Fifth: That I will strive to live closer to God, and to seek after holiness of heart, and leave providential events with God.

Sixth: That I will read this over every day or at least twice a week.

God help me, enable me to cultivate a spirit of self-denial and to yield myself a prisoner of love to the Redeemer of the world.

Amen and Amen
William Booth

"What do you think of that?" Catherine asked.

"I think it's wonderful," replied Mrs. Mumford. "But—" Hesitatingly, she looked around. "But, you know the story of the pendulum—"

"I'm afraid not." Catherine frowned.

"A clock's pendulum swings from one extreme to another. But it records time only when it crosses the center. When I first met your papa, he was just as radical for Christ as William Booth is now. Then he quit preaching. He began working for the Temperance Movement; and he was just as radical for them as he had been for the teachings of John Wesley. He used to say that he'd like to choke the devil with the last bottle of gin . . ." She sighed, shaking her head sadly. "Now he seldom goes to church and he drinks the horrid stuff himself." Her voice choked with tears.

"Maybe William Booth's different," Catherine commented hopefully. "At least I'm going to pray for him," she vowed. Glancing at herself in the mirror nearby and smiling one way and then another, she wondered what William thought about her. Finally, she spoke. "I think I'd better get out my Sunday dress and iron it," she said nonchalantly. *I wonder if he'll notice me,* she thought. *He's so—*

"But you ironed it just two days ago!" her mother exclaimed. "Why would you want to iron it again?" Mrs. Mumford gave her daughter a quizzical look. Then, an understanding light dawned in her eyes and a smile spread across her face.

Catherine blushed. "Oh, I want to be sure that it's just right," she answered, shrugging her shoulder. She walked to the stove and parked several irons near the front to heat. "The good Lord wants us to be neat." As she was leaving to get her dress, she asked, "Do you think Papa will go with us to the chapel tomorrow?"

"I'll do my best to persuade him, but sometimes he's very stubborn," replied her mother.

While Catherine was ironing her dress, she remarked, "William still has a Cockney brogue. You can tell when he's nervous because he says *'orse* for horse and *hother* for other. But I like it. It puts spice in his speech." She touched the bottom of an iron with a wet finger. Then as she started to press the white ruffles that circled the blouse, she added in a halfway mumble, "He's not very well-read—"

"What do you mean?" Sarah Mumford frowned.

"He never even heard of Dante or the *Divine Comedy!*"

"Now, Catherine, does that really matter?"

"Well, no. Still—" She carefully ironed a button hole. "Still, a preacher of the gospel ought to know a little about Dante, Milton, Shakespeare, Tacitus, Newton, Galileo—and others. Their thoughts and accomplishments could enrich his sermons."

"Oh, come now, Catherine; everyone isn't a bookworm! Remember, you were blessed with curvature of the spine, tuberculosis and a few other diseases. Those maladies kept you in bed so that you had time to read."

"Maybe so, Mama." She thoughtfully attacked the ruffles around the ends of the sleeves. "But please tell me, Mama.

Could a well-read person be happy living with a person who has little knowledge of books?"

"Of course. Each could complement the other. God in his goodness often puts opposite types together."

Catherine arranged her dress on a hanger, carefully smoothing it with her palms, and hung it in the closet. On her return, she stated, "William Booth may not know much about Dante. But he does love souls; and, Mama, that's what is *really* important!"

On Easter morning Catherine sat between her parents in the third pew from the front on the left side in Binfield Chapel. (She would have preferred to be closer to the pulpit, but her father had grumbled that he didn't want to be too conspicuous.)

As Catherine endured the preliminaries, she kept silently praying that Booth would provide a flame that would ignite a revival. She was especially concerned about her father. After what seemed to her a century, the announcements, hymns, offering and solos were over and William Booth stepped into the pulpit. He began by asking the congregation to open their Bibles to John 20:1–3.

This passage, which recorded how Mary Magdalene visited the empty tomb while "it was yet dark," brought smiles to the congregation. The story of the Resurrection was a story they loved to hear. Booth emphasized that when Mary found the sepulchre empty, she ran in order to relay this fact to Peter and "the other disciple whom Jesus loved." Then, after pausing until all eyes were focused on him, he thundered, "All of us know the Good News! It is now our duty to use every possible means to repeat that Good News to all who need to hear it. But, alas, most of us merely want to hear about the empty tomb, and not to repeat that Good News to others— especially to the underprivileged, many of whom haunted the pawnshops last night in order to have a few crumbs to eat today.

"To illustrate my point, I must relate to you a story from my own life.

"When I finished my apprenticeship at the age of nineteen, I spent every moment I could in telling the Good News to others. Will Sansom, a young man about my age, was a big help. We visited the sick. We preached on street corners. When we found an old lady who was starvin' we put 'er in a cabin and supplied 'er needs.

"One Sunday we marched a crowd of roughs we 'ad found in the slums to our chapel. The deacons didn't like that! One of 'em said, 'Booth, if you must bring 'em 'ere, bring 'em in a side door and put 'em as far back as possible.'

"Well, my Bible doesn't tell me that I should take anyone to a great feast by a side door! Jesus' feast is fer 'osoever. He said, 'Go out into the 'ighways and 'edges, and compel them to come in, that me 'ouse may be filled.' You'll find that in yer Bibles in Luke 14:23."

Catherine unconsciously sat with her mouth partly open. Some of the speaker's grammar was not quite correct. He frequently said *don't* instead of doesn't and used singular verbs with plural subjects. But he spoke with power. When he pointed, she was reminded of Isaiah. When he wept, she thought about Jeremiah. When he rebuked, she visualized another Amos.

Toward the close of his message, he said with deep feeling: "The churches are not doing what they should do. They should 'ave services in the East End. They should give 'ope to the wretches in Wappin' and Fryin'-pan Alley. They should sing and preach in the dark places, and in the places strong with a thousand smells. But we haven't done that. No, we only think about those who are comfortable. The bells in the great churches summon the well dressed. They mean nothin' to the outcasts. I just found a poem that records what the bells say to those who 'aven't a bite to eat nor a place to stay. Listen!

Oranges and lemons,
Say the bells of St. Clement's.

Brickbats and tiles,
Say the bells of St. Giles.
'alf-pence and farthings,
Say the bells of St. Martins.
Old Father Baldpate,
Say the slow bells of Aldgate.
Two sticks and an apple,
Say the bells of Whitechapel.
You owe me ten shillings,
Say the bells of St. 'ellen's.
When I grow rich,
Say the bells of Shoreditch.
Pray when will that be?
Say the bells of Stepney.
I'm sure I don't know,
Say the sweet bells of Bow.

" 'ow would you feel if you was starvin' and cold and the church bells at St. Clement's and St. Giles and St. 'ellens sneered at you with those words? Would they inspire you to repent or to steal?" Leaning forward, his eyes aflame, his beard sweeping his chest, his finger extended to its extremity, he methodically jabbed it at the well-dressed congregation. Then he paused until the silence was unbearable. At that point, he exclaimed, "It is our job to change the message of those bells! We need to tune them until they say to everyone, especially the poor: Come to the feast, Even the least. . . .

"And I have a feeling," he concluded after another dramatic pause, "that God has called me, William Booth, to help the church bells say just that. Let us pray."

As the Mumfords were leaving, Rabbits stopped them at the door. "Wife is expecting all of you and Preacher Booth at our house for dinner. Can you come?"

"Certainly," replied Catherine.

John and Sarah Mumford exchanged glances. "Yes, we'll be there," confirmed Mr. Mumford.

8
Two Sticks

Awaiting the call to dinner, Catherine and William sat on the sofa at the far end of the living room. "I really enjoyed your sermon," she said. "I was especially intrigued with the poem about the church bells—"

"Thank you," he returned, smiling broadly. "The church, Catherine, has forgotten its mission. Too many waste time arguing about fine points in theology. I'm not interested in how many angels can balance on the point of a needle!" He thoughtfully stroked his beard. "When Jesus began His ministry, He opened the Book of Isaiah in the synagogue and read: 'The spirit of the Lord is upon me, because he hath sent me to heal the brokenhearted, to preach deliverance to the captives, and recovering of sight to the blind, to set at liberty them that are bruised.'

"Kate, my dear, those are strong words. But we've forgotten 'em."

Catherine felt her heart jump when he used the words "my dear" and the unfamiliar name "Kate" that up until this point only her brother John had used. But with an attempt to hide her feelings, she replied, "As you were quoting the message of the bells, I thought of the bells of St. Sepulchre—"

"What about them?" Booth interjected, his hand brushing up against hers.

"On Execution Morning they used to ring the bells from six until ten. That way, those under sentence of death at Newgate Prison knew they were about to join the procession and be carted to Tyburn Hill and hanged."

"How horrible!" He shook his head and stared. "Instead of proclaiming life, those bells, those church bells, proclaimed death . . ." He shuddered. "Do—do they still do that?"

"No. Probably because of the Wesleyan influence, the last procession to Tyburn was in 1784."

Booth tipped his head sideways, looking at her intently. "How do you know all this?"

"I like to read."

Thoughtfully stroking his beard he murmured. "That's a dramatic illustration. It would stir sinners." He studied her for a long moment then asked, "Do you happen to have another illustration that I could use in a sermon on the new birth?"

After pondering for a moment or two, Catherine confessed, "I do. I just read it last week in Charles Wesley's diary. It's such a good one it brought tears to my eyes. Charles and John were puzzled about the doctrine of instant salvation, and about whether or not people could actually know they were saved. As you know, many Christians sing, 'Doubtful and insecure of bliss, since death alone confirms me His.' Then Charles made an experiment which proved to him that all seekers can be instantly saved and also know and feel assured that they are saved. Let me try and quote the notation Charles made in his diary for July 12, 1738.

" 'I preached at Newgate to the condemned felons, and visited one of them in his cell, sick of a fever; a poor black that had robbed his master. I told him of one who had come down from heaven to save lost sinners, and him in particular . . . He listened with all the signs of eager astonishment; the tears trickled down his cheeks while he cried, "What! was it for me? Did God suffer all this for so poor a creature as me?" '

"Later, Charles returned and was locked in a cell with all

of the ten who were to be hanged. He recorded what happened on July 18. 'All the criminals were present; and all delightfully cheerful . . . Joy was visible in all their faces. We sang:

> Behold the Saviour of mankind,
> Nailed to the shameful tree!
> How vast the love that him inclined
> To bleed and die for thee: . . .

" 'It was one of the most triumphant hours I have ever known,' he said. On the next day, the diary notes, 'At about half-hour past nine their irons were knocked off and their hands tied . . . I got into the cart . . .

" 'We had prayed before that our Lord would show that there was a power superior to the fear of death. Newington had quite forgotten his pain. They were all cheerful, full of comfort, peace and triumph, assuredly persuaded that Christ had died for them . . . Greenway was impatient to be with Christ.

" 'The black man had spied me coming out of the coach, and saluted me with his looks. As often as his eyes met mine, he smiled with the most composed, delightful countenance I ever saw. Read caught hold of my hand in a transport of joy. Newington seemed perfectly pleased. Hudson declared he was never better . . . None showed any natural terror of death: no fear or crying or tears. I never saw such calm triumph, such incredible indifference to dying. We sang several hymns.' "

(As was the custom at that time, a noose from the gallows was attached around the neck of each of the victims.) Catherine continued quoting from the diary:

" 'When the cart drew off [thus causing each to be strangled], not one stirred or struggled for life, but all meekly gave up their spirits. I spoke a few words to the crowd . . . *That hour under the gallows was the most blessed hour of my life.*' " (Italics mine.)

Wiping his tears, Booth said, "Kate, my dear, that is the greatest illustration I ever heard. It would really move the sinners. Do you have any more?"

"My head's full of them."

"Then we'll have to keep in touch with each other," he said, pressing her hand.

Their conversation was ended by Rabbits who suddenly appeared and announced dinner.

As usual in the Rabbits home the table was crowded with an armada of plates loaded with the best food an ample income could buy. After all had been seated, Rabbits invited William Booth to ask the Lord's blessings on the food.

Sitting next to William, Catherine kept wondering if the Lord had arranged this event, or if she, like her mother, was headed toward a disastrous heartbreak. Silently, and within the recesses of her heart, she prayed, *Lord, have Thy way*.

While they were eating, Rabbits related how he'd started in business. "Whenever I go to the office and survey the buildings that belong to me," he said, "I thank the good Lord for His goodness. I started with just a half crown [two and a half shillings] and that was borrowed—"

"What is your secret?" asked Booth.

"Taking advantage of every opportunity and putting out a fine product. I say to my workers, 'Don't let any except the best boots go out of this place.' You know the Lord told us to use our talents. That's what I've done." He speared a piece of steak, loaded the hump of his fork with mashed potatoes, added peas, covered them with gravy, and crowned the load with a thick slab of butter.

Catherine was spellbound by this maneuver. Would the five tiers of food tip over? Would they fit into his mouth? Like an experienced crane operator loading a ship at the docks, Rabbits had no problem. After three or four more fork-loads, the boot tycoon, speaking around a huge bite, said, "Now tell, Brother Booth, what do *you* want to accomplish?"

"I want to do exactly what the Lord wants me to do," replied the preacher. "As of now, I think the Lord wants me to preach to the poor. You know, someone has said, 'The sun never sets on the British Empire.' That is true. We have colonies around the world. But it is also true that the sun never rises in London's East End! The wretches over there need to know that God loves them."

Using the skill of an accomplished shoemaker, Rabbits carefully heaped his fork with another five layers of food, then said, "That's a great idea. But—" He looked doubtful. "But how will you support yourself?" He glanced at Catherine. "It costs a lot of money to live these days—especially if one is married and is raising a family. East-Enders don't have any money."

"Maybe the Lord will lay the need for support on the hearts of some of the more well-to-do Christians—"

"Like?"

Booth shrugged. "Maybe some of the Christians who live right here in Brixton would be moved to help."

"Do you believe that if a drunk is given a new shirt, he'll reform and become a useful member of society?" Rabbits eyed him scornfully.

"Certainly not! Drunks and women of the street first need to be born again. The new birth can change anyone. I'm going to preach on that subject next Sunday."

"Oh, but you won't be preaching here next Sunday. I'm arranging another appointment for you. We're having another guest preacher."

"I-I thought I was to preach here every Sunday for three months," managed Booth. Dismayed, he studied his benefactor with a look of horror.

"Oh, no," replied Rabbits. "I didn't engage you to preach here all that time. I merely said that I would pay you a pound a week for three months."

"I see."

Rabbits smiled. "Maybe we'd all better go into the other room where it's more comfortable."

After all had been seated, Rabbits brought in a bottle of port. "It will settle our dinner," he said.

Catherine lifted her palm. "No thank you, I'm a teetotaller." She spoke in precise, definite tones.

Booth also refused. "I only drink for medicinal purposes," he explained.

The solitary one to accept a drink was John Mumford. While Rabbits was drinking with Mumford, they discussed the way in which Benjamin Disraeli, a novelist and baptized Jew, and now a member of the Church of England, had become Chancellor of the Exchequer in the Derby administration. As Mumford was having his third refill, William and Catherine moved to the sofa at the far end of the room.

"I was disappointed that I won't be here next Sunday," admitted Booth. "But, I suppose, Edward Rabbits is in control." Then turning toward her he stated, "It is my opinion that the minister, not the congregation, should be in control."

"Then you don't agree with the Reformers?"

"Certainly not!" he exploded. "Methodism made its greatest progress when John Wesley was in control. But enough of that. You were speaking about Dante. Did he ever do or say something that could be used for an illustration to move sinners?"

"He certainly did."

"Tell me about it." He squeezed her hand.

Her heart fluttering at his nearness, she began. "The Roman poet Virgil met the wandering poet of the *Divine Comedy* on Good Friday in 1300. Virgil then led him through the woods where they had met into hell. On the gates of that dreadful place were these words: 'All hope abandon, ye who enter here.'

"Strangely, there's very little fire in Dante's hell. The flames are for heretics, violent opposers of God, counselors of fraud—and those who've bought and sold positions in the church for money."

Booth frowned, a shadow crossing his face. "My listeners couldn't understand that," he said. "But the idea that the gates of hell display the sign, *All hope abandon*, is crammed with possibilities." He released her hand, his heart moved by the illustration. "Yes, hell is a place without hope," he expounded, jabbing his finger at an imaginary audience, "and a lot of people in the East End have no hope." Then reaching for her hand again, he said excitedly, "Kate, you've given me a wonderful idea!"

"And here's another," she added, pleased at his response—both to her and her words. "A Dante scholar claimed that there are hundreds of ways to express the idea: abandon hope."

"Hundreds of ways?" Booth stroked his beard as he considered that statement. "What do you mean? Remember," he smiled at her, "I'm from the slums of Nottingham and I have not read all the books you've read."

"One could say: all hope abandon, or abandon all hope, or there is no hope, or hope is dead. There are many ways to indicate the tragedy of no hope."

Suddenly as if lightning had just flashed on a dark night, a new understanding illuminated his face. "I 'ave it!" he exclaimed, slipping into his Nottingham brogue. "Yes, I know 'ow to use it. And, Kate, it's an idea that will floor sinners—"

"How will you use it?"

"Easy. Most of the people I preach to 'ave never 'eard of Dante. Yet all of 'em know about 'ope or the lack of 'ope—" He stopped, smiled, rubbed his beard, shook his head. "No, me dearest Kate, I'm not going to tell you now. I'll use it in my sermon on the new birth when I preach here the next time."

"Please tell me now!" she urged.

"Sorry," he said, smiling. "You'll have to wait." Then standing up he stated, "Dante met Virgil on Good Friday. Right?"

"Right."

"And when did I have my first long visit with you?"

"On Good Friday."

"Do you think that means anything?" He looked searchingly into her eyes.

"It might. It just might," Catherine blushed. "But I trust it doesn't mean that we have to abandon hope!" They both laughed together.

"No, Kate, it doesn't mean that. But perhaps God arranged our meeting. Maybe He has a great work in store for us—a work in which we both need to work together as a team. That Good Friday, like the original Good Friday, was full of God's providence. Remember?"

"Of course."

"Do you believe the Lord arranged for us to meet?"

"Right now I don't know the answer to that. But I'll be praying about it."

"And so will I, Kate," he murmured softly.

And with her hand tucked in his arm, they joined the Rabbits and the Mumfords at the other end of the room. "How about a drink?" grinned Rabbits.

"Never!" emphasized Catherine.

The following Sunday, after Rabbits had introduced the student pastor who was going to preach that morning, he informed the congregation, "William Booth will bring the message next Sunday. Let's all pray that God will especially use him to stir our hearts."

Catherine had never experienced a week that crept by so slowly. It seemed as if the clock barely moved. To pass the time, she reread the first two volumes of Wesley's Journal, washed her hair twice, went for long walks, visited a neighbor, sent a bushel of corn to the still-thin horse three streets away, and spent hours each day kneeling at her bedside. She also searched a concordance for helpful promises.

After the noon meal on Friday, she said, "Mama, William Booth doesn't have a great speaking voice like George Whitefield, and he's not a reader. But he has great dramatic ability and everything he says seems to quiver with life."

"Are you in love with him?" Her mother cocked her head to one side.

Catherine's cheeks became crimson. "I-I don't know," she stuttered. "In a way I am and in a way I'm not. He's not a teetotaller; and I don't think he believes in equal rights for women as strongly as I do."

"Maybe you could change him."

"Do you really think so? You've not been able to change Papa—"

"True, but I'm still praying for him; and he told me that he really liked William Booth's sermon. I think he secretly wants to get right with the Lord."

"The thing that I admire about Booth the most is that he wants to do whatever the Lord wants him to do."

"That's fine. But should you marry him, how would you live? He hasn't been ordained. He's never been to Oxford or Cambridge—"

"True. But if he's God's servant, God will take care of him."

"Even if Brother Rabbits doesn't rehire him?"

"Yes, even if Brother Rabbits doesn't rehire him. David said in Psalm 37, 'I have been young, and now I am old; yet have I not seen the righteous forsaken, nor his seed begging bread.' "

On the third Sunday of April Catherine Mumford sat again with her parents in Binfield Chapel. William Booth read the story of the meeting between Nicodemus and Jesus as recorded in the third chapter of John. He then preached on the necessity of the new birth. Toward the close, he remarked, "Many have wondered if the new birth is a possibility. Even John and Charles Wesley wondered if a person could be instantly changed. Then Charles Wesley had himself locked in a cell in Newgate with some prisoners who were to be hanged at Tyburn. While there, he won them to Christ."

Catherine was moved as he related the story she had told him.

"On Execution Morning Charles went with the procession to Tyburn and there he talked with those who had accepted Christ and were about to die. To his amazement he found that none of them were afraid. Instead of being afraid of the noose, all of them were looking forward to being with Christ.

"Wesley said that that day under the gallows was the happiest day of his life. Why did he say that? Because those convicts proved to him that sinners can be born again!

"Of course I already knew that because when I was a lad in Nottingham, there was a notorious hoodlum in the city named Bensom Jack. While his wife and children starved, he wasted his money in the taverns. Then David Greenbury held some gospel meetings and Jack was converted. From that day on he was a changed man. I've heard him testify.

"Dante wrote that the gates of hell have written across them: 'All hope abandon, ye who enter here.' Being without hope is hell. But I'm here to assure you that you can have hope. Hope, the Good Book teaches, is for whosoever. Yes, whosoever!

"But there's no hope in just good works, and there's no hope without repentance, and there's no hope without going through Christ. There's only one way to hope—the Bible way!"

As the invitation to kneel at the mourner's bench was given, three young people went forward. Catherine prayed that her father would respond. But even though he wept, he didn't budge. Although disappointed that her father didn't seek reclamation, Catherine was extremely happy. Her knowledge had inspired the preacher; and the preacher had been mightily used by the Lord to win three people.

The successful service on that third Sunday of April was proof that she could be useful in the salvation of souls!

Since Booth preached elsewhere during the next two Sundays, our only knowledge of Catherine's contact with him is through several of her letters. The earliest of these is dated May 11, 1852. It began: "My dear Friend." Key sentences in that initial letter hint at some of the things Booth may have said or written:

> Don't pore over the past! Let it all go! Never mind *who* frowns if God smiles . . . Do try to forget me, as far as the remembrance would injure your usefulness or spoil your peace . . . 'Thy will be done!' is my constant cry . . .
> It is very trying to be depreciated and slighted when you are acting from the purest motives. But consider the char-

acter of those who thus treat you and *don't overestimate their influence.*

Catherine's letter, written two days later, indicates that some serious things had been discussed between them. The salutation was the same. But within the letter were some intriguing sentences:

I have read and reread your note, and fear you did not fully understand my difficulty. *I dare not enter into so solemn an engagement until you can assure me that you feel I am in every way suited to make you happy, and that you are satisfied that the step is not opposed to the will of God.*
Let us besiege His throne with all the powers of prayer . . . (Italics mine.)

Two days after that letter, William and Catherine had an opportunity to be together. On that Saturday evening, they each bared their souls to each other. Since neither could come to a definite conclusion about whether or not they should be engaged, they decided to use a method that even John Wesley had employed. After balancing a Bible on its spine, they agreed to let it fall open and to be guided by the first passage they read.

The Bible fell open to the 37th chapter of the Book of Ezekiel. Having read this prophecy many times, Catherine wondered how it could possibly speak to them. Then their eyes were drawn to the 19th verse. Silently they read:

Say unto them, Thus saith the Lord God; Behold, I will take the stick of Joseph, which is in the hand of Ephraim, and the tribes of Israel his fellows, and will put them with him, even with the stick of Judah, and make them one stick, and they shall be one in mine hand.

The final words, *and they shall be one in mine hand,* riveted their attention. But did that passage apply to them? After all, Ezekiel had written those words some twenty-four hundred years ago. Ah, but a decision had to be made. Catherine records what happened:

"However, this controversy could not go on forever with two hearts as ours, and consequently we . . . covenanted that come weal or woe we would sail life's stormy seas together, and on our knees we plighted our troth before the Lord."

Catherine's next letter, written a day or two after they had "plighted their troth," indicates that she was fully committed and looking forward to her marriage to William Booth. Her salutation had now changed. She wrote:

> My dearest William—the evening is beautifully serene and tranquil, according sweetly with the feelings of my soul. The whirlwind is past and the succeeding calm is in proportion to its violence.

Those words were followed by similar sentences. Still, the letter concluded with a most solemn declaration:

> The more you lead me up to Christ in all things, the more highly I shall esteem you; and if it is possible to love you more than I do now, the more I shall love you. You are always present in my thoughts.
>
> Believe me, dear William, as ever,
>
> > Your own loving
> > Kate

After Catherine had posted this letter and similar ones, she gradually descended from the high peaks of her dreamworld to the arid plains of reality; and some of the facts she faced on the parched plains below were grim indeed.

One startling fact was that she had committed herself to marriage after having known Booth for only a little over a month. Had not Jesus warned about the folly of starting to build a tower without first counting the cost? Of course He had! His admonition was in Luke 14:28–30. She slowly reread and marked that passage.

Had she made a fool of herself?

Another grim fact was that Booth had no money, no position, had not been ordained—and had never even stepped inside an institution of higher learning. Moreover, Rabbits was already getting tired of him. And, according to her husband-to-be's unwritten contract with the boot manufacturer, he was only due another six pounds. She calculated the amount on her fingers. Indeed, the tall man to whom she had pledged her troth was almost as poor as one of the paupers in the East End!

As she tossed and turned, trying to sleep, she kept visualizing the hole in the sole of Booth's shoe, which had been so evident to the congregation when he knelt with the youthful seekers who had bowed at the mourner's bench.

When the hands of the clock stood at 2 a.m. and she was still unable to forget the worn-out shoe, she lit a candle and opened her Bible to the Book of Judges. In the fourth and fifth chapters she reread a favorite story—the one about Deborah, Barak, and Sisera.

Frightened by the Canaanite commander Sisera and his nine hundred chariots, Barak went to Deborah. Afraid to confront the Canaanite, he was candid: "If thou wilt go with me, then I will go: but if thou wilt not go with me, then I will not go" (4:8).

Assured that the Lord was with her, Deborah accompanied Barak. Backed by ten thousand men, they faced Sisera and his army at Megiddo. Then a miracle took place. The rains poured and "the river of Kishon swept them away. . ." (5:21). Sisera's chariots floundered in the mud. The horses merely pranced about. Utterly defeated, Sisera fled. He was finally put to death by a woman who hammered a nail "into his temples and fastened it into the ground" (4:21).

Overwhelmed by God's providence, the Hebrew historian who recorded the event composed one of the world's most sublime lines of poetry: "The stars in their courses fought against Sisera" (5:20).

Closing her Bible, Catherine vowed to herself: "Like Deborah, I will team with William Booth; and Jesus Christ, God's only begotten Son, will guide—and provide for us." With that confidence, she was soon fast asleep.

9

Storms

Although some of the Reformers questioned Booth's belief that the pastor should make the major decisions, and Rabbits was concerned about William's passion to reach the poor, no one questioned his dedication—especially Catherine. The post yielded a typical letter.

After the ardent salutation, "My own loving Kate," Booth mentioned a dying girl who needed help. His letter included directions: "If you leave the omnibus at the Obelisk, at the end of the London, and at the foot of the Waterloo and Blackfriars Roads, you will be but a few yards from your destination, which is No. 3 or 4 Dyke Street, next door to a plumber and glazier's shop; it is up two flights of stairs." Remembering the horrible smells, he added, "Take with you a smelling bottle . . ."

Booth signed this letter in an even more passionate conclusion than his salutation:

> Yours in the closest alliance of united soul, spirit, and body for time and for eternity, for earth and heaven, for sorrow and for joy, for ever and ever. Amen.
>
> William

Each day Catherine and William became increasingly unhappy with the Reformers. In late May they faced each other across the dinner table in the Mumford home. William all but exploded: "I'm fed up right to 'ere." He slashed his finger across his throat.

"What happened *this* time?"

"I just met with the church leaders and had important plans I wanted to discuss about visiting the slums. I expected to preside. But Rabbits! God bless 'im . . . Rabbits said, 'Brother Booth, you're merely our 'ired preacher. You can't preside at any meetin' unless you've been elected to preside at that meetin'!'

"Kate, what am I to do?" He covered his face.

"Preach a good sermon on the way each congregation was governed in New Testament times. I'll help you prepare it—"

"But I can't do that! Rabbits just informed me that I'm not to preach here again until the first Sunday in June."

"Then there's only one thing to do."

"What's that?"

"Leave the Reformers."

"I've already left the Wesleyans! Where would I go?" He lifted his hands and gasped.

"To the Congregationalists."

"But they don't believe in *whosoever*! I'm not about to preach for any denomination that believes certain ones are born to be damned! God's redemption is for everyone. And everyone includes all the thieves, women of the street, wife-beaters—and the—the idle rich."

"They don't *all* believe that." Catherine's voice had a note of authority. "Why don't you let me speak to Dr. David Thomas, the pastor at the Stockwell New Chapel. He's an excellent preacher I've heard him several times."

"All right. I'll leave it up to you," Booth sighed contentedly. "After all, Kate, you're part of the team!"

Thomas suggested to Catherine that Booth should contact Dr. John Campbell, the distinguished editor of *The Christian Witness*, *The Christian's Penny Magazine*, and *Friend of the People*. Booth was reluctant to leave the Wesleyans. Both John and Charles were his heroes. But Catherine kept nudging until he finally knocked at Campbell's door in the manse which was attached to the Whitefield Tabernacle.

"I think the Congregational Church is just the place for you," concluded Campbell from behind a desk piled high with books and manuscripts.

"Ah, but Dr. Campbell, I want to preach *whosoever*—"

"And that's another reason you should come with us. Whitefield was a Calvinistic Methodist. True, he didn't use the word *whosoever* as much as it was used by John Wesley; but he won a lot of souls for Christ, and he is the one who inspired the Wesleys to preach out in the open air."

"Could I preach *whosoever* in the Congregational Church?"

"In most of them. As with all groups, we have a few radicals." He stood up and held out his hand. "Brother Booth," he stated, "I like you. You have great talent. Go to college. Study. Listen to one of our experienced pastors. Then preach what you like." He picked up his pen. "I'll write you a letter of introduction to Dr. William Massie, secretary to the Home Missionary Society of the Congregational Union. He'll tell you exactly what you should do."

With the letter of introduction in his hand, Booth approached Massie.

"Mmm-mmm," murmured the pontifical man as he scanned the letter. "Mmm-mmm. Have you ever been to college?" He peered at Booth over the top of his glasses.

"N-no."

"Do you know any Latin or Greek or Hebrew?"

"I'm afraid not."

"Mmm-mmm. Well, I'll tell you what I think you should do. Return to business for two years, attend a good Congregational Church where there's an intellectual minister; and then apply, through that church, for admission to college. But let me warn you, it will be quite difficult for you to be

admitted to any college, because we already have more ministers than pulpits—"

"Do you have any churches in London's East End?" ventured Booth, shifting his feet nervously, for Dr. Massie had
not offered him a seat.

"We have a struggling mission . . ."

"Wouldn't you like to have some churches among those
people?"

"Yes, I believe that you do have a constructive idea. But,
Mr. Booth, how would we ever support works out there? The
wretches in Frying-Pan Alley don't have any money." With
that statement he held out his hand. The interview was over.

Realizing that his three-month contract with Rabbits was
almost completed, Booth became thoroughly discouraged. In
utter despair he wrote to Dr. Campbell on June 25, 1852. His
letter was highlighted by the word *fear.*

"Perhaps the ministry is not my way," he lamented. "My
prayer, my constant prayer is, 'Teach me Thy will . . .' My only
fear is that I have not sufficient ability to be a successful
minister . . . I fear reaching a position which I should not be
able to fully sustain. I fear having formed an erroneous esti-
mate of myself, my capacities and powers, and I tremble at
the consequences . . ."

Negative though that part of the letter was, he clearly had
not "abandoned hope." In a paragraph near the end he waved
his banner of faith: "But the God whom I serve, and whose I
am, lives to direct, and in *Him* I put my trust, and on *Him* I
can lean."

After receiving his final pound from Rabbits, he was desperate. With no income, no place to preach, an enlarging hole
in his shoe, and the realization that the girl to whom he was
engaged was a semi-invalid, he felt walled-in by impossibilities. After presenting a girl who was dying of tuberculosis
with his last sixpence, he visited Catherine.

Over a cup of tea he wailed, "Kate, I don't know what to
do."

"Have you given up becoming a Congregational minister?"

"I have. Their doctrine of election frightens me—"

"Ah, but many of the greats, including George Whitefield, believed in election. After Whitefield's death, someone asked John Wesley if he thought he would ever see him in heaven. Wesley replied, 'Never!' That pleased his Arminian friend. 'Why won't you see him in heaven?' he asked. 'I won't see him,' replied Wesley, 'because he will be so much closer to the throne than I will be. My eyes will be dazzled by the glory surrounding him!' "

They both laughed; then Booth became extremely serious. "But, Kate, my dear, what *am* I to do? I'm desperate!"

"When God closes a door it's because He's opening another."

"I hope you're right." He thoughtfully stirred his tea. "But waiting is hard." He emptied the cup, picked up his hat, and headed for the door.

Hurrying after him, she grabbed his hand in both of hers and looked steadily in his eyes. "William," she encouraged, "everything will work out just right. God has a great work for you and me to do together. Mama and I will be praying for you. Remember the words of Tertullian, 'It is certain because it is impossible!' "

"Thanks, Kate. Thank you very much." He drew her close and kissed her tenderly. "You're a modern Deborah," he smiled, his eyes flashing his love. "I don't know what I'd do without you!"

Catherine watched him walk slowly down the street until he turned the corner. Closing the door with a sigh, she went to the bureau and picked up her shorthand book.

"What are you doing with that?" asked her mother.

"I'm going to learn shorthand."

"On your own?" She questioned, cocking her head to one side.

"Of course! Charles Dickens learned shorthand on his own."

"Why do you want to learn shorthand?"

"To help William when God finally gets him shaped up

and places him just where He wants him to be. I'm also going to learn to play the piano."

"You really believe in him, don't you?"

"Of course I believe in him! He's fully surrendered; and anyone who is fully surrendered to God has possibilities. Someday, William Booth will stir the world."

"Are you sure?" she asked doubtfully as she began to clear the table. "If Wellington had been as discouraged as Booth was this morning, he would never have defeated Napoleon."

Catherine shrugged. "True, and yet we must not forget that even though Barak was discouraged, he defeated the Canaanites in spite of their nine hundred iron chariots."

"And what was the secret of Barak's success?"

"His secret was that he and Deborah allowed God to use them!"

Mrs. Mumford smiled. "As usual, you're right. And now, 'Deborah,' you'd better get busy with your shorthand and piano lessons."

The next Sunday Booth had a speaking engagement just outside London. Three days later when he showed up at the Mumford home, he was sparkling with enthusiasm. "They gave me a pound, and five people were saved!" he exulted. "And look, a cobbler in the church resoled my shoes." He lifted his shoe for Catherine to see. "But, Kate, that isn't the best news. The best news is that I've been invited to assist Dr. Ferguson at Ryde on the Isle of Wight."

"Sounds interesting."

"It *is* interesting! And not only do they want me to be their assistant, but they've suggested that I might become the pastor after Ferguson is gone."

"Do you think you'll accept their invitation?" asked Catherine after she had motioned for him to sit with her on the sofa.

Patting her hand, he said, "I-I don't know. It's a real opportunity and I'm happy they considered me. But I don't think it's the kind of situation that I'd really like."

"Why not?" She questioned, leaning a little closer.

"Well, I think God wants me to be near an industrial center like Manchester or London. That way I could work with the outcasts. In my way of thinking a man may be down but he's never out. The Isle of Wight is just beyond our southern coast. If I go there we could get married . . . But, I want to be in God's will."

"Have you prayed about it?"

"Of course. And I want you to join me in prayer too. If it's God's will for me to go, then I'll go. But if it isn't His will, I won't."

A letter from Booth, written on July 28, reveals some of his feelings about the call to Ryde:

My Own Dear Catherine:
I have just received a letter (three sheets of note paper) from my friend in the Isle of Wight. He says very plainly that he cannot give me up, and prays me to reconsider . . .

He says, "Here is the place for your social and, I believe, loving heart to expand and quicken. Don't go to college."

This is my reason for writing. I am not *miserable*; do not fear that. I prayed earnestly all the way home last night for guidance. I believe it will be given.

Mysteriously, Booth did not accept the call to Ryde. The deciding factor is unknown. Perhaps it is indicated in the last sentence of this letter: "I am reading Finney and Watson on election and final perseverance, and I see more than ever reason to cling to my own views of truth and righteousness."

The barrier to Ryde may have been doctrine.

During August and September Catherine continued to pray that a worthwhile door would open for William. But it seemed that God had decided not to answer her just yet.

"When God closes a door He really closes it and bolts it shut," grumbled Booth. "I've about worn out me prayer bones prayin'. Maybe God doesn't want me to be a preacher! Maybe I should return to the pawnbroker business. Maybe—"

"Oh, but God *does* answer prayer!" interrupted Catherine. "I've found some scripture I want to share with you after I fix you a cup of tea."

While Booth was devouring his third cookie, Catherine said, "Now, William dear, listen to Isaiah 40: 'But they that wait upon the Lord shall renew their strength; they shall mount up with wings as eagles; they shall run and not be weary; and they shall walk, and not faint!' "

"Yes, I've read that many times. But it doesn't seem to apply to me—"

"Then you don't believe in whosoever!"

"Oh, but I do! It's just that—" He spread his hands in a gesture of despair. "It's just that I don't get an answer."

Almost automatically Catherine flipped her Bible to Ps. 27:14. "Here's another passage we can rely on. David said: 'Wait on the Lord: be of good courage, and he shall strengthen thine heart: wait, I say, on the Lord.'

"You see, William, he repeated the word *wait*, and, in between those words, he told us that we should have good courage. That means we should have courage—now."

"I have courage. But maybe I don't have enough."

"Here's a poem I found that was written by Thomas Ken, the author of the Doxology. I think the Lord must have guided me to it.

> Devote yourself to God, and you will find
> God fights the battles of a will resigned.
> Love Jesus! love will no base fear endure—
> Love Jesus! and of conquest rest secure.

"What do you think of that?"

He blew his nose and wiped his eyes. "It's great! Kate, what would I do without you?" He put his arm around her and cradled her head on his shoulder.

"Don't worry," she said, looking up. "God has His hand on you, William. Someday you will reach thousands. I just know it to be true."

After he had gone, Catherine retired to her room; closing the door, she sank to her knees and prayed for guidance.

When September passed without the tiniest door opening, Catherine became anxious. Her anxiety was increased by her father. One evening, his eyes aflame with gin, he cautioned, "Catherine, you'd better forget about this fellow Booth. There must be some sneaky reason why he can't get a church! Nottingham's a rotten town—"

"Oh, Papa, don't!"

"Truth hurts. But I'm right. Booth's been eating here so much, I think I'll start charging him for his board. I never ate one meal in my father-in-law's house. Not one!"

"That's because he threw you out—"

"I suppose your mama told you that one?" His red eyes slowly blinking demanded an answer.

Catherine nodded.

"Well, I won't charge him," he chuckled. "He is a good preacher, even though he says 'orse. But I hope he gets a church soon. I'm getting tired of seeing him around here."

Early one evening when Catherine had just gone to her bedroom for another handkerchief, Booth knocked at the front door. "Have I got wonderful news!" he exclaimed as he stood in the doorway. "The Reformers at Spalding need a man to ride circuit and I've been selected!"

"Spalding—Spalding," repeated Catherine. "That's Wesley country. You wouldn't be far from Epworth where John and Charles were born."

"Yes, it's in Lincolnshire. The circuit covers a twenty-seven-mile area. It's also not far from Lincoln Castle where Samuel Wesley was imprisoned for debt."

They both laughed and then rejoiced at God's provision.

10
Interlude

T he chilly winds of late November were lashing into Brixton as Catherine and William spent their last evening together in one of the finer restaurants in town.

Across an immaculate table lit by candles and sparkling with expensive silverware and china, Catherine said, "William, I'm convinced that your call to the Spalding Circuit was from the Lord. Just think, you'll be preaching in the same area in which the Wesleys preached! A while back, a friend who attends the Metropolitan Tabernacle heard Charles Spurgeon say, 'The character of John Wesley stands above all imputation of self-sacrifice, zeal, holiness, and communion with God.' "

"I am indeed fortunate," he murmured. Then tasting his salad, he added, "And I have you to thank. The call came because of your prayers—"

"*Our* prayers!" she corrected. "Jesus said, 'If two of you shall agree on earth as touching any thing that they shall ask, it shall be done for them of my Father which is in heaven.' "

"I agree," replied Booth as he cut a slice of fish. "And now that we're going to be separated by almost one hundred miles—and, Kate, that's at least a three-day journey!—we ought to agree on some important petitions we'd like to have answered. Any ideas?"

"I have a very important one," Catherine offered. "I think that both of us should pray that each of us will remain in God's perfect will."

"I agree. But, Kate my dear, suppose God calls us to work with the outcasts, say in London's East End, would you agree to obey Him?"

"Certainly."

"Even if it meant being cold and hungry?"

"Yes, even if it meant that. But, William, God would not let us go hungry—especially if we remain in His will."

Silently Booth manipulated a bone out of his fish. "What would you say if the people in Spalding provided us with a house and suggested that we get married right away?"

"The moment it's God's will for me to marry you, I will marry you." Catherine smiled and looked thoughtfully determined.

Booth almost dropped his fork. "You mean you have doubts about me?" He studied her face.

"Of course not! But the author of Ecclesiastes said, 'To every thing there is a season, and a time to every purpose under heaven!' "

Smiling Booth reached for her hand. "I was just teasin' you," he said tenderly. Following a fine dessert of creamed pudding, polished off with a pot of the finest India tea, Catherine asked, "When does your coach leave for Spalding?"

"Tomorrow morning at nine o'clock."

After William Booth had taken her home in a hired carriage, and while they were lingering together on the sofa, John Mumford staggered in. As he swayed on his feet, he focused his eyes on Booth and said, "Sho you're going to Shpalding . . . Wish I were going with you! My happiest days were when I was a preacher. The people up there really need you . . . They're a bad lot." He slowly shook his head. "I'd better go to bed. Had one too many." As he shuffled across the room, he swayed and then collapsed.

"Oh, Papa!" Catherine screamed as she rushed over to him. Gently helping him to his feet and leading him to his room, she promised, "Mama will help you get to bed."

Back on the sofa Catherine covered her face. "I'm so embarrassed. Papa is really a very fine man—"

"I know he is," comforted Booth, putting his arm around her. "Let's agree that God will convict and change your father." Kissing her goodbye, he stepped out into the night.

While struggling for sleep, the events of the day kept flashing through Catherine's mind. Suddenly she became aware that she had not had a final discussion with William about women's rights, nor had she repeated to him again that she felt he should become an absolute teetotaller. These two differences between them were becoming increasingly painful. But having prayed about the matter, she felt assured that they would be removed, or, at least, compromised. After praying for her father's restoration, she fell asleep.

In the morning, arriving early at the coach depot, Catherine was a little surprised that William wasn't there. But at five minutes to nine he strode up. His only suitcase was a black, worn-out bag with several patches on each side and a handle on the verge of coming off.

"I was afraid you'd be late," Catherine sighed.

"Oh, no," he assured. "I was watching my time." He drew out his watch and pointed to the minute hand. "I decided long ago that I didn't want to waste the Lord's time by bein' either late or early." He forced a smile.

In their last brief moment together before he stepped into the coach, Catherine whispered, "Be sure and remember Papa and be assured that Mama and I will be praying for you."

"I'll remember," William said as he looked lovingly into her eyes. Quickly giving her a brief hug and brushing his lips gently over her forehead, he turned to board the waiting coach.

Seconds later, the red-coated driver flicked his whip and the coach was on its way. Catherine waved her handkerchief until the coach had disappeared around a curve at the bottom of the hill. Choking with emotion and wiping her eyes, she made her way home.

Nearly a week passed before Catherine received a letter from William. Eagerly she opened it and soon her eyes were glowing with satisfaction. After the warm salutation, she read:

> My reception has been beyond my highest anticipations. Indeed my hopes have risen fifty percent that this circuit will be unto me all that I want or need.
>
> I do think it was the hand of the Lord that brought me here. I had a good day yesterday. The people were highly satisfied . . .
>
> On Sunday I preached at Holbreach . . . Strong men were completely melted down . . .

Catherine answered all of his letters immediately; and the longer they corresponded, the lengthier they became. In many of her "epistles" she not only encouraged him, but also filled them with words of caution.

> My dearest love, beware how you indulge that dangerous element of character, *ambition* . . ."
>
> Could you not provide yourself with a small leather bag or case large enough to hold your Bible and any other book you might require—pens, ink, paper, and a *candle*? And presuming you have a room to yourself, could you not rise by six o'clock every morning, and convert your bedroom into a study until breakfast time?
>
> Do not be overanxious about the future. Spalding *will not be your final destination* if you make *the best of your ability*.
>
> I fear, my love, you are not sufficiently careful as to diet; do exercise self-denial when such things are before you as you have any reason to fear will disagree with you.

In response to a letter in which Booth mentioned that he had taken some brandy for his upset stomach, and another in which he had asked her advice about using port wine for the same reason, she responded with an epistle which included some undiluted statements:

Now, my dearest, it is *absolutely necessary*, in order to save you from people's false notions, that you should have a settled, *intelligent conviction* on the subject, and, in order that you may get this, I have gone to the trouble of almost unpacking your box . . . to get out *Bachus*, in which you will find several green marks . . . and pencillings in three or four sections. I do hope you will read it.

It is a subject on which I am most anxious that you should be *thorough*. I abominate that hackneyed and monstrously inconsistent tale—a teetotaller in principle, but obliged to take a little for my stomach's sake. Such teetotallers aid the progress of intemperance more than all the drunkards in the land, and there are an abundance of them among the Methodist preachers.

I have far more hope for your health *because* you abstain from stimulating drinks than I should have if you took them; to one of your temperament they would be especially hurtful.

Goodnight, I must conclude tomorrow.

Mrs. Mumford frowned as she read this letter. "Aren't you afraid it will break up your romance?" she asked.

"Never! William and I have decided that we should be a team. This means that we should combine our strong points."

"You may be right, but as a popular preacher, William will be meeting many pretty and talented girls. Men don't like to be crossed. I know from experience!" She shook her head sadly.

Catherine's letters were not all temperance tracts. Woven into each were lines of warm affection. "I thought about you very much during the day." "Be assured, my love, I have confidence in you, I believe what you say, but you know, William, I shall give my all to you—my happiness, my pride . . ." "Bless you a thousand times, I only want to see you happy and useful, I care not where or how, provided it be according to God's will."

Each letter opened with an affectionate salutation. Sometimes it was "My Own Dear William." Other times: "My Beloved William." On each occasion, all the adjectives were capitalized!

But all of Catherine's book-length tomes were not addressed to William Booth! Having heard Dr. David Thomas preach a sermon in which he held that women were secondary to men, she filled her ink pot, selected several pens, and went to work. Her letter began:

> Dear Sir: You will doubtless be surprised at the receipt of this communication, and I assure you that it is with great reluctance and a feeling of profound respect that I make it. Were it not for the high estimate I entertain for both your intellect and heart, I would spare the sacrifice it will cost me.

Having filled many pages with her diplomacy, she then launched an attack. Although she never used invective or ridicule, she proved herself to be as effective with words as Napoleon was with artillery.

> All man-made religions indeed neglect or debase woman, but the religion of Christ recognizes her individuality and raises her to the dignity of an independent moral agent. Under the Old Testament dispensation we have several instances of Jehovah choosing a woman as a vehicle of his thought. And in the New Testament she is fully restored to her original position. In Jesus Christ there is neither male nor female.

Following page after page of similar examples, punctuated by grim exclamation points, she concluded:

> I have no sympathy with those who would alter woman's domestic and social position from what is laid down in the Scriptures! This, I believe, God has clearly defined, and has given the reason. And, therefore, I submit, feeling that in the wisdom of love, as well as in judgment, He has done it. But on the subject of equality of nature, I believe my convictions are true!

Her head and shoulders aching from the strain of concentration, she finished making a copy, placed it in an envelope with a letter and addressed it to William Booth. As she paid the postage on both thick envelopes, she began to wonder about the results of her verbal attack.

A response from Dr. Thomas has never been discovered. But within a few days she had an answer from Booth. After making herself comfortable on the sofa, she opened the letter.

Nervously skipping the normal chitchat, she finally came to the reply. Biting her lip, she read:

> From the first reading I cannot see anything to lead me for one *moment* to think of altering my opinion. You *combat* a great deal that I hold as firmly as *you* do—namely, her *equality*, her perfect *equality*, as a whole—as a *being*. But to concede that she is man's *equal*, or capable of becoming man's equal, in intellectual attainments or prowess—I must say *that* is contradicted by experience in the world and in my honest conviction. You know, my dear, I acknowledge the superiority of your sex in many things—in others, I believe her inferior. *Vice versa* with man.
>
> I would not stop a woman from preaching on any account. I would not encourage one to begin. You should preach if you felt moved thereto: felt equal to the task. I would not stay *you* if I had power to do so. Altho' *I should not like it.* It is easy for you to say my views are the result of prejudice; perhaps they are. I am for the world's salvation; I will quarrel with no means that promises help.

Rising and pacing the floor, Catherine was clearly upset after reading those paragraphs. As far as preaching was concerned, she had no desire, for in her heart she knew that she was far too timid to ever stand in the pulpit and face a congregation. But the idea that a woman was intellectually inferior to a man was almost more than she could bear! Still, she loved and respected William.

After a few frustrating minutes, she returned to the sofa. Yes, they disagreed at this point; nonetheless, she solemnly vowed to herself that she would change William Booth's thinking on this subject. Yes, she would change it even if it took years of subtle effort. The fact remained that without Deborah, Barak would never have defeated Sisera and his nine hundred chariots of iron!

Though the disagreement continued, it still did not mar their relationship. A new letter that just arrived moved her heart: "Tonight I go back to Spalding. Tuesday to Rinchbeck. Wednesday to Suttleton. Thursday a special sermon at Boston. I wish all this writing were at an end and you were in my arms, and yet I cannot help having fears and doubts about the future . . ."

From his many letters, Catherine knew that in spite of his great success, William had misgivings about the Reformers. True, they urged him to marry right away and had offered him a house, a buggy, and a horse. A letter, dated November 3, 1853, was intense with enthusiasm:

> I have today given myself afresh to God. On my knees I have been promising Him that if He will help me, I will aim only at souls, and live and die for their salvation. I feel a delightful and soul-cheering victory over what has often been of late very severe temptation.
>
> Wednesday . . . Two souls weeping very bitterly. I never saw persons in deeper distress. From about eight until half-past ten they wept incessantly on account of their sins.
>
> Sunday . . . In the morning very large congregation . . .
>
> Evening . . . Liberty in preaching. Fourteen persons came forward . . . Praise the Lord!

But even though William continued to describe his successes with glowing words, Catherine knew that he wasn't satisfied. The Reformers could never forget their grievances. In his view, they were more interested in rehashing the past than in summoning the lost to Christ.

While riding the Spalding Circuit, he continued to hear about the Methodist New Connexion and he liked what he heard. They were well-organized, methodical, successful. Intrigued, he asked Catherine to make a study of the group.

Her investigation revealed that this group was the first to break away from the main body after Wesley's death in 1791. Among the leaders at that time was Alexander Kilham, a capable man who believed that traveling preachers should be allowed to administer the sacraments, and that laity should have a vote in the administrative government of the organization.

Dominated by these suggested reforms, Kilham published pamphlets outlining his ideas. These less than diplomatic publications angered the main body and he was expelled by the Annual Conference of 1796. He then began to publish a monthly paper, the *Methodist Monitor*. Two years later, this publication became the *Methodist New Connexion*

Magazine. Eventually, this split-off bought the Ebenezer Chapel in Leeds from the Baptists.

Now, with their own church building, the Methodist New Connexion denomination became a reality. Booth liked them. Being almost fifty years old, their sore spots had healed and they were enjoying rapid growth. But even though he appreciated them, he also had some affection for the Reformers. Both groups were thoroughly Wesleyan in doctrine. The best solution, he believed, was for the Reformers to unite with the New Connexion.

With this view in mind, Booth published an article in the *Wesleyan Times*—the official organ of the Reformers. Friendly discussions followed. But since the Reformers insisted that most decisions in any situation be made by the laity rather than the clergy, and since the New Connexion refused to agree to this point of view, unity between the two groups became impossible. Nonetheless, Booth felt that he could have a more effective ministry by working with the Methodist New Connexion.

As Booth wrestled with the problem, he leaned heavily on Catherine's prayers and advice. There were many things to consider. He could continue with the Reformers. His ministry of more than a year in the Spalding Circuit had been satisfactory. If he united with the New Connexion, he would be placed on a four-year period of probation, would have to go to "seminary," and would not be allowed to marry for several years. Then in January 1854, an additional complication entered the situation. Wondering what he should do, he wrote to Catherine.

While the January snows were whitening the streets of Brixton, Catherine studied his letter:

> My Dearest Kate: The plot thickens, and I hesitate not to tell you that I fear, and fear much, that I am going wrong.
> Yesterday I received a letter asking me if I would consent to come to the Hinde Street circuit [London Reformers], salary one hundred pounds a year. I have also heard that the committee in London [is] about to make an offer. I would give a great deal to be satisfied as to the right path . . .

You see, my dearest, it is certainly enough to make a fellow think and tremble. Here I am in a circuit numbering 780 members, with an increase last year of nearly two hundred. Am invited to another group with nearly one thousand. And yet I'm going to join a church with but 150 members in London [New Connexion], and a majority of circuits with but a similar number.

I fear that with all my cautiousness on this subject, I shall regret it. Send me a letter to reach me on Friday. Bless you a thousand times! My present intention is to tear myself away from all and everything and persevere in the path I have chosen. They reckon it down here the maddest, wildest, most premature and hasty step that they ever knew a saved man to take.

I remain, my dearest love,

Your own
William

Catherine reread the letter many times and prayed about it. Then, her mind made up, she dipped her quill and thoughtfully wrote:

My Dearest William: I have with a burdened soul committed the contents of your letter to God, and I feel persuaded He will guide you. I will just put down one or two considerations that may comfort you.

First, then, you are not leaving the Reformers because you fear you would not get another circuit or as good a salary as the Connexion can offer. You are leaving because you are out of patience and sympathy with its principles and *aims*, and because you believe they will bring it to ultimate destruction.

Second, you are not leaving it to secure present advantages, but sacrificing present advantages for what you believe to be on *the whole* (looking to the end) most for God's glory . . .

Oh, if you come to London, let us be determined to reap a blessed harvest! My mind is made up to do my part toward it. I hope to be firm as a rock on some points. The Lord help me! We must aim to improve each other's minds.

I am living above. My soul breathes a purer atmosphere than it has done for the last two or three years. God lives and reigns, and this to me is a source of much consolation.

With deepest interest and sincere affection,

> I remain, your loving
> Kate

Convinced that he was making the right move, and encouraged by Catherine, Booth packed his things and headed for London.

11

A New World

Catherine was excited as she hopped out of bed that early Wednesday morning. After what seemed such a long time she would finally be seeing William at the Brunswick Chapel that night. Of course he had no idea that she would be there. That made it all the harder to wait.

After carefully pressing all the wrinkles out of her dress, Catherine sat down to wait for her mother to come and fix her hair. So preoccupied was she with her thoughts, she scarcely noticed when her mother entered the room. As though in a dream Catherine proclaimed, "The best thing about William is his complete dedication."

Somewhat startled by Catherine's outburst, Mrs. Mumford agreed. "But we must keep praying that he will continue to be so dedicated."

"What do you mean, Mama?" asked Catherine, frowning.

Her mother parted Catherine's hair in the center of her head and began to thoughtfully comb it out. "Your papa used to be all out for Christ. He'd do anything for the cause. Anything! Then he became too successful. I think success ruined him. Now he's such a slave to gin he's losing customers—"

"Is he having financial difficulties?"

"Yes. We're already dipping into our savings. But you must not tell anyone."

"Oh, Mama, I'm so sorry to hear that! William and I will continue to pray for him." Catherine winced as the comb caught a snag in her hair.

Having trimmed her hair until it circled just above her shoulders, Mrs. Mumford skilfully fashioned a heavy puff made of curls over each ear. "Your father reminds me of Demas. I was studying him this morning. He is mentioned only three times in the New Testament, but his career is a solemn warning to everyone." Opening her Bible she read:

" 'Luke, the beloved physician, and Demas, greet you' (Col. 4:14). 'Marcus, Aristarchus, Demas, Lucas, my fellow laborers' (Philemon 24). And finally, 'For Demas hath forsaken me, having loved this present world' (2 Tim. 4:10). Those passages parallel the life of John Mumford!"

Remembering the story of Paul's former helper, Catherine took a seat in the Brunswick Chapel that night. The clock on the side indicated that she was fifteen minutes early. Her heart pounded as she nervously looked around, wondering how William would react when he first saw her. Although the building was nearly full, William was not present.

"News spreads fast," whispered the plump woman next to her.

"What do you mean?"

"The news that William Booth is going to preach."

"Is that good news?"

"It certainly is. I've heard him in Spalding and he's the best."

"But where is he?"

"Don't worry. He'll be here. He doesn't like to waste a minute. Booth wants to save the whole world!" She chuckled while scratching a patch of hair on her lowest chin.

Thirty seconds before it was time to start, the door in the back of the platform opened, and William Booth stepped in. As he took his seat behind the pulpit, Catherine noticed that his beard was a little longer and that he was wearing a new suit.

Suddenly their eyes met!

Booth's face lit up like a lantern and he smiled and nodded toward her. He then bowed his head in prayer.

When it was finally time for him to speak, Booth stood in the pulpit. "Our text this morning, I-I mean this evening, is found in the third chapter of John, the sixteenth verse. L-let me—let me read it to you." He started to read. Then he stopped. "I-I'm sorry," he confessed, "my Bible was opened to the wrong chapter."

Catherine listened in horror. Never before had she seen him so confused. With eyes open, she silently prayed for the Lord to help him. Nonetheless, he continued to get worse. A child began to cry. A gust of wind blew his notes on the floor. He spilled the glass of water that had been placed on the pulpit for his convenience. Next, three more babies started to fuss. In utter panic, Catherine closed her eyes, lifted her hand and groaned, "Lord, help him!"

Providentially, Booth glanced in her direction as she did this. The effect was as if lightning had struck. He forgot his notes, his shoulders straightened, his eyes blazed, his finger pointed, his beard added emphasis. The sight of Catherine earnestly praying for him had transformed him into a prophet.

When the invitation was given, fifteen seekers knelt at the mourner's bench.

Catherine was overjoyed.

Following the service, William and Catherine faced each other across the dining room in her parents' home. "The Lord spoke to us tonight!" exulted William.

"What do you mean?"

"I was so tired, Kate, I was in a fog. My mind had quit working. But when I saw you praying, I felt like the nearly defeated Wellington at Waterloo when he saw Blücher and his Prussians coming. You really inspired me!"

"And what did the Lord say to us?" She smiled as she squeezed his hand.

"The Lord said that we should work together as a team."

"Like Deborah and Barak?"

"Yes, like Deborah and Barak!"

While they were ending their meal with her mother's famous Yorkshire pudding, William said, "I must thank you, Kate, for encouraging me to come to London and work with the New Connexion people. From a human point of view, I've made a mistake."

"Tell me about the school."

"It meets in Dr. William Cooke's home in Camberwell—"

"How many students are there?"

"As far as I know there are only four."

"Only four students!" Catherine almost dropped her fork.

"The number is small. But that's an advantage because that way Cooke has more time to spend with each of us. He's a distinguished man, has written many books, and is an excellent preacher. Besides, I'll do a lot of field work. In March I'll be preachin' in the East End."

"Would you ever like to go back to Spalding?" asked Catherine as she tasted her pudding.

"N-no. In a way, I had a bigger opportunity up there. But I'm satisfied that God wants me in London. And, Kate, even though we may have to wait four years before we can get married, you'll be able to help me in my work."

"Four years!" Catherine swallowed hard. "But how can I help you?"

"You know the Bible better than I do and you can help me with my sermons."

"But . . . four years is a long time."

"True, still, God must have His way!"

On March 19, 1854, Booth wrote in his journal:

Left home for Watney Street. Felt much sympathy for the poor neglected inhabitants of Wapping and its neighborhood as I walked down the filthy streets and beheld the wretchedness and wickedness of its people . . .

Felt much power in preaching. The people wept and listened with much avidity. Gave an invitation . . . and many came—fifteen in all . . . Tired and weary, I reached home soon after 11 o'clock.

Booth's success in the East End opened many doors. Soon he was advertised in Bristol, Guernsey, Lincoln, and other cities. Catherine missed him intensely, especially when he was preaching in places where she could not attend. But his letters demanding help made her feel that she was already a part of his ministry. One letter, a typical one, moved her heart:

Yesterday I preached to crowded congregations, and we had a crashing prayer meeting. I am more than ever attached to the people. They are thoroughgoing folks. *Just my sort.*

I have just taken hold of that sketch you sent me on "Be not deceived," and I'm about to make a full sermon on it. It is admirable. I want you to write some short articles for our magazine. I will look them over and send them to the editor.

I want a sermon on the Flood, one on Jonah, and one on the Judgment. Nothing moves people like the terrific. They must have hellfire flashed before their faces . . .

Am resolved to live near to God.

In response to such letters, Catherine got out her commentaries, made outlines, and suggested anecdotes. To the above letter, she replied:

Bless you! Bless you! Your note . . . touched the deepest chords in my heart . . . God is too good! I feel happier than I have for months . . .

Your words, your looks, your actions, even the most trivial and incidental, come up before me as fresh as life. If I meet a child called William, I am more interested in him than in any other.

Booth's letters were not as literary as Catherine's; but he, too, responded with intensification. One of his salutations made her catch her breath with joy. "My Dearest And Most Precious Sweet." In another letter, this one from a distant preaching appointment, his superlatives reached the limits: "My Dearest, My Own Precious Love—What a time it is since I heard from thee—and thou shalt have the first fruits of my pen and I send *thee* the offering of a loving heart . . . Oh, Catherine, *I do love thee* . . ." After continuing in this purple fashion, he added a P.S.—"I kiss this letter many times."

William did not enjoy reading the heavy books assigned to him on Greek, theology, or church history. But he longed for knowledge and frequently spent hours in the British Museum.

Dr. Cooke was disappointed with Booth's lack of fascination for those facets of learning that intrigued him; but his mind was broad enough to realize that his energetic student had the gift of evangelism. And because of this broad view, he overlooked his student's lack of interest in Greek and Hebrew.

Cooke's fascination with Booth reached a new peak when his daughter was converted through his preaching. Sitting with Catherine on the sofa in her Brixton home, Booth went over the sermon that had persuaded the resisting daughter to kneel at the mourner's bench:

"I described a wreck on the ocean with the affrighted people clinging to the masts between life and death, waving a flag of distress to those on shore, and in response, the lifeboat going off to the rescue . . . I reminded my hearers that they had suffered shipwreck on the ocean of time through their sins and rebellion; that they were sinking down to destruction, but if they would hoist the signal of distress, Jesus Christ would send off the lifeboat to their rescue."*

Then stepping out in front of Catherine, he dramatized what he did. "Jumping on the seat at the back of the pulpit, I waved my pocket-handkerchief round and round my head to represent the signal of distress I wanted them to hoist."†

"I wish I could have been there!" sighed Catherine. "In a certain way, you remind me of George Whitefield—"

"Oh, don't flatter me! How do I remind you of Whitefield? Do my eyes squint?" He crossed his eyes and chuckled.

"No, your eyes don't squint. But you have the same kind

---

*Booth's own words as recorded by his son-in-law Booth-Tucker.
†Ibid.

of drama that made him so effective. On one occasion, Lord Chesterfield was sitting in Lady Huntingdon's pew while Whitefield was preaching. At a dramatic point in his sermon, Whitefield described how a blind beggar was being led by his dog near the edge of a sharp precipice. Since the string to the dog's collar broke, the poor man had to depend on his stick. When the stick fell over the precipice, the unfortunate man groped forward, trying to find it. At that moment the immaculate Chesterfield, famous everywhere for his wickedness, leaped to his feet and cried, 'Good heavens, he's gone!' "

Booth laughed hilariously. "The great gift Whitefield had that no one else has ever had was his voice. Cooke told us that David Garrick, the famous actor, said, 'I would give a hundred guineas if I could say "Oh!" like Mr. Whitefield!' "

"You may not have his voice,* but you have his dramatic ability," added Catherine with confidence. "Remember, William, we are serving the same God George Whitefield served. What we need is a *cause*! Having a *cause* was the secret of the Wesleys, Charles G. Finney, and others."

"We have a *cause*, Kate; and that cause is to reach the poor with a vital gospel." He stood up and began to pace the floor. "Most people don't know what the Good News of Jesus Christ is all about. Just last week we were studying our laws of the twelfth century. In those days clergymen could not be punished. And that's the reason so many of them were so wicked.

"At that time when a criminal faced the judge, he could escape punishment by pleading 'benefit of the clergy.' All he had to do to claim that benefit was to be able to read—not quote!—the 'neck verse.' "

"What was the 'neck verse'?" Catherine smiled.

"The first verse of Psalm 51."

Catherine's eyes widened. Then she picked up her Bible and read that passage: " 'Have mercy upon me, O God, according to thy loving-kindness: according unto the multitude

---

*Booth had an excellent, low-pitched, pleading voice.

of thy tender mercies blot out my transgressions.' Well," she commented, "at least that is a strong verse. You should use it as a text sometime."

"Strong it is," affirmed Booth, nodding his head. "But the accused could only plead 'benefit of the clergy' once. To keep him from using that excuse again, he was branded with a red hot iron." He shuddered and drew in his breath. "Still there was a way out. Those who had connections or those who could manage a bribe were branded with a cold iron." He shook his head as he returned to sit near Catherine on the sofa. Holding her hand in both of his, he added, "We must teach that there is forgiveness for everyone; and that everyone can have a second and third and fourth chance—and more."

Catherine stood up and as she and William embraced, she said, "William, you and I have a *cause*. An unsurpassed cause! And to celebrate that fact, I'm going to make you some tea."

At the end of a class, Dr. Cooke summoned Booth to his office. "You'll never make a theologian," he announced. "Your gift is evangelism." He drummed the desk with his fingers. "Would you mind if I nominated you to become the superintendent of the London Circuit?"

"The London Circuit!" Booth gasped.

"Yes, the London Circuit. Why not?"

"I'm too young and inexperienced."

"Nonsense! You're just the man we need."

While Booth hesitated, the eager man added, "If you'll agree, I'll recommend that you be allowed to marry in twelve months. Catherine Mumford is a very nice young lady—"

"Y-your offer is interesting. And yet— And yet I don't feel qualified. I didn't do well on that last exam—"

"Will you pray about it?"

"I will."

Three days later, after having discussed the matter with Kate, he knocked at Dr. Cooke's door.

"Have you made up your mind?" asked the elderly principal.

"I have. I will take the position provided I'm merely an assistant to an older man."

Cooke nervously drummed the desk. "Why be an assistant? You can be the top man!"

"Well, sir, I need more experience. And— And—"

"And what?"

"I'd like to have time to get out into the field and conduct revival meetings. I love revival meetings and have many invitations."

Cooke studied him in silence for a long time. Finally he said, "I'll bring it up at the next conference."

"And will you also get their consent for Catherine and me to get married? We've already been engaged for about two years—"

Cooke smiled. "I'll do my best."

The Conference had a problem. There was just enough money to pay one man. How could they support an assistant? Edward Rabbits got to his feet. "I'll personally pay the assistant," he said, "provided the assistant is William Booth!"

Having been made a member of the Conference, Booth was also given special permission to get married within the year. Delighted with both decisions, Catherine wrote to William, "May God baptize you afresh with His love, and make you indeed a minister of the Spirit." After mailing the letter, she went to her bedroom and prayed for guidance.

Booth's superior in the London Circuit was T. T. Gilton. While visiting with Catherine, Booth complained, "Gilton is a very difficult man. He has no talent at all. Not a drop! When he faces a congregation, he doesn't preach, he wails!"

Catherine laughed. "Maybe God provided him to be your thorn in the flesh."

"Maybe. Ah, but I'll soon be out holding revival meetings. When I mentioned my next meeting, he objected. But he had to give in after I told him that that was part of the agreement.

After all, Kate, I could have had his job!"

All of Booth's revival campaigns were successful. In one city 1,500 turned out in the morning and 2,500 crowded the building at night. At one place he wrote to Catherine, "Tonight many went away, unable to get into the building. The aisles were crowded, and up to eleven o'clock it was almost an impossibility to get them to the communion rail, so great was the crush."

From another stop his report was equally as enthusiastic: "At night, notwithstanding the unfavorable weather, we had the place crammed in every nook and corner, and in the prayer meeting we had nearly twenty penitents . . . Two black women came, and altogether it was a good night."

As Catherine read these glowing reports, she rejoiced and spent more time on her knees. Charles G. Finney had credited much of his success to Father Nash, an illiterate layman who traveled with him and spent his time in prayer. He and Finney often prayed and fasted together.

Inspired by Father Nash's example, Catherine promised the Lord that she, too, would be a crusader in prayer. With this in mind, she followed William's schedule and prayed for him each time he preached.

That spring, William and Catherine were discussing wedding plans when Catherine's face grew tense. "There's one thing I want to know," she said across the table in the Mumfords' dining room, "and that is, do you still feel that men are superior to women?"

"How could I feel that way when the United Kingdom is being ruled by Queen Victoria, a woman?" He softened his evasive answer with a smile.

"You didn't answer my question!" she replied, a little fiercely.

"Queen Elizabeth was a woman—"

"William, I want a straight answer."

"George Eliot is a woman, and she's a great writer."

Catherine's eyes snapped with fire. "Don't tease me. I want an answer. Now!"

Pretending that he was Luther, facing Charles V at the Diet of Worms, Booth said, "My reply is that I have decided that you, Catherine Mumford, will decide the date of our wedding. On this answer I stand. I cannot do otherwise. Amen and amen!"

Smiling, Catherine could not help but answer, "It will be on Saturday, June 16, 1855."

"And who will perform the ceremony?"

"Dr. David Thomas."

"But he doesn't believe in women's rights. Are you compromising?"

"No, William Booth, I'm not compromising. Nonetheless, we have to be broadminded. When it comes to women's rights I'm—"

Their conversation was interrupted by her mother bringing in a heavily loaded tray of delicious smelling food. Turning to leave the two to dine privately, she could not help but wonder why Catherine's cheeks were so red.

While enjoying the paper-thin roast beef and potatoes, William continued, "I'm in utter ecstasy that you're about to become Mrs. Booth. But, Kate, there are some dark clouds approaching—"

"What is it, William?"

"Mother's ill and my sister Mary's been out of work for months. When I was preaching in Nottingham, I gave them five pounds. That reduced me to fifteen shillings and I need to buy a coat. Also, I don't know how long we can depend on Rabbits. The last time I saw him he seemed rather distant."

"I understand. It seems I have problems as well," replied Kate. "Papa's been drinking a lot. We're about out of money—"

"Oh, things will work out all right." William carefully piled his fork high with beef and potatoes and topped it with a knifeful of mustard. "I'll be in a meeting at Burslem. That's a pottery town. Place is full of Wesleyans. They'll be generous. The poor always are."

Catherine smiled. "All will be well as long as we are obedient!"

"How many days until June 16?"

Catherine touched her fingers. "Sixty-seven."

They both laughed.

12

A New Life

Both William and Catherine were twenty-six years of age when they stood before Dr. David Thomas in the Stockwell New Chapel in South London. Each had been a Wesleyan, a Reformer, and were now members of the New Connexion. Even so, he slipped a gold ring on her finger in a Congregational place of worship.

Denominationalism meant nothing to them!

Curiously, the only family members present were William's sister Emma and Catherine's father John Mumford. William listed his occupation on the marriage certificate as a Dissenting Minister.

Following the ceremony, the happy couple headed for Ryde on the Isle of Wight. After a week by themselves, they boarded ship for Guernsey where an evangelistic campaign had been arranged. Soon after the ship began its southwestern journey toward that island just off the coast of France, Catherine rushed to the rail.

"What's the matter?" asked William.

"I-I'm seasick," she groaned.

"Oh, you'll get used to it."

"Let's hope so!"

After Catherine had lost every bit of food and felt certain

she was on the verge of heaving up all her insides, she staggered into their cabin and collapsed on the bed. The quiet
helped, but the continuous up-and-down rolling motion of
the ship was too much. Even thoughts of food were nauseat-
ing. "Oh, I'm so sick!" she groaned again and again.

After what seemed a millennium, the ship dropped anchor at Guernsey. With effort, Catherine descended the ramp
and smiled at the eager crowd assembled at the pier to welcome them. "You'll be feeling better after a few hours of rest,"
assured the chairman as he drove them to their lodgings.

Even though she forced herself to attend several meetings, she became so ill she was unable to get out of bed. At a
low point during which she almost wished she were dead,
William burst into the room. "Kate, you'll soon be on the
mend!" he announced with enthusiasm. "It's just this terrible seasickness. It takes some people a long time to get over
it. I heard a chorus today that I think you'll like. It goes to
the melody of *My Bonnie Lies Over the Ocean*." Posing like
an opera singer, he sang:

> Me breakfast lies under the ocean,
> Me dinner lies under the sea,
> Me stomach is all in commotion,
> Don't talk about sailing to me.

"Now let's sing it together." He beat time with his finger.

"Oh, William, that's impossible. And, besides, I didn't
have any dinner!" She wiped her eyes. "I've been a near-in-
valid all my life. You've married a handicap—"

"Oh, Kate, don't say that!" Hastening to her side, he took
her in his arms and kissed her tenderly. "You're my inspiration," he encouraged. "You know more about the Bible in
a minute than I do in an hour. Without you I'd be like a ship
without a rudder. Every time I preach I feel the effect of your
prayers. You're even better than Finney's Father Nash, for
you're . . . you're . . . literate . . ." He laughed.

As the hands of the clock showed that it was time for the
evening service to commence, Catherine eased herself over to

the desk and addressed a letter to her mother. With difficulty she scribbled:

> William is preaching tonight. I feel so sorry that I am not well enough to hear him. The doors were to be opened at half-past five to admit the seat-holders *before the crush*. The interest has kept up through the services to such a degree as I have never witnessed before. There have been many conversions.

By the time she had sealed the envelope, she felt dizzy. Then slipping to her knees by the side of the bed, she began to pray for the services.

Their next meeting was at Jersey, an island about thirty miles southeast of Guernsey and a little over twenty miles from the French coast. Here, Catherine felt much better; but on the voyage back to England she once again became extremely ill.

Too weak to accompany William to his next appointment in York, Catherine returned to her parents' home in Brixton for a long rest. From York, he went to Hull—the hometown of William Wilberforce, the incredible near-hunchback who, influenced by the Methodists and the Quakers, eventually after a lifetime of struggle, got a bill through Parliament that ended slavery in the British Empire.

Feeling a trifle better, Catherine journeyed to Hull. There, she sat in a packed building night after night and witnessed the conversions of nearly three hundred. The strain was too much. William arranged a place for her to rest in nearby Caister. After spending two days with her, he returned to finish the campaign in Hull.

Lonely, ill, and a little disheartened, Catherine groped for her Bible. It opened to Second Corinthians. In a few minutes she was savoring a favorite text: "For my strength is made perfect in weakness" (12:9). Yes, that *was* a solemn fact to consider! Then, as she was resting, her mind was drawn to Wilberforce. Several who had attended the services in Hull had known him personally.

"That little shrimp was God's man!" a lady who sang in

the choir had bubbled. "I knew him personally." Then handing a book to Catherine, she had said, "This biography came out shortly after his death in 1833. Read it. It will inflame your heart."

As Catherine read the biography her eyes glistened, giving her new energy. Wilberforce, she learned, had been a living corpse. Having examined him, Dr. Warren remarked, "That little fellow with the calico guts cannot possibly survive twelve months." But instead of allowing his bad health and intense opposition to stop him, Wilberforce used those forces to increase his determination to eliminate slavery in the British Empire.

While campaigning in York, James Boswell, the biographer of Sam Johnson, went to hear him. Overwhelmed, he wrote to Henry Dundas, "I saw what seemed a mere shrimp mount upon the table; but as I listened, he grew and grew until the shrimp became a whale."

Fighting tears, Catherine kept wiping her eyes as she reread that paragraph again and again. What was it that changed the little man with "calico guts" from a shrimp into a whale, even in the eyes of a man who hated him? The answer was clear. *It was because William Wilberforce had become assured that his mission on earth was to put an end to Britain's participation in the slave trade.*

Born to wealth, Wilberforce could have continued his career as a pleasure-seeker. But when he learned the plight of the slaves who had become victims of the Caribbean Triangle, he was convinced that God wanted him to use his position as a member of Parliament to put an end to that business. His unwavering belief had transformed him from a high society-waster into a God-intoxicated crusader.

Since the 1493 *Line of Demarcation* bull issued by Pope Alexander VI barred Spain from Africa, Spain issued licenses to supply slaves for her colonies in the New World. Possessing this license, Britain entered the slave trade. Realizing that the public would be revolted by what they were doing, the traders developed the Caribbean Triangle. Their system was extremely simple.

The British man-on-the-street saw merchantmen on the Thames as the ships were being loaded with Manchester cloth, coils of beads, iron bars, and other trade items. Then, months later, they witnessed these same ships unloading sugar, rum, cotton, tobacco, and other New World products. What the uninformed did not realize was that the original cargo had been taken to Africa and traded for slaves. Then the slaves had been taken to the Caribbean where they had been exchanged for sugar and similar products from the New World.

The secret line of the triangle, the trip from the west coast of Africa to the Caribbean, was one of unspeakable horror. Calculating that a minimum of one-third of the slaves would perish on the way, the greedy owners packed each available inch with their recently purchased cargo. Of course there were loose-packers and tight-packers. Loose-packers believed it was more profitable to provide a few inches of extra space for each victim. That way fewer would die and have to be fed to the sharks.

The managers of the 320-ton *Brookes* were tight-packers. Their chart allotted a space sixteen inches wide and six feet long for each male, and a little less for each female. When this ship lifted anchor on its trip from Africa, it was packed with as many as 609 slaves. Like a majority of the owners, they wedged the slaves on their right sides. This procedure increased profits by protecting their hearts—or so it was believed.

The ventilation in the holds of many ships was so poor that there was not enough oxygen to enable a candle to keep burning for more than a few minutes.

Strangely, the largest British slaver in the sixteenth century was the heavily armed *Jesus*. It was twice as large as the *Niña*, *Pinta*, and *Santa María* combined.

All but fried by these facts, Wilberforce became so busy doing research, writing books, and making speeches that he forgot to die. Indeed, he stayed alive until the very day Parliament passed a bill to compensate slave owners for the slaves they would free the following year. The next year, 1834, on July 31 at midnight, approximately 800,000 slaves were granted their freedom.

When Catherine finished the book, she wiped her eyes, washed her face, and stretched out beneath the sheets. While meditating, she relived the life of the man God had so definitely used. In her mind's eye, she saw his twisted form as he stood before the House of Commons and spoke for three hours without a note. And as he spoke, she could almost smell the stench in the holds, hear the whistle of the lash as the slaves were flogged, and see the dark fins of the sharks as they sped toward the unfortunate beings tossed to them.

History was exciting. But she couldn't help wondering what she and William were to do. Slipping to her knees at the side of the bed, she pled for guidance. Still, the only answer she received was a deep impression that God in His own time would reveal to them day by day what they were to do.

"But how am I to help William," she implored, "when I'm sick all of the time?" As she prayed, her mind was directed to Prov. 3:5–7. There, she read:

> Trust in the Lord will all thine heart; and lean not unto thine own understanding.
> In all thy ways acknowledge him, and he shall direct thy paths.
> Be not wise in thine own eyes: fear the Lord, and depart from evil.

Suddenly a new confidence, like a puff of fresh wind, swept over her. Getting up, she dressed, went outside and walked around the block. The next day she told William, "I'm going with you to the services tonight."

Concerned, William exclaimed, "Catherine, my dear! Do you really think you ought to go? You're a little pale and the place is packed at every service—"

"Of course! God has given me new assurance. 'The Lord is my light and my salvation; whom shall I fear? the Lord is the strength of my life; of whom shall I be afraid?' (Ps. 27:1)."

Shaking his head, he turned her toward him, looking

deep into her eyes. As she melted into his arms, William murmured, "Kate, my dear, I love you more every day."

The meetings in Sheffield were scheduled for five Sundays. Again there was intense excitement, large crowds, and scores of converts. By now Catherine was feeling better, but she soon faced another problem. Hearing of her parents' dire financial need, she mailed them a postal order for two pounds. "Don't be harassed about the rent," she wrote. "When you have done what you can, I am sure William will help . . . Why don't you advertise for a lodger?"

Along with this worry, she received an unexpected surprise. Her article on training young converts, which had appeared in the *Methodist New Connexion Magazine*, had been reprinted in the *Canadian Christian Witness*. This reprint had reached thousands of new readers across the Atlantic. It proved that her pen had power. The excitement of that achievement gave her added confidence. Then, in a letter home, she revealed a newly discovered fact, a fact she wanted only her mother to know, for she didn't want to cause William undue worry.

She was with child!

From Sheffield they went to Chatsworth and then to Dewsbury. In this place she was stricken by a severe inflammation of the lungs. And so severe was her affliction she had to miss several services. "I seldom go on weeknights," she wrote. "Last night I could scarcely remain until the sermon was over. I am sorry for this, as I often render help at the communion rail. I have told William about the baby. He was so overjoyed, though concerned about my physical condition. However, I know the Lord will care for both of us. It has been such a joy to serve the Lord with William. God blesses us with souls wherever we go."

At the conclusion of the Dewsbury meetings, they went to Leeds. Then, following other engagements, they arrived in Halifax.

These campaigns had not been easy for Catherine, but

the blessing of seeing so many coming to the Lord compensated for any discomfort she suffered. William was a great encouragement and strength to her, though he found it difficult to restrain her activities, for she did have a strong determination in the face of any obstacle. Here in Halifax her time of delivery drew near. They had prayed much for the safety of both the baby and Catherine and believed God would see them through.

Then on Sunday, March 9, William dashed off an exuberant letter to the Mumfords: "It is with a feeling of unutterable gratitude and joy that I have to inform you that at half-past eight last night my dearest Kate presented us with a healthy and beautiful son. The baby is a plump, round-faced, dark-complexioned, black-haired little fellow—a real beauty. The Lord has been good to us. Poor Kate had a dreadful time . . ."

They named their firstborn William Bramwell after the well-known pastor-evangelist who had often preached in Nottingham.

With a baby in her arms, it was more difficult for Catherine to remain in the field. But, determined, she remained by William's side as much as possible. Finally, when her health was about to break, she moved in with her parents at Brixton while William continued on his own.

He missed her terribly. Each of his letters was laced with melancholy:

> I have not been in good spirits today . . .
> My preaching is more than ever . . . at a discount . . .
> The Lord have mercy on me . . .
> I care less for so-called society day by day . . .
> In this house there is not a congenial soul . . .

Each time Catherine read one of his pessimistic lines, she cringed. But what was she to do? Like Father Nash, she prayed for the meetings and wrote encouraging letters. Still . . .

At the conclusion of the meetings in Chester, William could hardly wait to return to Brixton.

"Oh, Kate, I've missed you so!"

"I know. It was lonesome here too."

"Nothing seemed to go right without you. How's the little one?"

"He's fine. But I've made up my mind. From now on I will travel with you."

William stared. "What about Bramwell?"

"I'll take him along."

Since Booth couldn't dissuade his wife, he took his family with him. But traveling with a baby was difficult. Trains were primitive. Carriages were cold. Long hours in waiting rooms were exhausting. There were few sanitary facilities. Eventually Catherine decided to leave Bramwell with her parents. Fearing that he would forget her, this was a heartbreaking decision.

Whenever it was possible, however, William and Catherine returned to Brixton for a few days of rest.

Soon, an unexpected problem presented itself: jealousy. Many New Connexion pastors found it difficult to tolerate the success of a fellow worker. Their grumblings took many forms: they didn't like his methods, the converts didn't last, too much money was spent on advertising, Booth was getting too famous. This agitation reached a climax in the 1857 Conference of the Methodist New Connexion.

One group of pastors believed that Booth had the "special gift of an evangelist" and that he should continue this type of work. The other group insisted that Booth's work should be confined to a circuit. When the problem was brought to the floor, the debate continued for five hours.

Forty members voted that he continue in evangelistic work. Forty-four members voted that he be assigned a circuit.

The committee's choice of a circuit was Brighouse, a little town twenty miles southwest of Leeds. Catherine was unhappy. "I can't say that I like the place," she wrote. "It is a low, smoky town, and we are situated in the worst part of it . . ."

But, being obedient to the "system," they had to make the

best of it even though Booth described the superintendent as a "somber, funeral kind of being."

Nonetheless, Brighouse had one blessing. There was a parsonage! Although the house lacked much in the way of comfort and convenience, Catherine had her second child in that dilapidated affair on July 28, 1857—just a few weeks after their arrival. They named him Ballington in honor of Sarah Mumford's brother.

As the days meandered by, Catherine looked forward to the next Conference, which was scheduled in Hull the following May. She not only hoped that William would be ordained, but also that he would be freed to become a full-time evangelist.

At the time, she had no way of knowing that her immediate future would be full of problems.

13
Gateshead: A Turning Point

Catherine was nervous as the date for the May Conference in Hull drew near. Her William was scheduled to be ordained! And the fact that he was to be ordained in the hometown of Wilberforce made the coming event even more significant for her.

On the way to Hull, Catherine and William discussed the possibility that he would be assigned to evangelistic work. "That is my special calling," he reaffirmed. But both were doubtful that their wish would be granted. Upon arriving, however, they were encouraged because many of their friends, including John Ridgway and Dr. William Cooke, were present.

As the moment for his ordination drew near, Booth asked all of his friends to stand near him while the hands of the special committee were laid upon his head. To him, this was an especially sacred moment.

During the ceremony, Catherine sat with her hands folded. It was one of the proudest occasions of her life.

Unfortunately, following Booth's ordination, a heated debate erupted.

"I think he should be assigned to a circuit," insisted Halliwell, his most determined opponent.

"I disagree. William Booth is our most gifted evangelist," countered another. "He should be used in that capacity. Hundreds are converted in each of his meetings. It would be a sin not to use him as an evangelist."

"Hear! Hear!" shouted those who agreed.

"No! No!" retaliated those who disagreed.

Realizing that he faced defeat, Halliwell offered a compromise. "I move that William Booth be assigned a circuit for one year; and after that one year, he be returned to the evangelistic field by the unanimous vote of our Conference."

The instant the compromise was accepted, Mr. Firbank, lay delegate from Gateshead, got to his feet. "Our recent minister has become an infidel," he said. "The cause in Gateshead is very low. Therefore, I suggest that William Booth be assigned to our circuit. He is the kind of man we desperately need."

Catherine squirmed. But after exchanging a glance with William, she agreed to go along with the decision of the Conference.

The Conference assigned the Booths to Gateshead.

Located approximately one hundred miles northeast of Hull and hugging the North Sea, Gateshead was a city of 50,000. It served as a railway center, and its numerous ironworks darkened the sky with smoke. Situated amidst several towns, including Newcastle-upon-Tyne, Gateshead was an ideal central location for a circuit.

Alas, Bethesda Chapel, the impressive building owned by the New Connexion, was as empty as the mouth of a man who had lost all but three teeth. It seated 1250, yet less than one-tenth of that number ever attended—especially at night.

"What'll we do?" wailed Booth as he surveyed the empty building with its U-shaped balcony.

"The gospel of Jesus Christ will fill it!" assured Catherine. "One of these days the seats and the aisles will be packed and many will be standing around the walls and sitting in the windows."

"Really?"

"Yes, really."

During the first Sunday night service, six people responded to the invitation. The size of the congregation grew. Soon the downstairs was filled. Then the balcony overflowed. A few weeks later every inch of space was occupied, including the aisles, the windows, the space around the walls—even the vestibule.

"Do you know how many we had tonight?" beamed Catherine across the table.

"How many?"

"Two thousand! And would you like to know something else?"

"What?" he asked as he stirred an extra spoonful of sugar into his tea.

"Bramwell and Ballington are going to have a healthy playmate."

The spoon slipped from William's hand and clattered into the cup.

"As you were giving the invitation tonight," she continued, "I could feel the child kicking."

"Oh, Kate, you amaze me," he said, giving her a glowing look of admiration as she poured him another cup of tea.

Not feeling well, Catherine wrote to her mother. "William was talking . . . about the different bodies we shall have after the resurrection. I replied, 'I should never want to find mine. I would leave it to the worms for an everlasting portion, and prefer to live without one!' "

Sarah Mumford may have been shocked by those lines because Catherine was seldom depressed. But from experience she realized that one of the side effects of pregnancy is discouragement.

The new baby arrived on September 18, 1858, and was

promptly named Catherine in honor of her mother. William wrote proudly to the Mumfords: "Baby is a little beauty, a perfect gem, healthy, and quiet." Since there were now three children in the house, quietness was a special attribute!

While Catherine was regaining her strength, William found her again counting on her fingers. "What's the problem?" he asked.

"I was just figuring out the length of time that was required for us to produce our first three children."

"And how long did it take?"

"Thirty-one months and ten days."

"Did you count an extra day for leap year?" William teased.

"No, I forgot. But with that extra day it took us thirty-one months and eleven days."

"And I hope they all enter the ministry," William added.

"Even Catherine?" Her eyes glistened with mischief.

"Well, she could be a pastor's wife," he replied evasively.

The question of women's equality was one subject on which William was not ready to yield. He bent over the cradle, picked up his tiny daughter and kissed her gently on her forehead.

About a year after the birth of her third baby, Catherine received an invitation to speak at a special prayer meeting in the chapel. Surprised, she refused without hesitation.

"But the vote was unanimous!" pleaded the chairman. "The people will be disappointed. They—"

"That doesn't matter," she replied adamantly. "My task is to help my husband, not to be a public speaker."

But after the chairman left, Catherine was troubled by thoughts about obedience. Did the Holy Spirit want her, a woman and a semi-invalid, to be a public speaker? As she pondered, Bramwell and Ballington began to tug at her skirt. Moments later, she heard baby Catherine cry as she awakened from her nap.

As Catherine attended her children, she silently prayed,

"Lord, show me in a clear and definite way what I am supposed to do."

While seeking guidance, a pair of American evangelists, Dr. and Mrs. Palmer, began to hold revival services in Newcastle-upon-Tyne. Mrs. Palmer did most of the preaching, and she was far more effective than her husband. This fact infuriated Arthur Augustus Rees, a local pastor. Determined that something must be done, he published a pamphlet which denounced women preachers.

Challenged by his paperbound collection of sizzling proclamations, Catherine fumed.

Dipping her quill again and again, Catherine filled page after page with sentences that demanded to be read. In a letter to her mother she described her project: "I am publishing a pamphlet in reply. It has been a great undertaking . . . Thirty-two pages . . . William has done nothing beyond copying for me, and transposing two or three sentences. I composed more than half of it while he was away . . . I have been at it from seven in the morning until eleven at night most of the week.

Her first pamphlet bristled with logic and scripture. Catherine searched the Bible for ammunition and then skillfully arranged her arguments just as she had arranged her arguments in her letter to Dr. Thomas:

> We commend a few passages bearing on the ministrations of woman to the careful consideration of our readers.
>
> Jesus said to the two Marys, "All hail! And they came and held him by the feet and worshipped him. Then said Jesus unto them, Be not afraid: go tell my brethren that they go into Galilee" (Matt. 28:9, 10). There are two or three points in this . . . narrative to which we call the attention of the readers.
>
> First, it was the *first* announcement of the glorious news to a lost world and a company of forsaking disciples. Second, it was as *public* as the nature of the case demanded . . . Third, Mary was expressly commissioned to reveal the fact to the apostles; and thus she literally became their teacher . . . Oh, glorious privilege, to be allowed to herald the glad tidings of a Saviour risen!

She then went on to show that there were women in the Upper Room on the Day of Pentecost: "And the Holy Ghost filled them *all*, and they spake as the Spirit gave them utterance." In conclusion, Catherine summed her arguments in a devastating blast:

> *He* [the devil] knows, whether the Church does or not, how eminently detrimental to the interests of his kingdom have been the religious labors of woman; and while her Seed has mortally bruised his head, he ceases not to bruise her heel; but the time of her deliverance draweth nigh.

With a look of extreme satisfaction on her face, Catherine mailed the first copy off the press to Pastor Rees. But as she slowly walked home, she wondered how she, Catherine Booth, would fulfill the thesis she had aimed at the general public. The answer came sooner than expected. Years later, she wrote about this turning point in her life:

"I was . . . in the minister's pew with my eldest boy, then four years old. I felt much depressed in mind and was not expecting anything particular, but as the testimonies proceeded, I felt the Holy Spirit come upon me. You alone who have experienced it can tell what it means. It cannot be described. I felt it to the extremity of my hands and feet. It seemed as if a voice said to me, 'Now, if you were to go and testify, you know I would bless it to your own soul as well as to the people!' I gasped again and said to my heart, 'Yes, Lord, I believe Thou wouldst, but I cannot do it!'

"A moment afterward there flashed across my mind the memory of the bedroom visitation when I had promised the Lord that I would obey Him at all costs. And then the voice seemed to ask if this was consistent with that promise. I almost jumped up and said, 'No, Lord, it is the old thing over again. But I cannot do it!' I felt . . . I would sooner die than speak. Then the devil said, 'Besides, you are not prepared. You will look like a fool . . .' 'Ah!' I said, 'this is just the point. I have never been willing to be a fool for Christ. Now, I will be one!'

"I rose up from my seat and walked down the aisle. My

dear husband was just going to conclude . . . He stepped down and asked me, 'What is the matter?' I replied, 'I want to say a word . . .'

"I stood—God only knows how—and if any mortal ever did hang on the arm of Omnipotence, I did. I felt as if I were clinging to some human arm, but it was a divine one which held me up. I just stood and told the people how it had come about . . .

"There was more weeping, they said, in the chapel that day than on any previous occasion. Many dated a renewal in righteousness from that very moment."

As soon as Catherine had stopped speaking, William Booth had a question. "Will you preach in my place tonight?" he asked.

"Yes, we want to hear you!" shouted a voice in the congregation.

"All right, I will preach for you tonight," agreed Catherine. But as she puffed up the hill from the chapel to their home, she was suddenly gripped by a feeling of terror. *What would she say? Was she a victim of clever deception?* During the last portion of the climb, the words of 1 John 4:1 hammered in her mind in rhythm to her steps: "Beloved, believe not every spirit, but try the spirits whether they are of God."

Terrified that she had mistaken her own desires for those of the Lord, she arrived home "drenched in perspiration." But as she prayed about the ordeal just ahead, she felt an assurance that God would help her.

In his *Life of Catherine Booth*, Booth-Tucker recorded what happened on that momentous occasion:

"The chapel presented a never-to-be-forgotten scene . . . It was crowded to the doors, and the people sat upon the windowsills . . . It happened to be the anniversary of Pentecost . . . Mrs. Booth took her subject: 'Be filled with the Spirit.' The audience was spellbound.

"The news spread . . . and invitations poured in . . . from all directions in greater numbers than could be accepted."

Catherine Booth had become a preacher!

But preaching was not the only ministry that beckoned Catherine at this time. Another summons was just as dramatic as her call to the pulpit. "One Sabbath I was passing down a narrow, thickly populated street on my way to chapel, anticipating an evening's enjoyment for myself, and hoping to see some anxious ones brought into the Kingdom, when I chanced to look up at the thick rows of small windows above me where numbers of women were sitting, peering at the passersby, or listlessly gossiping with each other."

While viewing this scene, a new idea flashed into her mind: "Would you not be doing God more service, and acting more like your Redeemer, by turning into some of these houses, speaking to these careless sinners, and inviting them to service, than by going [to chapel] to enjoy yourself?" I was startled; it was a new thought; and while I was reasoning about it the same inaudible interrogator demanded, 'What effort do Christians put forth answerable to the command, 'Compel them to come in that my house may be filled?' (Luke 14:23).

"This was accompanied with a light and unction which I knew to be divine. I felt greatly agitated. I felt guilty. I knew that I had never thus labored to bring lost sinners to Christ . . ." Convicted, she "stood still for a moment, looked up to heaven, and said, 'Lord, if thou wilt help me, I will try.' "

Noticing a group of women on a doorstep, she forced herself to stop and speak to them; and to her amazement discovered that all fear had left her, and that the women responded eagerly. Encouraged, she approached another group. Again, the results were positive.

As she proceeded down the street, Catherine experienced an intense joy she had never known before. "With a heart full of gratitude and eyes full of tears, I was thinking about where I should go next when I observed a woman standing on an adjoining doorstep with a jug in her hand."

Having learned that those who lived on the second floor had gone to chapel, Catherine asked, "And why didn't you go with them?"

"Oh, oh, I couldn't. Y-you see I have a problem."

"And what might that be?"

"Me husband drinks."

"May I come in and see him?"

"Oh, no. He's drunk right now." She shook her head and backed away.

"Let me in. He won't hurt me," insisted Catherine.

Eventually Catherine persuaded the dominated woman to unlatch the door. "The woman led me to a small room on the first floor where I found a fine, intelligent-looking man, about forty, sitting almost doubled-up in a chair with a jug by his side."

From his own lips, Catherine learned that at one time he had been a follower of Christ. As the conversation proceeded, the man became more and more friendly. Eventually he revealed that his brother was a Methodist preacher, that he feared their eighteen-year-old son had tuberculosis, and that their daughter, who had passed away two years before, had begged him with her dying breath to stop drinking and to prepare to meet her in heaven.

Catherine recalls: "I read to him the parable of the Prodigal Son while the tears ran down his face like rain. I then prayed with him as the Spirit gave me utterance, and left, promising to call the next day with a temperance-pledge book, which he agreed to sign."

Stirred to her depths, Catherine could hardly wait to get started the next day. Soon, she was at his door and he eagerly signed the pledge. Then she went out looking for others who needed help. "From that time I commenced a systematic course of house-to-house visitation . . . The Lord so blessed my efforts that in a few weeks I succeeded in getting ten drunkards to abandon their soul-destroying habits."

Each adventure into the streets produced new and often exciting experiences. "I remember . . . finding a poor woman lying on a heap of rags. She had just given birth to twins, and there was nobody of any sort to wait upon her. I can never forget the desolation of that room. By her side was a crust of bread and a small lump of lard.

" 'I fancied a bit o' bootter,' the woman remarked. 'My mon couldna git me iny bootter, so he fitcht me this bit o' lard.' "

Since there was no tub, Catherine washed the babies in a pie-dish. She wrote about the occasion: "The gratitude of those large eyes that gazed upon me from the want and shrunken face can never fade from my memory.

"In the long run . . . the work told on my health . . . The rooms were often hot and close, and going from them into the night air, I caught cold which finally resulted in a severe illness. But my whole soul was in it, and I became deeply attached to the drunkards whom I had been the means of rescuing."

Catherine had become almost impossibly busy. Her fourth child, born January 8, 1860, was named Emma Moss. Three months later, shortly after his wife had preached her first sermon, William suffered a complete physical breakdown.

The doctor was stern. "You need a prolonged rest," he announced. "I recommend that you go to Smedley's Hydropathic in Matlock—"

"For how long?" Booth nervously pulled at his beard.

"At least three months—"

"Three months! And who will look after the circuit while I'm gone?" He studied the doctor anxiously.

The doctor shook his head. "I'm afraid it's a matter of life or death."

"I'll take over," volunteered Catherine.

Startled, Booth stared unbelievingly at his wife. "That would be too much, Kate! Besides the children, you'd have to preach at Bethseda as well as the other chapels you made a commitment to. And you'd have to conduct the revival meetings I've scheduled."

"I am not afraid. God helped Deborah also. He'll help me!"

On September 13, 1860, Catherine, deeply concerned

about her husband's health, wrote:

> The difficulty in breathing of which you speak . . . alarms
> me . . . Your health is too important a matter to be trifled
> with . . . What shall I do if you don't get better? I dare not
> think about it. The Lord help me! . . . No human means
> must be left untried to bring about your restoration . . . If
> our money fails, I must try to get some more . . . I might
> arrange some lectures.

The novelty of a woman preaching in her husband's pulpit inspired newspaper articles as far away as Scotland. But all were not confident that she could fulfill her husband's duties. One semiliterate stood up in a crowded service and prayed, "Lord, we *must* trust Thee. May we have confidence in believing that Thou wilt help even the *weakest* instruments."

Catherine, however, became a spectacular success. In a note to her mother, she rejoiced: "I had a splendid congregation on Sunday night . . . I spoke . . . on the Prodigal Son . . . I felt discouraged, but I have heard nothing but the greatest satisfaction expressed by the people."

Due to the success of both William and Catherine, Bethseda Chapel was dubbed The Converting Shop. In addition to her successful ministry, Catherine had another reason to be ecstatic: William was recovering and would soon be on his way back to Gateshead. Then a totally unexpected calamity struck. All her children came down with whooping cough.

14
Crisis

Although still concerned about William and how she was going to manage since her children were all sick, Catherine wrote to her mother:

> You will be sorry to hear that all the children have the whooping cough! It never occurred to me that the cough Willie [Bramwell] had was the commencement of it. Now, however, it is beyond doubt, and very much it distresses me to hear them cough one after another. Katie and Baby have it the worst. I am giving them the appropriate homoeopathic remedies, with their feet in hot water and mustard at night and water bandages on their chest . . . Baby suffers the most as she is cutting her teeth . . . It takes me about an hour and a half before I have finished.

Another paragraph in the letter indicates that the Booths were very conservative in their dress, and they felt that their converts should also be at least moderately conservative.

> Accept my warmest thanks for the little frock you sent. We like it very much. There is only one difficulty . . . It is too smart . . . I feel no temptation to decorate myself. But I cannot say the same about the children . . . I must be decided and come out from among the fashion-worshipping . . . professors around me. Lord, help me!

William was only slightly better when he returned from Matlock. But he brimmed with ambition to go into full-time evangelistic work. "I know it's more convenient for you if we continue in a circuit," he said as he sat down on the couch, slipping his arm around Catherine. "But, Kate, I've spent a lot of time praying about it; and I've come to the conclusion that we must obey God."

"Evangelistic work is hard," agreed Catherine. She picked up Emma and gently patted her back until she stopped fussing. "But like you, I believe in obedience. Perhaps we could arrange our meetings in clusters. That way we could live in a central location and commute to the meetings."

"Then you are agreed that I should apply to the Conference to be appointed a full-time evangelist?"

"Oh, of course, William!"

Beaming, he said, "Then let's celebrate our agreement with a pot of tea. And be sure the milk is hot. Like my religion, I still like my tea strong, hot, and sweet."

Both of them chuckling, Catherine handed Emma to her husband and went into the kitchen.

The Converting Shop continued to prosper as well as the other churches in the circuit. Soon there was so much work, the Booths asked and received permission to employ a convert from their revival in Chester by the name of Shone.

This zealous assistant helped with the visitation, the preaching, and encouraged each chapel in the circuit to move forward. He lived with the Booths and they all got along well together like a happy family.

As their chapels bulged, Catherine received an answer to her many prayers. While visiting Gateshead, her father renewed his commitment to Christ, signed the pledge, and quit drinking. Triumphantly she wrote to him: "I hope, however, that my dear father will not stop at teetotalism. Why can you not speak a word for Jesus? . . . The mere recital of God's merciful dealings with you would . . . melt many a heart . . . Try it! Oh, let us all try to live to purpose!"

Local success did not satisfy William Booth. God had

called him to be an evangelist, and he was determined to be an evangelist. Since his next opportunity to be appointed to that task would be at the yearly Conference scheduled in Liverpool the following May, he made careful preparations. Still remembering the opposition led by Halliwell in the 1858 Conference, Booth prepared for the 1861 Conference with the utmost thoroughness.

On March 15, two months before the scheduled meeting, he addressed a letter to the retiring president, James Stacey, with Catherine's help. "For the last seven years I have felt that God has called me to this work." He then suggested that both of them meet in his home to discuss the matter.

After approving the wording of the letter, he dropped it in the mail, but when a week and then two weeks passed without a reply, he became increasingly concerned. "I wish he would make up his mind," he fumed.

"Maybe he didn't get it," suggested Catherine.

"He's 'ad plenty of time. The mails aren't *that* slow." Pacing around the room, he nervously asked, "What are we to do, Kate? Time is passing. Our future, our entire future, depends on the whims of the Liverpool Conference."

Catherine poured him another cup of tea and whitened it with hot milk. With the pot still in her hand, she went over to the window and stared at the shrubbery in the backyard. Then facing William, she said with confidence, "I have a plan."

"Tell me."

Returning the pot to the table she explained, "Since the Durham District Meeting is just before the Liverpool Conference, let's get the district ministers to agree on a resolution that the Conference appoint you to full-time evangelistic work."

"But what if the District refuses?" he questioned as he slowly stroked his beard.

"Oh, they won't refuse. We have a lot of friends. And, and—"

"Yes?"

"And there's something we can do that will really help—"
"Like what?"

"Let's announce a revival meeting right here in Gateshead. We're about ready for one, and it will generate so much enthusiasm the District will beg the Conference to appoint you as its evangelist."

Rising from his chair, William threw his arms around her. "Why, you little conspirator, you weren't born yesterday!" His hand touched the side of her soft flowing hair and drew it neatly under his chin. "Oh, my Kate, my Kate, what would I do without you! You are my help, you are my inspiration, you are my love!"

While the Booths were preparing posters announcing the forthcoming meetings, William received a letter from Stacey. His note explained that due to illness he had been unable to meet him. But it assured him that he had laid his request to become an evangelist before the Annual Committee.

Alarmed by the possibility of a snag, Catherine immediately copied William's original letter and mailed it to their friend, Dr. William Cooke, a former president of the Annual Conference.

The revival was a great success. Booth was as colorful as ever. The aisles were crowded and two hundred responded to the invitation to accept Christ. Excited, the officers of the circuit requested their district leaders to convey a message to the Liverpool Conference that William Booth be granted his wish and be appointed an evangelist. Moreover, William Love, a layman of the area, promised to supply the extra funds that might be needed to keep Booth in the field.

Feeling confident that his wish would be granted, Booth began meetings at Hartlepool on Easter Sunday. As usual, there were great crowds and many were turned away because of the lack of room. Catherine did some of the preaching. But the strain was too much. William described the problems to the Mumfords:

"She came home much exhausted and on Thursday she

had a day of violent pain. An attack of spasms came on at four in the morning and did not leave until two in the afternoon. In fact, the pain did not pass away until the next day."

But in spite of her illness, when Catherine learned that the Winlaton congregation had advertised her meeting with them, she insisted on fulfilling her engagement—refusing to rest.

After speaking in Winlaton, she occupied other pulpits. "On Sunday the Lord was gracious with me. I never felt more liberty. It was my twelfth public effort in Hartlepool, and on no single occasion did the Lord fail."

"Kate, you must rest," insisted William. "Remember we'll be in Liverpool on May 19. The Conference opens on the 20th."

"I know, but the harvest is white . . ."

Catherine was fully aware of the coming crisis. In a letter to her mother she was frank:

> My heart almost fails me in going to the Conference and leaving the children behind. But William would like me to be there to advise with in case he is brought into a perplexing situation. I shall be in the gallery while the discussion goes on.

She then went on to explain that she had personal reasons to fear the problems that would develop if William were appointed a full-time evangelist.

> I have many a conflict in regard to the proposed new departure—not as to our support. I feel as though I can trust the Lord implicitly for all that. But the devil tells me I shall never be able to endure the loneliness and separation of the life. He draws many pictures of a most dark and melancholy shade. But I cling to the promise, "No man hath forsaken,"* etc., and having sworn to my hurt, may I stand fast. *I have told William that if he takes the step, and it should bring me to the workhouse, I would never say one upbraiding*

---

*"And every one that hath forsaken houses, or brethren, or sisters, or father, or mother, or wife, or children, or lands, for my name's sake, shall receive an hundred fold, and shall inherit everlasting life" (Matt. 19:29).

word. No! To blame him for making such a sacrifice for God and conscience' sake would be worse than wicked! So whatever be the result, I shall make up my mind to endure it patiently, looking to the Lord for grace and strength. (Italics mine.)

As Catherine viewed Liverpool's Bethseda Chapel at the corner of Hotham and Bridport just off London Road, she tingled with the anticipation that William would have his way. Both Rabbits and Love were present, and she was confident that their advice—and money!—would be most persuasive. She reported to her mother: "We dine with Love today at the Royal Hotel, and I'm going to prepare him a bit . . ."

After days of debate over denominational problems, the decision about William Booth's new assignment came to the floor. From her place in the gallery, Catherine realized that many of those in power were totally against his being an evangelist. Indeed, one of his most outspoken antagonists was Henry Only Crofts, the president of the Conference.

Since it was Saturday and the Conference had been enduring dull speeches from early Monday, the delegates were tired, irritable, ready for argument. Many were anxious to go home for their Sunday services.

Each delegate had a firm conviction regarding Booth's request. The moment the issue was presented, the floor livened with various opinions. Philips James was against it. Rabbits was for it; but, being a layman, he lacked the eloquence of a preacher to present his viewpoint. Alexander McCurdy spoke highly of Booth and praised his gifts. And yet for some reason he contended that revival meetings accomplish more evil than good.

As speeches got louder, arm-waving more pronounced, and interruptions more numerous, Catherine kept her eyes on Love. Although he was worth two million pounds, he remained as silent as a lump of coal in one of his mines. Her pulse speeded as the debate grew louder; soon it was out of control. At this point Crofts banged his gavel. "I will leave the chair if we don't control ourselves!" he threatened.

Finally, after several more explosions, and several more threats from the chair, the venerable Dr. William Cooke stood up and faced the delegates. Catherine silently prayed for him. As principal of their school and editor of their paper, he had enormous prestige; and from his own lips she knew the old man was on their side. His daughter had been converted under William's preaching and he had always been grateful.

Catherine soon discovered, however, that Cooke was not himself. Tired and rattled, he offered a compromise—that Booth be assigned a circuit, but that he be given ample time to do evangelistic work along with his pastoral duties.

This suggestion ignited so much debate, arm-swinging and fist-shaking that Crofts banged his gavel again and again while he shouted more threats. Visitors in the gallery were ordered to leave.

Heartsick, Catherine got to her feet. But she did not leave. Eyes and ears focused on the confusion below, she lingered at the door at the top of the stairs. As she surveyed the scene and her lips moved in prayer, she saw Dr. Cooke face her husband. "William," he said, "you are extremely talented. You can fill larger halls than anyone else. But remember, 'in the multitude of counsellors there is safety' (Prov. 11:14). Take my advice. Accept a circuit."

Unable to control herself, Catherine responded to William's inquiring glance by shouting, "No! Never!"

During the stunned silence that followed, Crofts demanded, "Are the doors closed?" Then, before anyone could reply, he boomed, "Close the doors!"

But the chairman was too late. Catherine had already stepped out onto the porch where she was joined by her husband. As they headed toward their lodgings, the vote was taken. It was lopsided.

By a large majority, the Liverpool Conference had decided that William Booth should be assigned to a circuit.

As they walked down the street with their hands firmly clasped together, William's shoulders began to slump. "I hope we did the right thing," he muttered.

"We did," replied Catherine with forced enthusiasm.

"But how will we live?"

"We'll have revival meetings."

"Where?" William, discouraged, stopped and turned toward Catherine.

"We're always getting calls. We—"

"We won't get any more!"

"Why not?" Catherine tightened the grip on his hand and peered into his face.

"The Wesleyans won't call us because we left the Wesleyans. The Reformers won't call us because we left the Reformers. The Congregationalists won't call us because we don't preach their doctrine. And the New Connexion pastors won't call us because we've left the New Connexion."

"Oh, but we haven't left them yet . . ."

"True, and I don't want to leave them." His tones had become emphatic. "But we've come to a fork in the road."

Quietly they turned and headed down the street toward their lodging.

The Booths had been sitting in the living room of their apartment for less than an hour when there was a sharp knock at the door. Opening it, William faced Dr. Cooke and another minister.

"You are too valuable a man for us to lose," said his former principal.

"But what are we to do?" interjected Catherine. "We've offered to give up our salary and to depend on the income from our meetings."

"Yes, I know." He drummed his fingers on the book in his hand. "Still, you ought to pray about it. Why don't you come back on Monday? That's the last day of the Conference and everyone will have a better perspective."

"I'll be there," promised Booth.

Cooke paused with his hand on the brass doorknob. "The Conference has great respect for you," he said.

"Then why don't they let William become a full-time evangelist?" demanded Catherine.

"I-I don't know. But they've elected William to be the superintendent minister of the Newcastle Circuit, and that's a mighty fine circuit."

Giving Cooke an understanding nod, Catherine smiled. "We'll be praying about the matter," she promised.

The next day, the Booths held services in Chester, a thriving town some twenty-five miles to the south. The building was crowded and a number responded to William's plea to accept Christ. Encouraged, they returned to the Conference. But although the atmosphere was friendly and tempers had cooled, the verdict remained that William Booth was assigned to take charge of the Newcastle Circuit.

Dismayed, Catherine wrote to her parents:

> William hesitates. He thinks of *me and the children* . . . But I tell him that God will provide . . . Oh, pray for us yet more and more! We have no money coming in . . . Nor has William any invitations at present. The time is unfavorable. I am much tempted to feel it hard that God has not cleared our path more satisfactorily. But I will not charge God foolishly. I know that His way is often in the whirlwind, and He rides upon the storm! I will try to possess my soul in patience and to wait on Him.

That July, William Booth resigned from the Methodist New Connexion after having worked with them for seven years. This meant that they had to vacate the Gateshead parsonage immediately. Being almost penniless, they sold their only possession—a piano.

Fortunately for them, the committee in Newcastle invited them to occupy their parsonage, for it was standing empty. While there, each hoped to receive an invitation to conduct a meeting. Both watched for the postman, but each day they were disappointed.

"We've been completely forgotten," grumbled William.

Eventually William decided to go to London. "Perhaps Evangelist Hammond will tell me how to get started as an independent minister," he explained. Catherine relayed the news to her mother:

> My dearest is starting for London. Pray for him. He is much harassed. But I have promised him to keep a brave heart. At times it appears to me that God may have something very glorious in store of us and when He has tried us He will bring it forth as gold . . .
>
> Of course there are some who would brand us as fanatics for so persistently pursuing our course. But I am prepared to "endure the cross and despise the shame" if God sees fit to permit it to come.

A few days after he had gone, the postman handed Catherine a letter. The return address indicated that it was from William. "Thank you very much!" she exclaimed to the slender postman as she quickly vanished through the front door of the house.

15

In the Wilderness

Making herself comfortable on the end of the couch, Catherine ripped open the envelope and unfolded the letter. Her dark eyes dancing with fire, she read:

> I saw Mr. Hammond yesterday, found him in a beautiful mansion . . . He is a very agreeable gentleman . . . He starts for America on Monday on the *Great Eastern*. His success has been very considerable in Scotland, and they have acted most generously toward him. He has only been a public evangelist for the last twelve months . . .
>
> Almost his first advice after hearing my position was, "Cut the denomination and go to work for Jesus, and He will open your way."
>
> I must say I was pleased with him, though I far from agree with all he said. Still, the interview was such a contrast to the discouraging looks and desponding words of everybody I have come in contact with for the last two months, save one (my Kate), that it quite cheered me. I shall not, of course, decide on any plan until I see you.
>
> Mr. Hammond said, "If you have power to hold a large audience, and exhibit the truth and bring home the gospel to their hearts, you may go forth and God is sure to provide for you. All Britain is open to you."
>
> Whatever comes, we must live for God—close to God! Oh, let us give ourselves afresh to Him, and covenant anew to walk in His ways and keep His commandments!

As Catherine daydreamed of the great success that would eventually bless her William, she heard Bramwell's little voice say, "All you sinners need to come to Cheesus. Cheesus is the only one who can set you free!"

Smiling, she hurriedly jammed the letter into an envelope and quietly tiptoed over to the door of the playroom. Cracking it open a few inches, she observed an astonishing sight. A revival meeting was in progress! Five-year-old Bramwell was standing behind a cardboard box, pleading with the sinners spread out in front of him to come forward and kneel at the mourner's bench.

The sparce congregation included Ballington, Catherine, Emma, together with their dolls, a stuffed dog, a one-eyed tom cat, and a green pillow with a frayed corner. Emma, crawling around on her hands and knees, obviously needed to be changed; and the cat, unconcerned about the sermon, was polishing his whiskers. The pillow, however, was under such deep conviction it just sat there without expression. Bramwell faced this miserable drunk.

While wagging his finger in his face, he exhorted, "If you'll accept Cheesus and sign da pledge, you can stop dwinking." When the pillow still didn't respond, Bramwell continued. "Think of your wife and children! While you're out dwinkin', they're at home starvin'. You're so dwunk now you're gween! Oh, why don't you come? Cheesus can change you. How do I know? Because he changed me!"

Since the stubborn pillow refused to even weep, Bramwell grabbed it by the ear (the frayed corner) and plunked it in front of the mourner's bench—a rolled-up rug.

This was too much for Catherine!

Having stuffed her mouth with a handkerchief, she fled into the bedroom. There, the door closed and her head under the blanket, she laughed until the bed shook. As she mused over what she had seen, she realized she had four extremely talented children—potential evangels. Getting on her knees, she prayed for each and asked the Lord to help her inspire them to make their lives worthwhile.

After many prayers and long days of discussion, Catherine and William decided to return to London and stay with her parents until a door opened. But as the days passed and no calls came, William became impatient. "Maybe the Lord's through with me!" he decided.

"No, He's not through with you," replied Catherine as she heated some milk for his tea. "The Lord is merely teaching us patience."

"Maybe, but we're running out of money. Ballington needs new shoes. Bramwell has only one pair of pants. Catherine's dresses are getting too short. Emma isn't feeling well."

"Don't worry. God has chosen you to do His work. A door will open."

In the midst of their conversation, John Mumford entered the room. His red-rimmed eyes studied William. "Any calls?"

William shook his head.

"Why doesn't Rabbits help? He could pay the national debt!"

"I don't know."

Mumford pinched his beard. "Work's shlack. Pantry's nearly empty. Rent's due. We're shcraping the bottom. Eight mouths consume a lot of food. Even the baby—"

"Oh, Papa! Everything will be all right," interrupted Catherine.

"Letsh hope sho." Stomping out, he slammed the door.

Catherine and William exchanged glances.

"Has Papa started drinking again?" Catherine asked her mother, who had just entered the room.

"I'm afraid so." Sarah Mumford wiped her eyes. "Your father stayed sober for almost six months after he signed the pledge. Those were happy days!" She sighed. "We even saved money . . . Then when work slacked, he started tippling again." She blew her nose. "But God answers prayer. Let me read my standby passage." She turned to Matt. 18:19 and read, " 'Again I say unto you, that if two of you shall agree on earth as touching any thing that they shall ask, it shall be

done for them of my Father which is in heaven.' Now, let's
kneel and do just that."

More weeks went by without a hint of a call. Then one
afternoon William burst into the room. "Look what the postman just delivered!" he all but shouted as he waved an im-
portant-looking envelope in front of Catherine.

"Ah, it's just a bill," scoffed Mrs. Mumford, waving her
hand.

"No, it's from Cornwall!" William pointed at the return
address.

"Well, open it," urged Catherine.

Booth slit the envelope with a knife. Suddenly his face lit
up. "It's from Shone, our former assistant at Gateshead. Now
he's stationed at Hayle. He— He— Listen to this. He wants
us to conduct revival meetings throughout his entire circuit
in Cornwall . . ." He shook his head and all but shouted,
"Amen! Amen! Amen!"

Catherine frowned. "Isn't he still with the New Connexion?"

"He is. But he's a little independent."

"Let's go. We've been praying for an open door and this is
an open door."

"True." William became thoughtful. "But first let me finish
reading the letter. Listen: 'We're in a very sparsely populated
area. Our buildings are small. The people are poor. We can't
even guarantee you transportation. Still, we'd love to have
you. Answer immediately."

He handed the letter to Catherine. "Now what do you
think?"

"I say, let's go."

"Cornwall is in the extreme southwest of England," continued Booth. "Some call it Britain's tail." Trying to hide the
smile on his face with his hand, he looked at her teasingly
and added, "We'll probably starve."

"Nonetheless, we've had a call; and, like Elijah's cloud, it's
a sign from the Lord." She stood up. "I'm ready. Let's go."

"Why don't you leave Catherine and the children here," suggested Mrs. Mumford.

"Oh, Mama, I couldn't do that! We're a team. William needs me. Where William goes, I go . . ." She closed her eyes. "But we will leave the children with you. At least for a time . . ."

The first meeting was at Hayle, a little town on the northern shore of the final joint in the tail—and about fifteen miles east of Land's End on the most western tip. William opened the meeting on Sunday morning, August 11, 1861. The building was comfortably full, but he was not at his best.

After the service, the gaunt fisherman who took Catherine and William to a lady's house for dinner said, "You almost capsized us! I hope your wife will preach this afternoon and give us a little cheer."

At the table, another member of the congregation had a similar comment: "Before you came my husband and I had a very good opinion of ourselves." She sighed. "Now we see we are nothing—absolutely nothing—and worse than nothing."

As Catherine listened, she prayed that the Lord would give her a burning message for the afternoon service. Charles Finney had insisted that revival could not come until the fallow ground was broken. *Could it be that William's sermon had helped to break such ground?*

Years later, Catherine remembered: "In the afternoon the place was jammed . . . At night there was another crowd, and a powerful impression was made . . . There was, however, no immediate break . . .

"The next night the result was much the same. In spite of the strongest appeals not a single person would go forward . . . Knowing that there were many present who were deeply convicted of their sin, the invitation was repeated again and again without eliciting the slightest response."

Just before Booth was ready to close the invitation, "the silence was broken by the loud cries of a woman . . . She pushed through the crowd, fell upon her knees at the penitent form, and thus became the firstfruits of what proved to be a glorious harvest."

. The crowds increased after this break, and at each service the mourner's bench was filled. Catherine rejoiced, but her thoughts kept going back to her children in Brixton. Four days after the opening of the Hayle meeting, she addressed a letter to her oldest:

> My dearest Willie: I promised to write you a letter all to yourself . . .
>
> I have been thinking a great deal about you, my dear boy, and about Ballington, Katie, and Baby; but most about you because you are the oldest. I hope you are praying to the Lord every day . . .
>
> I often wish you were here with us. It is a beautiful place; such nice fields and lanes, where you could run about and play . . . and sing and shout without troubling anybody, and such a nice place to fly kites, without trees about to catch them.

A month later, Catherine sent him another letter:

> It won't be long before you come. So try to learn as fast as you ever can . . . When you get here Papa and I will take you onto the cliffs and show you the great and beautiful sea. In fact, you will perhaps live just opposite to it, where you can see the ships and the boats from your nursery window . . . You can show them to Ballington, Katie, and Baby, and tell them the names of the ships that sail past.
>
> I often wish . . . that you were here. I am quite tired of being without you all, and I sometimes cannot help crying about it. But then . . . the Lord knows best.

Revival enthusiams at Hayle continued to rise. Both Catherine and William faced crowded aisles at nearly every service. Reporters kept busy. The news spread. The meetings were discussed in the boats and ships, at the tin and copper smelters, in the depths of the mines, in the fields. Several walked as far as twenty miles to be present.

But all were not pleased.

By a vote of 56 to 15 the 1862 Conference of the Methodist New Connexion voted to accept Booth's resignation. The Wesleyans closed their chapels to him; and the Primitive Methodists did the same. Their resolution urged "all their station authorities to avoid employment of revivalists, so called."

Although shocked by this opposition, William confided to Catherine, "That won't stop us. We'll use the independent chapels." These chapels had and were being built indirectly through the influence of John Wesley who had often preached in Cornwall, and also through the efforts of men like Billy Bray. Bray, loved by everyone in Cornwall, was one of the most eccentric preachers who ever pounded a pulpit.

Before his conversion, Billy got drunk every payday. Being, in his own words, "the worst of the lot," he allowed his wife and children to remain hungry while he shoved his last farthing across the bar.

Completely transformed, Billy expressed his happiness by leaping and shouting. He named one of his legs Glory and the other Hallelujah.

Billy felt that it was his special duty to build chapels, and he had a unique way in getting the local people to provide the land as well as all the materials and to do the work. His chapels, along with those of others, were all over Cornwall. But William and Catherine discovered that they could not use many of them because frequently those who opposed them had the keys!

Nevertheless, some courageous pastors called them; and, as a result, experienced revival. The pastor at St. Ives, a New Connexion man, rejoiced in seeing 1,028 seekers kneel at his mourner's bench.

At one church they experienced "a gale of saving grace." But while there they were disappointed to learn that numerous converts at St. Ives "had been turned back by the moderate use of liquor." Dismayed, the Booths returned and "spoke plainly on the subject." Catherine's eyes sparkled when she counted 157 signed pledges. Also, she was ecstatic in noticing that her William had seen the light on teetotalism.

Catherine enjoyed the crowded services, but her heart

ached for her children. In each letter to her mother she mentioned them:

"I wonder how the dear baby is getting along. Do you think she has forgotten me? I hope not. You must talk to her every day about Papa and Mama. . . Bless her little heart."

"I am glad Ballington likes to say his lesson. Bless him! He has the most perseverance of them all."

"Please read my letter to Willie, and read it to him two or three times just before he goes to bed at night so that it may affect his heart the more. Bless him!"

After eight months of separation, the children joined their parents at St. Ives. Then the Booths rented a home at Penzance, a former pirate-port less than a dozen miles from Land's End. Here, amidst the rocks and fog and fronted by the sea, they headquartered in a rented home. The family enjoyed the sea, the circling gulls, the sand. Catherine especially enjoyed having the children with her. Soon the local dialect began to seep into Bramwell and Ballington's speech. "Little" became "li'l." "From" was twisted into "verum." "School" was hardened into "skule."

But with church authorities against them and the keys to the chapels in the tight fists of opposers, the Booths began to run short of money. Often with no invitations to preach and no money in hand, they worried how they would pay the rent, or even buy food. In spite of their poverty, however, Catherine always had something cheerful to say; and since Billy Bray had frequently preached in Penzance, his trusting ways were a great encouragement to her.

Billy often said, "If Billy gets work, he praises the Lord; when he gets none, he sings all the same. Do'e think that He'll starve Billy? No, no, there's sure to be a bit of flour in the bottom of the barrel for Billy. I can trust in Jesus, and while I trust 'im, He'd as soon starve Michael the Archangel as He'd starve Billy."

During the first part of August while money was desperately needed, William was so pressed for cash, and his calls were so few, he had to content himself by conducting services at Mousehole, a fishing village four miles from Penzance.

While William was preaching to the fishermen, Catherine had her fifth child, whom they named Herbert Henry. (Six months later they changed it to Herbert Howard, but they were too late for the change to be official.)

At a time of financial desperation just after Herbert was born, William was summoned by the Free Methodists for special meetings in Redruth. Other calls occasionally drifted in. When there were no more calls, the Booths learned to rent buildings on their own and provide their own publicity. In this fashion, they preached in tents, barns, theaters; and sometimes, in the manner of John Wesley and George Whitefield, they preached outside in parks and open fields.

At Cardiff they rented an empty circus building. And again, in Wales on the southern west coast of Britain, they conducted their meetings in an empty circus building. Here, they met two families who would become financial supporters across the years—J. E. Billups, a prosperous contractor, and John Cory who together with his brother Richard, owned a number of coal mines and a large shipping business. These businessmen appreciated the work the Booths were doing.

During the Cardiff meeting, Catherine noticed that seven-year-old Bramwell was under deep conviction. In the midst of the invitation, she approached him. "Wouldn't you like to be saved?" she asked.

Bramwell faced his mother in silence. Then he firmly replied, "No."

But in the meeting at Walsall, Catherine noticed him kneeling with some other children at the mourner's bench. He had responded entirely on his own! From experience she had learned that a totally independent decision was the most worthwhile.

Bramwell was the first of the Booth children to accept Christ, and his parents were delighted.

The Walsall meeting, however, did not produce enough money to pay their traveling expenses; and William did not have sufficient funds to pay the rent. Then he sprained his ankle, developed an ulcerated throat, and finally collapsed with shattered nerves.

The doctor was definite: "Brother Booth, if you want to live you'll have to rest. I recommend that you return to Smedley's Hydropathic in Matlock."

"But, Doctor, I-I . . ."

"There's no alternative. You will either rest or you'll die," he repeated.

Knowing that she was pregnant with her sixth child, Catherine became the victim of the deepest despair she had ever known. After wiping her eyes, she composed a note to her mother: "I feel a good deal perplexed, and am sometimes tempted to mistrust the Lord. But I will not allow it."

In her blackest moments Catherine's mind went back to the jail in Boston where the Pilgrim Fathers had been imprisoned. A total outline of their troubles returned to her. Kneeling by her bed, with the Bible opened before her, she prayed for guidance.

16

That Leaky Tent in a Graveyard

While breakfasting on scraps one morning, Catherine noticed the deep lines of discouragement on William's face. After pouring the last bit of tea into his cup and whitening it with the last drop of milk, he said, "It seems that God has forsaken us." He groaned and stared into space.

"Don't you believe in Rom. 8:28?" Catherine asked, forcing herself to sound cheerful.

"Kate, I've reread that passage until I've almost worn a hole through the page." Wiping his eyes he continued, "Maybe I've been trying to be too famous. Maybe I should have listened to my superiors and taken a circuit. Maybe —"

Catherine got up and put her arm around his shoulders. "Don't say such things!" she cried. "God led us into evangelistic work and God will see us through. God has a special work for us . . . I'm as certain of that as I am that He made us for each other."

Pulling her onto his lap, William maintained, "Kate, I appreciate your optimism. But we must be realistic. Have you ever considered the trouble we're in? Even when we have meetings, we don't get paid enough to keep a sparrow alive. We're behind on our rent. The children need clothes. I have to go to Matlock for a long rest. You're not well and a lot of people are criticizing you because you preach. My own mother is almost destitute, your father is drinking again, and we'll soon have six children to feed—"

"All you say is true," she interjected, running her fingers through his hair. "But have you thought of the 7,000 who made decisions for Christ when we were in Cornwall? Have you considered how wonderful it is that Bramwell has accepted the Lord and that all of our children like to play church?"

"Oh, Kate," he murmured, "you make me feel so ashamed." He rubbed his beard and the trace of a smile brightened his lips.

"When I first saw those cells in Boston under the Guildhall," continued Catherine, "I read every book I could find about the Separatists. As you know, they sold all their possessions in order to pay their way to Holland. But just as they were about to sail, they were arrested and locked in jail. The captain had betrayed them! Ah, but they didn't give up.

"A month later they tried again. This time they planned to board a ship from a secret place in the marshes just south of the Humber. But after only one boatload of men had boarded, a band of armed horsemen swooped down on them.

"Terrified, the Dutch captain from Hull weighed anchor and sailed—"

"And what happened to their wives and ch-children?"

"They left them behind."

"All of them?"

"All of them! And all of them were immediately arrested. Then the ship was caught in a storm. Its compass was ruined and they were blown up to the Norwegian coast. It was fourteen days before they got to Holland."

"But tell me, Kate. What happened to the women and children who were left behind?" He twisted the end of his beard.

"As I said, they were arrested. But since the people sympathized with them and they couldn't find a judge to condemn them, they were eventually freed and joined their husbands in Holland.

"The Separatists prospered in Holland and were gradually joined by others from England. But within a few years they tired of Holland and determined to migrate to America—"

"So they arranged to sail on the *Speedwell* and the *Mayflower*," interjected William. He stood up and poured himself a glass of water.

"That's right," continued Catherine. "The two ships sailed from Southampton. But the *Speedwell* leaked like a sieve and so both ships returned. They dropped anchor in Dartmouth. After repairs, they sailed again. But about 300 miles from Land's End, the *Speedwell* began to fill with water. Both ships returned—this time to Plymouth.

"There it was decided the *Speedwell* was overmasted and that all its passengers should transfer to the *Mayflower*. This discouraged many and so they returned to London on the *Speedwell* and gave up the trip.

"Eventually the overcrowded *Mayflower* sailed again. But as it neared land the winds kept blowing it off course until the captain finally dropped anchor in Massachusetts rather than Virginia where they had permission to set up a colony and where they would be governed by the laws of England."

"And so," interjected William again, "they drew up the *Mayflower* Compact, which was the beginning of American democracy—the best in the world." He thoughtfully stroked his beard.

"That's a nice story, Kate. But what does it have to do with us?"

"It just shows that God often takes a long time to do something. It took the children of Israel forty years to get from Egypt to the Promised Land. Paul was saved in A.D. 34, but he didn't go on his first missionary journey until A.D. 47—"

"So?"

"So, we must be patient."

"Kate, we've been very patient! We're now out of money. And we're almost out of food. Besides, the churches are against us, I'm a sick man—and I'm out of patience. We're not only facing a stone wall, we're surrounded by stone walls, and the waters are rising!"

"It does seem that way," agreed Catherine. "But have we ever been hungry?"

"N-no. Still I don't know how I can finance a trip to Matlock and pay all the medical bills."

"God's invisible fingers are shaping us for an important work ahead. I'm as certain of that as I am of the second coming of Christ."

William frowned. "How could rejection and poverty be shaping us?"

"By helping us to understand the poor. William, you're a unique person! You've been a pawnbroker. You've stared poverty in the face. God is equipping us for the future."

"But how will we pay our bills?" William threw out his hands in despair.

"God knows our needs and He will faithfully take care of them. We must learn to trust in the same way in which Billy Bray trusts. When a lady approached him and asked the size of his clothes, Billy replied, 'And why do you want to know that?' 'Because,' she answered, 'my husband just died and I want to give you his Sunday suit.' 'Did the Lord tell you to give me that suit?' asked Billy. 'Yes, He did.' 'Then bring it right over, for the Lord knows my size exactly!' "

William laughed. His face brightened. Arms around Kate, he exclaimed, "God gave you to me for a purpose. You're my lighthouse! Let's kneel and thank God for all His blessings."

Three days after this crisis, the Booths received two unexpected letters from Cardiff. One was from Mrs. J. E. Billups and the other was from the Cory brothers. Each contained a generous postal order.

"See, God has answered our prayers," said Kate, "and the best part is that both Mrs. Billups and John Cory have promised that they will send us more money from time to time." Then getting out some paper she sent each one a warm letter of thanks.

Since their gifts were so generous, Catherine accompanied William to Matlock and took personal advantage of the hydropathic treatment. Soon after William's recovery, additional calls came for his services as an evangelist. The entire Midlands opened to them and they headquartered at 12, North Field Terrace in Leeds, a large city with many factories. While there, Catherine gave birth to her sixth child on May 19, 1864. They named her Marian Billups in honor of the Billups family.

Five weeks after Marian's birth, Catherine went out on her own and began to conduct a series of revival meetings. But she was tiring of the Midlands. The crowded East End and the Thames continued to beckon. In a letter to her mother, she said, "I should like to live in London better than any place I was ever in." Her heart in London, she hoped that she would receive an invitation to conduct meetings there, and she prayed that God would open appropriate doors.

Catherine's prayers were answered by an invitation from the superintendent of the Southward Circuit of Free Methodist Churches in London. In his letter, he pointed out, "Rotherhithe is a good chapel. When I knew them they were the warmest-hearted people in London." As she discussed the call with William, she mentioned to him that she would like to move to the big city. He was doubtful about moving there, but agreed to meet her in London and discuss such a move at the conclusion of her meetings.

The meetings in Rotherhithe Chapel began on February 26 and continued through March 19. A convert wrote an impression of the services:

> A friend . . . gave me a handbill on which the words were printed, "Come and hear a woman preach!" I accepted the invitation. Mrs. Booth took for her text, "Now advise and see what answer I shall return to him that sent me" (2 Sam. 24:13). She asked if there were any present who had promised on a bed of sickness to give their hearts to God, and whose promise had remained . . . unfulfilled. I realized that her words applied to myself and I resolved to redeem my vows that very night.
>
> There were many . . . conversions . . . Among others there were the two daughters of a publican who kept the "Europa." When one sister was saved the other went to the

chapel . . . to ridicule . . . But she was seized with such an agonizing realization of her sins that she came down from the top gallery to the communion rail . . . Soon afterwards their father gave up the public house . . . and they became members of Mr. Spurgeon's Tabernacle.

But even though Catherine often had as many as thirty seekers in a single service, everyone in London was not happy with her. R. C. Morgan, a Plymouth Brother and co-publisher of *The Revival*, a weekly publication, persuaded his partner to join with him in sending William Booth a letter of complaint. Diplomatically, he wrote Booth on March 8, 1865:

> Beloved Brother: We are completely overdone with business of various kinds, nevertheless we hope at least once to hear dear Mrs. Booth . . .
> Let us now say a word on the subject of female preaching. We quite feel that it is to be defended in principle, but we are greatly led to question . . . whether it be right for mothers of families to be away from their home duties on any account, not excepting this most important work . . . Besides . . . the instances of harm done . . . it appears questionable on scriptural grounds (see St. Paul to Timothy, 1 Eph., and Titus). We are only anxious that the Lord's will in the matter be done.
>
> Believe us, dear brother,
Ever very affectionately,
MORGAN AND CHASE

Did such letters disturb Catherine? Apparently not, for she continued her meetings; and later had the joy of having Mr. Morgan in the chair at many of them!

Catherine was not only an effective peacemaker, she was also a dynamic speaker. Likewise, she knew how to persuade both individuals and the masses without relying on her feminine charm. The *Gospel Guide* described her platform appearance:

"In dress nothing could be neater. A plain black straw bonnet, slightly relieved by a pair of dark velvet strings; a black velvet loose-fitting jacket, with tight sleeves, which appeared exceedingly suitable to her while preaching, and a black silk dress constituted the plain and becoming attire of this female preacher . . .

"Mrs. Booth is a woman of no ordinary mind . . . Her delivery is calm, precise, and clear . . . Her language is simple."

While conducting meetings in the London area, Catherine was invited to speak at a service of the *Midnight Movement*. The goal of this organization was to rehabilitate the vast number of prostitutes who worked in the brothels and solicited on the street. Many of them, she learned, had been trapped into this profession by white slavers.

The Wesleyan Times reported her address: "She identified herself with them as a fellow sinner, showing that if they supposed her better than themselves it was a mistake, since all had sinned against God. *This*, she explained, was the main point, and not the particular sin of which they might be guilty."

At the end of Catherine's message, it was announced that there were homes which would welcome them, and where they could start a new life.

That evening, Catherine found it almost impossible to sleep. As she rolled and tossed, individual faces came before her. Each of which, she knew, was extremely valuable to the Creator who had made it. Her eyes closed, she visualized the useful lives these women could have if only someone would show them, and help them find the way. Yes, they had possibilities. All of them! On her knees by the side of her bed, she prayed for guidance. She also prayed that God would direct William about moving to London.

While Catherine was preaching in the great metropolis, William was conducting meetings in Louth—some seventy miles east of Sheffield where he had planned to make his headquarters. But Catherine's prayers and God's providence persuaded him to move to London.

Their first home was in Hammersmith in the West End, just north of the Thames.

"Now that we've moved to London, what will I do?" asked William.

"Don't worry, the Lord will open a door," assured Catherine.

Then it happened that the evangelist who had been engaged to conduct meetings in an abandoned Quaker cemetery in Whitechapel had become ill and William was asked to take his place. *The prospects for an effective meeting in this place are extremely low*, thought William as he walked over to the area. The sight—and smells—of poverty were everywhere.

William watched as drunks staggered down the streets. He saw them lying in the gutters, on doorsteps, on the sidewalks. He watched people in rags searching through garbage cans for a bite of food. He noticed prostitutes tapping at their windows, hoping to lure a customer. Then he went over to the tent where the services were to be held. The shabby canvas obviously leaked, for some of the makeshift benches and chairs were still wet.

William felt like Dante when Virgil led him to the gates of hell and he viewed the dimly colored sign with its words: *All hope abandon, ye who enter here.*

Ah, but he had prayed for an open door and this was an open door!

On July 2, 1865, William Booth chose his text and began his first service in the leaky tent. As he preached, he was overwhelmed by the way the people listened. Many who had abandoned hope began to brighten. And when he gave the invitation to come forward, several responded.

After walking home, he confessed to Catherine, "Oh, Kate, I have found my destiny! These are the people for whose salvation I have been longing for all these years! As I passed by the doors of the flaming gin palaces tonight, I seemed to hear a voice sounding in my ears, 'Where can you go and find such heathen as these? and where is there so great a need for your labors?' And there and then in my soul I offered myself and you and the children to this great work. Those people shall be our people, and they shall have our God for their God.' "

Years later, Catherine recorded what she had thought on this occasion. "I remember the emotion that this produced in my soul. I sat gazing into the fire, and the devil whispered to me, 'This means another departure, another start in life!' The question of our support constituted a serious difficulty. Hitherto we had been able to meet our expenses out of the collections which we had made from our more respectable audiences. But it was impossible to suppose that we could do so among the poverty-stricken East Enders—we were even afraid to ask for a collection in such a locality.

"Nevertheless, I did not answer discouragingly. After a momentary pause for prayer, I replied, 'If you feel you ought to stay, stay. We've trusted the Lord *once* for our support; we can trust Him *again.*' "

Catherine had been praying for exactly this type of opening. Now the reality of her answered prayer was terrifying. In addition, she was pregnant for the seventh time. Each evening Booth conducted two services: one in the open at Mile-End Road, the other in the tent. On Sunday he had four services. One evening he placed a hand on the shoulder of a lad who had been helping with the lights. Speaking with great confidence, Booth said, "The time will come when they will be stringing lights like these around the world."

Although his pockets were empty, he spoke in a confident way. The lad, deeply impressed, never forgot that statement.

Then just as the meetings were reaching their peak, disaster struck.

Early on the third Sunday, William was horrified to see that the tent had collapsed.* A hurried examination revealed large rents. Convinced that the tent could not be repaired, he wondered what he should do; for quite obviously, he had no money with which to buy a new one.

---

*An Irish prize-fighter, the first East-End convert, assured Harold Begbie that the "cords had been cut by a gang of roughs." Feeling that Booth had enough burdens, he allowed him to think that the wind had blown it down. See *God's Soldier,* p. 282.

17
The Christian Mission

Although the tent was reerected, the rains made it almost impossible to continue services in it. William was desperate. "After a time, " he wrote, "we secured an old dancing room for Sunday . . . But, there were no seats in it, so our converts had to come at 4 o'clock on Sunday morning to bring the benches in, and work till midnight, or later still, when the day's meetings were over, to move them out again. For our week-night meetings we . . . hired an old shed, formerly used to store rags in, and there we fought against the obstacles for months."

While William was still using the tents, an article came out in *The Christian*, under the byline of William Booth. Having explained the success he was experiencing, he added:

> We have no definite plans. We wish to be guided by the Holy Spirit. At present we desire to hold consecutive services for the bringing of souls to Christ in different localities of East London all the year round. We propose to hold these meetings in halls, theaters, chapels, tents, open air, and elsewhere, as the way may be opened . . .
>
> In order to carry on this work we intend to establish a "Christian Revival Association," in which we think a hundred persons will enroll themselves at once. We shall also require some central building in which to hold our more private meetings . . .

To work out these plans it will be manifest to each reader that funds will be required . . . We appeal for help . . . I beg to be regarded as your brother in the Lord.

While Catherine and William waited for a response to their appeal, they kept busy with meetings. Each second of time allotted to them, they felt, should be used to proclaim the Good News of Christ. On the corner of Cambridge and Whitechapel Roads, there was a tavern called the Vine, and back of this area, dubbed The Waste, there was another den known as the Blind Beggar. The space in front of these establishments became favorite spots for Booth to preach.

Dressed in his black clergyman's coat, and wearing his stovepipe hat, he made a habit of taking his place on the sidewalk and preaching. A few listened, but most of the crowds merely glanced in his direction and pushed through the tavern doors or staggered down the streets to the place where they were staying. Frustrated by the insignificant effect he was having, Booth made a monumental decision. St. John Ervine wrote about this decision, which ultimately revolutionized Booth's career:

> He soon realized that he was a voice ineffectively crying in the wilderness, and since he had no wish to beat the air, he resolved to have an organization and a hall. One man, passionately banging a Bible and waving an umbrella to attract attention, in a dismal tract of derelict land in a slum, might cause a few sinners to repent, but without an establishment, his influence would go no further. *Booth was not the man to rejoice over the sinner that was found, when there remained ninety-and-nine that were lost: he longed, not for units, but for millions;* and as he stood on the Waste, his tall, thin body awkwardly swaying to the tune of his harsh, uneducated voice, which failed to rise above the noises of the street, his mind began to get busy with plans.*
> (Italics mine.)

He had no idea what his organization should be like. But he was convinced that he needed to inspire former drunks and former prostitutes to help him reach the masses they

---

*God's Soldier, p. 285.

understood in greater depths than himself.

The beggars in the East End had no money to give; but Catherine continued to preach in the West End where she was amply rewarded with both success and money. As before, her pregnancy did not stop her. In October when she lacked only two months of being full term, she conducted meetings in Kennington, just a short distance from the first pawnshop where William had worked when he first moved to London in the fall of 1849.

While Catherine was busy in this meeting, William called on her with exciting news. "I just received a letter from Samuel Morley, M.P.!" he exclaimed.

"And who is he?"

"His family was one of the rich families in Nottingham; and, although 'e lives in London 'e was just elected to Parliament as their representative," he stated, slipping into his Nottingham brogue.

"And what does that mean for us?"

"He wrote that when 'e gets back from Scotland, 'e wants to interview me about the work in view of supporting us. 'e likes to support Christian causes, and 'e 'as bags and bags of money!"

"That's wonderful. God has answered prayer." Feeling movement within, Catherine groped for a chair.

"Of course, it's wonderful. And, Kate, we're goin' to move!"

"M-move?" she stared with unbelieving eyes.

"Yes, Kate, we *must* move," he said quietly but firmly. "We need a permanent headquarters with a permanent address." He glanced at her bulging abdomen. "Soon there will be nine of us."

Catherine's eyes dropped. "All we do is move, move, move. I don't know if I can stand the strain. It takes a lot of effort to move."

"True, but this time we'll get a permanent house on the East End—a house we can be proud of. A house where the children can play and where we can meet our supporters."

He put his arms around her and lifted his hand to stroke her hair.

"Don't ruin my curls! I have to preach tonight." Then returning to the subject at hand, she sighed, "Well, I guess we'll have to move. You're the man of the house. When do we start packing?"

"The first week in November."

"The first week?" She looked at him in exasperation.

"Oh, it won't be that hard. You're always telling me about the Separatists. And no one moved more than they moved. From Scrooby they moved to Boston, then to Leyden in Holland, then to Southampton, then to Dartmouth, then to Plymouth. At Plymouth those on the *Speedwell* moved in with those on the *Mayflower*. Then they set out to Virginia and ended up in Massachusetts." He curled the end of his beard with his finger. "We haven't done *that* bad!"

"Oh, no?" Catherine fanned the fingers of her left hand. "Let's see how often we've moved." She touched her thumb. "First—"

Taking her hands in his, William interrupted her. "Don't do that, Kate. We have moved a lot. But we've been directed by the Lord! And, you see, I'm a Booth. That word has a Teutonic root that means *temporary structure* or *tent*."

"Oh, William!" she cried as they both laughed. She knew he was right.

The November weather was cold and most of the oak leaves had fallen when the Booths moved to 1 Cambridge Heath, South Hackney. Their home was a substantial two-story building with a basement, several fireplaces, and a large living room with a built-in flower container at the base of the main front window.

Shortly after they were settled, William called on Samuel Morley and explained to him the kind of work he planned to do. After probing him with numerous questions, the distinguished philanthropist handed him a substantial check.

Now that they were living in a new home and such men as Morley were supporting them, it seemed that the road ahead was perfectly clear. Catherine smiled every time she read Rom. 8:31: "If God be for us, who can be against us?" But she soon learned that although she could count on ultimate victory, there were almost always incredible problems along the way.

Many East-Enders did not appreciate what the Booths were doing at all; and frequently as William or Catherine led the crowd they had gathered at The Waste, a gang of hoodlums would shout obscenities at them, pelting them with garbage—and sometimes stones. Then, when the newly gathered congregation was seated, they would have additional fun tossing lighted firecrackers inside.

Both Catherine and William often suffered minor bruises and had their clothes torn. But neither of them wavered from the goal which they had stated: "We are moral scavengers netting the very sewers. We want all we can get, but we want the lowest of the low."

In order to win as many as possible, they organized and encouraged others to follow the systems they were developing to reach the lost. In these efforts, they encouraged new converts to almost immediately give testimonies. Many of these converts were nearly illiterate. But that didn't matter. Their rough language was understood by those who used rough language; and their sober lives and shining faces were quite convincing.

When a derelict approached a young convert who was testifying on a corner, he tried to embarrass her by saying, "What does an ignorant girl like you know about religion? I know more than you do. I can say the Lord's Prayer in Latin."

The former down-and-outer, who had been convinced that she might be down but not out, replied, "I can do better than that. I can say that the Lord saved me in English!" This bit of wit was appreciated by the crowd, and they stayed with her until she was finished.

Another convert, a former fisherman, was preaching to a large crowd of men in London on the parable of the Pounds. When he read the text, "I feared thee, because thou art an austere man" (Luke 19:21), he misread the word "austere" as "oyster." He then went on to explain the difficulties faced by oystermen. "They are compelled to work in bad weather," he preached. "They have to dive deep and they often get their fingers cut. But they don't give up until they bring in a load of oysters." At the conclusion of this exposition, he extended an invitation to accept Christ, and twelve men stepped forward and knelt by the curb.

After the service was dismissed, a man stopped him. "The word is *austere*, not *oyster*," he explained.

"Oh, well," replied the new convert, "we got a dozen oysters anyway!"

Being a mother of six children and expecting her seventh, Catherine faced her own set of problems. Like most people in those Victorian days, the Booths employed a number of servants and tutors for the children. But these people had to be supervised. Also, there were bills that had to be paid and letters to be answered.

Catherine, a bit under stress, had just gotten settled in the new house when one night she woke up screaming.

"What's the matter?" asked William.

"Oh, there's a horrible spider crawling over my face!" she cried.

William lit the gaslight. "Let me see," he said. He studied her face carefully and brushed it with a handkerchief. "I don't see a spider," he assured her.

"Maybe it was only a dream," she murmured, closing her eyes and snuggling close to him. But a few minutes later she sat bolt upright. "Oh, William," she cried, "it was such a *vivid* dream! I could feel the nasty thing crawling. Ugh!" She was quiet for several more minutes and then she sat up again. "I do hope I didn't m-mark the baby."

"You didn't," he reassured her, kissing her softly and holding her close. "Now go to sleep, my love."

A gentle snow whitened the roofs and streets all around

them that Christmas Eve, while the children looked forward to the festivities of the next day. As darkness deepened, groups of carolers began to sing before the various homes. While Catherine listened she wondered if her baby might be born on Christmas Day, and a few hours later she went into labor. Summoning William, she announced, "You'd better call the midwife."

Downstairs, Bramwell and Ballington and Herbert and their three sisters had no idea what was going on in their parents' bedroom.

As Catherine waited and suffered and waited and suffered, the bells of a nearby church began to chime. It was Christmas Day! Some time later a wee little girl started to cry.

"Examine her carefully and make sure she doesn't have any spider marks on her," Catherine whispered, breathing out the words with effort.

The midwife held her to the light. "She has no birthmarks and looks just like a Booth," assured the rotund lady with a chuckle.

"What are you going to name her?" asked William as he tenderly smoothed back her hair and wiped her forehead.

Catherine glanced at the second volume of *Uncle Tom's Cabin* on the stand by her bed. Then with a tired but determined smile, she replied, "Her name is Eveline Cory Booth."

Puzzled William speculated, "I suppose the Cory is in honor of the shipping brothers in Cardiff. But why Eveline?" He frowned.

"Eveline is almost like Evangeline, and we need another Eve in our home." (Years later, Eveline changed her name to Evangeline.)

The next morning while the children were having their breakfast, William Booth, dressed in his black clerical coat, came down the steps with an oblong basket lined with straw. "Last night the Lord sent us all a Christmas present," he announced. His voice was tender, laced with excitement. Lifting the blanket, he pointed to a pinched little face and dab of hair. "Her name is Evangeline Cory Booth. You can call her Eva."

"But why is she in a wastepaper basket?" demanded Bramwell.

"That's not a wastepaper basket. That's her temporary cradle," replied Booth.

Less than two months after Eva had made her appearance, Catherine booked the longest meetings of her life—a ten-week series in Peckham. The hall, filled with sinners, responded. But while she was personally dealing with the penitent, she frequently had to get up from the mourner's bench and rush to the ladies' room.

She had become a victim of chronic diarrhea.

By the end of the meetings, William was so concerned by her loss of weight that he took her to Tunbridge Wells. "Now, Kate," he admonished, "you must do nothing but rest." As she rested, the workers in London prayed; and, within weeks, although not fully recovered, she was able to return home.

While she was gathering strength in London, she discovered an old pamphlet which advocated a certain preparation of charcoal for her condition. She tried it. It worked. Nonetheless, her nerves remained shattered.

But in spite of shattered nerves, she could not refuse the many calls that came for her to preach. However, she did select those places that were by the sea. Even so, she continually had to force herself to keep going. But strong as her will remained, she could not cope with her nerves. Frustrated by every unnecessary noise, she returned to London.

Facing defeat, Catherine locked herself in her room in Hackney. Alas, she discovered that she had leaped from a cell onto a gallows. Their house was near a large new church that was being built! She remembered: "What I suffered from the building of that church no tongue can tell. There was a large amount of stonework . . . The chipping of those stones, the laying of the bricks, and the putting down of the floors cost me what only those who have been similarly afflicted can understand . . .

"I padded the windows, but that was useless. It came

through the glass and reverberated through the walls. I plugged my ears with cotton wool dipped in oil. But this only brought the sound of the rushing of my blood, which was still more difficult to endure."

While Catherine suffered, she made use of her time by praying and studying. The many forward moves at this time caused her to rejoice. Samuel Morley supported a bill in Parliament that eventually saved Bunhill Cemetery from housing developers by preserving it in memory of the Dissenters. At a time of crisis, that cemetery, across from Wesley Chapel, had been a great encouragement to her. She had never forgotten the occasion when she and her mother had paused before the graves of Daniel DeFoe, Isaac Watts, John Bunyan, and Susanna Wesley.

The Christian Mission was also expanding. Enough money was now coming in for William to rent the Effingham Theater, seating three thousand. Better yet, the new place of worship was so filled, a critic wrote: "On the arrival of the mob . . . a rush took place to get a first seat . . . The result was that the boxes and stalls were filled with as idle and dissolute set of characters as ever graced a public resort."

The sight of those "dissolute" characters from off the street inspired Booth with an almost unending supply of new energy. And soon he was able to boast to Catherine, "We now have eight thousand free seats, and thirteen preaching stations."

As Catherine listened to these glowing reports, she prayed that the Lord would so inspire her children that each one would find a niche of usefulness in dredging the slums for the lost. The Lord had spared her first seven children; and now she was nearing the time when the eighth child would be born.

On April 28, 1868,* William Booth gathered his children around him. "God has sent us a most beautiful present," he

---

*St. John Ervine has pointed out that both Booth-Tucker and Begbie were mistaken. The date was 1868, *not* 1867.

announced with considerable excitement.

"Is it alive?" asked the children.

"Yes. It's alive."

"Is it a dog?" ventured Bramwell.

"No."

"A donkey?" inquired Ballington.

"No."

"A cat?" asked Emma.

"A horse?" suggested another.

"No, it's a baby!"

The children then insisted on going upstairs to see it. As they viewed the new arrival, Ballington said, "That's what I've been praying for—a baby." But Jane Short, who was present, noticed that he spoke without enthusiasm, and she remembered that he had actually been praying for a donkey.

"What's her name?" asked little Catherine.

"Lucy Milward Booth," replied her father.

Catherine's nerves still hadn't healed, so every noise, the barking of a dog, the sound of traffic, or even loud conversation brought tears to her eyes. Then, while on a walk with the children, she noticed a large empty house near Victoria Park. Interested, she examined it more closely. The three-story building had numerous large rooms, was surrounded by a well laid brick wall and topped by a heavy iron fence in excellent condition.

There was also a large garden and a number of magnificent trees. Best of all, it was for rent.

Excitedly, she said to the children, "How would you like to live here?"

"It would be wonderful," said Ballington.

"And it would also be quiet," added Bramwell, glancing at the park.

"Could we afford it?" asked Ballington doubtfully.

"I don't know. But I'll speak to your father tonight."

"D-do you think he'll agree?" Bramwell's voice was hopeful.

"I-I don't know. We've been having a lot of expenses."

"Let's all pray about it," said Bramwell.

"Yes, we must all pray about it," agreed Catherine.

18

The Birth of an Army

William Booth toyed with the end of his beard as he listened to Catherine's description of the house across from Victoria Park. "Sounds interesting," he finally responded, "but how would we pay the rent?"

"We could take in another lodger."

"True . . ."

"It's a very quiet place. There's a big garden and wonderful trees. We could raise vegetables and take walks in the park . . ."

"I suppose . . ."

"The children need room to grow."

"You have a point there, Kate."

A few weeks later the Booths moved in. Their new address was 3 Gore Road, Hackney.

With plenty of room and quietness, the Booths settled down to a somewhat normal routine. When Jane Short started working for them, she realized that Booth's statement, "Sister Jane, the Booths are a queer lot," was very true and that their "queerness" had a purpose.

William's determination earned him the title, "The General." This was a shortened form for his real title, "General Superintendent."

"You could never say *no* to the General," recalled Jane. "It was he who decided, not I, that I was to live with them. When he said a thing had to be done, it was done—quickly, too . . . He couldn't bear beating about the bush. Procrastination, like stupidity, exasperated him. Everything had to go like clockwork, but very much faster than time. I always say that he got forty-eight hours' work out of twenty-four."

Catherine's task was to run a smooth household, inspire the General—and keep an eye on the children. In addition, she made and mended all their clothes. Although helpers bathed the children until they could bathe themselves, Catherine insisted on washing their heads. In the midst of all this, she continued to preach.

All meals were served on time, and anyone who was late without adequate excuse was in trouble. Jane recalls: "The General never sat at the head of the table when Mrs. Booth was present. He always sat beside her. She carved at dinner, or poured . . . the tea." (Although they later avoided meat, they often had fowl.)

The food was extremely simple. After they became vegetarians, there were always several vegetable dishes. And there was always a rice pudding. On special occasions, the pudding was embellished with currants. Table conversation was encouraged, and minor disputes were allowed, provided they were debated calmly and without anger. Sometimes when a letter came in with a donation for the work, the General would immediately sink to his knees and thank the Lord.

Games were encouraged. A favorite was fox and geese, during which the General was always the fox. The regular sport was to tie him up; and this he allowed without protest while he calmly read a book. Jane remembered when this activity had an unusual variation. She reported to Harold Begbie:

"His daughter Emma, then about six, amused herself by putting his long hair into curl papers. She worked . . . until the whole head of the General was covered with little twists of paper . . . When she had finished her work, the door opened and a servant entered, announcing a visitor. Up sprang the General, and was all but in the hall when the children flung themselves on his coattails, screaming with laughter."

All the children with the exception of Evangeline made an early decision for Christ. They did so as a matter of course. Eva adored her parents. Her most cherished spot was on her father's lap. But although she loved to hear them preach, and was thankful when the mourner's bench was filled with the penitent, she never responded to one of their invitations.

As the years went by, Eva continued to refuse to make a public decision for Christ; however, a trip to an art gallery changed her life. There, a famous painting became the perfect catalyst. Eva loved to retell the story:

"For some reason my mother suggested that I visit the gallery where the paintings by Gustave Doré were on exhibition in London. The artist was . . . enjoying his greatest vogue. I was ten years old and had no particular taste in art, save that I did strongly object to the vivid red of the cook's hair and was corrected by my mother for being too outspoken in the matter . . . However, holding our housekeeper's hand, I found myself gazing at the immense picture of Christ standing before Pilate. There, before my eyes, was the unyielding majesty of Jesus, infinite patience and tender forbearance manifest in His firm and silent lips. The slender figure in the seamless robe, the eyes that looked on the screeching, maddening mob with fathomless compassion. I shivered as if I were cold.

"My mother had told me in words of the crucifixion . . . I now saw the scene. I burst into tears."

Eventually a night came in which she was unable to sleep. She rolled and tossed as she struggled with the pleadings of the Holy Spirit. Thoroughly miserable, she finally rushed into her parents' bedroom. There they knelt by her side and wept as they listened to her accept Christ as her personal Savior.

Every moment in the Booth household was exciting. Although the General had an extreme dislike for such public sports as cricket and rugby, he was extremely fond of the children's menagerie. He liked to watch them as they went from cage to cage feeding their rabbits, mice, rats, guinea pigs, and various kinds of fowls. He was especially fascinated with Bramwell's silkworms. One night when everyone was disturbed by the meowing of a kitten, he searched until he found it.

Bramwell was the first to announce that he was not going to be a preacher. "Then, what will you be?" asked his mother. "A surgeon," he replied with enthusiasm. In order to learn the ins and outs of this profession, he dissected a mouse that had died. Following this postmortem, he decided to operate on Emma's doll.

Emma wept when she noticed the sawdust pouring out of its abdomen. "Silly child," scorned the surgeon-to-be; "do you think you can have an operation without blood?"

The Booths lived very strict lives, and they expected their children to follow their example. Each was encouraged to sign a pledge never to drink alcoholic beverages. While visiting Jane Short's father, who both drank and smoked, Ballington noticed a glass of gin and water on the table. For a long time he had wondered what the forbidden liquid tasted like. Now was his chance to know. Succumbing to the temptation while the old man was out of the room, he drank some of it. Instantly his conscience bothered him. The moment he got home, he tearfully sobbed, "Oh, Papa, I've broken my pledge!"

The General responded by kneeling with him and listening as he begged God to forgive him.

Both the General and Catherine preferred to reason with the children rather than to whip them. Still . . . Jane Short remembered a minor crisis when the General said to one of the boys, "I'm going to give you a choice. Which would you rather that I do, pray for you or whip you?"

"Pray for me," pleaded the one in trouble.

"We'll see what prayer will do," replied his father. "If that doesn't make you a good boy, I will whip you."

One Christmas season the General decided that his family would have a real old-fashioned Christmas. For once, he forgot about expense. There was a tree properly arrayed with tinsel and candles. The living room was tastefully decorated. Gifts were colorfully wrapped. Bowls were filled with candy. Special ornaments were arranged in appropriate places. And there was plenty of food. But when the General returned from preaching at Whitechapel just before the festivities were to begin, he was utterly downcast.

"What's the matter, William?" asked Catherine.

"Oh, the poverty that I just saw," he replied, wiping a tear from his eye. "Here we are with a tree, food, presents, and a warm house. But out there the streets are full of those who have nothing. Nothing, Kate! Some of them have even pawned their watches in order to have a crust of bread . . ." He wiped his nose. "The church bells mean nothin' to them." He slowly moved around the brightly colored living room, thoughtfully fingering one of the table decorations.

"Today, as they sup, the bells will be mockin' them. As I mentioned when we first met, those bells speak another language to the poor."

After a pause he said, "Kate, we have to do something!"

"And what shall we do?"

"I just don't know."

This old-fashioned Christmas was the last Christmas the Booths celebrated in the normal way. From then on each member of the family honored Christmas by going into the slums and distributing plum puddings to those in need.

The children soon discovered that this new type of Christmas celebration gave them more lasting satisfaction than the old-fashioned type.

William and Catherine's opportunities to help others increased as they continued to minister to the needy. Moreover, their ideas became a part of their children's ideas. While eating lunch, Eva noticed a ragged man huddled outside near their house. Seeing that he was in need, she excused herself from the table and went outside. Soon she returned. "Mama, the man outside is hungry. Would it be all right if I gave him my lunch?" she asked.

"That's up to you," replied Catherine.

Plate in hand, Eva made her way out of the dining room, through the living room, and onto the front steps, where she gave her lunch to the man. As she received his nod of thanks, she noticed his wet, downcast eyes. Her heart overflowed with compassion as he slowly shuffled across the street to a nearby park bench.

At thirteen, Bramwell was surprised when his father took his hand and led him into a gin palace in Whitechapel Road. As they passed through the swinging doors, he pointed to the men sitting at the bar. "These are the people I want you to live and labor for," he challenged.

Catherine continued to believe that God had sent her all of her children in order that she might train them to do His work. And, just as she studied to prepare sermons that would move people to Christ, she thought of ways to motivate her children. One of her methods of teaching responsibility was to encourage the older children to care for the younger. Her granddaughter recalls:

> When Marie [Marian Billups] fell ill with smallpox, all the other children were packed off to Billups' country house at Lydney; Bramwell, fifteen, was in charge of them. His mother, in a friendly letter that indirectly revealed much about her own method of managing the children, wrote: "Your somewhat graphic epistle cheered me a good deal this morning. I am glad to find you in such good spirits. What a pity you lost your hat! However, it was better than losing your head, which would not have surprised me, seeing you are fond of poking it where it should not be . . . Very much depends on you as to the ease and comfort of managing Ballington and Herbert . . . Do all you can; be forebearing . . . and don't raise unnecessary controversies; but where their obedience to us, or health is at stake, be firm and un-

flinching in trying to put them right. Mind Emma's medicine—two teaspoonfuls twice a day—and her feet kept warm. I will send the overboots . . .

The Lord bless you all. Pray for us. Your loving anxious Mother.*

Catherine believed in writing to her children. While Ballington was away at school, she sent him a warm, motherly letter:

I do hope you are industrious . . . Remember, Satan steals his marches on us little by little. A minute now and a minute then . . . Do, my boy, work as hard as your health will allow . . . All your little trials will soon be over . . . Never forget my advice about listening to *secrets*. Don't hear anything that needs to be whispered; it is *sure* to *be* bad . . . I enclose six stamps for extra letters. Papa is nearly killed with work; pray for him. Katie is a dear girl; she loves you very much, so do they all, and so does your own Mother.†

The Booths believed in order and cleanliness. They were among the few to have a bathtub in their home. Moreover, each of them used it! The current styles meant nothing to them, but Catherine believed that her family's clothes should be of excellent quality. Whenever she shopped for cloth, she asked to see the best.

Although Catherine wore the acceptable wedding ring, the Booths, like many radical Christians of the time, had their convictions about jewelry. During an afternoon tea, Ballington appeared sporting a ring. That cheap ring (he had purchased it with a shilling someone had given him) produced a painful silence. Everyone stared. Then the children burst into a chant: "Ballington is a backslider! Ballington is a backslider!"

The chant was cut short by the General. "Silence!" he demanded. Then, with deep emotion, he announced: "His mother will deal with him later." Afternoon tea continued, even though the atmosphere was a little awkward. After the

---

Catherine Booth, by Catherine Bramwell-Booth, pp. 276, 280.
†Ibid.

194

General had left, Ballington and his mother entered a closet. When they emerged after a few minutes, his eyes were red and his finger was minus a ring.

Since William and Catherine both advocated a strict economy, nothing was wasted. In addition, they refused to go into debt. But this abhorrence did not stop them from helping their parents. William's mother, Mary Moss Booth, was a frequent visitor.

During one of her visits, the more than eighty-year-old lady went to hear her son preach. While relaxing in their home, she said, "William, you preached a beautiful sermon."

William smiled. Then with a gleam in his eye, he said, "You've just heard your son preach. How would you like to hear him pray, just as he used to pray when he was a boy?" He then sank to his knees, buried his face in her lap, and prayed with unusual intensity. When he got up, his eyes were beaming. Turning to Jane, he said, "Haven't I told you that we're a queer lot?"

The year 1867 was the beginning of a difficult period for Catherine. During that Christmas season she learned that her mother had cancer. Now, whenever she had a fragment of time, she hurried over to Brixton. None of the remedies worked, and Sarah Mumford continued to worsen. As the disease progressed, Catherine lingered by her side; and when the pain became intolerable, she gave her mother injections of morphine.

The end came on December 16, 1869. As she was dying, it seemed to Catherine that her mother attempted to say, "Jesus." Since, probably because of the morphine, she was unable to do so, Catherine repeated the words she had often heard her mother say, "Jesus, precious Jesus." Moments later, she was gone.*

---

*The death certificate indicated that Sarah was a widow. This was not the case. John was still alive. St. John Ervine was correct: "The cause of the error is not known, but it may be supposed that Mumford, because of his drunken habits, had not been living in the same house with his wife, although there was no formal separation." See *God's Soldiers*, p. 307.

As was customary, the Booth children wanted to dress in mourning for their beloved grandmother. Their father would not allow this, for he had seen many poor families ruin themselves financially by going into debt in order to be dressed in black.

In spite of her grief, Catherine continued to drive herself in order to help William fulfill his dreams. Because of his periodic depression, she always had to be ready with a cheerful word. In addition, she continued to preach, write, and manage their children.

While conducting a meeting in Chatham in October 1873, she was stricken by a heart attack during a service, and had to be carried out on a stretcher. But after two weeks she was again announcing texts and preaching to the masses. It was a mere interruption when her children came down again with the whooping cough. Even before they recovered, she managed to find time to preach at the Royal Circus where 2,500 crowded in to hear her.

By 1870 William Booth proudly announced that the Christian Mission had 265 unpaid preachers. And by the end of the year he reported that 3,220 people had made professions of their faith. Encouraged by this, he published a pamphlet entitled *How to Reach the Masses with the Gospel.*

George Scott Railton was stirred by this eighty-six-page work, for it was filled with revolutionary ideas. Fascinated, he read:

> We believe that God has given us a mission to the throngs in the great thoroughfares . . . Our experience tells us that, although their aversion to churches and chapels is strong . . . they will, nevertheless, eagerly listen to any speaker who, with ordinary ability, in a loving and earnest manner, sets before them the truth of the Bible in the open air . . . *Hence we continue our open-air work all the year round.*

Further on, he began to feel a special attraction to the new movement. His eyes burned as Booths' ideas leaped at him:

If you will stop quietly in your church or chapel or meeting place, you may talk religion for ever, and beyond a little passing ridicule, the ungodly will let you alone. *But go out to them*, spread your feast by the highway side, proclaim the truth at the gates of the city, or in the crowded marketplace, and they will gnash upon you with their teeth, and hate you as they hated Him who went about all the cities and villages of Palestine . . . We cannot describe the kind of opposition we suffer better than by giving a few extracts from the journals of some of our workers:

"So soon as our brethren commenced the open-air service, a policeman came and ordered them away, saying he would take them to the station if they did not desist. Brother R. said he should deem it an honor to be locked up for his Master, whereupon the policeman took them off. By this time, a great crowd had gathered, and as they went along they sang—

I will sing for Jesus,
With his blood he bought me . . .

At the station they gave tracts to each of the policemen, who were just going on their beat. They then commenced reading the Bible, but being told to sit down, they knelt down and prayed aloud."

Deeply stirred, George Railton made immediate contact with the Booths. After some discussion, it was decided that he should move into their home on Gore Road for a few days in order that he and his hosts might become better acquainted. Booth was delighted that this young man was eager to be supervised; and Railton was delighted that the Christian Mission was dedicated to the salvation of the lost.

In March 1873, the twenty-four-year-old Railton gave up his previous job and became William Booth's secretary. He then moved in with them and remained in their home for the next eleven years. Catherine often smiled at his eccentricities—he had queer table manners and he always signed his letters with just the letter R—but he was a hard worker and she loved him in the same manner in which she loved her own children.

During the Christmas season of 1878, William Booth,

dressed in a yellow gown and wearing felt slippers, paced back and forth, dictating a letter to Railton. "We are a volunteer army," he said.

While Railton was jotting this down, Bramwell leaned back in his chair and exclaimed: "Volunteer? I'm not a volunteer. I'm a regular or nothing!"

Booth hesitated for a long moment. Then, leaning over Railton's shoulder, he crossed out the word "volunteer" and above it wrote "salvation." The sentence now read, "We are a salvation army." The effect of that phrase, "salvation army," was so startling, Railton and Bramwell jumped out of their chairs. With glowing eyes, Bramwell exclaimed, "Thank God for that!"

After the name Salvation Army had been agreed upon, a new letterhead was printed. On the left there was a list of the forty-seven meeting places, and at the top was the name, General William Booth. When Booth saw the proof, he scribbled in the margin, "Can't this form be altered? It looks too pretentious."

The name, however, stuck; and soon military terms were being used throughout the organization. Meetings were no longer advertised as revivals. Armies did not conduct revivals. They launched campaigns! In one city where Booth was to preach, flaming placards announced:

THE GENERAL OF THE HALLELUJAH ARMY IS COMING TO REVIEW HIS TROOPS. GREAT BATTLES WILL BE FOUGHT.

In another area, his recruits carried banners on which had been written the sensational lines:

BOMBARDMENT AND SHELLING OF HECKMONDWICKE. TROOPS WILL ARRIVE SATURDAY NIGHT. FIRST BOMBARDMENT ON SUNDAY MORNING. FIRST VOLLEY FIRED AT SOUND OF BUGLE AT 10 A.M.

Preachers were now identified as officers, and when they met for discussions, they were advertised as having "Councils of War." Meeting places became "citadels" or "outposts." The doctrines of The Salvation Army were titled "Articles of

War." (They also included a code of ethics, and the required lifestyle.) The second in command to the General was "The Chief of Staff." And students in the training colleges were enlisted as "Cadets."

Many workers did not like the new terminology and resigned. But a great many others were inspired to march with the General. It was in this manner The Salvation Army was born.

19

The Army Attacks

The leaders soon realized that an army isn't an army unless it's uniformed. General Booth understood this immediately. Discarding his clerical coat, he donned blue regimentals brightened with a crimson sash across his heart.

But what were the other officers, especially the lady officers, to wear? The design was left to Catherine. Her thoughts returned to the women Separatists with their Quaker-like bonnets. Inspired, she got busy. The result was a similar bonnet encircled with a red band. The bonnet was sturdy, distinctive, plain. Volunteers manufactured hundreds. Officers clothed in red jerseys along with smart skirts and topped with these bonnets were impressive. At first, the crowds gaped. But when it was learned the lassies could be trusted, they were viewed with appreciation.

The General planned the flag. The red, he explained, represented the blood of Christ; the blue, holiness; and the yellow star, the baptism of the Holy Ghost. Catherine designed it.

The new uniforms intrigued thirteen-year-old Eva. Glancing at a bolt of cloth while feeding the monkey, her creative mind leaped into action. Having noted that her mother was gone, she found a pair of scissors and summoned the redheaded cook.

"Let's make a uniform for Jeannie," she suggested.

"You mean the monkey?" The cook asked in alarm.

"Of course. Isn't she a member of the family?"

Within an hour the pet marmoset, who sometimes leaped on lady visitor's hats and then escaped to the top of a curtain and made faces at them, was sporting a Salvation Army uniform.

Suddenly, while Eva and the cook were enjoying her antics, the door opened and Catherine Booth stepped inside. Viewing the entire scene in a glance, she said in a firm commanding voice, "Take it off. Take it off right now."

"But why?"

"Because Jeannie doesn't live the life! Once a monkey, always a monkey."

At fifteen Eva put on a sergeant's uniform. Like all beginners, her father assigned her a job at the bottom. "You will sell the *War Cry!*" he decreed.

Standing at the Liverpool Street Station, she peddled them like a typical newsboy: "Get the War Cry! Read how a wife beater was converted and his home restored!" Soon her sing-song cries were producing more sales than almost anyone else.

Convinced that she didn't understand the poor, Eva dressed in rags and sold flowers on the steps of the fountain in Piccadilly Circus. As she worked, she listened; and what she heard brought tears to her eyes. But she wanted to explore an even lower depth, so she began to sell matches in Rotherhithe.

Utterly worn out, she stopped before a potato vendor. He was selling hot potatoes for a ha'penny. While she wearily held out a coin, he studied her carefully. "Why don't you go to The Salvation Army?" he suggested sympathetically.

Making her voice sound as coarse as possible, she asked, "Do you think they could 'elp me?"

"Of course! I was worse than you. I was a real bad 'un.

They took me in hand and pulled me out of it. You go to them. They'll 'elp you."

In the manner of an army general, William Booth demanded absolute obedience. If an officer questioned an order, his immediate response was, "Do what I say. Don't argufy!" And many of his orders were issued by telegram.

Mary Ann Parkin, a semiliterate waitress nicknamed Polly, received a Salvation Army commission. Her first order was blunt:

PROCEED KING'S LYNN. NO HOME, NO HALL, NO FRIENDS, NO MONEY. YOU MUST SUCCEED. WRITING. WILLIAM BOOTH.

With no idea where King's Lynn might be, Polly secured a map. Unable to find it, she consulted others. They didn't know. In time she discovered that it was a historic watering place in Norfolk. Fearlessly, she rented a hall. She now had only a sixpence left. But during her first open-air meeting, someone tossed her three half-pence. Nervously, she led her outdoor crowd into the hall. Shaking his head, a listener reported that she prayed seventeen times in that initial service.

But Polly persisted and after three months, a local pastor enrolled one hundred of her converts. Eventually a thriving Salvation Army corps was established. In due course, her telegrams from the General were addressed: Adjutant Mary Ann Parkin. Her rise in rank was in spite of the fact that she persisted in writing "dun" instead of done, and in spelling triumph "trimhumph."

William Booth used every opportunity to reach the masses. Elijah Cadman, a tiny man and former chimney sweep, loved to preach in the midst of persecution. He reported: "At night we had a glorious time of it, and weeping sinners came to Jesus. We were often pelted with dead cats and rats . . ."

After his transfer to Whitby, Cadman, along with several others, faced an opportunity for the most sensational meeting they had ever had. The morning John Starkey was to be hanged for murdering his wife,. they distributed five thousand handbills to the crowds that had gathered outside the jail, waiting for the black flag to be hoisted. The bill announced:

STARKEY'S FUNERAL SERMON will be preached this evening, Tuesday, at 8, by Wm. Booth in The Salvation Army Warehouse . . .

That night as he stood before the crowd of roughs packing the warehouse, he was almost drowned out by the unruly crowd. But General Booth knew how to handle them and soon they were in the palm of his hand. He began: "As I take my stand beside the gallows and look at that rope, that poor murderer, and that executioner, I can't help my mind wandering back to the early training of the victim. If the report in your papers is true, John H. Starkey never had a praying mother."

That beginning nailed everyone's attention. When the invitation was extended, many, including some who had never been in any church, knelt at the mourner's bench.

Doing the unexpected was a part of Booth's personality.

Aboard ship in a South Sea port, Kipling was drawn to the rail by a spectacular scene. Peering through his heavy glasses, he noticed that General Booth was about to board the ship. He wrote, "I saw him walking backward in the dusk over the uneven wharf, his cloak blown upward, tulip fashion, over his gray head, while he beat a tambourine in the face of the singing, weeping, praying crowd who had come to see him off."

Disturbed, the future Nobel Prize winner for literature told Booth he didn't like it. He never forgot the General's reply: "Young feller," he said, bending great brows at him, "if I thought I could win *one* more soul to the Lord by walking on my head and playing the tambourine with my toes, I'd—I'd learn how."

The famous author was momentarily shocked. But overwhelmed by Booth's sincerity, he admitted, "He had the right of it, and I had the decency to apologize."*As The Salvation Army grew in numbers and spread to other nations, the Booth children became a part of the team—each person's talents being used in the most advantageous way. Catherine rejoiced as each one filled a place of responsibility.

At the age of fourteen, young Katie accompanied Bramwell to an open-air meeting at the *Cat and Mutton*. There, Bramwell surprised her by asking her to speak to a company of men. She did so well that she was soon addressing other meetings—and was quite effective. Bramwell recalls a difficult meeting Katie had when she was sixteen:

> Rows of men sat smoking and spitting . . . while many with hats on were standing in the aisles and passages bandying jokes. This went on throughout the first part of the service. Then my sister rose and commenced to sing with such feeling it is impossible to describe. There was an instantaneous silence over the whole house. After singing she announced her text . . . While she did so, nearly every head was uncovered . . . For forty minutes her clear, young voice rang through the building. No one stirred, and when she concluded and called for volunteers to begin a new life . . . a man arose up in the midst of the throng in the gallery and said, "I'll make one." There were thirty others that night.†

After finishing school, Katie became an official evangelist.

Herbert's unique talents led him to compose music; and he was the originator of The Salvation Army bands. His hymns were popular. Even so, the General wanted him to make them more militant. While Herbert was composing, his father pointed out, "Herbert, I like the tune. But the words need less trumpets and more fight!"

Emma also became useful as an evangelist. Likewise, she made herself helpful to her mother by arranging her train schedules. But her main task was to head the Training Home for Women Officers. Six months after this school was opened, Ballington headed a similar school for men. This one met in

---

Something of Myself, by Rudyard Kipling, pp. 109–111, Doubleday, 1937.
†*Catherine Booth*, by Catherine Bramwell-Booth, pp. 284–286, Hodder and Stoughton, 1970.

the former Booth home on Gore Road, the Booths having moved to 114 Clapton Common.

The schools were successful. After the first year thirty-nine candidates had been graduated and sixty-four were in training. In a brochure, Catherine explained the purpose of the training centers:

"We try to train the *head* . . . To this end we teach the three Rs, and the rudiments of history, geography, and composition . . .

"The next point is to instruct the candidates in the principles, discipline and method of the Army . . . Not only is this done in theory in the lecture room, but they are led out into actual contact with the ignorance, sins, and woes of the people. This is done by means of open-air marches, meetings, house-to-house visitation, *War Cry* selling, slum, attic, garret work, the hunting up of drunkards . . ."

Soon the men in the men's school were falling in love with the women in the women's school. This created a problem, for the men were inclined to be from a lower class than the women. The General helped solve the problem by teaching the male candidates how to use their knives and forks, and how to behave while they were eating.

Catherine was delighted to learn that her husband agreed that both the men and women were equal. She even smiled when it was announced that at a marriage the one of lower rank was elevated to the rank of his partner. Thus, a lady captain who married a major immediately became another major.

Meanwhile, as the Army was spreading overseas, establishing soup-kitchens, giving out free meals, providing work, and countless other helpful things, a problem presented itself, which ultimately sent a leading editor to prison and increased the legal age of consent from thirteen to sixteen.

Few could motivate a group of dedicated people better than General Booth. Radiating enthusiasm, he would thunder, "Will you leave them as you found them? Heaven forbid! What will you do? Go! Go, and compassionate them! Go, and represent Jesus Christ to them! Go, and believe for them! Go! . . . and a great Army shall stand to live and fight for the living God!"

Such statements inspired his officers to risk their lives doing incredible things. Energized by his vision, officers and cadets in the Women Officers' Training Home organized the *Cellar, Gutter, and Garret Brigade.* Dressed in "humble and mean attire," this shock force followed "Mother" Webb and her husband.

The Webbs went to Walworth and secured rooms "above a haddock-cleaning and curing shed." Their furniture consisted of "three broken chairs and two old bedsteads tied together." A report, written by Mrs. Webb, appeared in an 1889 *War Cry*:

> The condition of slum babies is so dreadful . . . We begged a lot of egg boxes and I had them scrubbed and covered with chintz—and made some little mattresses to fit, and bed clothes. We keep the children twelve hours—that gives their mothers a good day's work. Those who can talk learn little songs, and the greatest delight of the older children is a march around the room, singing as they go . . ."

During the next year, the *Slum Evangels* reported: "Over 6,000 children have been through our nurseries during the year, only one of whom died while with us."

Contact with mothers of slum children revealed additional horrors. A seventeen-year-old wearing a crimson gown was discovered at the main gate of the Army on Victoria Street. Questioning revealed that she had responded to a newspaper ad for a "general servant." She had awakened to learn that she was an inmate in a brothel.

Alarmed, the wife of Bramwell Booth began to investigate the traffic in women for immoral purposes. She soon learned that British girls were constantly being trapped and then shipped to brothels on the Continent.

The well-oiled wheels of white slavery were cruel. Innocent girls were enticed to London. There, they were chloroformed, violated, and eventually sent to Paris, Berlin, Rome, or some other city. Many of the victims were only thirteen. Even worse, some of the girls were cold-bloodedly sold to the procurers by their parents. The usual price was less than five pounds.

As Bramwell and his wife uncovered these horrors, Catherine did all that she could to help. Remembering her own youth and her own daughters, she identified with the problem; and each day she spent additional time on her knees praying that a solution would be found.

The Booths were not alone in their concern over this national disgrace.

As early as 1881, Lords Dalhousie and Shaftesbury had tried to interest the House of Lords in this problem. The next year, the committee appointed to study the situation reported that "in other countries female chastity is more or less protected by law up to the age of twenty-one. No such protection is given in England to girls above the age of thirteen. The evidence . . . proves . . . that juvenile prostitution from an almost incredibly early age is increasing to an appalling extent and especially in London."*

According to the current law, a ravisher was protected if the girl was at least thirteen. But if the girl was younger than thirteen, he was still protected, for at that age she would not be qualified to take an oath or testify!

In 1883 a bill setting the age of consent at sixteen passed the House of Lords but was defeated in the House of Commons. In 1885 the Lords tried again. This time the age of consent had been lowered to fifteen. Again the House of Commons refused to pass it.

Bramwell Booth, then Chief of Staff, realized that the only way to get the bill through both houses was to stir up public opinion. And the best way to do this, he knew, was to acquaint W. T. Stead with the problem. Stead was the editor of the often sensational *Pall Mall Gazette*.

---

*The History of the Salvation Army, by Robert Sandall, vol. 3, pp. 25–26, Nelson, 1955.

At first, this son of a Congregational preacher wasn't interested. But, being sympathetic to the Army, he eventually showed up at headquarters. Bramwell recorded what followed:

"I introduced him to Benjamin Scott, who explained the legal situation and also the Continental traffic . . . After Scott had gone I told Stead that I had three or four women in the next room, together with a converted brothel-keeper . . . These women were brought in one by one, and Stead put them through their stories . . . With the exception of Rebecca Jarrett, they were all under sixteen.

"When the interrogations were ended and the girls had withdrawn, there was a pause, and I looked at Stead. He was evidently deeply moved by what he had heard. It had shaken his vehement nature, and presently his feelings found vent. Raising his fist, he brought it down on my table with such a mighty bang that the very inkpots shivered, and he uttered one word: 'D____!' This explosion over, I said, 'Yes, that is all very well, but it will not help us. The first thing to do is to get the facts in such a form that we can publish them.' Stead agreed; we not only took council together, we prayed together."*

Stead decided to publish in-depth articles about the situation in the *Pall Mall Gazette*. Realizing that those who were growing rich out of white slavery would challenge every word, he determined to record only facts that he, or his staff, uncovered.

Cooperating with Stead, Bramwell introduced him to a young woman who agreed to spend ten days in a brothel and report the details of what took place. Since this fearless girl did not allow herself to be used by any of the customers, the madam was financially compensated. The information provided by this girl indicated that prostitution in London was more widespread than even the police had indicated. But the

Echoes and Memories, by Bramwell Booth, pp. 121–123, George H. Doran Company, 1925.

most shocking part was not the employment of the girls themselves. Bramwell wrote: "It was not the immorality that stung us so much, horrible as it was; it was the deliberate scheming and planning whereby mere children were bought and sold . . . as in a slave market."*

Wanting more information, Rebecca Jarrett, a woman who had personally been a victim of the system and then had been converted through The Salvation Army, was asked to be a part of the scheme to expose the system. (Prior to her conversion, she had been raped when she was fifteen; and had then served for fourteen years in a brothel.)

Rebecca arranged for a child to be purchased, examined to prove that she had not been violated, left alone in a room with Stead, sent to a safe place in France, reexamined to make certain that she had not lost her purity, and then returned unharmed to her mother.

Following this plan, Eliza Armstrong, aged thirteen, was purchased for £5. She was examined by a physician and sent to France where she spent a few days of relaxation in a Salvation Army Rescue Home at Nimes. Eventually, she was returned to England, certified by a physician not to have been harmed, and returned to her mother.

On July 6, 1885, the first of four articles was published in the Gazette under the overall title, *The Maiden Tribute of Modern Babylon*. Each article sizzled with revelations. The pace was sustained with screaming subtitles: *The Confessions of a London Brothel-Keeper. A Child of Thirteen Bought for £5. How Girls Are Bought and Ruined.*

As Catherine read and reread these articles, she became sick at heart. Although the burden of the investigation rested on Bramwell and his wife, she felt again like Deborah when she stepped into Barak's chariot. Each day Catherine had a word of encouragement for them.

Stead was never pornographic. But he did reveal how cer-

Echoes and Memories, by Bramwell Booth, pp. 121–123, George H. Doran Company, 1925.

tain brothels charged a premium for the privilege of ruining a girl. His anger overflowing, he explained how in ancient Greece maidens, used as tribute, were sent once every seven years to their deaths in the Labyrinth of Crete. Then, using all the talent he possessed, he pressed home a startling comparison.

Every night in London, he explained, many times seven "will be offered up as the Maiden Tribute of Modern Babylon. Maidens they were when this morning dawned, but tonight their ruin will be accomplished, and tomorrow they will find themselves within the portals of the maze of London brotheldom."*

This statement was followed by another sharpened with sarcasm: "If the daughters of the people must be served up as dainty morsels to minister to the passions of the rich, let them at least attain an age when they can understand the nature of the sacrifice which they are asked to make."†

The response was immediate. The area around the PMG offices darkened with buyers. Each edition was exhausted the moment it was torn from the press. Letters streamed in. Sarcastic statements were answered by even more sarcastic statements. Referring to the open and closed seasons of the game laws, Stead demanded, "Why not let us have a [closed season] for bipeds in petticoats as well as for bipeds with feathers?"‡

Other papers entered the battle. Headlines countered headlines. Celebrities expressed opinions. George Bernard Shaw stood with Stead. A single issue of the *Gazette* brought as much as half a crown.

Neither the General nor Catherine had had part in the Eliza Armstrong affair. But each took part in the campaign to raise the age of consent.

Catherine corresponded with Queen Victoria. And, ne-

Crusader in Babylon, by Raymond L. Schults, p. 133, University of Nebraska Press, 1972.
†Ibid., p. 133.
‡Ibid., p. 139.

glecting a current illness, she addressed a "for women only meeting" at Prince's Hall. Eyes flashing, she was at her eloquent best. She was reported to have said, "The legislature took care that . . . a child should not be empowered to dispose of her money or property until she attained the age of twenty-one; and how came it that they gave her power to dispose of her virtue when she was too young to know the value of it—indeed to know what it meant?" She then demanded, "Is there anything worse than that, think you, in hell?"*

Convinced that it was time to strike, the Booths prepared a petition and sent it to all their halls for signatures. The document outlined four points:

1. The age of responsibility for young girls should be raised to 18.
2. Procuration of young people for seduction or immoral purposes must be made a criminal offense, having attached to it a severe penalty.
3. Right of search by which a magistrate shall have power to issue an order for entry to any house wherein there is reason to believe girls under age are detained against their will.
4. Equality of men and women before the law; seeing that whereas it is now a criminal act for a woman to solicit a man to immorality, it shall be made equally criminal for a man to solicit a woman to immorality.†

Within three weeks, 393,000 had signed the petition. Additional thousands also signed, but they were too late for the deadline. When the sheets were attached to one another, they formed a stream of paper two and a half miles long. Wrapped in Salvation Army colors, this package of petitions was transported to the House of Commons on July 30. The procession entrusted with this task was as colorful as it would be pos-

---

*The History of the Salvation Army, by Robert Sandall, vol 3, pp. 35–36.
†Ibid.

sible for anyone to assemble at that time.

Three distinguished men on horseback spearheaded the column. They were backed by a fifty-piece band that was trailed by two additional horsemen. One hundred Life Guards, each wearing a white helmet and red jersey, thumped behind. The center attraction, bearing the petition, was an open car. It had been decorated to resemble Noah's Ark. This car displayed a huge banner which proclaimed:

IN THE NAME OF GOD AND THE PEOPLE AND THE QUEEN MOTHER, THE SALVATION ARMY DEMANDS THAT THIS INIQUITY CEASE.

The car was guarded by eight colorfully dressed soldiers. It was followed by another fifty Life Guards, among whom was Wong Ock—a Chinese cadet who was being trained to "invade" China. The guards were reinforced by a long stream of soldiers.

It being against the law to parade within a mile of the Houses of Parliament, the procession stopped at Trafalgar Square. Eight Life Guards then carried the rolled-up document to the House of Commons. There it was presented to James Stuart, M.P., while the entire House stood up in order to get a better view of the amazing sight.

Bramwell Booth, together with Stead and others, was eventually asked to speak to the House. The bill went to Committee. The House of Lords decided that the age of consent should be "no less than fifteen." But, as a result of a motion by the Home Secretary, the House of Commons raised the age to sixteen.

The final vote was 179 to 71. The bill became law.

Elated by their victory, William and Catherine left the city in order to conduct special meetings. In the midst of their campaigns, sensational news sent them back to London. Bramwell, along with Stead, Rebecca Jarrett, and some others, had been indicted for "unlawfully taking Eliza Armstrong, aged thirteen, out of the possession of her parents and against her will."*

*Echoes and Memories, by Bramwell Booth, p. 115.

20
The Chariot Is Coming

As their train raced toward London, Catherine and William were extremely worried. "Just think, our son, the Chief of Staff, is going to be in a criminal dock!" wailed the General.

"God will take care of everything," replied Catherine confidently.

"Let's hope so!" The General began to look around anxiously. "All of this could ruin the Army. At this very moment our enemies are licking their lips, writing editorials, spreading lies."

"True," replied Catherine. "But remember, William, God still rules. He helped us before and He will help us again. Let's just trust Him." Having calmed a bit, the General took her in his arms. "You're right, Katie. God *will* take care of us. We are just His servants. *He* created the Army!" William kissed her soundly and returned to his newspaper.

To their intense relief, the Booths learned that neither Bramwell nor Stead was in prison.

The trial was scheduled at the Old Bailey for November 9.

On the evening of the 8th, the General addressed an all-night prayer meeting. With a shaky confidence, he declared: "If we win, we win. If we lose, we win." He said this because he knew he had the ear of the masses. Nonetheless, he spent a sleepless night.

Praying for guidance, Catherine sent a long telegram to Queen Victoria. Her Majesty's reply was that she could not interfere with a trial while it was in progress. Still, she assured Catherine that if there was a conviction, an appeal could be made for a remission of sentences.

Bramwell was acquitted. Jarrett and Mourez were given six months. Stead was sentenced to three months with an understanding that the period of the trial could be deducted from his term. While in prison he had a reasonably good time, and continued to edit the PMG from his cell. Many of his friends visited him. Since his imprisonment was over the New Year holidays, he prepared a card with a line drawing of the prison on the left, and his own portrait on the right. And just beneath his picture, he inscribed this line: "God, even my God, hath anointed me with the oil of gladness above my fellows." Cheerfully, he mailed this card to all on his list.

Upon release, the now famous Stead published five illustrated articles about his prison experiences. He closed the final article on a note of exuberance: "I have been the spoiled child of fortune, but never had a happier lot than the two months I spent in Happy Holloway."

Charles Spurgeon had indicated his sympathy during the trial; and, upon Stead's retirement, mailed him a warm letter of approval. It concluded: "I wish joy to your heart and power to your arm." Instead of hurting The Salvation Army, the trial had given it worldwide publicity. All fair-minded people readily acknowledged that it was because of them that the twice-defeated bill had become law. This fact was another indication that the Army was dedicated to the betterment of mankind.

Each year afterward Stead celebrated the anniversary of his incarceration by donning his prison garb. Years later, he received a letter from Eliza, reporting that she was happily married and the mother of six children.

The ordeal had not harmed her, nor had it harmed Rebecca Jarrett even though she was obliged to finish her entire sentence in prison. She spent the remaining part of her eighty years serving the Army.

October 1883 featured three events Catherine Mumford could not have imagined as she fought for health during her youth. The *War Cry* advertised the three celebrations with bold headlines. Its tens of thousands of readers rejoiced when they read:

GREAT THANKSGIVING
EXETER HALL   Monday, October 22
11:00 a.m., 2:30 p.m, and 6:30 p.m.
Miss Booth will speak on the Army's Victories and
Prospects in Switzerland.
The General will preside and Mrs. Booth will speak during
the day.
The Chief of Staff's child will be presented to the Lord on
this occasion.
Admission by ticket only

As Catherine sat in Exeter Hall that seats four thousand, she was overwhelmed by nostalgia. Nearly a quarter of a century before, while they were in Gateshead, she had given birth to the speaker-to-be. And now this first daughter was leading the invasion of Switzerland. Incredible! As she thought about it, chills raced through her body. This feeling of amazement continued during the evening service.

Soon the time came when her first grandchild, the daughter of her first son, now the Chief of Staff, was to be dedicated to the Lord. Eyes on the podium, Catherine watched. Facing the sea of faces, her husband, the former pawnbroker and now the General of the Army, said, "It is the principle of The Salvation Army that everything we possess belongs to God." He then turned to Bramwell.

"Are you willing that this dear child of yours should be thus consecrated to God, and will you . . . train her for this service?"

After Bramwell had agreed to this, the General addressed his daughter-in-law with an additional set of questions:

"Are you willing, my dear girl, that your child shall be consecrated to the service of the living God after the fashion I have described, and will you join with your dear husband in keeping from her everything in the shape of strong drink, or tobacco, or finery, or wealth, or hurtful reading or dangerous acquaintance, or any such thing that would be likely to interfere with the effect of such training and such education?"

Florence, the mother, replied, "Yes, I promise with joy to train her for The Salvation Army and God alone."

At this point Catherine could not keep from smiling; for she remembered how Florence's father, a successful Welsh physician, had been ardently opposed to his daughter's activities in The Salvation Army.

With his granddaughter nestled in his arms, the General pronounced his dedication:

"Then, my dear children, in the name of The Salvation Army, in the name of the God of The Salvation Army, I take this child and present her to Him. I take this child for Him and receive her for The Salvation Army; and I pray, and your comrades here I am sure pray, that Catherine Bramwell-Booth may be a true saint, a real servant, and a bold, courageous soldier in The Salvation Army."

He then handed Catherine Bramwell-Booth back to her mother, and added: "Take her, Mother, take her. The Father will help you train her for God and The Salvation Army. Let us pray . . ."*

That evening as Catherine and William lingered hand in hand alone by the fireplace, they reminisced about the past. "The Army is really growing," he sighed. "We now have 528 Corps, or Stations, and 245 Field Outposts, together with 103 Corps abroad. And our overseas work is leaping forward. This year we've already opened works in Ceylon, South Africa,

---

*Catherine Bramwell-Booth, by Mary Batchelor, pp. 17–18, Lion Publishing Corporation, 1986.

the Isle of Man, and India; and last year we invaded Canada, Switzerland, and Sweden." Running his fingers through his graying hair, he continued. "I can hardly believe that God has been so good to us."

"And I rejoice in our children," murmured Catherine as she poked the fire. "Already all of them are officers. Even Marion, invalid though she is, is a Staff-Captain!" She shook her head.

"Tell me, Kate," William added, "did you ever doubt that the Lord would use me?"

"Never! I've always believed in you even though you drop your h's sometimes."

William laughed. "I don't do that anymore unless I'm really excited." He pulled off her wedding ring and then replaced it. "Kate, other than getting saved, the best thing I ever did was to slip this ring on your finger. Without you, I'd never 'ave amounted to much—"

"You mean you never would *h*ave amounted to much," corrected Catherine.

"That's right. I would never *h*ave amounted to much. Your prayers and support were always there when I needed them. Now, I'm having a new dream." His eyes glowed with fresh determination.

"Tell me about it."

"I will after you've fixed me a cup of tea. And remember to put hot milk in it together with a lot of sugar." He laughed.

"Yes, General Booth, I'll do just that." Snapping to attention she gave him an exaggerated salute.

"Now tell me about your dream," she urged later, while he was enjoying his tea.

"I want to write a book."

"You've already written several—"

"Yes, yes, I know; and so have you. And I've heard that your new book of sermons is selling very well.* But this book

---

*It was entitled *Life and Death*. This and five other books of her sermons have just been reprinted by The Salvation Army.

will be something special. I want it to open the eyes of the
entire civilized world. As everyone knows, the East End of
London is a hell-hole. In spite of all that we've done, and
others have done, people out there are starving. It's a terrible
place. It reeks with more than a thousand smells. It crawls
with vermin. The East-Enders have nothing but their gin
palaces . . .

"And, as I said before, 'The sun never sets on the British
Empire, and yet it never rises in London's East End.' This
isn't right. And there's no excuse for it. None!

"The British Empire is the largest empire the world has
ever seen, and in this empire there are millions and millions
of acres of fertile soil that have never been used." Pouring
himself some more tea, he began to pace back and forth. "I
want to suggest a scheme that will enable us to send these
poor people to Canada, Australia, New Zealand, and other
places.

"Right now, Kate, there are many out there who are planning on killing themselves. Why? Because they have no food,
no money, no work. And, as The Salvation Army has demonstrated a thousand times, no one is really down and out.
Jesus Christ can help people to smile again and to live useful,
creative lives."

"And when are you going to start your book?"

Lifting his hands in despair he confessed, "Oh, I don't
know. I get glimpses of it now and then. But there are so
many other things to do."

"It's a great idea, William," encouraged Catherine, "and I
will help you in order that it may be fulfilled."

Gathering her in his arms, William gave her a reassuring
hug. "We do make a good team, don't we?"

William Booth was an organizational genius; however, he
frequently made mistakes. Nonetheless, he was always willing to acknowledge his errors. But the older he became the
more determined he was that an order was an order and that
there was no reason to "argufy." To him, even seconds were
important.

Early one morning, while still in his dressing room, he faced his son. "Bramwell!" he thundered, "did you know that men slept out all night on the bridges?"

"Yes," replied his Chief of Staff. "A lot of poor fellows, I suppose, do that."

"Then you ought to be ashamed of yourself to have known it and to have done nothing about it."

Bramwell replied with a number of excuses. The General ignored them. "Go and do something!" he ordered.

"What can we do?"

"Get them a shelter!"

"That will cost money—"

"Well, that's your affair! Something must be done. Get hold of a warehouse and warm it, and find something to cover them. But mind, Bramwell, no coddling!"*

William never issued orders to Catherine. That wasn't necessary! Like him, she made every second count. Moreover, they always pulled together.

Twenty-two years after her father had sent her to Brighton in order to regain her health, Catherine had been summoned back to this city on the sea for a series of meetings. Her services began in a concert hall that seated fifteen hundred. Taking advantage of the fact that his building was jammed, the proprietor demanded higher rent. Convinced that he was unreasonable, Catherine rented the Dome.

The Dome seated three thousand!

As Catherine studied the two thousand who had gathered to hear her, she did so with trepidation. Would they all be able to hear her? They did. Better yet, many stepped forward and accepted Christ.

Impressed by her meetings, Father Ignatius wrote: "What a glorious woman! What a mother of giants in Israel! What an astounding *Fact* is The Salvation Army! What a shame and what a glory to the churches!"

Echoes and Memories, by Bramwell Booth, pp. 1–2.

Whenever Catherine spoke she had crowded houses. Her sermons were gathered into books and were eagerly purchased. Great cities and great churches were constantly begging her to favor them with meetings. Dr. Joseph Parker, pastor of the famed City Temple, especially admired her, and frequently asked her to fill his pulpit.

While Catherine was writing an article for the *War Cry* during a pause between meetings, William laid his hand on her shoulder. "I've found something that is inspiring me to begin my new book right away," he said. He opened a pamphlet entitled *The Bitter Cry of Outcast London.* "Listen to this:

"Here is a filthy attic, containing only a broken chair, a battered saucepan and a few rags. On a dirty sack in the center of the room sits a neglected, ragged, bare-legged girl of four. Her father is a militiaman, and is away. Her mother is out all day and comes home late at night more or less drunk, and this child is left in charge of an infant that we see crawling about the floor; left for six or eight hours at a stretch—hungry, thirsty, tired, but never daring to move from her post." He paused, and then with additional emphasis read the final sentence in that paragraph:

*"And this is the kind of sight that may be seen in a Christian land where it is criminal to ill-treat a horse or an ass."**

After shaking the pamphlet, Booth asked, "And what do you think of that?" But before she could answer, he began another paragraph:

"Every room in these rotten and reeking tenements houses a family, often two. In one cellar a sanitary inspector reports finding a father, a mother, three children, and four pigs! In another room a missionary found a man ill with smallpox, his wife just recovering from her eighth confinement, and the children running about half naked and covered with dirt. Here are seven people living in one under-

---

The Bitter Cry of Outcast London, by Andrew Mearns, Leicester University Press, 1970, p. 76.

ground kitchen, and a small child lying dead in the same room. Elsewhere is a poor widow, her three children and a child who has been dead thirteen days. Her husband, who was a cabman, had shortly before committed suicide."*

"I have witnessed things just as bad as that, and even worse," commented Catherine as she glanced at her manuscript.

"And so have I." He thoughtfully wound the end of his beard around his finger. "This author did a good job. But, Kate, he merely diagnosed the problem. He didn't offer a cure! Jesus Christ alone is the cure. And you and I know that. The Salvation Army knows that." Pacing back and forth, he continued. "And we have examples to prove that Jesus Christ is *the* solution. What better examples could anyone have than the way the lives of Bones and Old Born Drunk were changed. "Kate, I've got to start writing that book!"

Catherine nodded. "You're right, and you must start writing it immediately!"

As Catherine began to think of ways in which she could help her husband with his new book, she began to notice a lump in her breast. Since her mother had died of cancer of the breast, she was concerned. On February 21, 1888, she made her way in her carriage through the snows to Sir James Paget's office.

"I'm afraid you have cancer and you should have an immediate operation," concluded Sir James.

"I—I've never known anyone to be cured of cancer by surgery," replied Catherine.

Sir James shrugged.

"How—how long do you think I have to live?"

"I really don't know." He evaded a direct answer.

"Come. Give me an answer. I want to make the best use of the time I have left."

*The Bitter Cry of Outcast London, by Andrew Mearns, Leicester University Press, 1970, p. 69.

The famous physician breathed deeply. Then, in as calm a voice as he could manage, he admitted, "It is possible that you have another two years. That's up to God."

William was shocked. "I'm scheduled to speak in Holland," he stated. "I'll cancel the trip."

Catherine squeezed his hand. "No, William. Keep your appointment," she insisted. "I'm ready to die. Many of those people are not."

Hoping that Sir James was wrong, Catherine consulted other physicians. None gave her hope. She tried the Mattie treatment, which employed intermittent currents of electricity. It provided a brief, temporary relief. With her remaining strength, she continued to preach. At the City Temple she spoke for an hour to an audience that filled every available space.

During her struggles, she kept encouraging William to start his book. As he wrote, she made suggestions, and helped him with his spelling and grammar.

Eventually the doctors persuaded her to submit to surgery; however, it was too late. Through the generosity of a friend, she was finally moved to a fine home at Clacton-on-Sea about seventy miles east of London. The sea always invigorated her and she felt better.

Booth had plenty of raw material for his book. But he felt he needed literary help in order that this latest volume might have the maximum effect. W. T. Stead volunteered his services. At this time the General was facing many crises. New buildings had been purchased, and others were being built. This meant he had to raise vast sums of money, and raising money provides unusual opportunity for misunderstandings.

The Booths were accused of living in luxury when, as a matter-of-fact, they had to take in lodgers in order to pay their bills. One critic insisted that The Salvation Army was clearly Antichrist.

The newspaper *Globe* probed the bottom when it reported

that Army men had displayed a banner which asked, "Why give tenpence a pound for lamb when you can get the Lamb of God for nothing?" Booth denied this horrible blasphemy in the *War Cry*. Nonetheless, it was believed by many. The General's advice was, "Don't answer your critics. Carry on with your work." But sometimes the load became too heavy even for him.

Noticing his depression, Catherine, ill as she was, said, "Don't let them get you down. When I was a girl I was fascinated by Joan of Arc. After she had helped the French defeat the English and had enabled Charles VII to be crowned King of France, the French sold her to the English, who burned her at the stake. Nonetheless, fifteen years later she was proclaimed innocent; and now the date of her death is a feast day in France, and the Roman Catholic Church considers her to be a saint."

"So?"

"And so, you may be damned today; but tomorrow you will be praised."

"So?"

"Do the work of the Lord and forget your critics."

Then William showed her a set of notes he'd been writing. "Read them, Kate. Tell me what you think."

Day after day Kate studied the notes and made suggestions. Each day she became more inspired. "This book can change the world," she remarked. "But to reach the masses it must be properly packaged. What are you going to name it?"

"I don't know." He pulled his beard. "I want a name that will shock the reader out of his complacency. I want a name that will slam people to their knees and make them dip into their pockets."

"God will supply a name," Catherine said confidently. "I'll make it a matter of prayer. When will Stead start helping you?"

"Next week. He has the right touch and he won't take a penny."

As the manuscript piled up, Catherine's pain increased. She tried to ignore it, for she didn't want to upset William. But as the months passed it became so severe she could not keep from crying out. Again and again she groaned, "Oh, these fiery scorpions, these fiery scorpions! Oh! Oh! Oh!"

At such times William always rushed to her bedside. "Why don't you let the doctor give you morphine?" he begged.

"Because I want to help you with your book! I saw what the drug did to Mother. It so deadened her mind she couldn't even say Jesus. She—" Unable to complete the sentence, she took a deep breath and all but screamed, "Oh, these scorpions! These fiery scorpions! Oh! Oh!"

"Kate, you must take some morphine—"

"I'll pray about it."

"God gave it to us to use."

"Yes, yes, yes! I'll think about it."

As Catherine pondered, she remembered the time in her girlhood when she had first become acquainted with the exploits of Deborah. Although Deborah didn't make it into Hebrews 11, her support of Barak had placed him in that famed list. In the same way she had supported William, and now that he was facing even more than nine hundred chariots of iron, she was determined to continue to support him until her last breath.

Yes, the General was her man; and his book was her book!

Catherine's pain continued to deepen. Even so, she was constantly coming up with brilliant statements. At Stead's suggestion, a screen was placed by her bed, and a stenographer, without her knowledge, was assigned to record her remarks.

Once, as Emma was dressing Catherine's wound, inflamed by a new hemorrhage, she said in a matter-of-fact tone, "You need not hurry, Emma; there is plenty of time. I have no train to catch. I have nothing to catch now but the chariot."

Late one evening as William watched Catherine struggling with pain, he came to her side. "The Lord has answered your prayer," he murmured.

"Which one?"

"He's given me a title for our book—"

"Yes?"

"Stanley's new book, *In Darkest Africa*, is creating a sensation. Everyone's reading it! My new book, I mean *our* new book, will be entitled *In Darkest England and the Way Out*. You see, Kate, our book not only outlines the disease; it also suggests a workable remedy."

"Oh, William," she exclaimed, "that is a great title! I can already visualize stacks and stacks of the books in the stores."

At night when her pain became excruciating, she often wondered why God didn't ease her suffering. *Did He answer prayer?* When fighting doubts, she made it a habit to count answered prayers on her fingers. A spectacular one concerned her father.

She had prayed hundreds of times for his deliverance from alcohol. While helping in her meetings, he had often signed a pledge. But on each occasion he had broken it. Then, when he was seventy-five, he signed again. This time he kept it and was sober when he died.

As the fall season of 1890 approached, Catherine continued to worsen. Knowing that their mother's death was near, the children left their various posts and lingered by her bedside. To each she spoke a blessing. Pulling Evan down to her lips, she whispered, "My Christmas box! Don't fret; you'll follow me. I will watch for you!" Then, remembering another concern, she added:

"And, Eva, don't you forget that criminal you spoke to with the handcuffs on . . . Tell him that your mother, when she was dying, prayed for him . . ."

The year before, on December 19, she had sent the following message to the *War Cry*: "The waters are rising, but so am I. I am not going under but over."

As she neared the end, she took off her ring and slipped it onto William's little finger while she said, "By this token we were united for time, and by it we are now united for eternity."

The night of October 3 was one of torrential rain. Thunder shook the windows. But the next day was calm. Larks could be heard, and there was the soft beating of the surf against the nearby shore. One of her favorite mottoes, featuring the words *My Grace Is Sufficient for Thee*, had been removed from the wall and placed in a position where she could see it.

The sun was just flaming red in the west when William realized that her summons was near. He pressed his lips to hers and she was gone.

Epilogue

Catherine's body was placed in a plain wooden coffin that had been fitted with a glass through which her remains could be viewed. As it lay in state in the great Olympia auditorium where the memorial service was conducted, tens of thousands filed by for a farewell glance.

The Salvation Army flag had been draped over the coffin and her hand placed on her favorite portrait of the General. A crowd four miles long stood with uncovered heads as the procession moved slowly toward Abney Park Cemetery.

The procession, made up of three thousand officers, finally reached the cemetery where the police had limited the attendance to ten thousand. The fog lifted and the sun in the west was sinking toward the horizon when General Booth stood up and addressed the huge crowd that pressed close to the opened grave. The *Daily Telegraph* recorded the scene:

> It was a most touching sight when the tall, upright General came forward in the gathering darkness to tell his comrades of the loss he, their chief, had sustained. He spoke manfully, and without the slightest trace of affectation . . . He spoke as a soldier should who has disciplined his emotions . . . Few wives who have comforted their husbands for forty years have received such a glowing tribute of honest praise.

After speaking for fifteen or twenty minutes, the General concluded:

"My comrades, I'm going to meet her again. I have never turned from her these forty years for any journeyings on my mission of mercy but what I have longed to get back, and have counted the weeks, the days and the hours that should take me again to her side . . .

"What then is there left for me to do? My work plainly is to fill up the weeks, the days, and the hours, and cheer my poor heart as I go along with the thought that, when I have served my Christ and my generation according to the will of God—which I vow this afternoon I will to the last drop of my blood—then I trust that she will bid me welcome to the skies, as He bade her.

"God bless you all."

A brass plate bearing the following inscription was placed over her grave:

Catherine Booth
The Mother of
THE SALVATION ARMY
Born 17th January, 1829
Died 4th October, 1890
"More than conqueror"

It was hard for the General to face the empty chair at home. But he kept busy. Fourteen days after Kate's passing, he was handed the first copy of his new book.

"How's it selling?" he asked.

"Extremely well," replied the manager. "We printed 10,000; and today, October 20, the first day of publication, we've sold all of them and the orders are streaming in. We've already ordered a new printing. We'll have to run extra shifts to meet the demand."

Opening his copy, the General unashamedly wiped his tears as he read the dedication:

TO THE MEMORY
of the
COMPANION, COUNSELLOR, AND COMRADE
Of nearly 40 years
The sharer of my every ambition
for
The welfare of mankind
My
Loving, faithful, and devoted wife
This book is dedicated

Unable to sleep, the General got up and opened Kate's Bible. He turned to the fourth chapter of the Book of Judges and reread the story of Deborah and Barak. *Yes, Kate had been another Deborah!* Without hesitation she had ridden with him into every conflict. He then paused at the 20th verse in the next chapter. There, he read the song of triumph the people sang after Barak's triumph. Realizing that the Canaanite commander had been annihilated because of an unexpected deluge of rain which had immobilized his nine hundred chariots, they sang:

"The stars in their courses fought against Sisera."

General Booth had no reason to complain. The Salvation Army was enjoying unusual success all over the world. Nonetheless, no spectacular phenomenon had ever come to his aid. Indeed, it had seemed that the stars in their courses had worked against him! The ship which the Cory brothers had named *William Booth* and whose profits were to be turned over to the Army had gone down in a storm. Rich men who had supported him had withdrawn their support. Even a large section of the Christian press had turned against him.

Ah, but perhaps his time had not come!

Booth continued to work, to pray, and to have hope. And then it seemed that the stars began to work in his favor. His new book was discussed all over the country. It went into many translations. Money poured in. Colonies for the benefit of the poor were established. And instead of the crowds pelting him, they began to praise him. Many an enemy even suggested that he might be—just might be—God's man! Some

300,000 copies of the *War Cry* were circulated each week;
and for the week ending on September 13, 1890, the headquarters in London received 5,574 letters and telegrams.

On June 24, 1904, the General was summoned to Buck-
ingham Palace to meet with King Edward VII. During their
conversation, the King asked Booth what he did for recrea-
tion.

"Sir," replied Booth, "some men have a passion for art,
others have a passion for riches. I have a passion for souls."

Booth was interviewed by various kings and queens. On
each occasion, the monarch, together with all who were present, knew that he was a scavenger for souls. "I want to reach
the lowest of the low," he repeated again and again.

Having concluded his conversation with Winston
Churchill about prison reform, he was asked by Churchill,
"Am I converted?"

Arching his brows, the General replied, "No, I'm afraid
you are not converted, but I think you *are* convicted."

On his return from speaking engagements abroad, the
General received a letter from Lord Curzon, chancellor of Oxford University. Puzzled why such a distinguished man would
wish to communicate with him, he opened the envelope.
Then his dark eyes glistened as he read: "I should like the
famous and ancient university, of which I am now the head,
and which has played so notable part in the history of our
country—to have the privilege of setting its seal upon the
noble work you have done . . . a work excelled in range and
beneficence by that of no living man."

While arrayed in a scarlet robe, the former pawnbroker
was presented with a Doctor of Laws degree. Upon seeing
Rudyard Kipling, he strode forward and grasped his hand.
"Young feller, how's it with your soul?" he demanded.

Ascending from one honor to another, the General was
welcomed at the White House by President Theodore Roose-
velt. Next, he was asked to open the United States Senate
with prayer.

Booth enjoyed the honors he received because he knew

that they were helping The Salvation Army. As he crossed into his eighties, his friends urged him to slow down. He refused. Not once in his life had he taken a vacation and he didn't want to break that record. There were just too many souls needing to be saved and far too many slums.

By 1912 his eyes had become so dim he finally agreed to submit to the surgeons if they would perform the operation in his home. Concluding his sermon to ten thousand in London's Royal Albert Hall, he stated, "I am now going into dry dock for repairs."

On May 23, the day scheduled for the second operation, he was unusually cheerful. He went to his study, dictated several letters and signed some documents. Then he had his picture taken along with Colonel Kitching and his faithful sheep dog, Gyp.

Two days after the last surgery, it was discovered that infection had set in. Hating to tell him the bad news, the surgeons summoned Bramwell.

Entering the dark room, Bramwell said, "Father, I'm—I-I'm afraid that you w-will never see again."

"You mean that I'm blind?"

"I think so."

"Does this mean I'll never see your face again?"

"Not in this world."

After a long pause, the General broke the silence. In an unbelievably calm voice, he proclaimed, "God must know best."

Following another pause, the old warrior squeezed his son's hand while he said, "Bramwell, I have done what I could for God with my eyes. Now I shall do what I can for God and the people without my eyes."

Noticing her father standing by the window facing a glorious sunset, Eva stood by his side and described it in word pictures. When she finished her word painting, he gave her a fatherly squeeze and murmured. "That's all right, Eva. I can't see the sunset, but I shall see the dawn."

In the afternoon on August 20, 1912, there was a violent thunderstorm. The storm passed and the evening was quiet. That night at thirteen minutes past ten, the old veteran of a thousand battles closed his eyes for the last time.

His last coherent words were uttered under great difficulty. He had been reclining in his chair and was talking about an incident of the day. Suddenly he exclaimed, "Bramwell—the promises! . . ." He tried again. Again he could not complete the sentence. Still determined, he made a third attempt. On this try, he only managed to say, "The promises . . ." Another voice added "of God." As stubborn as ever, he made a fourth try. This time he was successful. "The promises—of—God—are sure—are sure—if you will only believe."

The next morning, newspapers around the world carried the headline: "THE GENERAL HAS LAID DOWN HIS SWORD."

Sixty-five thousand marched by for a last look.

Forty bands assembled for the final services and played the songs he loved so well. That Thursday, with ten thousand Salvationists marching behind, he was taken to Abney Park Cemetery and laid to rest by the side of his wife. A simple shield was placed over his grave. It had on it a humble inscription:

William Booth
Founder and 1st General of
The Salvation Army
Born 1829
Born again of the Spirit 1845
Founded The Salvation Army 1865
Went to heaven 20th August 1912

Both giants were at rest. Still, The Salvation Army kept maturing and expanding. Many years later when their daughter, General Evangeline Booth, was in London, a policeman told her that a man in a car wanted to see her. At the time she was extremely tired, and since her car had broken down, she remained on the platform protected from the drizzling rain by a blanket.

"If he wants to see me, let him come to the platform," she replied.

"Oh, but he can't. He's ninety-three. And he told me that he's come two hundred miles to see you."

Finally persuaded, Eva made her way through the drizzle to the car. There, she saw an extremely bent old man with thin snowy hair.

"I'm a lamplighter," he wheezed. "I-I'm the l-l-lad who h-h-helped your father in the old tent in the Quaker cemetery."

"And how did you help?"

"I s-strung t-the lights on a r-r-rope. One day your father said to me. 'Someday—' " The old man struggled with his memory. "H-he said, 'Someday they will be stringing lights like this 'round t-the w-world.' Yes, Miss Eva, that's what your father said."

When Booth was preaching in that leaky tent, the sun never set on the British Empire. Today, that empire, like many previous empires, is gone. The sun sets daily on its few remaining possessions. But in our time the sun never sets on the tricolor of The Salvation Army. That pattern of blue for purity, red for the blood of Christ, and yellow for the Holy Spirit now hangs, and is respected, in eighty-six countries of the world.

The indomitable Catherine Booth was a major reason for this accomplishment. Like Deborah, she was undaunted by the nine hundred iron chariots of the enemy. In the depths of her heart she believed that "the stars in their courses" would eventually come to her aid.

Chronology

1829	Jan. 17	Catherine was born to John and Sarah Mumford at Ashbourne.
1831		Viewed the corpse of newly born brother.
1832		Began to read at three years of age.
1834		Told and confessed first lie at age four.
1834		Together with family, moved to Boston. John Mumford became an ardent temperance worker although he had given up the ministry.
1839		Catherine accompanied an arrested drunk to jail.
1841		Elected secretary of Juvenile Temperance Society. Began to attend school.
1843		At 14 dropped out of school because of severe spinal attack.
1844		First love, age 15. Moved to London and began to attend services in the nearby Wesleyan Chapel.
1846	June 15	Catherine converted.
1846		Started to participate in class meetings.

1847		John Mumford began to drink. Catherine stricken with tuberculosis—fled to Brighton.
1851		Expelled from the Wesleyans because she openly favored the Reformers. Heard William Booth preach at Binfield Chapel. Attended "tea" at the home of Edward Rabbits and heard Booth recite *The Grogsellers Dream*.
1852	April 10	Booth was appointed Catherine's pastor.
	May 15	Catherine became engaged to Booth.
1853		Booth joins Methodist New Connexion and attends seminary.
1855	June 16	Catherine and William are married.
1856	March 8	William Bramwell born at Halifax.
1857	July 28	Ballington born at Brighouse.
1858	May	Booth ordained at Hull.
	Sept. 18	Catherine born at Gateshead.
1859		Catherine (Mrs. Booth) publishes *Female Ministry*—her first pamphlet.
1860	Jan. 8	Emma born at Gateshead.
1861		John Mumford experiences spiritual renewal.
	May	Catherine exclaims, "No, never!" from the gallery at the Liverpool Conference when William was ordered to take a circuit.
	July	Booth resigns from New Connexion.
	Aug. 11	Booths begin meetings in Cornwall.
1862	Aug. 26	Herbert Howard born at Penzance.
1864	May 19	Marian Billups born at Leeds.
1865	July 2	William Booth began a tent meeting in London. Later moved meetings to new Road, Whitechapel.
	Nov.	Booths move to South Hackney (London).
	Dec. 25	Eveline (Eva) Cory born.

1868		The *Christian Mission*, born in 1865, starts work in Scotland.
	April 28	Lucy Milward born at Hackney.
1869	Dec. 16	Sarah Mumford dies of cancer.
1870		Booth published: *How To Reach the Masses*.
1878		The *Christian Mission* legalized.
1879		First Salvation Army band.
1880		Official publication renamed the *War Cry*. Headquarters moved to Queen Victoria Street. Branches opened in United States and Australia.
1885		Age of consent raised to 16.
1886		A branch opened in Germany.
1887		1000th corp established in Britain.
1888		Catherine learns she has cancer.
	June 21	Catherine gives last public address.
1890		Catherine refuses morphine.
	Oct. 4	Promoted to glory.
	Oct. 6–11	Catherine's body viewed by 50,000 at Congress Hall.
	Oct. 13	Catherine's body moved to West End. 36,000 pay their respects.
	Oct. 20	*In Darkest England and the Way Out* published.
1912	April 15	W. T. Stead goes down on the *Titanic*.
	May 23	Operation on the General's remaining eye.
	Aug. 20	The General lays down his sword.

Bibliography

Those who wish to know more about Catherine Booth will find the following books useful:

Batchelor, Mary. *Catherine Bramwell-Booth*. Lion Pub. Corp., 1986.

Begbie, Harold. *The Life of William Booth*, vols. 1, 2. Macmillan, 1920.

Begbie, Harold. *Twice-Born Men*. Fleming Revell, 1909.

Boon, Brindley. *Sing That Happy Song*. Salvationist Publishing and Supplies, 1978.

Booth, Bramwell. Echoes and Memories. George H. Doran, 1925.

Booth, Catherine. *Aggressive Christianity. Papers on Godliness. Life and Death. Popular Christianity. Papers on Practical Religion. Highway of Our God*. The Salvationist Army Supplies, Atlanta, 1986.

Booth, Charles. *Life and Labor in London*. Augustus M. Kelly, 1969.

Booth, Evangeline and Hill, Grace Livingston *The War Romance of The Salvation Army*. J. B. Lippincott, 1919.

Booth, William. *In Darkest England and the Way Out*. Funk and Wagnalls, 1890.

Bramwell-Booth, Catherine. *Catherine Booth*. Hodder & Stoughton, 1970.

Booth-Tucker, F. de L. *Catherine Booths*, vols. 1, 2. Fleming Revell, 1892.

Chesham, Sallie. *Born to Battle*. Rand McNally, 1965.

Ervine, John. *God's Soldier, William Booth*, vols. 1, 2. Macmillan, 1935.

Kipling, Rudyard. *Something of Myself.* Doubleday, 1937.

Ludwig, Charles. *General Without a Gun*. Zondervan, 1961.

Ludwig, Charles. *The Lady General*. Baker Book House, 1965.

Malvern, Gladys. *Valliant Minstrel, Sir Harry Lauder*. Julian Messner, 1943.

Mearns, Andrew. *The Bitter Cry of Outcast London*. Leicester University Press, 1970.

Nelson, William H. *Blood and Fire*. The Century Co., 1929.

Orsborne, Albert, CBE. *The House of My Pilgrimage*. Salvationist Publishing and Supplies, 1958.

Pearson, Hesketh. *G.B.S. A Full Length Portrait*. Harper and Brothers, 1942.

Railton, George S. *The Authoritative Life of General Booth*. Salvationist Publishing and Supplies, Ltd., 1912.

Sandall, Robert. *The History of The Salvation Army*, vol. 3. Thomas Nelson, 1935.

Shultz, Raymond L. *Crusader in Babylon*. University of Nebraska Press, 1972.

Stanley, Henry M. *In Darkest Africa*, vols. 1, 2. Charles Scribner's Sons.

Stead, Estelle. *My Father*. William Hieneman, 1913.

Stead, W.T. *Catherine Booth*. Salvation Army, Toronto, 1979.

Stead, W.T. *General Booth*. Salvation Army, Toronto, 1980.

Steele, Harold C. *I Was a Stranger*. Exposition Press, 1954.

Waldron, John D. *Women in the Salvation Army*. Salvation Army, Toronto, 1983.

Wilson, P.W. *General Evangeline Booth*. Scribner's Sons, 1948.

CHAMPION
OF
FREEDOM

CHARLES LUDWIG

BETHANY HOUSE PUBLISHERS
MINNEAPOLIS, MINNESOTA 55438
A Division of Bethany Fellowship, Inc.

Published by Bethany House Publishers
A Division of Bethany Fellowship, Inc.
6820 Auto Club Road, Minneapolis, Minnesota 55438

Printed in the United States of America

Library of Congress Cataloging-in-Publication Data

Ludwig, Charles, 1918–
    Champion of freedom.

    1. Stowe, Harriet Beecher, 1811–1896, in fiction,
drama, poetry, etc.   I. Title.
PS3523.U434C5   1987   813'.52   87–20884
ISBN 0–87123–965–5

To the memory of "Auntie" Elizabeth Hetrick, my parents' housekeeper who helped raise me. When I was eight she kept me spellbound as she read *Uncle Tom's Cabin*. A year later, she inspired me to make my life count by pointing out a sculpture of Harriet Beecher Stowe in New York City's Hall of Fame.

Acknowledgments

F rom the time Harriet Beecher Stowe's *Uncle Tom's Cabin* was read to me when I was eight, I've been interested in the author, wanting to know how such a tiny fragment of humanity was able to stir the world. Following my fascination, I visited Litchfield where she was born and where her father preached. Then I went to Brunswick, Maine, where Harriet Stowe had a "vision" of Uncle Tom—and there wrote the book.

Intrigued by Tom and Eliza, my wife and I photographed the famous John Rankin House in Ripley, Ohio. Perched on a cliff overlooking the broad Ohio River, this preacher-house was a stopping place on the Underground Railroad. It was from this residence that help was extended to Eliza after she had managed to leap from one cake of ice to another in her escape. It was also near this house, during a minister's convention, that Harriet began her romance with Calvin Stowe.

Crossing into Kentucky, Mary and I drove to the plantation that had allegedly belonged to Simon Legree—the man who owned Uncle Tom. We also stopped at the nearby cemetery where, according to legend, Legree is buried. Legend also insists that on three occasions lightning shattered the slab of cement over his grave.

In gathering material, I've used many books, both from the University of Arizona, and the Huntington Library in San Marino, California, which contains the largest collection of Harriet Beecher Stowe material in America.

Miss Sue Hodson, the Curator of the Harriet Beecher Stowe collection, was most helpful, as were all the other members of the staff.

How much of this book is true? I did take the liberty to name two of the many cats at the Beecher home in Litchfield, and I invented one character, the former slave, Sam. Otherwise, all the other names and events are actual.

I must also extend my thanks to the editors at Bethany House Publishers for their interest in publishing this work.

Table of Contents

Preface

C ongressman Philip Greeley of Boston settled himself in the night train for New York and Washington. Then to pass the time, he began to read volume one of the cloth-bound book just presented to him by Professor Calvin Stowe.

Although he had not read any of the story as it was being published in serial form in the *National Era*, he halfway expected to be bored. Indeed, when the publisher, fearing its failure, had offered to share the profits if Calvin would put up half the money, Greeley had advised against it. A ten percent royalty, he was convinced, was a much better proposition for the over-lengthy novel.

Opening to the first page, the Congressman began to read: "Late in the afternoon of a chilly day in February, two gentlemen were sitting alone over their wine in a well-furnished dining parlor in the town of P——, in Kentucky." Soon the book became alive. The rhythmic beating of the carriage wheels retreated into silence. The pages quickly shuffled beneath his eager fingers. He became conscious of tears coursing down his cheeks and of people staring curiously at him. But in spite of the scene he was creating, he could not lay the book down. In desperation he got off the train at Springfield, checked into a hotel and wept his way through both volumes.

Uncle Tom's Cabin, by Harriet Beecher Stowe, was on its way! Soon the presses were rumbling day and night. Twenty thousand copies alone were sold in three weeks. This was the mere beginning. It was translated into one language after another. It became an instant hit on Broadway. It was pirated

11

in England. More importantly, it became the leading cause for the abolition of slavery.

No one was more astonished by this success than the author. After the contract had been signed, she timidly remarked, "I hope it earns enough money so that I may have a silk dress."

To an admirer she replied with typical modesty, "I am a little bit of a woman—about as thin and dry as a pinch of snuff."

All eleven of Lyman Beecher's children made an impact with their lives. His seven sons were preachers. Catherine won renown as a pioneer in women's education. Isabella etched her mark as a suffragette, Mary became the wife of a leading attorney. And Harriet blossomed into one of the world's most famous authors.

Busts of both Harriet and Henry Ward are in the Hall of Fame.

So successful was this family that Theodore Parker declared: "Lyman Beecher was the father of more brains than any other man in America." And Dr. Leonard Bacon of New Haven commented that America is "inhabited by saints, sinners, and Beechers."

Both men were right. And even though Lyman's mother died at his premature birth, he possessed a secret: He *expected* his children to succeed—and raised them in a Christian atmosphere.

1
Litchfield

Harriet rubbed her eyes, stumbling toward the kitchen. She had no idea that she would grow up to become the most famous author in America, and that she would write a book that would help free millions of slaves. Nor did she understand that her father had a unique way of raising children, a way that would help make all of them useful—and several of them famous. The one thing she understood was that she had been awakened by the tangy aroma of bacon.

Bacon and eggs meant dawn. Dawn meant that it was time for all the Beechers in Litchfield to get up and start changing the world.

"Breakfast's 'bout ready," announced Zillah, one of the two black teenagers in charge of the kitchen. Skillfully Zillah broke more eggs on the edge of the skillet. While they bubbled and spat, she added, "Better wake your pa while the food's hot."

Complying with a squeal of delight, Harriet barged into her father's room. Waking him on Monday morning was almost as exciting as watching the parades on the Fourth of July. This morning she had no idea that she was gaining experience for a time nearly a half century later when she would call on a former rail-splitter and urge him to issue the Emancipation Proclamation. "Pa," she squeaked, "bwakefast's almost weady."

Lyman Beecher did not respond.

Harriet raised her voice. "Git up, Papa!"

No answer.

"Git up! Git up! Git up!" she sang.

America's most distinguished preacher refused to budge. Desperately Harriet peeled a corner of the covers from his face. Then, while pinching the end of his nose, she repeated, "Bwakefast is almost weady."

The sleepy man pushed out his big toe.

Encouraged, Harriet climbed down off the big bed and started to leave. She had just reached the door when he groaned and jerked his toe back to safety under the covers. "I can't get up. I can't get up." His voice shuddered with terror.

"Why not?" Harriet grinned, for this answer was part of the routine.

"B-b-because there's a hungry lion under the b-b-bed."

"There's no lion under the bed," assured Harriet.

"A-are you sure?"

"Papa, I'm sure."

"Maybe you'd better crawl under the bed and make sure. I d-don't relish being e-eaten—especially this early in the morning." Shuddering at this imminent possibility, he crunched even deeper into the bed.

Thoughtfully, Harriet paused with her hand on the door-knob. The smells of breakfast were becoming more tantalizing, and since they were required to have family worship *before* they could eat, she realized that she needed help. Knowing she'd have to crawl under the bed, search out the closet, look behind the cupboard, and examine all the corners before her father would get up, there was only one answer.

Stepping out the door, she called for her six-year-old brother George, and her ten-year-old sister Mary. Following her directions, they finally assured America's most noted theologian that there were no lions or even tigers in his room. Bouncing out of bed, he inwardly rejoiced in knowing that he had helped sharpen his children's imagination.

Following worship, all eight Beecher children, their mother Roxana, the three boarders who attended Sarah Pierce's school for young ladies, Betsy Burr, the orphan cousin of Lyman's assistant Mr. Cornelius, along with several guests, took their places at the enormous table.

After grace, and after he had eaten several eggs and a few pieces of bacon, Lyman Beecher began to reminisce. "As most of you know, my first church was in East Hampton, Long Island. The first pastor received one fourth of the whales stranded on the beach, was allowed to be first in line to have his grain ground, did not have to pay taxes on his land—and was paid forty-five pounds a year.

"I didn't fare so well. I only received four hundred dollars a year and firewood. Roxana had to open a school." He exchanged glances with his wife.

"Here, I get twice as much money. And they bring my firewood. But when they bring it they cause a big problem for me." Frowning, he helped himself to another egg and some fried potatoes.

"When they bring the wood, they're not careful about where they drop it. Now, as you know I've been in a contest with the president of Yale. Doctor Taylor thinks he can raise cucumbers faster than I can. He can't. I always have more and bigger cucumbers than he has, and I have them on the table before he does." He nodded assuringly.

"I have a secret." My secret is that I start my cucumbers in cold frames. The frames protect them from the frost. But now my friends have piled wood on those frames." He shook his head sorrowfully. "This means I'll need your help to move the firewood . . ."

Roxana neither smiled nor frowned, for she realized that Lyman was far more interested in raising useful children than in producing cucumbers; and that he had a subtle way of teaching them without their knowledge. Experience had taught her to conceal this understanding.

Since everyone was eager to help, the preacher continued eating in silence. Then his eyes lit up. "I really enjoyed preaching yesterday," he confessed. "God *is* sovereign! Still, I believe in free will. Those opposites cling together like bacon and eggs. It's as Jonathan Edwards says: you cannot have light without heat." Carried away, he thumped the table with such force the knives and forks jumped. "Had not Moses *obeyed* God, His providence would not have separated the Red Sea. . . .

"God hates dueling. But His providence cannot stop this type of murder until *we* do something about it. That's the reason God directed me to preach my sermon against dueling. Forty thousand copies of that sermon were distributed! In time God's providence will put an end to dueling . . ."

Annoyed that few were listening, he pointed to Harriet. "Hattie listened more closely than any of you. Her eyes never moved from the pulpit. And she's only four!"

The rest of the children glanced at Harriet and then down at their plates. The silence was finally broken by Roxana: "Catherine has a poem we ought to hear. It might inspire us to put an end to one of our worst problems—"

"What's it about?" asked Harriet, bursting with pride.

"Rats," replied Roxana.

"Rats?" questioned Mary.

"Yes, rats!" confirmed their mother.

"All right, let's hear about the rats," nodded Lyman, exerting his authority as head of the house.

Standing in front of her empty plate, Catherine, the oldest of the Beecher children, cleared her throat and read from the back of the envelope in her hand:

> One rat slipped on Miss Katy's shoes
> And danced about the room
> While with tongs and candlestick
> Two others kept the tune.
>
> One rat jumped onto Harriet's bed
> And began to gnaw her nose.
> The other chose another extreme
> And nibbled Mary's toes—[1]

After the clapping, Roxana said, "Lyman, we must do something about those rats!"

"Any suggestions? We already have a dozen cats."

"I'll tell you what I think we should do," Roxana laced her voice with authority. "We should stop feeding them! Look at Thomas Junior. He's so full of bacon and eggs all he can do is sit and scrub his whiskers."

Unconcerned that he was the center of attention, the black tomcat continued to preen, his pink tongue moving in and out as he licked his paw and carefully polished his face.

"He could at least frighten a few mice if he ever got hungry," added Roxana. "I doubt if he's even tried to catch the tiniest mouse. But why should he? Look at his plate! It's nearly full. Soon he'll be so fat he'll begin to stagger . . ."

"Maybe so," Lyman chuckled. "But in the meantime it's time to move that firewood. Catherine will be leaving for school in less than an hour, so let's get busy."

It had always bothered Harriet that her father wished she were a boy. Now, deciding to please him, she wrapped up in one of Edward's outgrown coats. She had just started for the woodpile when her father, not noticing how she was dressed, commented, "Hattie, I've lost my hat."

Since the preacher lost his hat almost every day, Hattie had become an expert at finding it. If it wasn't by the fire-

---

[1] *The Beechers*, by Milton Rugoff, p. 42.

place, it was generally near the big chair where he liked to study. Having located the hat, Harriet gave it to her father. Beecher stuffed it on his head and began to show the children just how the wood was to be moved and stacked.

As saws cut and axes chopped, Lyman watched. Then, as he helped with his own axe, he said between puffs, "I'm the happiest man—in the world. I have—the best family—in the world; and I—have the best church—in the world."

"Pa, a-are we better than Piskerpalians and Lutherans and Baptists?" asked Harriet.

"Of course not. But the Congregationalists or Presbyterians *are* the Established Church in New England." Placing the log he had just severed onto the woodpile, he continued. "Like all the other Footes, your mother was an Episcopalian before I married her. And so is her grandfather, General Ward.

"You see, Hattie, during the Revolution George III was the head of the Church of England. That's what they call the Episcopalians over there. Since he was our enemy, some Colonists tore down his statue in Bowling Green and dumped it in Litchfield. It was melted and molded into 42,088 bullets."

"But I like the Piskerpalians," argued Harriet.

"The word is Episcopalians," corrected Beecher. "Why do you like them?" He began to shorten another log.

"Because they celebrate Christmas. Catherine and I peeked through the windows of their church last December. It was full of flowers and there was a tall tree in front and it was lit with candles. Papa, you should have heard them sing! Can't we celebrate Christmas?"

"We celebrate the Fourth of July and Thanksgiving. Isn't that enough?"

"Maybe," replied Harriet thoughtfully. "Still, I like Christmas." Suddenly she changed the subject. "Papa, why did you want me to be a boy?"

Lyman leaned on his ax. "I like girls, Harriet," he said, smiling at her. "But I'm especially fond of boys because they can become Congregational or Presbyterian preachers. Preachers, Hattie, can change the world and help bring the millennium. So far, I have five sons—preachers-to-be. William Henry, Edward, George, Henry Ward, and Charles.

"But, Hattie, I love you very much. We named you after the first Harriet. She only lived about a month."

"I know all about it," acknowledged Harriet. "Catherine told me." Then she asked another question, totally unrelated to the present subject. "Pa, why did you tell Judge Reeve that although I wasn't very p-r-e-t-t-y, I was very s-m-a-r-t?"

When he hesitated she added, "Sometimes you and Ma forget that I've already learned to read."

"Hattie, as usual you ask too many questions."

Harriet smiled. Then she repeated the word her parents hated to hear, especially if she repeated it three times in a row. That word was *why.*

"Well, you see"—Lyman hesitated as he searched his mind for a diplomatic answer—"you look just like me; and I'm not very good looking. Your mother is the pretty one! That's why I married her." He rubbed his chin. "Hattie, you're a fast learner. You *are* bright. Even Judge Reeve's wife said so. If you will use that brilliant brain God gave you, and not be discouraged because of your firm Beecher nose, you'll really go far in life. I'll never forget how you listened to my sermon on Sunday morning. Your eyes never moved."

His comment about her listening to the sermon stung, for she knew that she hadn't listened to a word of it. She longed to confess the truth, but lacked the courage. Finally, she said, "Papa, I know I can't be a preacher."

"True. Still there are other things you can do." He handed her a trimmed log to put on the pile. "You can teach school like Sarah Pierce. Today her school is the most famous lady's school in all of America. You might even become a writer." He handed her another piece of firewood.

The children kept working long after Catherine had left for school. After all the firewood had been neatly piled and the cold frames leaned against the house, Beecher said, "Now, let's go swimming. Run along, change your clothes and be ready to go in half an hour."

Harriet and the others squealed with approval and disappeared immediately through the back door.

Located on a plateau in the northwest section of Connecticut, Litchfield was the fourth largest town in the state; and it was considered by many to be the loveliest town in all of New England. Harriet recalled:

"My earliest recollections of Litchfield are those of the beautiful scenery. . . . I remember standing often in the door of our house and looking over a distant horizon where Mount Tom reared its round blue head against the sky, and the Great and Little Ponds, as they were called, gleamed out amid a steel-blue sea of distant pine groves. To the west of us rose a smooth bosomed hill called Prospect Hill. I spent many a pensive, wondering hour at our playroom window watching the glory of the wonderful sunsets that used to burn themselves out amid the voluminous wreathings or castellated turrets of clouds—vaporous pageantry proper to a mountainous region.

"Litchfield sunsets were famous . . ."

Mount Tom and similar peaks intrigued the Beecher children, for they knew that when this was Indian country, the Bantam and other Connecticut tribes used them to communicate to one another by smoke signals. These signals were especially useful when settlers were attacked by the Mohawk. Mount Tom, dubbed by the Indians *Mackimoodus*, meaning "the place of noises," had the curious habit of rumbling. And sometimes its rumblings could be heard as far as Boston. Indians explained its angry scoldings by saying that it was the home of *Hobbamocko*, the originator of human calamities.

In the years to come, Harriet frequently spent hours thinking about these superstitions.

Settled in 1720, Litchfield was named after an old cathedral town in Staffordshire, England. The major difference in the name was the spelling. The Colonists added a *t* in their version. With his hunting and fishing instincts always near the surface, Lyman Beecher loved the nearby forests, streams and lakes. His gun and fishing pole and skiff were always within reach. The magnificent forests abounded with ducks, raccoons, rabbits, quail, partridges, fox, minks—and, alas, muskrats. The streams and lakes were also alive with fish: suckers, eels, catfish, trout, perch, pickerel. Pickerel weighing as much as five or six pounds sometimes stretched out on his table.

But hunter though he was, Lyman's intense love for Litchfield centered in the fact that it was a living museum of the Revolution—a museum that could inspire his children to make their lives count. Brimming with pride, he liked to lead them down the broad avenues and point to the houses where the celebrities had either lived or were still living. Waving his hand at a freshly painted house, he would say, "That's the home of Colonel Benjamin Tallmadge. He was a member of Sheldon's regiment of Horse. He guarded George Washington. He fought in the battle of Monmouth and was the leader of the guards when Major André, the spy who worked with Benedict Arnold, was hanged.

"Over there is the home of Oliver Wolcott. He signed the

Declaration of Independence. His son was the secretary of the U.S. Treasury." A favorite building was the Sheldon Tavern, less than a block from where he lived on the corner of North and Prospect. "Washington spent a night there," he said, his voice trembling with emotion.

Harriet enjoyed viewing all these famous homes; and sometimes, along with her father, she went inside. Each time she visited the home of Judge Tapping Reeve, just two blocks south of their own home, her father said, "Aaron Burr used to live here. But never mention his name in the presence of either Judge Reeve or his wife."

"Why?"

"That's a long story."

"Will you tell me when I'm older?"

"Probably."

"Why not now?"

"Because I don't want to tell you right now."

"Why?"

Instead of answering, Lyman knocked at the door.

Inside, Harriet listened in silence as her father and Judge Reeve discussed politics.

Holding Henry Ward by the hand, Harriet followed her brothers and sister to the swimming hole. While the others swam, Harriet remained on the bank with Henry.

"Why don't you come in with the rest of us?" asked Mary.

"Because I don't want to leave Henry Ward."

"He'll be all right. We'll keep our eyes on him."

"No, I'll just sit here and watch him."

"She wants to think about Pa's sermon," teased Edward.

As Harriet endured the teasing, her conscience bothered her more than ever. Yes, she had taken credit for something she did not deserve. *But what was she to do?* She did not want to disappoint her father, nor did she long to be ridiculed. While the others laughed, she struggled with her tears. Her conscience bothered her so much she had a hard time getting to sleep that night.

2

The Fourth

For over a month before the calendar would indicate that it was July 4, 1815, Harriet's excitement began to mount. She already knew that the famous date would be on Tuesday, and that the celebration this year would be extra special.

Lyman Beecher spoke more about the Fourth than any other holiday. A reason for this was that he had been born on October 12, 1775—less than nine months before the Declaration of Independence had been signed in Philadelphia. He familiarized himself with all the battles and the way God's providence had helped the Continental Army. "Sometimes," he thundered from his pulpit, "God used a storm or a fog or a missing letter. There were even occasions when He saved the life of General Washington by causing the sharpshooters to miss although he was only a few yards away."

During the middle of June, Beecher held the congregation spellbound as he related one of the dramas that took place in 1777. "Having ordered Sheldon to send him all the effective men in his regiment, George Washington waited with tense anxiety for their arrival. Four companies under Colonel Tallmadge passed through Litchfield. Since it was Sunday, they attended services here in the old meetinghouse on our village green.

"Those were perilous times, for Cornwallis was approaching the coast with a large fleet. It seemed that the Revolution would be over within a few weeks. But Pastor Judah Champion of this congregation was a man of great faith. Facing his people, he prayed:

" 'O Lord, we view with terror the approach of the enemies

21

22

of Thy holy religion. Wilt Thou send storm and tempest to toss them upon the sea, and to overwhelm them upon the mighty deep, or to scatter them to the uttermost part of the earth. . . .

" 'Should any escape Thy vengeance, collect them together again as in the hollow of Thy hand, and let Thy lightnings play upon them. We do beseech Thee, moreover, that Thou do gird up the loins of these thy servants who are going forth to fight Thy battles. Make them strong. . . .

" 'Hold before them the shield with which Thou wast wont in the old times to protect Thy chosen people. Give them swift feet that they may pursue their enemies, and swords terrible as that of Thy destroying angel that they may cleave them down.

" 'Preserve these servants of thine, Almighty God, and bring them once more to their homes and friends, if Thou canst do it consistently with Thy high purposes. If, on the other hand, Thou hast decreed that they shall die in battle, let Thy Spirit be present with them, and breathe upon them that they may go up as a sweet sacrifice into the courts of Thy temple, where are habitations prepared for them from the foundation of the world.' "

As Harriet waited impatiently for the tediously long days to pass, she tried to hurry the time by picturing the excitement she would soon be experiencing. Each moment would be unique.

Early in the day there would be a colorful parade complete with battle flags waving in the breeze. Bands would strike up with "Yankee Doodle" and other snappy marches. Then there would be a mock battle between the Redcoats and the Continental Army. Leaders were already gathering recruits.

Signing volunteers for the Continental Army was easy. But hardly anyone was willing to be a Redcoat; for, according to the usual script, the men in red were required to suffer a humiliating defeat. When approached to be a drummer boy, an acquaintance of Harriet snapped, "Not me. I don't want to be a loser!"

Thinking as well of the small fortune she and each of her brothers and sisters would receive to spend as they wished, Harriet felt chilly waves scoot down her spine. Six cents was a lot of money! Interesting ideas about how she would spend it danced before her eyes. The stalls, she knew, would be overflowing with tiny flags, ribbons, cookies, wooden swords, firecrackers, and other delights.

When the Fourth was only five days away, Harriet found it almost impossible to sleep. Visions of parades and bands kept marching through her mind. Having rolled and tossed most of the night, she barged into her father's room even before the bacon and eggs had started to sizzle. "Pa," she shouted, "it's time to get up!"

Her father did not answer.

"Get up! Get up! Get up!" she sang.

There was no response.

After raising her voice and repeating her usual song, she watched the bottom of the bed for the emergence of his big toe. When the toe did not emerge, she lifted the covers from his face. Then she heard a voice groan, "Oh, Hattie, I'm so sick. Call your mother."

"What's the matter?" asked Roxana a moment later.

"I-I don't know. I'm s-so sick."

Roxana placed her hand on his forehead. "Is there anything that I can do?"

"Nothing. My work on earth is finished. The Lord is beckoning me home. M-maybe you'd better call the children so that I can bid them farewell."

"Nonsense! You'll be all right," assured Roxana. "You just have an upset stomach. Maybe it's something you ate. I'll send for the doctor."

"No, no. Don't call a doctor. It would be a waste of money. The Lord has summoned me. I'm ready to go."

Within minutes the children had gathered around his bed. As his groans increased, their tears began to flow. The only one who remained calm was their mother; and the reason for her composure was that she had seen her husband in this situation before.

Lyman was born two months early—so tiny and frail that the midwife commented while she was washing him, "It's a pity he ain't goin' to die with his ma." His mother died of tuberculosis two days later.

Few thought the fragment of life would live. After viewing him and noticing that he could almost be placed in a German beer mug, a lean cattle buyer drawled, "He ain't hardly worth raisin', be he?"

A young mother was employed to nurse him. Unfortunately, her milk curdled in his stomach. His father, David Beecher, a blacksmith, son of and grandson of blacksmiths, placed him in the care of a thirteen-year-old by the name of Annis. She saved his life by feeding him, spoon by spoon, with milk. Patiently and diligently she worked, hovering over him like a mother hen. As he began to thrive, she added other nourishing foods. He was then raised by his uncle and aunt, the Lot Bentons, on their farm in south central Connecticut. But in spite of the fresh farm milk and vegetables, he continued to have an erratic digestive system.

While Roxana pondered what to do, Lyman's groanings increased both in volume and intensity. "I'm dying. I'm dying," he insisted. Convinced that he would soon be gone, the children began to confess their sins and implore his forgiveness.

"Pa, I want you to forgive me. I got into a fight with Edward," confessed Mary. Catherine's confession had more substance. She had played ball on Sunday night before the third star could be seen. Soon it was Harriet's turn.

Sobbing, she held her father's hand. "I-I didn't listen to your sermon at all—I-I-I—"

"Then what *were* you doing?" questioned her mother.

"I was watching a m-mouse that put his head out of a hole just beneath the pulpit."

"A mouse?" demanded her father. His voice had become almost normal.

"Yes, a mouse! Someone had been eating in the church and they-they left a few crumbs of cheese near that hole."

"Mmmm," responded Lyman ominously.

"Mmmm," repeated Roxana with even more concern.

Eyes on Harriet, her father asked, "And what did that mouse do?"

"He seemed to be listening to your sermon."

"Are you sure?" His eyes flashed with their usual brilliance.

"Yes, Papa, I'm sure. When you talked about peace, his eyes brightened; but when you talked about hell and the judgment, he backed deeper into his hole."

After a long silence, the supposedly dying preacher exploded, "That's wonderful!"

"What's so wonderful about it?" demanded Roxana. Her frown and raised voice indicated that she had begun to worry about her husband.

"It's wonderful because it proves that Paul was right. In Romans 8:22 he said, 'For we know that the whole creation groaneth and travaileth in pain together until now.' That mouse has shown us that the millennium is on the way! I'm feeling better already. Go on down to the kitchen while I get dressed."

After breakfast, Lyman Beecher wiped his mouth, summoned his dog, Trip, grabbed his gun, and went hunting. Later that evening he returned with six rabbits.

Early on Monday, the day before the Fourth, Roxana summoned Harriet to her bedroom in order to fix her hair. After she had secured a cloth around her daughter's neck, Harriet questioned. "Ma, do you believe in slavery?"

"No, of course not."

"But aren't Zillah and Rachel slaves?"

"No, they're not slaves."

"They're black."

"All black people aren't slaves. Many blacks are born free. Others buy their freedom. Rachel and Zillah are merely bound servants."

"What does that mean?"

"It means they've agreed to work for so many years, and after their time is up, they can do anything they like. As it is, they're like members of the family. They may leave next year. Many whites are bound servants. But there are those who own slaves."

"Do they own them like cows and horses?"

"Yes, they own them just as others own farm animals."

Harriet was silent as her mother fashioned the first curl by her left temple. Then she burst out, "Ma, do slave owners also own the children of their slaves?"

"They do."

"Does that mean that if somebody owned you and pa, they'd also own Henry Ward, baby Charles, and all the rest of us?"

"It does."

"That's awful."

"Of course it's awful. I wish you could have known my younger sister, Mary. She married John Hubbard, a West Indian planter whom she met in New Haven. When she got to Jamaica she found that he had fathered a large family of children by black women. Since these children were neither black nor white, they were called mulattoes. But instead of considering them his children, Mr. Hubbard thought of them as his possessions. Like a cattle rancher, he could sell them whenever he chose. Aunt Mary was so horrified she returned to Litchfield and lived with us. She died of tuberculosis two years ago. Some of her stories gave me the chills."

"Ma, do you think there will be a time when there will be no slaves?"

"I hope so. There are some states in the United States where no one can own slaves. But six of the original thirteen states and several of the new states permit slavery. The other states are free."

"Is it allowed in Connecticut?"

"It is. But only a few families practice slavery."

"Why?"

"Because as good Christians they don't believe in it."

"What will end slavery?"

"The gospel of Jesus Christ."

While her mother was fashioning her curls, Harriet noticed several new books on her shelves. Two of them were in French. One was by Antoine Laurent Lavoisier. Pointing at it, she asked, "Ma, what's that book about?"

"It's about chemistry. Lavoisier, the author, improved gunpowder and he helped develop the new French metric system. He also showed that we can neither create nor destroy—"

"What does that mean?"

"He proved that when a candle is burned, it is not destroyed; it merely changes form."

"Oh, Ma, that's not true! The wick in my candle gets black and disappears." Harriet spoke with emphasis.

Roxana chuckled. "Hattie, my dear, you're just as willful as your pa. But you are wrong. The wick is never destroyed. It merely turns into ash and gas and heat. That's what Lavoisier taught us, and he's the father of modern chemistry."

"Ma, can you read French?"

"Of course."

Harriet's eyes lit up. "Do you know everything?"

"No. I just like to learn." She placed her comb and curling apparatus on the desk. "Now you'd better rest. Tomorrow is the big day. I still have to fix both Catherine's and Mary's hair."

Pausing at the door, Harriet exclaimed, "Ma, you may not know everything, but you're the best ma in the whole world! You're also the prettiest." She then hurried to her room. Since it was impossible to rest, she went outside.

The next day Harriet woke up excited.

Holding Henry Ward by the hand, she stood with the other Litchfield Beechers at the edge of the wide avenue fronting the village green. Lined with huge elms and already-thinning buttonballs, this magnificent avenue was one of the finest in America. Since Lyman preached as many as nine times a week in any pulpit opened to him, a constant stream of visitors from other towns and counties waved at them.

Soon they heard the distant sound of drums beating. "They're coming! They're coming!" shouted Harriet as she squeezed her little brother's hand. As the band marched on, they began playing their favorite song, "Yankee Doodle." When they neared Harriet, she struggled to lift Henry Ward so he could see over the top of the children in front of them.

Numerous cannons drawn by horses followed the band, and behind the cannon marched the cannoneers, each equipped with the long wooden ramrod that had been used to load the weapon. One of the cannoneers was a woman. She held a ramrod in one hand and a pitcher in the other.

Pointing at her, Harriet turned to her Father. "Pa, look," she exclaimed, "that's a w-w-woman!"

"Yes, I know; and you'll learn more about her in the battle that will be fought. I've read the script."

Next came Colonel Benjamin Tallmadge, the speaker for the day. Dressed in a blue and buff uniform, this hero, who had guarded George Washington, fought in the Battle of Monmouth, and had escorted the spy, Major André, to the gallows, was so loved by the people that they cheered wildly as he passed by.

Marching immediately behind the colonel were the troops. Like the others in the parade, they wore three-cornered hats; and each had his powdered hair combed in a long triangle which streamed halfway to his shoulders. These queues, as they were called, ended in a ribbon bow.

Trailing behind the better dressed veterans were a number of men dressed in rags. One was even clad in a tattered blanket. Many were barefoot and several had streaks of blood painted on their legs and feet. These poor troops drew more applause than anyone else, for everyone knew that they had endured the dreadful winter of 1777 and 1778 at Valley Forge. Although 10,000 had been stationed there, each of the spectators remembered that George Washington had written: "We have this day no less than 2,873 men in camp unfit for duty because they are barefooted and otherwise naked."

As the ceremonies proceeded, no one sang "My Country,

'Tis of Thee." It had not yet been written. Nor did they sing the "Star-Spangled Banner." This anthem had been written in 1814, but it had not yet been adopted as our National Anthem. Instead, with lusty voices and a few brimming eyes, they sang:

> Let children hear the mighty deeds
> Which God performed of old;
> Which in our younger years we saw,
> And which our fathers told.

After Lyman Beecher had led in prayer, Colonel Tallmadge stood up. "Every year on the Fourth," he began, "we honor our veterans. But this year I want to honor our women. In 1776 the Continental Army not only ran short of ammunition, but we were also short of lead with which to make bullets. Then some wise people pulled down the statue of His Majesty King George III in Bowling Green and brought it here to Litchfield.

"That enormous lead statue was dumped in Governor Wolcott's apple orchard on South Street. Wondering what to do with it, two of the governor's daughters, Laura and Mary, decided to turn it into bullets. Good organizers, they persuaded many ladies to help them.

"Up at dawn, they cut the statue into sections, melted each part, and molded it into bullets. By sunset, according to Governor Wolcott's official records, they had made 42,088. Some of those Litchfield women burned their fingers and ruined their curls. But they didn't give up. Because of them, His Majesty's own statue helped to defeat his own army.

"Another lady we must honor is Mary Ludwig, the heroine of the Battle of Monmouth, a battle in which I had the honor of participating. Most of you don't remember her by that name. That is because she is remembered by the nickname the soldiers gave her, Molly Pitcher.

"Whenever they were thirsty, the men shouted, 'Molly, pitcher!' Molly would then hurry to a nearby spring and bring them a pitcher of water.

"As the battle neared the climax, Molly kept providing water for the soldiers. She had just returned from the spring with her pitcher when her husband was wounded near the cannon he was firing. Seeing him lying there, Mary handed the pitcher to a thirsty man, grabbed the ramrod, loaded the cannon, and began firing it herself.

"The next morning, after the battle was over, General Greene presented the powder-burned Molly to Washington.

The Commander in Chief was so proud he made her a sergeant on the spot. The French soldiers were also proud. They filled her chapeau with silver coins.

"Mary Ludwig's husband died of his wounds. But Pennsylvania didn't forget her. They voted her a forty-dollar-a-year pension. And she deserved it. We would have lost that battle had it not been for George Washington himself and brave people like Mary."

After a thundering ovation in which Harriet joined, Tallmadge said, "Now I'll read the Declaration of Independence as written by Thomas Jefferson."

When he had finished reading the document, Colonel Tallmadge said, "We now break for an hour to picnic. At one o'clock we'll see Molly Pitcher in action at the Battle of Monmouth."

After the Beechers had settled on the grass just behind the cannon Molly was going to fire, Harriet turned to her father. "Papa," she asked, speaking very seriously, "will there ever be a time when someone will read a paper like that which will say that all the slaves have been freed?"

"I-I don't know. If we do, such a document would have to be signed by the president."

"Would one of our presidents do that?"

"I hope so. But before an important document like that could be signed, there would have to be many little documents signed."

"Who will write those little papers?"

"I don't know. Maybe one will be written by an abolitionist."

"What's an abolitionist?"

"Harriet, you ask too many questions! Let's stop talking and start eating. Just look at those cucumbers," he chuckled. "I wish Doctor Taylor could see them."

While Harriet was eating and feeding Henry Ward, she inched as close to the cannon as her mother would allow. After what seemed forever, forty or fifty Redcoats took positions at the edge of the green. Then a smaller number of Continental soldiers formed a zig-zag line behind the cannon. As they crouched with their muskets ready, a determined man took his place behind the big gun.

Suddenly the Redcoats began to fire. The determined man responded. The cannon leaped forward with a roar. When the smoke cleared, Harriet noticed that three Redcoats had fallen. Still, King George's men continued to advance.

While guns fired and the air quivered with the yells of the soldiers, loud voices shouted, "Molly, pitcher! Molly, pitcher!"

Molly rushed from one group to another and then returned to the imaginary spring for more water. Suddenly the cannoneer groaned, "I've been hit!" As he sprawled to the ground, Molly ran to his side. "Never mind, darling," she said. "I'll take your place." Then, without a wasted motion, she poured powder into the barrel, pushed it home with her ramrod, pretended she was rolling in a cannonball, took aim, and fired. And even before the smoke was gone, she reloaded. *Whoom! Whoom!* responded the black monster as it spat fire.

Soon the Redcoats were tossing away their guns as they fled.

"Three cheers for Molly!" shouted the crowd.

As both "armies" disappeared, Harriet said, "I'm sure glad I'm a girl."

"Why?" asked Roxana.

"Because when I grow up I'll be a woman, and it was the women who won the Revolution!"

While everyone laughed, Harriet, with Henry Ward by her side, hurried over to one of the stalls to spend their six cents.

3

Sorrow

In the midst of the evening meal, Lyman Beecher announced, "Now is the time for each of you to tell me how you spent your six cents."

All but Harriet and Henry Ward had purchased candy.

"And what did you and Henry Ward buy?" asked Lyman, focusing his eyes on them.

"Henry bought a flag," replied Harriet proudly. "I'll have to call Rachel and Zillah to show what I bought."

With bright smiles dominating their black faces, the girls pointed to blue ribbon bows in their hair.

"How do you like them?" inquired Roxana.

"We love them!" exclaimed Zillah. "They make us know that we are appreciated," added Rachel.

Lyman beamed. "Henry Ward and Harriet were the best stewards. The candy is gone. But the ribbons will last."

Being the winner, Harriet proudly beamed at her other brothers and sisters.

The older children made faces at her. But they didn't say a word, for their parents looked approvingly at Harriet.

After thoughtfully cutting a square of beef and covering it with tomato sauce, Lyman said, "Brother Spence and I have arranged to exchange pulpits next Sunday. This means you'll hear an interesting sermon. Brother Spence follows the *Old Light* idea about fore-ordination. Still, he's a good man. He's just mistaken. And don't stare at his missing ear. He's very sensitive about that."

"What happened to it?" asked Catherine, her eyes sparkling with interest.

31

"He was a chaplain in the war. A bullet tore it off."
"Poor man. That must have really hurt."

Two days later, Harriet discovered what she thought was a sack of onions in the nursery. She tasted one. "Ummm, that's good," she said as she took another. It was a little sweet, and she decided it must be a different variety from those her father raised in his garden. Generously, she shared her find with the other children. They all dug in, enjoying the feast. What a picnic! Mary had just devoured the last one when Roxana appeared at the door.

"Look what we found!" exclaimed the little Beechers, holding up the empty sack of peelings.

Roxana's normally serene face clouded. "Oh, my dear children," she said, sadly. "What you have done makes Mama very unhappy. Those were roots of beautiful tulip flowers, not onion roots. If you had left them alone, next summer Mama would have had great big beautiful red and yellow flowers in the garden such as you never saw."

"I'm sorry, Mama," Harriet murmured.

Feeling sorry about what she had done, Harriet followed her mother to her room. Then viewing the beautiful pictures on the wall, the rug on the floor, rows of ivory miniatures, a half-knitted sweater, and a dress she was making to give to a friend on Thanksgiving, Harriet forgot about her misdeed and became captivated by her surroundings. "Mama," she said, "why do you work so hard making beautiful things?"

"Because I love the Lord and am His child. And since the Lord made the trees and the birds and the flowers and all the lovely things, I want to do the same."

"But Mama, how do you do it? Did you make that pretty carpet in the east room?"

Roxana smiled. "Yes, I'll tell you what I did. When your pa and I moved to East Hampton, no one in the entire little town had a carpet. Many of our congregation had never seen one. When your Uncle Lot sent me some money, your pa took that money and bought a bale of cotton. I spun the cotton into coarse thread and had the thread woven into a huge sail-like sheet that was as thick as my little finger.

"But that white 'carpet' didn't satisfy me. I thought it should have some color in it, so I sent to New York for some bright colors and made them into paint. After I had decided how big I wanted the carpet, I had your pa tack it down on the floor in the garret. Then I got busy.

"I painted roses and other flowers in the center and made a beautiful border around the edge. We then laid it on the parlor floor. The carpet is still beautiful, but you should have seen it!" she smiled, a faraway look in her eyes.

"One day a deacon came to visit. Your pa pointed him to the parlor and told him to go in. Hesitating at the door he exclaimed, 'I-I can't go in 'thout steppin' on't!'

" 'It was meant to be stepped on,' replied your pa.

"After the deacon had walked over it, he said 'Brother Beecher, d'ye think ye can have all that and heaven too?' "

While they were laughing, Roxana lifted Harriet onto her lap and showed her the ivory miniature she had painted of her mother. Aiming her finger at her long, straight nose and cupid lips, she said, "Hattie, you look so much like your Grandma Foote. She's a wonderful woman."

After studying the miniature, Hattie said, "I sure wish I could paint like that. How do you do it?"

"I work at it every day. Painting isn't easy. Anyone who wants to do something well must work hard at it. God has given you a good mind, Hattie. Be sure and use it." Slipping Harriet off her lap, she stood up. "And now I must get to work on my painting so run along."

At the door, little Harriet stopped and turned, "Almost every time we have family worship, Mama, you quote a favorite scripture. It begins, 'But ye are come unto mount Zion—' I don't remember the rest. Why do you say those words so much?"

"That passage goes like this, 'But ye are come unto mount Zion, and unto the city of the living God, the heavenly Jerusalem, and to an innumerable company of angels.' That verse is found in Hebrews 12:22."

"What does it mean?"

"Oh, it means many things. To me it especially means that God is alive, that there is a heavenly Jerusalem where we will go, and that that heavenly Jerusalem is filled with angels. Those words help to keep a smile on my face. But now I must get busy. Last week I bought Miss Edgeworth's new book, *Frank*. Tonight I'm going to read a part of it to you and the children. Tell them to come to my room on time."

As Sunday drew near, Harriet kept wondering how she would manage to listen to Brother Spence without staring at the place where his ear had been. Well, she would try anyway. Dressed in her Sunday best, she sat down in the boxed pew set aside for the pastor's family.

While the meetinghouse filled, Harriet began to wonder when the guest preacher would arrive. Judge Reeve and his billowy wife took their places in the pew just to her left. Then the students from his law school occupied the pews under the left balcony. A moment later they were followed by the girls from the Pierce Academy, who filled the section beneath the right balcony.

Harriet kept wondering when the one-eared preacher would arrive. Since the clock showed that it was only three minutes to the time for the services to open, she began to think perhaps the poor man had gotten lost. Forcing herself not to turn around, Harriet focused her mind on the interior of the building and the members who sat in front and on either side. This Congregational meetinghouse made an indelible impression on her mind.

In an article which became a part of her first book, she wrote: "To my childish eye, our old meetinghouse was an awe-inspiring thing. To me it seemed fashioned very nearly on the model of Noah's ark and Solomon's temple, as set forth in my Scripture Catechism—pictures which I did not doubt were authentic copies. . . .

"Its double row of windows, of which I knew the number by heart; its doors, with great wooden quirls over them; its belfry projecting out the east end; its steeple and bell—all inspired as much sense of the sublime in me as Strasbourg Cathedral itself; and the inside was not a whit less imposing.

"How magnificent, to my eye, seemed the turnip-like canopy that hung over the minister's head, hooked by a long iron rod to the wall above! And how apprehensive did I consider the question: what would become of him if it should fall? . . .

"The glory of our meetinghouse was the singers' seat, that sublime place for those who rejoiced in the mysterious art of fa-so-la-ing. There they sat in the gallery that lined three sides of the house: treble, counter, tenor, and bass—each with its appropriate leader and supporters. . . ."

Although it was time for the worship period to begin, the pulpit-chair remained empty. Suddenly the choirs were on their feet. Each did its assigned part. Then, just as they were blending together in a mighty finale, Lyman Beecher strode onto the platform and dropped down in the pulpit-chair. His face radiated the appearance of absolute determination.

Harriet stared. Nudging her mother, she whispered, "W-what happened to Brother One-Ear?"

"Shhh," cautioned her mother. "We'll soon find out."

After what seemed to Harriet an eternity, Lyman Beecher stood in the pulpit. "Brother Spence," he began, "was to preach for us this morning and I was to preach for him. But it so happened that when I was halfway to his place, we met. After we had greeted one another, he said, 'Brother Beecher, I wish to call to your attention that before the creation of the world God arranged that you were to preach in my pulpit and I in yours this Sabbath.'

"Those words twisted me the wrong way. I replied at once, 'Then I won't do it.' And so I am here this morning. My subject being 'The Providence of God.' "

Solemnly, he opened the large pulpit Bible, slipped on a pair of steel-rimmed spectacles, read his text, waited until the silence in the pews was almost unbearable, and then began. He had mastered the techniques of great oratory and spoke with the skill of a Shakespearian actor.

"If Brother Spence thinks I do not believe in Providence, he is mistaken." That first sentence was stated in such a low voice the people had to strain in order to hear. As he continued, his volume increased. "My life was shaped by God's providence, and my children's lives are being shaped by God's providence. Signs of God's providence are everywhere. That fact was dramatized in last week's Fourth of July celebrations. Had it not been for God's providence, we would still be a British Colony."

As her father gathered the audience into the palm of his hand, Harriet glanced at Colonel Tallmadge. Shoulders erect, he was listening with the intensity of a thirsty man with a cup of cool water at his lips.

"Whenever I pass the home where Ethan Allen was born," continued Lyman as he glanced at his family, "I think of Almighty God. All of us are proud that he was born in Litchfield. But he is not remembered as a pious man. When he passed away in 1789, Ezra Stiles, the president of Yale, wrote in his diary: 'Died in Vermont the profane and impious Deist, General Ethan Allen, author of the *Oracles of Reason*, a book replete with scurrilous reflexions on revelation.' President Stiles then added: '*And in hell he lifted up his eyes, being in torment.*'

"Nonetheless, this impious man provided the *human* action that allowed God's providence to take charge. On May 10, 1775, he inspired the entire Continental Army by taking Fort Ticonderoga without the loss of a single man. And what did this blasphemous man say when the British commander demanded, 'By what authority have you entered His Majesty's fort?' He answered: 'In the name of the Great Jehovah and the Continental Congress!'

"At that time," said Lyman, raising his voice, "the Continental Congress was less than a year old. Many Colonists— even loyal Colonists—had never even heard of it. But that didn't matter, for the Great Jehovah had been overseeing the affairs of men from the beginning."

As the inspired congregation held on to every spoken word, Lyman pushed his spectacles high above his forehead, lifted his head and continued.

"God's providence," he explained, "was especially demonstrated when General Washington crossed the Delaware the second time and faced the Hessians at Trenton. Those were terrible days.

"After losing nearly three thousand men at Brooklyn Heights, Harlem, Manhattan, and Fort Washington, what was left of the Continental Army under Washington's direct command fled south across New Jersey. Panic-striken, they abandoned much of their artillery. They were in such a hurry they left their soup kettles bubbling over a fire with the day's ration of soup untouched.

"As those ragged men fled, Washington spurred them on by flailing his sword in the air, and shouting, 'Run! Run! Faster!'

"For seventeen days Washington's men retreated. And during all that time the Redcoats pursed them. Well trained, the determined veterans from England were rapidly approaching even though their artillery was constantly sinking into the mud and Washington had destroyed all the bridges behind them.

"Eventually Washington and his remnant reached the Delaware just north of Trenton, but had no means to cross."

Lyman put on another pair of spectacles. "It was already December 7. If Washington couldn't get his men across the Delaware, the war would be over. Standing on the bank, the tall man from Virginia prayed for a solution. As he pondered, he thought of the Durham boats. These huge boats had been built to freight iron ore between Riegelsville and Philadelphia.

"They got a hold of the boats and soon those long, shallow transports were poled into place and the tattered army managed to cross. And just in time, too, for the last group of men were sure they had heard the Scottish bagpipes of General Howe's men.

"Comparatively safe on the west side of the river, Washington had to decide his next move. He was beset with problems and desertions. In addition, the term of duty for most of his men would be up at the end of the month."

Lyman pushed the second set of spectacles up on his head next to the first pair and put on another set. "The events of the next two weeks were crowded with almost unbelievable providential acts. We don't have time to mention all of them. But we will consider some of the most humanly apparent ones."

Surprisingly, Lyman continued to hold his congregation spellbound—even the children.

Pausing briefly, he went on. "Since Howe didn't like the weather in Trenton, and since he had a mistress in New York, he decided to return. To him, this seemed logical; for, after all, the war was practically over and he would soon be returning to England.

"Because of this thinking, the Redcoats in Trenton were replaced with Hessians under the command of Colonel Rahl—the bloodthirsty man who boasted that he had killed more rebels than anyone else."

Shuddering, Lyman shook his head.

"As Washington planned and prayed and consulted with his staff, he decided on a brave move. Against expert advice, he determined to recross the Delaware during the night of December 25 and take the Hessians by surprise. To make sure his attack would be effective, he arranged that while he crossed at McKonkey's Ferry, General Ewing with the Pennsylvania Militia would cross a mile below Trenton, and Colonel Cadawaladar would cross at Dunk's Ferry—four miles southwest of Burlington. Having crossed, each would attack Trenton from his position.

"The password that night was *victory or death!*"

Long sermons bored Harriet. But this account was so exciting she visualized everything. She saw men huddled in boats, felt sleet on her face, and watched the ice swirl by.

"Washington," emphasized the preacher, "had many reasons to be worried. Huge chunks of ice ramming into their boats had been terrifying. One boat loaded with vital cannon balls nearly sank. His already tired men didn't get to the east bank until two-thirty on the morning of December 26. This meant he could not attack under the safety of darkness. Then an even worse hazard faced them. *It had started to rain and snow at the same time.* This wet snow and rain had so dampened the priming pans on their guns that it would be impossible to fire them. Still, even though the muskets could not be fired, the charcoal boxes prepared to operate the cannon continued to glow as vigorously as when they were lit.

"As Washington advanced toward Trenton, many of his barefoot men left trails of blood. Others were so tired they marched in semi-sleep. Washington hoped that he and his army would surprise the Hessians, who would undoubtedly be drunk because of Christmas celebrations. Unfortunately the Hessians had been informed in advance about his plans! This meant that the Continental Army was marching into a trap; for, being able to fire from cover, Colonel Rahl's men would have the advantage of dry priming pans."

Beecher paused and slowly moved his eyes across the audience. As Harriet watched him she felt her heart speed.

"This could have been the end of the Continental Army," continued the preacher, raising his voice. "But at this point God's providence took hold. As Washington was advancing, a group of no more than twenty Colonists attacked the Hessians. After the Hessians drove them away, they supposed that they were the Continental Army! (Even today no one knows who they were.) Flushed with victory, the Hessians emptied more barrels of liquor.

"While they were drinking, another chapter of God's providence unfolded. Knowing what Washington was up to, a Tory went to see Colonel Rahl. When Rahl refused to see him, this British sympathizer sent him a letter by the hand of a servant. Deep in his stupor, Rahl put it in his pocket without reading it.

"But God's providence was not completed with this negligence. As Washington marched with his mud-caked, half-naked troops, a new confidence surged through him, even though at this time he did not realize that neither General Ewing nor General Cadawaladar were cooperating with him. Ewing had not crossed the Delaware. Cadawaladar, on the other hand, had crossed, but when he found it difficult to move his cannon, he retreated over the river into Pennsylvania.

"The battle began at about eight in the morning. Sleepy and drunk from their Christmas celebrations, the Hessians were completely defeated. Colonel Rahl was mortally wounded. While he was dying, and after his uniform was removed, he pointed to the letter and murmured, 'If I had read this, I would not be here.'

"Washington's victory at Trenton gave the Continental Army the boost of enthusiasm they needed. Their victory can be attributed to only one source: *The Providence of God!*"

Lyman swept his spectacles to the top of his head and put on a fourth pair. Then after a painful silence during which Harriet almost stopped breathing, he concluded: "*Each of us was made for a purpose. Our sovereign God has a task for all of the elect. I don't know what your assigned task may be. Perhaps it's to put an end to slavery. I don't know. But I do know that if we'll get busy, God's providence will come to our aid.*"

Harriet did not understand all the moves in the Battle of Trenton that her father had described. But she was caught by the idea that God has assigned a task to each individual, and she determined that she would discover what her task was as soon as possible.

Arousing from her contemplating, she took Henry Ward by the hand and headed home. The moment she stepped into the kitchen she knew something was wrong. She looked over at Zillah, who was quietly adjusting her apron.

"Miss Hattie," she said softly, "Thomas Junior is dead."

Harriet rushed outside where the furry black corpse lay in the backyard. Kneeling beside her favorite pet, she burst into tears. That very morning, he had purred and rubbed up against her. As she tenderly stroked his fur, she saw the crimson wound in his head. This little friend, who had never caught even a mouse, had been cruelly shot.

Later at the dinner table, Catherine noticed that Harriet wasn't eating. "Never mind, Hattie," she comforted, "we'll have a nice funeral for him tomorrow." Thus consoled, Harriet managed to finish her dinner.

The next morning Edward prepared a grave beneath the largest apple tree while Mary tucked the beloved pet in a shoe box their mother had provided. Following the hymns, scripture reading, sermon, and a final prayer, William H. dropped some dandelions on the closed box while he murmured:

> "Earth to earth,
> Ashes to ashes,
> Dust to dust."

After the grave had been filled, Catherine read a poem she had written for the occasion:

"Here lies our kit,
Who had a fit
      and acted queer.
Shot with a gun,
His race is run,
      And he lies here."

Thinking about the shortness of life and the fact that all of God's creatures had an assignment, Harriet became even more concerned about the real purpose of her own life. Thomas Junior had obviously been created to protect them from rodents. That he had failed this assignment was especially apparent to her mother. And now that his life was over, he was nothing but a dead cat.

While revisiting his grave, Harriet wondered whether she had been created to be a servant like Zillah or Rachel; or, perhaps, a housewife like her mother. As young as she was, in the depth of her heart she knew that she longed to be another Mary Ludwig. But, if she couldn't be that, she decided that she would be glad to be a duplicate of one of the Wolcott girls. The way they had organized the women to transform the statue of George III into 42,088 bullets was a real challenge. Inspired by what Laura and Mary Wolcott had done, she went over to their home and envisioned the huge pile of bullets it must have made.

That night Harriet dreamed about bullets—42,088 bullets.

Days later at the conclusion of family worship, Lyman Beecher informed his family, "We may be facing difficult days ahead. Up until now the Presbyterians and the Congregationalists have been supported by taxes. But now some radicals are trying to put an end to all that. If these radicals succeed, we'll have to raise our own money.

"Judge Reeve and his wife are coming over this afternoon to discuss this problem with me. If you want to sit around and listen, it will be fine." He then turned and shook his finger at Harriet. "But please, Hattie," he said, using the tone of voice he frequently employed when he was warning about the wiles of Satan, "I don't want you to ask about either dueling or Aaron Burr."

Harriet gave an exhausting sigh, "But, why not?"

"Because it would upset the judge."

As Judge Reeve seated himself in their best chair, Harriet's eyes followed his hand as he ceremoniously laid his gold-headed cane on the floor. With long, snowy hair drooping to his shoulders, the judge radiated the appearance of another Solomon.

Although she tried not to stare when Mrs. Reeve sank into the sofa, Harriet unconsciously held her breath. This animated Mount Tom of cultured and smiling flesh was so huge it was impossible for her to walk the short distance from her home to that of the Beechers'. Invariably she came in a horse-drawn chaise.

While the judge and his wife were having tea, the conversation centered on the possible elimination of their church support from the tax rolls. "It isn't right!" Lyman grimly exclaimed. "Connecticut is a theocracy ruled by the church. And since the Congregationalists and Presbyterians are descended from the Puritans, we are God's spokesmen. It is our duty to decide the affairs of state!"

"True," agreed the judge. "But we must remember that this is a democracy." (Reeve had lost his voice, but his whisper was clear enough for him to continue teaching in the law school he had founded in 1784.[1])

"True," Lyman exploded heatedly, "but if we lose the revenue we'll be hindered in our God-assigned task." Thoughtfully he rubbed his chin, smiled and added, "When my uncle Stephen Benton refused to pay the church portion of his taxes, the sheriff sold his heifer at an auction."

After the conversation drifted to the law Judge Reeve was attempting to squeeze through the legislature which would enable married women to dispose of their property, Harriet lost interest and slipped out the back door.[2]

Early that fall while Lyman was returning from a pastoral visit, Roxana murmured, "I have a feeling that I won't be with you long." Remembering the occasion, he wrote: "I saw that she was ripe for heaven. When we reached home she was in a sort of chill."

Roxana's illness and death made an indelible impression

[1]This, the first law school in America, is distinguished for having graduated 101 members of Congress, 34 Chief Justices of States, 40 Judges of Higher State Courts, 28 U.S. Senators, 14 Governors of States, 6 Cabinet members, and 3 Justices of the U.S. Supreme Court.
[2]That legislation: *Law of Baron and Femme, of Parent and Child*, etc., was passed in 1816.

on Harriet. Helping her father with his autobiography, she painted this picture:

"I remember . . . when everyone said she was sick . . . when I saw the shelves of the closets crowded with delicacies which had been sent in for her, and how I used to be permitted to go once a day into her room, where she sat bolstered up in bed, taking her gruel. I have a vision of a very fair face, with a bright red spot on each cheek, and a quiet smile as she offered me a spoonful of her gruel; of our dreaming one night, we little ones, that mamma had got well. . . . Our dream was indeed a true one. She was forever well; but they told us that she was dead, and took us in to see what seemed so cold, and so unlike anything we had ever seen or known of her.

"Then came the funeral. Henry was too little to go. I remember his golden curls and little black frock as he tried to follow us, like a kitten in the sun in ignorant joy.

"I remember the mourning dresses, the tears of the older children, the walking to the burial ground, and somebody speaking at the grave. . . .

"They told us at one time that she had been laid in the ground, at another that she had gone to heaven. . . . Henry, putting these two things together, resolved to dig through the ground and go to heaven and find her. . . .

"Although mother's bodily presence disappeared from our circle, I think that her memory and example had more influence in moulding her family, in deterring from evil and exciting to good, than the living presence of many mothers. . . .

"Even our portly old black washerwoman, Candace, who came once a week to help . . . would draw us aside and, with tears in her eyes, tell us of the saintly virtues of our mother."

The words of her father at the funeral remained with Harriet and often they came back to her as she sat grieving. With a broken voice he had said, "Roxana, you are now come to Mount Zion, unto the city of the living God, the heavenly Jerusalem, and to an innumerable company of angels, to the general assembly and church of the firstborn, which are written in heaven, and to God the Judge of all, and to the spirits of just men made perfect, and to Jesus the mediator of the new covenant, and to the blood of sprinkling, that speaketh better things than the blood of Abel."

Roxana's last hours made a deep impression on her children and those who lingered at her bedside. Judge Reeve's wife considered the last moments she spent with her extremely precious and she never forgot how Roxana admonished her sons to become missionaries.

After seventeen years of marriage, and giving birth to nine children, this daughter of Eli and Roxana Foote had passed away at the age of forty-one. But her influence remained; and, across the years, flowered. Henry Ward moved his congregation to tears when he would refer to her. "She died when I was three years old that she might be an angel to me all my life. . . . No devout Catholic ever saw as much in the Virgin Mary as I have seen in my mother." And Charles Beecher indicated his deep devotion by saying: "Roxana Foote is my madonna!"

Harriet never forgot the comfort she received from the blacks. Their sympathy and understanding helped shape her life. She reminisced: "I recollect [Candace] coming to wash our clothes when the family was assembled for prayers in the next room, and I for some reason lingered in the kitchen. She drew me toward her and held me quite still until the exercises were over. Then she kissed my hand and I felt her tears drop upon it. There was something about her feeling that struck me with awe. She scarcely spoke a word, but gave me to understand that she was paying homage to my mother's memory."

Harriet Foote, Roxana's sister, had moved in with the Beechers during Roxana's illness; and now that her sister was gone, she insisted on taking Harriet back with her to Nutplains. Little Harriet was reluctant to leave Litchfield and go with her aunt. But Aunt Harriet, after whom she had been named, was a favorite; moreover, she knew that Grandma Foote had a large collection of interesting books.

Thus, with mixed feelings Harriet mounted the coach that was to take her to Nutplains, a short distance from Guilford, nearly forty miles southeast of Litchfield. As the coach bounced over the difficult roads, Harriet fought a fresh flood of tears. She had no way of knowing that God's providence was guiding her into a wonderful future.

4

New Worlds

Living in the country in a small wood farmhouse was a new and unique, experience. Both Aunt Harriet and Grandma Foote were convinced Episcopalians, and each morning and evening read prayers out of a black book, something Harriet's father would never do. Lyman Beecher believed that effective prayers were spontaneous.

"Grandma, I know that you love Papa very much," Harriet began one day. "But when you're in Litchfield you pass our meetinghouse and go to the Episcopal church. Don't you know Papa is the greatest preacher in America?"

"Your pa is a *great* speaker," she replied as she brushed her silvery hair back with her hand, "but you see, as a member of the Church of England, I believe in Apostolic Succession."

Harriet's face was puzzled. "What's *that*?"

"Apostolic Succession means that a minister must be ordained by another who, across the centuries, was ordained by one of the original apostles. Lyman Beecher is a fine man. He has lots of ability. I'm proud that he's my son-in-law. Nonetheless, he was *not* properly ordained.

"You see, Hattie, your grandfather, my husband, Eli Foote, was an attorney. But after the Revolution, he abandoned the law to become a businessman. After we had ten children, Grandpa died of yellow fever. Since we were penniless, my father, General Ward, invited me and all my children to move here to Nutplains. He then adopted all of my children with the exception of John—"

"And why didn't he adopt John?" asked Harriet.

"Because John had already been adopted by Eli's brother, Justin Foote. Justin was a New York shipper. But now let's get back to your father. While he was attending Yale in New Haven, he used to ride over on his horse. I remember those days very well. All of us liked him. Soon, he fell in love with your mother.

"Your mother was convinced that he was the greatest man that ever lived. But, they did have a problem; you see, Hattie, your mother was an Episcopalian and he was a Congregationalist. This difference in faith made it hard for them. Soon, trouble developed. I learned about it a few years after they were married.

"Your papa worried because your dear mother had *always* prayed and had *always* gone to church and had *always* considered herself a devoted Christian. He was afraid she had mistaken the *natural* goodness in her character for real salvation. So he wrote her several long letters about it. I know that because she used to share the letters with me," Grandma Foote adjusted her glasses.

"One afternoon when I heard the sound of his horse, I had a feeling that he was a troubled man. And I was right. As he dismounted I could see dark shadows in his face. That evening while he held your mother's hand, he asked an awful question."

"What was the question?" Harriet asked, almost breathlessly.

"He said to her, 'Roxana dear, would you be willing to be damned if it was for the glory of God?'

"That question shocked your mother. But, as always, she had a ready answer and said, 'Is it wickedness in me that I do not feel a willingness to be left to go in sin? When I pray for a new heart and a right spirit, must I be willing to be denied, and rejoice that my prayer is not heard? Could any real Christian rejoice if God should take away from him the mercy bestowed?'

"Lyman was stunned by her brilliant answer. When he finally came to himself, he exclaimed, 'Oh, Roxana, what a fool I've been!' He was never quite the same after that."

Little Harriet returned to her room after tea and cake. Although she remembered the gist of what her grandmother had told her, she did not quite understand the theology that was involved. The world in which she now lived in Nutplains was completely new to her. She later wrote about the long months she had spent with her grandmother and aunt.

"Aunt Harriet was no common character. A more energetic human being never undertook the education of a child. Her ideas . . . were those of a vigorous Englishwoman of the old school. . . .

"According to her views, little girls were to be taught to move very gently, to speak softly and prettily, to say, 'Yes, ma'am' and 'No, ma'am,' never to tear their clothes; they were to sew and knit at regular hours, to go to church on Sunday and make all the responses, and to come home and be catechized.

"I remember those catechizings, when she used to place my little cousin Mary and me bolt upright at her knee, while black Dinah and Harvey the bound-boy had to stand at a respectful distance behind us. For Aunt Harriet always impressed it upon her servant 'to order themselves lowly and reverently to all their betters.' That portion of the Church Catechism always pleased me, particularly when applied to *them*, as it insured their calling me 'Miss Harriet,' and treating me with a degree of consideration that I never enjoyed in the more democratic circles at home."

Two other influences at Nutplains helped shape Harriet: her uncles, George and Samuel Foote. Although George labored on the farm all day and had calloused hands, he loved a game of chess, and had a passion for knowledge. Harriet was especially drawn to him because he was never afraid to at least try to answer her questions. In the midst of a chess game in which she was losing badly, Harriet's eyes suddenly wandered. Then she said, "Uncle George, what's dueling?"

"Ah, that's a good question," he replied after making the decisive move. "Let's go to the Rees *Cyclopedia* and see what it has to say."

As he looked up the reference, Harriet had a question. "Uncle George, can you learn about anything in those books?"

"Not *anything*. But they are crammed with knowledge. Next to the Bible, an encyclopedia is my favorite reading. . . . Ah, here's the story on dueling. 'Dueling is a system in which two people who have an argument can agree to settle it by having a fight with a deadly weapon. During their fight, they must obey certain rules. If they obey the rules, the one who kills the other is not punished. Dueling goes back to ancient times. In the fifteen hundreds four thousand duelists were killed in France in eighteen years.'

"Someday this legalized system of murder will be stopped. At least it will be stopped in America. But I'm afraid it won't be stopped until another Aaron Burr affair shocks the people into action. I—"

"Tell me, Uncle George," Harriet interrupted, "why is it that when Judge Reeve visits us, Pa tells me not to mention Aaron Burr?" Her eyes brimmed with excited curiosity.

"Don't you know?" He spoke in a tone of unbelief. "Aaron Burr ran for the presidency of the United States against Thomas Jefferson. Since the electoral vote was a tie, the House of Representatives decided on the 36th ballot that Jefferson was President. Thus, according to the law of that day, Burr was the Vice-President. Burr believed he lost because of the influence of Alexander Hamilton. Later, Hamilton also kept him from being elected governor of New York. This so angered Burr he challenged Hamilton to a duel and killed him."

"But why shouldn't I mention Aaron Burr in front of Judge Reeve?"

"You don't know?"

Harriet shook her head.

"Judge Reeve, Hattie, was married to Sally Burr, Aaron Burr's sister. Aaron even lived with them."

"Oh!" exclaimed Harriet. "Now I understand."

Uncle Samuel was completely different than George. He was the captain of a square-rigged clipper and sailed to distant ports over much of the world. He was fluent in French and Spanish; and, on his return from a long voyage, he liked to bring home things that would excite comment; frankincense from Spain, the latest books from England, swords from Turkey, mats and baskets from Morocco. He also liked to relate breathless stories about his trips and to insist that there were many brilliant people in the world who were not white.

Harriet loved to visit with this uncle and as the candles burned late into the night, her horizons were pushed back again and again. Because he seemed to know more family history than anyone else, she plied him with questions, over and over again, much to his pleasure.

In addition to her uncles' influence, Harriet succumbed almost immediately to the charm of her radiant always-smiling grandmother. Mrs. Foote's influence on her granddaughter was permanent. Years later Harriet wrote: "Her mind was active and clear; her literary taste just, her reading extensive. My image of her in later years is of one always seated at a great round table covered with books, among which nestled her work basket. Among these books, the chiefest was her large Bible and prayer-book; other favorites were Lowth's *Isaiah*, which she knew almost by heart, Buchanan's *Researches in Asia*, *Bishop Heber's Life*, and Dr. Johnson's *Works*.

"We used to read much to her: first many chapters of the Bible, in which she would often interpose most graphic comments, especially in the Evangelists, where she seemed to have formed an idea of each of the apostles so distinct and dramatic that she would speak of them as acquaintances. She would always smile indulgently at Peter's remarks. 'There he is again, now; that's just like Peter. He's always so ready to put in!' She was fond of having us read Isaiah to her in Lowth's translation, of which she had read with interest all the critical notes."

Like her grandmother, Harriet also fell in love with Isaiah. Intrigued by Isaiah's vision as recorded in the sixth chapter, Harriet studied it until it became a part of her being. She read it over and over again.

The sublime imagery in those words fascinated Harriet. In her imagination she saw the whole scene.

But it was the eighth and ninth verses that moved her to the very depths. With a mixture of questioning and worship she read that part of the drama:

> Also I heard the voice of the Lord, saying, Whom shall I send, and who will go for us? Then said I, Here am I; send me. And he said, Go, and tell this people, Hear ye indeed, but understand not; and see ye indeed, but perceive not.

Bible in hand, Harriet approached her grandmother. "Grandma," she asked, "what are the first nine verses of the sixth chapter of Isaiah all about?"

Roxana Foote laid down her knitting. "Since the Lord needed a prophet to preach to His people, and since He knew that Isaiah was the person to preach to His people, and since He knew that Isaiah was the person He wanted, he sent him a vision. Those nine verses relate what Isaiah saw in that vision."

"And what did the Lord want Isaiah to do?"

"He wanted him to warn the people about many things

and to tell them about the coming of Jesus Christ."

"Did Isaiah do that?"

"He certainly did! In the fifty-third chapter and the second through the fourth verses we read:

> For he shall grow up before him as a tender plant, and as a root out of a dry ground: he hath no form nor comeliness; and when we shall see him, there is no beauty that we should desire him. He is despised and rejected of men; a man of sorrows, and acquainted with grief: and we hid as it were our faces from him; he was despised and we esteemed him not. Surely he hath borne our griefs, and carried our sorrows: yet we did esteem him stricken, smitten of God, and afflicted.

"Those words, my child, describe the coming of Jesus Christ, who came some seven hundred years later. Isaiah was one of God's chosen people."

"Grandma, does the Lord still speak to people in our time?"

"Of course. But He does not always speak to each of His children in the same way. He spoke to Moses through the burning bush. He spoke to Saul of Tarsus in a vision while he was on his way to Damascus. He sent the angel Gabriel to tell Mary that she would be the mother of Jesus."

"Does the Lord ever speak to you?"

"Many times. But never in a dramatic way. I've never had a vision."

"Do you think the Lord might speak to me?"

"Of course."

"Why?"

"Well, the Lord has many things He wants done; and each one of us was made for a purpose. Perhaps the Lord wants you to do something special for Him."

"Do you really think He does?"

"We'll have to be patient and see."

During the months Harriet was at Nutplains, Catherine kept a stream of letters moving to her grandmother and Aunt Harriet. In her notes she often referred to Hattie and how they, especially Henry Ward, missed her. Harriet was therefore not surprised one day when her father pulled in with his carriage.

"Hattie," he announced after he had lunched, "it's time for you to come home. You will soon begin going to school."

"And where will I go?" Harriet's eyes danced with excitement.

"Since Sally Pierce won't take anyone until they're twelve, I'm sending you and Henry Ward to Widow Kilbourne's school."

Lyman was ready to leave when he suddenly stopped at the door. "I've lost my hat," he said.

Harriet looked for his hat all over the living room and kitchen. Unable to find it, she said, "Papa, maybe you left it in the carriage." Skipping outside, she soon returned with the missing ministerial top piece. After putting it on his head, he remarked, "Hattie, I don't know what I'd do without you!"

5

A Churning World

Widow Kilbourne's school on West Street was only a few blocks from the Beecher home. There, on its split-log benches and with Henry Ward in tow, Harriet began her formal education.

The teacher was strict. She relied on two systems to force knowledge into the minds of her little pupils. Both were effective. "Repeat after me," she liked to say in her cracked-bell voice: "Cat is spelled C A T. How is it spelled? C A T. Altogether now. C A T." Her other method was threatening *with* and *often* applying a hickory stick.

Henry Ward rebelled at the idea of school. Feeling responsible for him, Harriet assumed the task of keeping him going. A letter indicates the progress the future Shakespeare of the pulpit made under that teacher.

> Dear Sister
> We are al well. Ma haz a baby. The old cow has six pigs.

Since Lyman knew that Henry would have to do better than that if he were to become a Congregational or Presbyterian preacher, he had him transferred to the nearby district school. But Harriet's favorite brother hated this one as much as he did the previous one. In later years, he wrote about those early experiences in his series of articles, *Star Papers*, published in *The Independent*:

> In the winter we were squeezed into . . . the farthest corner. We read and spelled twice a day. . . . All our little legs together . . . would fill up the corner with such a noise the

51

master would bring down his two-foot hickory stick on the desk with . . . a clap that sent shivers through our hearts. He would cry, 'Silence in that corner!' "

In the next school—for his father had him transferred—he learned to exercise his wit. "Now, Henry," said the teacher, "*A* is the indefinite article, you see—and must only be used with a singular noun. You can say *a man*—but you cannot say a men, can you?"

"Yes, I can. I can say amen, too," replied Henry. "Father always says it at the end of his prayers."

"Come, Henry, don't be joking. Now, decline *He*."

"Nominative *he*, possessive *his*, objective *him*," replied Henry.

"You see," emphasized the teacher, "*his* is possessive. Now you can say his book—but you cannot say him book."

"I do," scorned Henry with a huff. "Every Sunday I say hymnbook!"

Keeping Henry content was not Harriet's only concern. Within hours after her return, she discovered that her father's home was not the serene place she had remembered before she went to Nutplains. Zillah and Rachel were both gone and she missed their familiar presence. Their places had been taken by Aunt Esther, her father's half sister, and Grandma Beecher, his stepmother.

Feeling the need to help with the housework, Catherine dropped out of Miss Pierce's school. Her father, Catherine recalled, had a talent "of discovering and rejoicing over unexpected excellence in character and conduct.

"Thus stimulated, I for the first time, undertook all the labor of cutting, fitting and making all the clothing for the children as well as for myself." She also learned to cook.

The Beecher household ran with more efficiency than when Roxana was alive. But Harriet chafed under the new system. Esther and Grandma Beecher were dominated by two mottoes: "A place for everything and everything in place," and, worse yet: "Waste not, want not."

In desperation, Harriet fled to her father's study. There, in the attic, amidst the smell of curing hams of bacon, and with stacks of sermons and shelves of books nearby, she sat and watched as her father labored on sermons, articles, and correspondence. As the day went by she noticed that his zest for life was not as keen as it had once been. Knowing that she was an encouragement, she spent long hours with him in his study. One day while fingering through his books on theology, she noticed a thick volume entitled *Arabian Nights*. As she began to read, she became enchanted.

The first chapter related how Sultan Shahriyar insisted that whatever girl he married during the day should be executed the next morning. This was interesting! Soon Harriet's gray-blue eyes were leaping from one word to another. While the schedule of death-in-the-morning was being carried out, Scheherazade, daughter of the grand vizier, shocked her father by offering to marry the Sultan.

"He will kill you the next day!" exclaimed Father.

"Maybe so, but I want to marry him," insisted Scheherazade.

Sheherazade had a plan and was not worried. Her simple plan was to start telling her husband a story every day, then always stop in the most interesting place and not end it until the following morning. Then she would immediately start a fresh one even more exciting than the previous one, and again stop when she reached the highest peak of interest.

Breathlessly, Harriet began to read the young wife's stories. *Sinbad the Sailor* speeded her heart, while *Aladdin and the Wonderful Lamp* held her with such intensity she lost all sense of time.

Each story was more spellbinding than the previous one. One day as she was in the midst of an adventurous tale, she was told that Judge Reeve and his huge wife were coming over in the afternoon. Fearing that she might miss something important, Harriet put a marker in the book at the beginning of *Ali Baba and the Forty Thieves* and curled up in a corner of the living room.

Facing the judge, Lyman Beecher was extremely troubled. "This is about the most serious crisis I've ever faced," he groaned. "For years the Congregational church in Connecticut was *the* political force. We ran the state. We were supported by taxes. And now all that power is gone. Gone! And it's all gone because the Sabbath-breakers, rum-selling, tippling folks, infidels, Unitarians, and ruff-scuff got together."

"True," agreed Reeve in a throaty whisper. "Still, Lyman, they won the election! And all of our states, all twenty of them, are required by law to obey the majority."

"I know. I know. I know. But, Judge Reeve, how will we pay our bills?"

"Haven't you always preached that God would take care of His children?"

"I have."

"And haven't you told us to rely on Romans 8:28: 'And we know that all things work together for good to them that love God, to them who are the called according to his purpose'?"

"But, Judge, I'm a widower! I have eight children to clothe and feed and they have to be educated." He bowed his head in discouragement. "Things seem to be getting worse for the preachers," he murmured. He closed his eyes and shook his head.

"Lyman, God is still on His throne," replied Reeve as he took his wife's hand and helped pull her out of her chair. "God will show you what you should do. Didn't Calvin teach that God never fails?"

After the Reeves had gone, Harriet watched her father as he sat immobile in his chair. His eyes had lost their fire, and dark shadows smudged his cheeks. He appeared as if he had been forsaken by everyone. Worried, Harriet ventured, "Papa, what are you thinking about?"

Following an almost interminable silence, he replied, "I'm thinking about the Church of God!"

"Are we all going to starve to death?"

Instead of answering, one of America's greatest theologians got up, shuffled into his bedroom, and noisily closed the door.

Harriet was almost frantic. From the time she had returned from Nutplains, she had noticed how much her father had changed. No longer did she have to search under his bed for hungry lions. He had even stopped getting out his fiddle after the Sunday evening service and happily dancing a jig in his stocking feet as he sawed out a tune.

Worried, she approached her grandmother. "What's the matter with Pa?" she asked.

"All the Beechers are hypochondriacs," she divulged, nodding her head with confidence. "Lyman is just suffering with the hypos. He'll be all right in a day or two."

The next day after breakfast when Harriet crept up to her father's study she found him busy at his desk.

"Papa, what are you doing?"

"Hattie, I'm organizing some committees to raise money in the church. We've depended on taxes too long. Now we'll pay our own way! Sometimes the Lord has to teach us by closing a door. . . . The New Testament church wasn't supported by taxes. Paul said, 'Upon the first day of the week let everyone of you lay by him in store, as God hath prospered him, that there be no gatherings when I come' " (1 Cor. 16:2). He dipped his pen and filled another page with names. Then he turned to Harriet.

"One of the things I've learned," he said, speaking with more enthusiasm than Harriet had heard since her return, "is that God sometimes has to guide us with a club. Hattie, do you know why I'm a preacher and not a farmer?"

Harriet shook her head.

"As you know my mother died when I was born. Her name was Esther Lyman. She was Father's third wife. I was then raised by my uncle and aunt, the Lot Bentons. They had a hilly farm near Guilford. Because they didn't have children, they decided that I was to inherit their farm. But since I was always dreaming and thinking about books, I couldn't plow straight. One day as I was plowing, the old wooden plow jumped out of the furrow. Still, I kept going because my mind was on something else. This was too much for Uncle Lot. He said, 'Lyman Beecher, you'll never make a farmer! But since I'm your uncle I'm going to send you to Yale.' It was thus, Hattie, that I became a preacher. That experience proved to me that often our failures are far more important than our successes."

Eventually the Congregationalists were glad that Connecticut had been cut off from income tax. In his autobiography, Lyman confessed: "For several days I suffered what no tongue can tell, *for it was the best thing that ever happened to the State of Connecticut.* It cut the churches loose from dependence on state support. It threw them solely on their own resources and on God.

"They say ministers have lost their influence; the fact is, they have gained."

This crisis over, life continued on without ups or downs in the Beecher home. In a letter to Aunt Harriet Foote in Nutplains, Catherine mentioned the latest news: "Edward continues at South Farms. William is at Mr. Collins' store, but boards at home. Mary goes to Miss Pierce, and George to Miss Collins. Henry is a very good boy. . . . Charles is as fat as ever. He can speak a few words to express his wants, but does not begin to talk."

The smoothness in the home, however, did not continue. Early in the fall Lyman made a sudden announcement. "I am going to Boston. I may not get back for several weeks, so just keep busy."

There was a gleam in his eye when he stepped into his carriage. After it had disappeared, Harriet asked, "Why is Papa going to Boston?"

"I don't know," replied Catherine.

Esther shrugged.

"Maybe he's gone to get us a new ma," suggested Mary.

"You may be right," added Grandma. "My husband had five wives and David was the father of Lyman." She smiled.

With a book to finish, Harriet didn't speculate about her father's intentions. She had read *Ali Baba and the Forty Thieves* and now she continued with the next stories.

After several weeks of continuous reading, Harriet completed the final story. The unexpected solution widened her eyes.

"My master and sultan," said Scheherazade, after she had kissed the ground at his feet, "for one thousand and one days I have told you all the stories I know. May I, as a reward, humbly ask a favor?"

"Your wish is granted."

Scheherazade summoned a servant.

"Bring my children," she said.

The oldest child could already walk. The second could merely crawl. The youngest was confined to his crib. "Sir," she said "here are your sons. For their sakes grant me my life. Do not let the poor boys grow up without a mother." She then threw herself at his feet.

Overwhelmed, the sultan lifted her up. Then he said to her, "You are to reign at my side as my spouse as long as Allah grants us life."

That ending lifted Harriet's heart. The fact she appreciated most was that Sheherazade's stories had inspired the sultan to change the law that required each of his successors to have each wife killed the day after he married her.

When she was chided for wasting so much time reading fiction, Harriet replied, "Reading fiction is *not* a waste of time. The stories in the *Arabian Nights* changed the world!"

Later in the fall, Harriet was almost asleep when she heard a strange sound at the door. As an adult, she recalled: "We knew Father had gone away somewhere on a journey, and was expected home, and thus a sound of a bustle or disturbance in the house easily awoke us. We heard Father's voice in the entry, and started up, crying out as he entered our room, 'Why, here's Pa!' A cheerful voice called out from behind him, 'And here's your ma!'

"A beautiful lady, very fair, with bright blue eyes and soft auburn hair bound round with a black velvet bandeau, came into the room, smiling, eager, and happy-looking. Coming up to our beds, she kissed us and told us she loved little children and would be our mother. We wanted to get up and be dressed, but she pacified us with the promise that we would find her in the morning."

Harriet Porter was only twenty-seven when forty-two-year-old Lyman Beecher proposed to her. She came from a well-known family that had settled in Portland, Maine. Her father, Doctor Aaron Porter, was a distinguished physician. An uncle was Maine's first governor, another uncle, a state's senator, and, on two occasions, minister to Great Britain, while still another uncle was a congressman.

Hattie described her new mother with affectionate words: "She seemed to us so fair, so delicate, so elegant that we were almost afraid to go near her. . . . She was peculiarly dainty and neat in all her ways and arrangements; and I remember I used to feel breezy, and rough, and rude in her presence. We felt a little in awe of her, as if she were a strange princess rather than our own mama; but her voice was very sweet . . . and she took us up in her lap and let us play with her beautiful hands, which seemed wonderful things, as though made of pearl, and ornamented with strange rings."

Harriet Porter provided Lyman with a new enthusiasm for life. And the next year a college in Vermont added to his dignity by honoring him with a D.D.

Like many other fathers Lyman Beecher was concerned about the spiritual lives of his children. In 1819 he wrote to William H:

> I have no child prepared to die; and however cheering their prospects for time may be, how can I but weep . . . when I realize that their whole external existence is every moment liable to become an existence of unchangeable sinfulness and woe. My son, do not delay the work of preparation. . . . Time flies; sin hardens; procrastination deceives. . . . A family so numerous as ours is a broad mark for the arrows of Death. . . . To commit a child to the grave is trying, but to do it without one ray of hope concerning their future state . . . would overwhelm me beyond the power of endurance. . . . Let me not, if you should be prematurely

cut down, be called to stand in despair by your dying bed, to weep without hope over your untimely grave.

Lyman expressed this same concern to all of his children. But he always did so in a gentle and loving way. The second decade in the 1800s were convulsive years. The hated War of 1812—dubbed by many as Madison's War—had been fought. New states had entered the Union and these changes had inspired debates.

From the time of Harriet's birth until 1819, Louisiana, Indiana, Mississippi, Illinois, and Alabama had been admitted to the Union. Their admission had not created much of a stir. But immediately afterward when Maine and Missouri applied for admission, a nest of deadly hornets began to whirl. This was because eleven states permitted slavery and eleven states prohibited slavery. This division provided each group with twenty-two senators—an even balance. However, if Missouri were allowed into the Union as a slave state, the balance would be broken. Such a possibility frightened the states where slavery was prohibited.

By 1820 the debate had become acute. Many distinguished men such as Judge Reeve came to the Beecher home to discuss the matter. Sitting in a corner, Harriet, by now nine years old, listened to the discussions with intense interest. Some of the finer points were over her head. Nevertheless, she acquired a bold outline of the history of slavery in America.

The importation of slaves into the United States, she learned, had been prohibited in 1808. That was three years before she was born. Slavery at that time was on the decline. Then Eli Whitney's cotton gin, invented in 1794, became popular. This machine enabled a slave to produce fifty times more clean cotton than he had previously produced. And since cotton flourished in the South, the southern states gradually whitened with vast fields of cotton.

In less than ten years the export of cotton multiplied thirty times. Cotton production increased the demand *for* and the price *of* slaves. Harriet read that a southern newspaper had advertised a fifty-pound male slave for $500. Meaning he would be sold for ten dollars a pound! Harriet was horrified. The child would be about the same size as her little brother Charles.

The problem of allowing Missouri to enter the Union as a slave-state continued to churn. Henry Clay, speaker for the House of Representatives, pointed out that if Missouri were barred from statehood, southern senators would bar Maine from statehood. The Missouri Compromise, which he authored, restricted slavery from the territory secured in the Louisiana Purchase north of 36° 30' latitude with the exception of Missouri.

Clay's compromise was duly passed. Maine became a free state in 1820 and Missouri would become a slave-state in 1821. After Lyman had explained all of this to Harriet with a map, he added. "This does not end the problem over slavery. Tom Jefferson has dubbed the compromise 'A firebell in the night.' And I'm afraid, Hattie, the old man is right even though a balance of senators has been maintained."

From the time Harriet had noticed that Zillah and Rachel were black and that Grandma Foote insisted that her black servants stand at a distance even during family prayers, she had thought about the injustice of slavery. But what could she, a mere girl, do about the terrible wickedness?

Although Harriet's life seemed uneventful, she brightened it by constantly curling up with a book. She was fascinated with Cotton Mather's *Magnalia Christi Americana*. Its tales of witches, Indian raids, and God's providence kept her mind active. Then one day she opened a book of Lord Byron's poetry. That book to her was like the secret door opened to Ali Baba by the Forty Thieves. It revealed huge caches of treasure. Spellbound, she read:

> Maid of Athens, ere we part,
> Give, oh give me back my heart!
> Or, since that has left my breast,
> Keep it now and take the rest.

Later, when she learned that Byron had a crippled foot, she loved his works all the more. *If such a handicap could not stop him, maybe her handicap of being a girl would not stop her!* But she was afraid her father would not approve of Lord Byron. Then, in the midst of her doubts, she found him reading from Byron just as he often read from Milton.

"Do you like him?" she asked eagerly.

"Hattie, I love him. Just listen to this." He then read from *The Destruction of Sennacherib*:

> For the Angel of Death spread his wings on the
>   blast,
> And breathed in the face of the foe as he
>   passed;
> And the eyes of the sleepers waxed deadly
>   and chill,

And their hearts but once heaved and forever
grew still.

"That is a talented man!" he proclaimed. "Just think about what he could do if he would use that talent for the Lord. But I'm afraid, Hattie, that Lord Byron is a very ungodly man."

"Do you mind if I read him?"

"Of course not. Although he leads an ungodly life, his poetry, on the whole, is rather clean."

"Papa, do you think a girl might have enough talent to make some changes in the world?" Harriet eagerly studied his face.

"Certainly. Some of the world's most talented individuals have been women."

It seemed to Harriet that an eternity would pass before she was old enough to enroll in Sarah Pierce's school. Finally, however, she met the age and was duly seated with the other young ladies—many of them from wealthy homes and distant places.

Sarah's school was famous all over America. Not only did she teach the three R's, but she also graduated polite and dedicated scholars. She took a special pride in each of her charges and made a habit of questioning them about those things which she considered vital: Have you prayed? Have you been neat in your person? Have you spoken an indecent word? Have you combed your hair with a fine-toothed comb? Have you brushed your teeth?

John Pierce Brace taught composition and Harriet paid special attention to everything he said, because she hoped to become a poet someday. Strangely, the fact that she remained indifferent to correct spelling for the rest of her life became evident the day she enrolled. By a curious slip she was registered as Harriet F. Beecher instead of Harriet E. Beecher. Unconcerned, she made no effort to correct the error.

Harriet never achieved the honor roll even though her sister Mary was constantly listed as "Head of Papers." Like her father, she was unique. Unaffected by peer pressure, the fashions of the times meant nothing to her. She read what she wanted to read whether it was a part of her assignment or not.

When she was twelve, an occasion arose to submit an essay in competition with others, knowing that the three best essays would be publicly read to the literati in Litchfield. Her chosen subject was a difficult one: *Can the Immortality of the Soul Be Proved by the Light of Nature?*

Harriet studied, wrote, and rewrote. On the day the essays were to be read, she noticed that her father was sitting on the platform next to Mr. Brace. As she waited, someone began to read her essay. She remembered: "Father brightened and looked interested. At the close I heard him ask, 'Who wrote that composition?'

" 'Your daughter, sir,' was the response.

"It was the proudest moment of my life. There was no mistaking Father's face when he was pleased, and to have pleased him was past all juvenile triumphs."

6

The New Flower

Alexander Fisher had entered Yale at fourteen and graduated at the top of his class at eighteen. His genius glowed in many subjects. He published a book on astronomy, wrote another on Hebrew grammar, composed music, was a talented poet, and had ample finances.

His fame spread abroad to Europe.

Fisher had first become acquainted with Catherine when he read one of her poems in *The Christian Spectator*, a magazine published by her father. And, being an admirer of Lyman Beecher, he made frequent trips to Litchfield where he was always invited to stay for dinner. A relationship developed and soon the couple became engaged. Lyman was delighted about the match. But he was also concerned, for the young professor had not taken a stand for Christ.

After an up-and-down romance, which was broken and then mended, Catherine and the young professor agreed that they would be married after he spent a year touring the universities in Europe. That spring he set sail on the *Albion*.

Two months later, Lyman was attending a ministers' meeting in New Haven when he learned that the *Albion* had lost a rudder and crashed into the cliffs on the west coast of Ireland. There were only two survivors, but Professor Fisher was not one of them. Without waiting for his return to Litchfield, Lyman wrote to Catherine:

> My dear Child:
> On entering the city last evening, the first intelligence I met filled my heart with pain. It is all but certain that Professor Fisher is no more.

Thus have perished our earthly hopes, plans and prospects. Thus the hopes of Yale College—and of our country and, I may say, Europe, which had begun to know His promise—are dashed. The waves of the Atlantic commissioned by heaven have buried them all.

And now, my dear child, what will you do? Will you turn at length to God, and set your affections on things above, or cling to the shipwrecked hopes of earthly good? Will you send your thoughts to heaven and find peace, or to the cliffs and winds and waves of Ireland, to be afflicted, tossed with tempest and not comforted?

Till I come, farewell. May God prepare you, and give me the joy of beholding life spring from death.

Having never experienced conversion, Catherine found it extremely difficult to face life. She lamented:

If I attempt to turn the swift course of my skiff, it is only to feel how powerful is the stream that bears it along. If I dip my frail oar in the wave, it is only to see it bend to the resistless force.

There is One standing on the shore who can relieve my distress, who is all powerful to save; but He regards me not. I struggle only to learn my own weakness, and supplicate only to perceive how unavailable are my cries, and to complain that He is unmindful of my distress.

Feeling Catherine's anguish, Lyman poured out his heart:

My rod has been stretched out and my staff offered in vain. While the stream prevails and her oar bends, within her reach is My hand, mighty to save, and she refuses its aid.

Eventually Catherine received help from the writings of John Newton, converted slave trader and author of *Amazing Grace*. While she was overcoming her grief, she learned that Fisher had willed her his library and $2,000. When the books arrived in Litchfield, Lyman examined them carefully to make certain none of the volumes would be detrimental to his children. At first he hesitated about the novels of Sir Walter Scott. But after a thorough examination, he became assured that they were clean—and educational. From then on, the Beechers were addicted to Scott. Harriet especially loved *Ivanhoe*. One summer she allegedly read it through seven times.

Each year Lyman conducted work projects to get some of the special chores done. One of these consisted of preparing apples and quinces in order to make apple butter for the winter months. Since several barrels of what Harriet called "cider applesauce" were required each year, the entire family was kept busy. As the apples were peeled and cored Lyman kept everyone's mind occupied.

"Why," he would challenge as he brought out another basket of apples, "did Matthew write that two sparrows cost a farthing, while Luke wrote that five sparrows cost two farthings?"

As the problem was discussed, he prodded them with numerous questions, challenging their imagination. "Was Bookkeeper Matthew better at figures than Doctor Luke?" "Why didn't an editor make their figures agree?" "How can we believe the Bible if it is full of contradictions such as this?"

Eventually someone would conclude, "Both Luke and Matthew were right. The difference is because a merchant would throw in an *extra* sparrow for two farthings."

Pleased with this solution, Lyman would praise the one who had solved the problem and then change the subject.

In this manner the apple-bee, or work project, continued until the barrels were full and stored in the basement where the cider applesauce eventually froze and was thus preserved.

Having returned to Litchfield after visiting Alexander's family, Catherine decided that her best opportunity "to do good" was to become a teacher. Her brother Edward, who was heading the Hartford Grammar School, encouraged her. Financed by the capital she had inherited, Catherine, together with her sister Mary, opened what was described as a school "intended exclusively for those who wish to pursue the higher branches of female education."

Their institution occupied the second floor of a harness shop at the Sign of the White Horse on Main Street. It was well located, for Hartford was on the stage route between Boston and New York City. Moreover, stages frequently stopped at the nearby Ripley's Coffee House.

Neither Catherine nor Mary was adequately trained to teach the subjects they announced. But that did not deter them. Having Beecher determination, they learned quickly. After school, their candles burned late into the night while they pored over Latin, rhetoric, chemistry, logic, history, and other subjects.

The school prospered.

One day, Catherine approached Harriet and asked, "Why don't you attend our school?"

"I would love to," answered Harriet. "But how would I pay my tuition and board and room?"

Lyman Beecher solved the problem. He had made a deal with Isaac Bull, a Hartford wholesale druggist, to board his daughter Catherine so that she could attend Sarah Pierce's school in Litchfield. Now he asked if he would do the same for Harriet. Catherine also agreed to waive the tuition requirement.

Upon her arrival in Hartford, Harriet learned that she had an entire bedroom all to herself. This was a new and wonderful experience. Two classmates, Catherine Cogswell, the prettiest girl in school, the daughter of a distinguished physician and Georgiana May, who had lost her father and had a special need for companionship, became lifelong friends.

Hartford, with its population of 5,000 was, to Harriet, a huge metropolis. Window-shopping with friends was like walking down the main street of heaven. Fashion shops with their silk dresses were especially attractive. Pausing in front of one of them, Harriet pointed through the picture window. "Do you see that silk dress?" she said. "Someday I'm going to have one of them. And it's going to have a bustle."

"That's just a dream," replied Georgiana, slowly shaking her head. "Only the rich can afford silk dresses with bustles."

"Maybe so. But someday Harriet Elizabeth Beecher is going to have a custom-made silk dress complete with a bustle."

One day during an outing with Georgiana to Hartford's Park River, Harriet confided in her friend. "I have one ambition," she said, "I'm going to be a writer."

"What kind?"

"I'd really like to be a poet, especially if I could be a great one like Lord Byron. But if I can't do that, I'd be willing to become a novelist like Sir Walter Scott."

On their way home, passing a magnificent grove of trees, the girls agreed that when they were rich and famous they would build magnificent dream-houses in the midst of that grove. "And my house," boasted Harriet, "will be a large one surrounded by flowers and trees. It will have a garden and gables. There will be an enormous parlor where I can entertain famous authors and editors. I will have paintings on the walls, and shelves bulging with the latest books. All the servants will wear bright uniforms—"

Georgiana began to laugh. "Harriet, you have such an imagination; but I hope all your dreams will be fulfilled," she added as they started home.

"They will be," Harriet determined. "Just give me time!"

The fame of Lord Byron increased every day. His books and portrait were in almost every home. Young people copied his manner of dress and went on diets in order to attain his thinness. Conversations were embellished with his lines. If an admirer began with the quote: "I know only we loved in vain; I only feel—farewell! farewell!" the reply might be: "Fools are my theme, let satire be my song."

Harriet continued to admire him; and being aware that his poem *Childe Harold's Pilgrimage* had made him famous overnight, she decided to write a drama that might duplicate his success. Pondering her chances of impressing the literary world, she decided that her poem needed at least three ingredients: a dramatic setting, a dynamic hero, and a constant description of extravagant living. At the desk in her bedroom, she outlined the source of each ingredient.

The hero would be a rich Athenian who was also an Olympic champion. The setting would be Nero's court in Rome. And her description of extravagant living would be based on the way the Caesars wasted millions of sesterces on a single feast, which sometimes ended with a serving of hummingbird tongues.

And who would be the model for the rich Athenian and victor at the Olympics? The answer was simple. Her model would be none other than Lord George Gordon Byron! Having named her poem *Cleon*, she lifted her pen and excitedly began:

> Diversion is his labor, and he works
> With hand and foot and soul both night and day:
> He throws out money with so flush a hand
> As makes e'en Nero's waste seem parsimony.

Harriet was making progress with the poem when her notebook was discovered by Catherine. After confiscating it, she stormed: "If you have so much spare time, you can begin studying Butler's *Analogy* so that you can teach it next fall."

"Yes, ma'am!" replied Harriet sarcastically.

Brokenhearted, Harriet turned to the analogy. But she continued to dream about her lame-footed hero. Then she began to learn shocking things about him. Yes, her hero, who was more proud that he had swum the Hellespont than that he had written his greatest poems, was an ungodly man. He lived with his half sister. He chewed tobacco. And it was claimed that he had staged an orgie in which he and some friends donned long, black cossocks in the manner of medieval monks, and drank wine out of polished human skulls.

Then came the shattering news that Byron had died on April 19, the day after Easter 1824. Like his father, he died at the age of thirty-six.

Harriet wept.

That summer she returned to Litchfield. One Sunday morning while sitting in her regular pew, she immediately noticed that her father was unusually moved. Even before shoving the first set of spectacles to the top of his head, he stated sadly, "Byron is dead—gone."

Shocked to attention, Harriet and the rest of the congregation waited with bated breath for his next statement.

"I'm so sorry," he continued after a few moments and gaining control of his emotions. "I did hope he would live to know Christ and to do something for Him. What an impact he might have made." Again he hesitated while he struggled with his words. Then, with a catch in his voice, he added: "If only Byron could have talked with Taylor or me, we might have helped him out of his troubles."

Several weeks later, while her father's words about Byron were still stirring within her, Harriet again turned her gray-blue eyes to the pulpit. This Sunday her father was preaching what he called a frame sermon. Instead of weaving complex arguments about some profound aspect of one of the five points of Calvinism, he ad-libbed from the overflow. His subject was: "I call you not servants, but friends."

Harriet wiped her eyes as her father spoke from his heart. An overwhelming conviction of sin settled upon her. Then she remembered the way of forgiveness as taught in the New Testament. Overwhelmed by the fact that Christ had willingly died for her, and remembering Roxana's concern for her salvation, she quietly surrendered her life to Him.

That afternoon Harriet climbed the steps to her father's study. There, with the pungent smell of hams and bacon about her, and with Mama Kitty nursing her kittens nearby, she told her father how she felt, and related the commitment she had made. As she spoke, she felt his arms tighten about her shoulders. While his tears dropped on her head, she heard him say in a broken voice, "Then a new flower has blossomed in the kingdom today."

Hearing those words, it suddenly dawned on her that she

had been freed from guilt, that she had become a joint-heir with Christ—and, best of all, that she had been created for a purpose. Tingling with anticipation, she descended the steps two at a time and went outside. She noticed that the grass was greener, the blue head of Mount Tom on the distant horizon was more glorious than it had ever been, and the sun that evening as it courted the west with its thousand colors was far more breathtaking than she had ever noticed it to be before. Yes, Harriet Elizabeth Beecher had been born again!

Sleep was impossible as she pondered how God would use her, as a girl, in His plans and purposes. Did He want her to be a teacher, a missionary, a housewife, a writer?

As she wrestled with her thoughts, her mind went back to the time she had been with Grandmother Foote in Nutplains. During those months she had been overwhelmed by Isaiah's vision in the sixth chapter of his book.

At that time she had been too young for it to be vividly clear to her. But now, as she recalled the occasion, Isaiah's words glowed with a new meaning. Slipping out of bed, she lit a candle and studied the first nine verses of that chapter. As she reread them, she became aware of the fact that Isaiah's lines were far greater than the best lines of Lord Byron. Comparing them was like comparing a mouse to a lion. Fighting tears, she read:

> In the year that kind Uzziah died I saw also the Lord sitting upon a throne, high and lifted up, and his train filled the temple.

After she had completed the passage she returned to the fifth verse. Lingering on each word, she read:

> Then said I, Woe is me! for I am undone; because I am a man of unclean lips, and I dwell in the midst of a people of unclean lips: for mine eyes have seen the King, the Lord of hosts.

After praying for understanding, she studied the following three verses, which especially impressed her.

> Then flew one of the seraphims unto me, having a live coal in his hand, which he had taken with the tongs from off the altar: and he laid it upon my mouth, and said, Lo, this hath touched thy lips; and thine iniquity is taken away, and thy sin purged. Also I heard the voice of the Lord, saying, Whom shall I send, and who will go for us? Then said I, Here *am* I; send me. And he said, Go, and tell this people, Hear ye indeed, but understand not; and see ye indeed, but perceive not.

Getting on her knees, Harriet prayed, "Lord, touch my lips with a coal from off the altar, and show me what I am to do."

As she waited, she did not receive a specific answer. Still, she felt an assurance that her prayer had been heard, and that the Lord was preparing her for a specific purpose. With new confidence, she pinched out the candle and was soon asleep.

A few years later, having recalled this occasion, Harriet wrote to her brother Edward, "He has given me talents and I will lay them at His feet, well satisfied if He will accept them. All my powers He can enlarge. He made my mind and He can teach me to cultivate and exert its faculties."

7
Darkness at High Noon

Knowing that she would be leaving for Hartford the next day, Harriet slipped over to the cemetery to where her mother, her little sister, the first Harriet, and her stepbrother Frederick were buried.

Lingering a long moment in front of Roxana's grave, Harriet pondered about her recent conversion, and how it assured her that she and her mother would be together again someday. Remembering her father's words, "Then a new flower has blossomed into the kingdom," she vowed that she would live and work in a way to honor her mother, the dearest friend she ever had.

Still sobbing, she walked over to her sister's grave. Had she lived she would be seventeen now—three years older than herself. Moved by thoughts about what her sister might have accomplished, Harriet prayed that she might "double up" and complete both her sister's assignments and her own.

Finally, she went over to the grave of Frederick—her stepmother's first child. Born in 1818, he had passed away two years later. Viewing the still-raised mound of earth, Harriet reflected on the uncertainty of life.

Since it was still late afternoon, Harriet wandered over to the fence enclosing the backyard of the Walcott home.

"May I help you?" asked Sam, the tall black gardener, walking toward her.

"Oh, no. I'm just thinking about the way the women melted George III and turned him into bullets."

Sam leaned on his hoe and chuckled. "The women did a good job," he smiled. "Those 42,088 bullets helped earn our freedom." He picked up the hoe and started to walk away. Then he stopped. "You know, Miss Hattie," he added, speaking very thoughtfully, "I wish we had some more statues we could turn into bullets."

"You mean you'd like to start another war?" Harriet frowned.

"Oh, no. I'm against war. Nevadaless, somethin' has to be done 'bout slavery. Miss Hattie, it ain't right for one man to own another. My old pappy was a white man, but I was sold as a slave."

"How could that be?" Horrified, Harriet stared.

"Because my mother was black."

"Who sold you?"

"My pappy sold me. Sold me in 'Orleans for one thousand dollars."

"Your own father sold you?" Harriet's eyes widened in disbelief.

"Yep. My own pappy sold me."

"Why?"

"Because he was in debt."

"Are you a slave now?"

"No, ma'am. I bought my freedom."

"Well now, Sam, if you had some statues to melt, what would you do with them?"

"Don't know, Miss Hattie. 'Deed I don't." Digging out a weed as he considered the problem, he continued. "But ah'll tell you what ah tinks. Ah tinks if someone could turn a chunk of history into a statue as Lot's wife was turned into salt, and den change dat statue into words, da words could change people's hearts."

"What would you do with the words?" asked Harriet, curiously.

"String 'em into stories. Mebbe a book. Miss Hattie, everyone has a tender spot inside him. Even da meanest slaveholder has a soft spot. If somebody could touch dat soft spot, he could change his ways. 'Deed, he could."

"Ah 'member when I was bein' sold down in 'Orleans. It was a summer day just like dis and da birds were singin' just like dey is singin' here now. As I was waitin' for someone to buy me, ah seed a fair-skinned woman who was holdin' a little boy by the hand. While I was watchin', da auctioneer pointed at her with his mallet.

"Speakin' through his nose, he said, 'Sasaphras is a might nice gal. Has religion. Don't steal. Sews. Has good

teeth. Works hard. Cooks. Her pancakes melt in your mouth.'
Den da man turned and spat a stream of terbakker juice.
Next, he pointed to the ball and chain around her ankle.
'She's also good lookin'!' he added as he winked at the men
who was a-crowdin' round the platform. He spat again. 'But
da owner has a problem. His problem is dat he don't want to
separate da mother from her son. Because of dat, we'd like
to sell 'em together. Both together would make a fine buy. The
young'un is a mighty fine boy. He'd look nice in a smart uniform by a front door.

"' 'But if none of you gentlemen comes up with 'nuff
money, ah'll be forced to sell 'em separately. Ah don't wanna
do dat 'cause ah'm a kindhearted man. Deed ah am. Dat little
boy needs his mammy!' Da brute hesitated. Den he said,
'Sometimes ah goes to church.'

"When he said dat, Miss Hattie, da whole crowd howled.
Day 'bout split dere sides 'cause dey knew what kind of a
critter he was."

He stepped closer to the fence. Mimicking the stance of
the auctioneer, he pointed at Harriet and boomed in a nasal
tone, "Wal, now, ladies and gentlemen, let's keep a-goin'. This
good-lookin' gal and her son are bein' sold together. Do I have
a bid? Five hundred dollars. Who'll make it six? Six hundred.
Who'll make it seven?"

Harriet was spellbound.

"Dat's da way it went," explained Sam, shifting back into
his normal voice. "When da bids stopped at twelve hundred
dollars, da man decided to sell 'em separately. Ah'll never forget how Sasaphras busted up. She got on her knees. 'Please
sell us together,' she begged. 'Please! Please! Please! If you'll
sell us together ah'll work mah fingers to da bone. Ah'll do
anything. Deed ah will.'

"But, Hattie, no one would go high 'nuff; and so she was
sold to one man, while her son was sold to da other. Ah'll
never forget how she screeched when dey dragged him away.
While she was a-weepin', I saw dat hardhearted auctioneer
turn his back to da crowd. But dis time, Miss Hattie, he didn't
spit even though he had a fat wad in his cheek. No, Hattie,
he didn't spit—"

"What did he do?" demanded Harriet, leaning against the
fence.

"He wiped his eyes. Yes, Miss Hattie, dat's what he done.
He wiped his eyes. Den he blew his nose. Words, Miss Hattie,
words like bullets have power. Terrible power. Sometimes

words, dramatic words, have even more power den bullets."

Deeply moved, Harriet was almost in a trance as she slowly returned home. The impromptu drama and Sam's statement about the power of words had lodged in her heart.

As the coach made its way toward Hartford, Harriet leaned back in her seat to enjoy the luxury of daydreaming. It was a lovely day. Cumulus clouds formed into patterns overhead. The countryside was green. Birds circled. Cattle and sheep grazed near the freshly painted barns. It was a day meant for dreams, and Harriet quickly became lost to hers.

It was great to be a flower in the kingdom! Better yet, it was exciting to be a *special* flower, a flower that had been planted for a special purpose. Searching her heart, she discovered that she was quite willing for God to make that decision. Still, she longed to be a poet. Oh, if she could only be another Byron—a good Byron. If she could merely approach his greatness, her greatest joy would not be that she had swum the Hellespont. Oh, no. It would be that at the age of fourteen she had accepted Christ.

Carried away, she visualized bookstores displaying her latest volume—a slender hardback with her name Harriet Elizabeth Beecher in gold letters on the spine. What would be the title of her latest, which a series of presses could not produce fast enough for an eager public? She imagined herself sitting at a desk heavy with books and hearing a buyer saying, "Miss Beecher, I have all your books; and I think *The Lord's Harp* is by far the best one. Husband says you remind him of Lord Byron. As for myself, I think you're better."

In the midst of her dream she was shaken into reality when the carriage stopped in front of an inn and she was at her destination.

After arranging her room, Harriet went over to see her father's friend, Dr. Joel Hawes, pastor of the First Congregational Church in Hartford.

"Please, sir, I want to join the church," she said.

"Mmmm. Have you ever been converted?"

Harriet related the story of her conversation and her father's words when she met with him in his study.

"Mmmm. I see." He studied her in the manner of a judge about to pronounce a death sentence. "Harriet, do you feel that if the universe should be destroyed, you would be happy with God alone?"

Harriet's heart sank. But she managed a feeble, "Y-yes, sir."

His face still grim, the pastor continued, "You realize, I trust, in some measure at least, the deceitfulness of your heart, and that in punishment for your sins God might justly leave you to make yourself miserable as you have made yourself sinful?"

The question pushed Harriet's spirits almost into her shoes, but she managed to whimper, "Yes, sir."

That answer brightened the pastor's face. "Since you are certain about your conversion, I'm glad to welcome you as a member into this congregation."

Although crushed by the interview, Harriet forced herself to smile. Secretly fighting her tears, she murmured, "I'll see you in church next Sunday."

While slowly descending the steps, the minister's words about the deceitfulness of her heart and the punishment she deserved for her sins pounded in the depths of her being. The memory of each statement was like a dagger. As she stepped onto the sidewalk, she noticed a robin tugging at a worm. Studying the drama, she wondered, "Am I no more important than a worm?"

Depressed, Harriet addressed a letter to her brother Edward, now twenty-three, who was studying for the ministry. Maybe he could help her. "My whole life is one continual struggle," she wrote. "I do nothing right. I yield to temptation almost as soon as it assails me. . . . I am beset behind and before, and my sins take away all my happiness."

She had just sealed the envelope when Georgiana knocked at the door.

Sitting on the edge of the bed, Harriet bared her soul. "The happiest moment in my life," she said, "was when Pa embraced me and assured me that I was a new flower that had blossomed into the kingdom. That idea filled me with joy and I began to think of all the fine things I could do with Christ. But now the pastor has convinced me that my heart is full of deceit." She wiped her eyes.

"Could it be, Georgiana, that my heart has deceived me about being useful in the kingdom?"

"Oh, I don't think so. You're just in a bad mood. You'll feel better tomorrow. I sometimes feel the same way. Depression is a part of life—especially for talented people."

"What do you mean?" Harriet's eyes widened.

"It takes talent to see trouble where there is no trouble.

That's the reason all the Beechers get so depressed. They're just too talented."

Harriet laughed. "What's the best way to get rid of depression?"

"Faith. Prayer. Work."

Harriet had no need to worry about having something to do. Catherine's school was growing, and she needed teachers. After discussing the matter with Catherine, it was decided she should teach. But Harriet was surprised and upset with Catherine's decision. "Next year, Harriet, I want you to teach Virgil," she said without blinking.

"Virgil!" Harriet exclaimed.

"Yes, Virgil."

"But I've never read Virgil, and my Latin isn't that good."

"That doesn't make any difference. Brush up on your Latin and study Virgil."

Harriet learned Virgil and taught him. Still, she remained discouraged. Addressing another letter to Edward, she wrote:

> I wish I could describe to you how I feel when I pray. I feel that I love God—that is, I love Christ—that I find comfort and happiness in it, and yet it is not that kind of comfort which would arise from free communication of my wants and sorrows to a friend. I sometimes wish that the Savior were visibly present in this world, that I might go to Him for a solution of some of my difficulties. . . . Do you think, my dear brother, that there is such a thing as realizing the presence and character of God, that He can supply the place of earthly friends? Do you suppose that God loves sinners before they come to Him? Some say that we ought to tell them that God hates them, that He looks on them with utter abhorrence, and that they must love Him before he will look on them?

An additional problem smote her. Almost all of the girls had a boyfriend. But no one was attracted to her. As she studied her face in the mirror, she asked herself, Was it because of her squarish face, or because of her prominent Beecher nose? Maybe it was her hair! Turning her head from side to side she studied her reflection.

Finally she rearranged her hair to fit the current style. The new coiffure made no difference. The young men continued to ignore her as if she were a symbol of the plague.

In order to get her mind off her despair she took long walks, read current books, and forced herself to laugh even amidst heartbreak. She listened closely to the pastor's sermons, went to parties, lingered on her knees, and studied the Bible.

Remembering the inspiration she had received from the sixth chapter of Isaiah, she reread the first nine verses. They were as glorious as ever. Isaiah's vision, she remained convinced, was still the most inspiring incident in the entire Old Testament. At one time she had been convinced that God would favor her with a similar vision in which He would indicate what she was supposed to do with her life. But no such vision had ever come to her—and time was passing. She was already fifteen!

Pondering why she seemed to have been ignored, she wondered if she were similar to Luke's fifth sparrow—fit for nothing but to inspire a buyer to part with an extra penny.

Harriet's feelings of uselessness remained. She felt useless when she prepared for bed. She felt useless when she read her Bible. Even her dreams impressed her with her uselessness, and when she shuffled off to school her feelings of uselessness intensified. A single question dominated her mind: "Why, oh why, was I born?"

Once in a mood of deep despair while she was sitting with Georgiana on the bank of the Park, she confessed, "I know I'm a preacher's daughter, and I hate to say it, but I almost agree with the words of Lady Macbeth."

"And what was that?"

"Don't you remember? She wailed:

'Out, out brief candle!
Life's but a walking shadow, a poor player
That struts and frets his hour upon the stage,
And then is heard no more; it is a tale
Told by an idiot, full of sound and fury,
Signifying nothing.'

"I know that's pretty strong, but—"

"Oh, Harriet, don't talk like that! You're just in one of your moods."

"Maybe so, but Georgiana, do pray that God will show me what I'm to do with my life. I'm terribly afraid that my heart has deceived me. I sort of feel that I'm enduring a darkness at high noon."

But in spite of her feelings of uselessness, Harriet continued to work without pay in order that her brothers might continue studying for the ministry. Deep down inside she was convinced that none of her brothers were quite as useless as she. Moreover, she enjoyed a great satisfaction in helping them.

Following a long session with Virgil, Harriet eagerly responded to the sharp rap at the door. "Have interesting news," announced Catherine as she stepped inside. "Pa is moving to Boston."

"Boston!" exclaimed Harriet.

"Yes, Boston."

"But Boston is full of Unitarians."

"True. Nonetheless, the Hanover Congregational Church has elected him pastor. And they really want him. They're starting him out at two thousand dollars a year. That's almost three times as much as he received in Litchfield."

"But what will he do with the Unitarians?"

"Fight them of course! As you know, Pa enjoys a good fight." Catherine turned and added, "Well, I must go now. I'll see you in church on Sunday."

Since the next day was Saturday, Harriet insisted that Georgiana go with her for a long walk. Uptown, Harriet stopped at the dress shop. Pointing at a fashionable silk dress in the window, she said, "Georgiana, it won't be long until I'll walk in there and say, 'Please measure me for a dress like that, and make it wide enough at the bottom so that it will support a wide bustle.' "

"And what will you do for money?"

"Money? Money won't mean anything. Georgiana, I have a secret."

8

Boston

Harriet was nervous as she settled in the horse-drawn stage bound for Boston. The frightening story of her father's deeper-than-usual attack of hypochondria had alarmed the entire family. That story had originated in a letter William H. mailed to Edward on April 18, 1826.

In his factual and yet descriptive way, William wrote:

> I spent a week in Boston at the installation. Father was quite unwell with dyspepsia; he suffered from fear, and still does. I never knew him more cast down. He felt as though his course was finished. He had serious thoughts of sending for you, and had even written the letter, but concluded to wait and see how he got over the Sabbath. This was Friday.
>
> He took a chair, turned it down before the fire, and lay down. "Ah, William," he said, "I'm done over! I'm done over!" Mother told him he had often thought so before, and yet in two days had been nearly well again. "Yes, but I was never so low before. It's all over with me! I only want to get my mind composed in God—but it is hard to see such a door of usefulness set open and not be able to enter. . . !" I never saw him so low before.

Harriet not only worried about her father's health, but was also concerned about his continual acceptance in Boston. This cultured city, sacred to the Pilgrims, had a population of 50,000—a number so vast she found it impossible to comprehend. In addition, it was a dominion of highly intellectual people.

In contrast to this city of concentrated brilliance, Litchfield was a countrified village. Although the native had rich historic beginnings, they were still common folks and didn't

78

object when her father preached with his boots on, climbed trees to shake down the walnuts, covered his head with spectacles, or pronounced creature *creetur*, and referred to Nicolo Paganini as *Padge-a-nigh-nigh*. But how would the Brahmans of Boston accept such crudeness? Harriet shuddered. In her imagination she visualized a leader of the church saying, "Doctor Beecher, it seems that you have forgotten that this is Boston and not Litchfield. You're just a country preacher and we're disappointed. Since we don't want to embarrass you, we'll give you the privilege of resigning next Sunday to take effect in six weeks."

The thoughts raced through Harriet's mind.

After changing horses five times, the almost one-hundred-mile journey was nearing an end. Harriet was excited that she would soon be with her parents. Finally the stage rattled into the depot and came to a stop. From the window, she spotted her father. A moment later she stepped onto the pavement and he cried, "Welcome to Boston!" Gathering her into his arms, he kissed her on both cheeks.

While leading her to his shiny new carriage, Lyman Beecher said, "Your stepmother and I are delighted that you'll be spending the summer with us."

"How are you feeling?" asked Harriet.

"Fine."

"I heard that you were pretty low when you first came."

"Indeed I was. The devil had me by the nose. But after I started preaching I felt better. My six sermons on temperance really shook them up. But the Lord has blessed us with revival and I've been baptizing and taking in members ever since. Since I'm free this afternoon, I'll take you around. Have you had your lunch?"

"No."

"Fine. Your Ma has prepared a big feed. She can't wait until you get home."

All of the Beecher children, with the exception of Henry Ward and the older ones who were in school studying for the ministry, were present when Harriet stepped into the living room. After they had greeted her, she asked them to tell their ages.

Charles, with whom she and Henry Ward had shared a room when they were small, replied a little boastfully, "I'm eleven."

"And how about you, Isabella?"

Eyes on the carpet, Isabella shyly held up four fingers.

After picking up Thomas and smoothing his hair, Harriet kissed him and inquired his age.

"He doesn't know his age," scoffed Charles. "He's only two."

(Isabella and Thomas were her father's children by Harriet Porter.)

"And where's Henry Ward?" asked Harriet after she had seated herself by the fireplace.

Lyman laughed. "Henry's afraid that his mother's prayers will be answered and he'll become a preacher," he said, rubbing his hands. "When we first came to Boston he wasted his time in school. All he really wanted to do was to go down to the wharfs and watch the ships. One day the rascal dropped a note addressed to his brother in a place where he knew I'd find it.

"The note mentioned that if he couldn't get my permission to go to sea he'd run off, that he was determined to be a seaman."

"The sea!" exclaimed Harriet. "Henry Ward going to sea? I can't believe it."

"Yes, the sea. The next day I asked Henry to help me saw wood. While we were working, I said, 'Henry, what would you like to do with your life?'

" 'Go to sea,' he replied.

" 'Do you want to be just a common sailor, or would you rather be an officer in the navy?'

" 'I want to be a midshipman and finish as a commodore,' he said.

"I then replied, 'In order to do that you must begin a course in navigation and study mathematics.'

" 'I'm ready,' he answered with great enthusiasm.

" 'Well, then,' I said, 'I'll send you to Amherst. There, you can start your preparatory studies; and if you do well, I'll try and get you an appointment at Annapolis.'

"Henry agreed to all that, and now he's enrolled at Mount Pleasant Collegiate Institute."

"How's he doing?"

"Very well. His hero is Lord Nelson. He's working hard. He's discovered the joy of learning. The boy doesn't know it, but I'll soon have him studying for the ministry! Ah, but that raises a problem. Training my boys for the ministry costs a lot of money." Shaking his head he continued. "If it weren't for yours and Catherine's generosity, I'd be sunk."

The table was crowded with dishes loaded with vegetables and meats. Harriet merely picked at her food.

"What's the matter?" asked her stepmother. "Are you ill?"

"Oh no. I guess I'm just tired," managed Harriet. "It was a long trip. We stopped to change horses five times and the roads were so rough."

"You'll probably be all right in a day or two. Next week we'll go shopping and I'll show you the new styles that are coming out."

"Are clothes expensive here?" asked Harriet, perking up.

"They're dreadfully expensive." She shook her head and stroked the side of her face. "Last week I found a black silk dress. It had covered buttons and was just what I need for weddings, and your pa has many weddings. But it was too costly. The price was higher than Henry's tuition! Lyman makes three times as much money in Boston as he did in Litchfield. Even so, we're squeezed for cash. Milk and eggs cost a fortune." After studying Harriet for a moment, she added tenderly, "Hattie, you look tired. You'd better rest."

Leading the way upstairs she paused at the top and motioned with her hand toward a door at the end of the hall. Opening the door, she pointed inside. "This is your room," she said, speaking rather proudly. "You'll be all by yourself. Now get some rest. Your father has to finish an article for his new magazine. He'll be down in an hour or two and show you around."

Wearily, Harriet hung her dress in the closet and stretched out on the bed. It seemed to her that she had barely closed her eyes when there was a tap on the door. "'I'll be ready to go in half an hour," announced her father.

As the horse clip-clopped down the street, Lyman kept pointing to items of interest. "We live on the north side," he explained. "At first your mother didn't think she'd like this side. Now she loves it. For one thing we're near Copp's Hill—"

"Copp's Hill?"

"It's a cemetery where dozens of Puritans are buried."

Moments later, he tethered the white mare at the meetinghouse and unlocked the door. Flinging his hands at the row upon row of pews, he said, "Hattie, when I first came and saw all those empty pews, a vacuum formed in my stomach. I was fearful. Since the congregation only had thirty-seven members, I wondered how we'd ever fill them." He laughed. "I need not have worried. Today, we have people in the aisles!"

He led the way up to the pulpit.

"At the last auction, choice pews brought as much as thirteen hundred dollars—people are that eager to come to church. Yes, Hattie, my dear, the good Lord wanted me here in Boston, and He's bringing many into His kingdom."

After a hurried tour around the inside of the building, he said, "Now we'll climb Copp's Hill." As the mare struggled up the cobbled street, he continued, "Boston is built on three hills: Beacon Hill, Fort Hill, and Copp's Hill. To me, Copp's Hill is the most important one—"

"Why?"

"When I first came to Boston I was so low in spirits I almost died. I loved the people in Litchfield and I wondered how I'd ever compete with all the intellectualism and wealth on Beacon Hill. Then when I was about to give up, I followed this road right to the top. Each gravestone in the cemetery spoke to me. Many Puritans are buried there; and as I moved to each marker, I thought of their lives. It seemed to me that I was treading on sacred ground."

After tethering his horse at the graveyard, he wound his way over to the grave of Cotton Mather. "Born in 1663, died in 1728," he read.

Harriet bent over the tablelike tomb resting on an oblong foundation of bricks. "I adored his *Magnalia Christi Americana*," she confessed. "That book inspired me to become a writer. He must have worked day and night. I read that his name was on four hundred and fifty publications."

"He *was* brilliant," agreed her father. "Entered Harvard at eleven and finished with honors at fifteen. Ah, but Hattie, he ruined his reputation by being so hardhearted at the Salem witch trials. No one will ever forget how they burned those poor women. The Salem trials were a blot on America." He stepped over to another marker. "Even so, Cotton Mather, God bless him, was a Congregational preacher," he sighed.

While they moved from one marker to another, Harriet became very serious. "Papa, do you remember when you told me that I was a new flower that had blossomed in the kingdom?" she asked.

"I do."

She then related the statements made by Joel Hawes.

"That was wrong, Hattie. Terribly wrong! Jesus said, 'But whosoever shall offend one of these little ones which believes in me, it were better for him that a millstone were hanged about his neck, and that he were drowned in the depth of the sea' (Matt. 18:6). Still, you must forgive him. Joel doesn't know any better. I used to be just like him. I remember when anyone told me that they were anxious about their soul, I immediately asked them about their digestion—"

"Digestion! Why?"

"Because I wanted to know if their anxiety was caused by the Holy Spirit or a stomach. Your mama and stepmother straightened me out on that. They made me understand that God is love, and that He never—never—turns anyone away."

"Pastor Hawes also told me that my heart is deceitful—"

"It is. All hearts are deceitful. That's why Cotton Mather wanted the accused women burned. But only God really knows our heart."

Harriet frowned. "But, Papa, how could such a wise man as Mather be deceived?"

"Easy. Many are deceived. They trust in their feelings rather than the Word. If our brother had gone to the Bible he would have read that Jesus taught us that we should love them and show them where they are wrong, not burn them."

"I'm still confused."

"About what?"

"I-I keep wondering whether I really did blossom into a flower and become a part of God's kingdom."

After putting his arm around her shoulders, Lyman said, "Do you not know that you cannot love and be examining your love at the same time? Some people, instead of getting evidence by running in the way of life, take a dark lantern, get down on their knees, and crawl on the boundary up and down to make sure they have crossed it. If you want to make sure, *run*, and when you come in sight of the celestial city and hear the songs of the angels, then you'll know you're across."

"In other words, you mean I shouldn't worry about it and simply get busy?"

"Of course! I keep very busy. I've started a Bible society, a Tuesday night prayer meeting, a missionary organization—and a few other things. I believe the Lord is coming soon, and we must hurry up and get ready for His coming reign." He helped Harriet get into the buggy. While they were going down the hill, he continued in a serious tone of voice. "The Puritans who are buried in Boston gave their lives for the truth. But now the Unitarians are trying to take over. They've already captured more than one hundred of our churches." He shook his head.

"The Unitarians are polished and quick-witted. They've already dominated Harvard. But they don't believe in the Trinity or the divinity of Jesus; and anyone, Hattie, who doesn't believe in the divinity of Jesus is an infidel!"

"I know, Papa, but what am I to do with my life?" Her face creased with anxiety.

"The Lord will tell you."

"How?"

"By opening or closing doors."

"Do you think I might have a vision the way Isaiah did?" She studied him carefully.

"You might. But I wouldn't count on it."

"Have you ever had a vision?"

"No."

After they arrived home and the horse had been unharnessed, Lyman suggested, "Hattie, if I were you I'd go to bed early and sleep in and relax all day. Sunday will be a busy day and I have a lot of things I must do."

Hattie had just seated herself at the table for lunch the next day when her father rushed into the room. "Had a strange experience this morning," he announced after he had tossed his hat on the floor by the door.

"Believing I'd stepped into this house, I sank into a chair near the fireplace and pondered over a sermon. As I was outlining it in my mind, I noticed a French clock on the mantlepiece. Puzzled, I said, 'Wife, where did you get that clock?'

"My question was answered by a strange voice! 'Dr. Beecher,' it said, 'I fear you've made a mistake.' Looking around, I discovered that I was peering into strange faces. Worse yet, those smiling people were Unitarians!" He laughed. "Ah, but they were very gracious. They even invited me to visit them again."

After everyone had stopped laughing, Harriet said, "Papa, you've been working too hard. Why don't you rest and then later today prepare for Sunday?"

"Rest!" he exploded. "I've no time to rest. There are three people I must visit. One is anxious about his soul. And I've a committee meeting this afternoon at four. I also have to work on my sermon." Rising up he headed for his attic study. At the foot of the steps, he paused. "Hattie, God made the Beechers in order to help change the world. Don't forget that. And if we're to change the world we have to keep busy."

Mrs. Beecher smiled. "That doesn't mean that you should

not rest, Harriet. Now, go to your room and get some sleep."

After a short nap, Harriet was awakened by the sound of voices downstairs. Wide awake, she thought about the Sunday services and all the new people she'd meet and because of this she removed her Sunday dress from the hanger and crept down the steps and into the kitchen.

"Mama," she whispered, "I must iron my dress."

Pointing at a dozen irons at the rear of the stove, her stepmother said, "They're already hot."

After testing the iron with a wet finger, Harriet asked, "Mama, are there many young people in this congregation?"

"Many. Your father really attracts young people."

"Are—are any of them studying for the ministry?"

"Of course. If Pa had his way, every young man would be a Congregational preacher," she laughed. "Why do you want to know?"

Harriet blushed. "Well, I know Papa wants all my brothers to be preachers, and so . . ." Her voiced trailed as she attacked a bit of lace.

Moments later having finished the ironing, Harriet asked, "Mama, do you think I should have a different hairdo?"

"What's wrong with the way it is?"

"Nothing. But I think that since I'll have to redo my curls anyway, you might fluff it up a wee bit."

"Why would you want to do that?"

"I'm barcly five feet tall! A little fluffing would make me look taller."

"All right. Just sit down in front of the mirror and I'll see what can be done."

9

A Dog, A Petticoat, and Two Lanterns

As in Litchfield, the Beechers had family worship before breakfast. On Harriet's first Sunday in Boston, she paid special attention as her father knelt with them and prayed in the most intimate way:

"Come, Lord Jesus, here where the bones of the fathers rest, here where the crown has been torn from thy brow, come and recall thy wandering children. Behold thy flock scattered on the mountain—these sheep, what have they done? Gather them, gather them, O Good Shepherd, for their feet stumble on the dark mountains."[1]

Breakfast over, he rushed off to finish getting dressed. Harriet smiled as he bellowed, "Ma, where's my collar?" and a little later, "Ma, where are my suspenders? Ma, where's my coat?"

Fortunately, on this occasion, the long-tailed coat was located in the closet and in good condition. As he slipped into it, Harriet remembered another occasion that had become a family legend. On that never-to-be-forgotten Sunday he had located his ministerial coat without difficulty. Unfortunately he couldn't wear it. On the previous Sunday as he was rushing to the meetinghouse from an emergency, he passed the creek and noticed a fish darting close to shore. Reaching for his pole he kept tucked by a nearby tree for such opportunities, he caught it. Not knowing what to do with his prize, he slipped it into his coat pocket. Forgotten, it remained there

---

[1]Autobiography by Lyman Beecher, Vol. 2, p. 112. This prayer as it was remembered by Harriet Beecher Stowe.

all week. That Sunday when he slipped the coat on, the putrid smell drenched the entire room.

While the family held their breath, Roxana produced another coat that she had just repaired and deposited the other in a nearby laundry bag.

Lyman Beecher's dilemma this morning was worse than the previous near-disaster. The problem was that he hadn't prepared his sermon! In her reminiscences, published in her father's autobiography, Harriet accounts the way he composed sermons.

"The time that he spent in actual preparation was not generally long. If he was to preach in the evening he was to be seen all day talking with whosoever would talk, accessible to all, full of everybody's affairs, business, and burdens, till an hour or two before the time, when he would rush up to his study, and throwing off his coat, after a swing or two with his weights to settle the balance of his muscles, he would sit down and write quickly, making quantities of hieroglyphic notes on small, stubbed bits of paper, about as big as the palm of his hand. The church bells would begin to ring, and still he would write.

"They would toll loud and long, and his wife would say, 'He will certainly be late,' and then she would be running up and down the stairs to see that he was finished, till just as the stroke of the bell was dying away, he would emerge from the study with his coat in disarray, come down the steps like a hurricane, stand impatiently protesting while female hands, always lying in wait—adjusted his cravat and settled his coat collar. Then he'd call loudly for a pin to fasten together the stubbed little bits of sermon notes, drop them in the crown of his hat, and, hooking his wife or daughter like a satchel on his arm, would start on such a race through the streets as left neither brain nor breath till the church was gained."[2]

This morning, the single-purposed preacher snagged his wife with one arm and his daughter with the other. As he whizzed down the streets, his coattail flying, Harriet was alarmed about her hair. Totally forgetting the women he was towing, he barged through the church door, elbowed his way through the crowds searching for a seat, and puffed up the pulpit stairs.

Left to fend for themselves, Harriet and her mother

---

[2]Beecher, op. cit., p. 114.

wedged into the pastor's pew toward the center. Seconds later, a nearly bald man bent down and pled, "If you good folks will squeeze together just a wee trifle more, I will have a seat." The people complied and with a sigh of relief he sank into the remaining space at the end of the pew next to Harriet.

"Thank you very much," whispered the grateful man. "I'm terribly tired and I was afraid that I'd have to stand." Smiling at Harriet and studying her through his steel-rimmed spectacles, he added confidentially, "I'm William Lloyd Garrison. And I suppose you're—"

The tired man's speech was interrupted by the organ.

Harriet was fascinated with her father's sermon. According to custom, he laid a solid biblical foundation and carefully buttressed it with strong, logical reasoning. Then, after pushing his spectacles high on his forehead, he outlined what the scripture meant, and what it did not mean. This accomplished, he announced numerous formidable objections to his thesis, all of which he demolished with two or three skillful blows.

As this old formula was proceeding, Harriet noticed that Garrison was taking notes. Watching out of the corner of her eye, she noticed the intensity of his lean face, thin triangular nose, straight mouth, firm, smoothly shaved chin.

Now that her father was sporting his fourth set of lenses, Harriet knew that he was about to press his arguments home—and plead for commitment. So far, he had done well; and Garrison's interest had remained. *But would this continue?* She knew that when her father drew in his nets, he was sometimes so carried away, he often fell into his old habbit of mispronouncing words and even using faulty grammar. Silently she prayed that he would not make any embarrassing slips this time.

But even as she was frantically directing petitions to the heavenly Father, he leaned forward, and while shaking his finger, stormed, "We must never forget *Padge-a-nigh-nigh*. That slender *Eyetalian* is one of God's choice *creeturs*. God put in his *natur'* the passion to play a violin."

Embarrassed, Harriet lowered her head, closed her eyes and sighed.

"*Padge-a-nigh-nigh*," continued her father, "had just started to play when the A string broke. Ignoring this, he continued on without hesitation. Then the E string snapped. The audience groaned. Many had waited for months, paid good money, and stood in line in the rain in order to hear the one and only *Padge-a-nigh-nigh.* Now their money was wasted! But ignoring his loss, the maestro kept playing. And his improvisation was so sublime many were pulled to the edges of their seats.

"Ah, but that wasn't the end of his troubles; for just as he was climaxing an aria, the D string parted. This meant that all he had left was the slender G string. Did he give up? Never! Stepping forward, he poured his soul into his playing. Soon, scores were wiping their eyes. Why? Because *Padge-a-nigh-nigh* could squeeze three octaves out of a G string and it seemed to them that they were listening to a choir of angels.

"In spite of the other strings, that single G string—that lonely G string—was faithful.

"Many of us are like a violin. Some have broken strings. Others have strings that are out of tune. Those problems don't really matter. What really matters is for us to be fully yielded to Jesus Christ, the truly great musician. *Padge-a-nigh-nigh* is charming Europe by rubbing a few strands from a horse's tail over the insides of a cat. But we—you and I— are God's masterpiece; and we are joint-heirs with His only begotten Son."

After the service, Garrison beamed at Harriet. "Dr. Beecher is truly a great preacher." He shook his head. "By mispronouncing Paganini's name he made his illustration stick. It was like adding a barb to an arrowhead. What a man! What a man!"

Harriet stared, swallowed, shifted her feet, and finally murmured, "Dr. Beecher is my father. He's very unique." Then turning she accompanied her mother out of the sanctuary.

After the noon meal Harriet rose and went up to her father's study. "Pa," she said, "excuse me. I don't want to disturb you. But, do you know a man named William Lloyd Garrison?"

"Oh, he's a very zealous young man. A printer, I believe. Someone mentioned he's looking for work. I like the fire in his eyes. Someday he'll stir the world."

"Pa, I loved your sermon. That wonderful story about Paganini stirred me. But—" she bowed her head and her eyes became shiny. "But I'm afraid that there isn't even a broken string in my life—"

"Nonsense. As I've told you before, God made you for a purpose."

"But what is it?" A note of desperation edged her voice.

"I don't know."

"When will God tell me?"

"Give Him time."

"But, Papa, last June 14 I was fifteen and now I'm going on sixteen! I'm getting old. If the good Lord would tell me what He wants me to do, I could start preparing so that I could do it more effectively." She wiped her eyes and blew her nose.

"How do you know that He's not preparing you now?"

"In what way?"

"I really don't know. But God didn't call Moses until he was eighty, and yet He arranged for him to be prepared across many years in Pharaoh's court. Hattie, God works in mysterious ways." He smiled and then changed the conversation. "I understand that Ma is taking you sightseeing tomorrow. She really knows the city and I'm sure you'll have a good time."

Having tethered the horse in Dock Square, Harriet's mother said, "It was in this area, just a few blocks from our church, that the Revolutionary War started. The trouble began on March 5, 1770. There had just been a heavy snow. The streets were white. Snow had always been a temptation to some of the young people, for the British red-coats were excellent targets. And that night they were especially zealous because a lobsterback had been quoted as saying, 'Them in Boston as would eat their suppers Monday night would never eat another.' And remember, Hattie, this was Monday night!

"About eight o'clock four young men were sauntering down the street when they came upon a hot-tempered Irish sentinel armed with a club. After telling him he shouldn't be armed at that time of night, they tried to pass him without answering his challenge. This started a fight.

"One of the men was knocked down and another had his clothes torn and his arm slightly wounded. Soon a group of soldiers poured out of their barracks. Since they were not supposed to have guns, they were armed with shovels.

"As the confusion increased, church bells began to ring; and since church bells often signalled a fire, hundreds poured into the streets carrying leather buckets filled with water. While the half-dressed crowds milled around, more arguments erupted. Eventually a group of redcoats armed with guns appeared.

"Frightened, Henry Knox pushed through the crowd to the side of Captain Preston. 'Take your men back,' he warned. 'If you don't there'll be bloodshed and you'll be held responsible.'

" 'I'm sensible to that,' the captain agreed.

"Then Crispus Attucks, a giant mulatto slave who bought and sold cattle for his master, began to wrestle with a soldier over a musket. While they wrestled, the shouting increased. Finally someone cried, 'Fire!' Attucks was the first one killed. Altogether, five Americans died. Others were wounded.

"That, Hattie, was the flame that started the Revolution. Since it's close by, let's walk over to the home of Paul Revere. It's just a little way up the street."

"Wasn't Paul a bell-ringer at the Old North Church?"

"Yes, he was. He began ringing them when he was fifteen. Later, when he became a silversmith, he made their silver chalice, which is still used to this day when they serve communion."

"Then Paul Revere was a Congregationalist?"

"Of course. The Old North Church used to be called Christ's Church. Some even call it Mather's Church. That's because four generations of Mathers preached there. Your father told me that he took you up on Copp's Hill where Increase and Cotton Mather are buried. Both of them preached at Old North Church and were great men."

After viewing the Revere home, Harriet and her mother walked over to the famous church on Salem Street. As they were walking, Mrs. Beecher continued. "It's important to know why that old meetinghouse is so important in the story of the Revolution. This is what happened:

"The news that General Thomas Gage had assigned 700 men to seize the ammunition and cannon stored at Concord had leaked out. (Some think his American wife couldn't keep the secret.) But no one knew whether the raid would be by land or by sea. Thus it was arranged for Paul Revere to have lanterns hung high in the steeple of Old North Church. One lantern would warn that the British were coming by land. Two would warn that they were coming by sea."

When Harriet and her mother reached the church, they found a guide showing a group of tourists around the interior of the building. Pointing to pew number 62, the stout man said, "That is where General Gage and his wife used to sit." Then, aiming his finger at the organ loft, the colored windows and numerous marble busts, he related an interesting story about each item. "The communion plate," he explained, "was presented by King George II." Next, after leading the group to the base of the high pulpit, he added, "His Majesty also presented the congregation with the *Vinegar Bible*—"

" 'Vinegar Bible!' " exclaimed Harriet. "What's that?"

"It was called the Vinegar Bible because in the 1719 printing, the word vineyard in the Gospel of Luke was printed vinegar. But, as it turned out, his gift was a prophetic one; for, due to the lanterns in the steeple, this church became vinegar to His Majesty's grandson, George III!" He laughed. "Come to the steps leading to the steeple and I'll show you what I mean."

Opening the door and waving his hand upward, the guide continued, "Contrary to popular belief, Paul Revere did not hang the lanterns in the steeple on the 18th of April, 1775. Instead, they were placed there by Robert Newman, an outspoken Son of Liberty and known to the British. Newman risked his life by lighting and hanging them there.

"Since it was known that the British intended to arrest Samuel Adams and John Hancock, Paul Revere agreed to dash over to Lexington and warn them. To save time, he asked young Newman to hang the lanterns for him.

"Newman agreed without hesitation.

"Robert was in a very dangerous position, for he lived with his mother in North Square. Their home was just a short distance from the church. In addition, a number of British officers had been billeted with his mother. How was he to perform his task at such a tense moment without raising suspicion? He went to bed early. Then, while the officers in the living room below were laughing over their cards, he slipped out the window and dropped to the ground.

"John Pulling, a vestryman from the church armed with the key, was waiting for him. Together they went to the church. Pulling unlocked the door, relocked it after Newman entered, and stood guard.

"Having climbed the steeple before, Newman knew just how to proceed. From the closet he selected two lanterns and slowly eased his way up through the darkness to the bells. There he rested. Then he continued higher and higher until he reached the top window. From this vantage point he could see the shoulder of Copp's Hill, the outline of Charleston where he knew eager men were awaiting his signal, and the dark hulk of the battleship Somerset which had been anchored in the Charles River to keep an eye on anyone who crossed.

"He then lit both lanterns and allowed them to shine briefly. He had to be careful. He knew that Paul Revere had, or would be, crossing the Charles in order to get to Lexington and warn Adams and Hancock to go into hiding. He didn't want to alert anyone on the Somerset."

"Were the lights seen?" asked a lady at the end of the pew.

"Yes, ma'am, they were seen. And because they were seen, the men at Concord were prepared. Without Newman's lanterns the Revolution might have ended right then. And if it had ended that day all of us would be subjects of Silly Billy, better known as George IV!"

"And we'd all be paying a tax on tea," added Harriet.

Everyone laughed.

"Now I'll tell you about Paul Revere and his famous ride," continued the guide. He wiped his face with a fresh handkerchief. "But since his ride was not in this church, it might be more comfortable if all of you were seated on this front pew."

Standing before them, the man continued. "After Revere was assured that Newman would light the lanterns, he put on his heavy boots, kissed his wife goodbye and crept into the street. The entire area that night was heavily patrolled. Ignoring the British soldiers, Revere headed to the house where his friend Thomas Richardson lived. While he was hurrying through the alleys, he discovered that his dog was following him.

" 'Go home!' he ordered. "But instead of going home, the brown spaniel faithfully remained. Finally, he got to Richardson's house; and there both Richardson and Joshua Bentley, the boatbuilder, were waiting for him just as it had been arranged.

"According to their agreement, these men would row him across the Charles where he would mount the horse John Larkin had agreed to furnish and start on his ride. The trio had reached the corner of North and North Centre Streets when Revere stopped. 'I-I forgot to bring some cloth to muffle the oars,' he said.

" 'That's all right,' whispered one of the men. 'My girlfriend lives upstairs in that house.' He made a secret whistle and when she opened the window, he told her what he needed. She tossed them her petticoat. (Years later, Revere told his children that it was still warm.) The men were about to head for the hidden boat when Revere stopped again. His problem this time was that he had forgotten his spurs! Ah, but he had a solution.

"He wrote a note to his wife, attached it to his dog's collar and sent him home. That brown spaniel headed home like a streak of lightning. And when the dog returned the spurs were attached to his collar.

"After the oars had been muffled, Revere's boat took off. They rowed by the Somerset without being detected. The horse was ready and Revere was on his way. There were two roads from Charleston to Lexington, Revere took the road that led by the gibbet—"

"What was that?" asked Harriet.

"Twenty years before, a slave who had tried to escape was executed, placed in an iron cage, and left hanging in his chains at that place. When Revere got there, only his bones were left. . . . That grim reminder indicated to Revere what would happen to him if he were caught! Instead of discouraging him, it encouraged him to ride faster. But let me read to you what happened in Revere's own words." Taking a worn book out of his pocket, he read:

" 'The moon shone bright. I had almost got over Charleston Common toward Cambridge when I saw two Officers on Horseback, standing under the shade of a tree, in a narrow part of the road. I was near enough to see their Holsters & cockades. One of them started his horse toward me and the other up the road, as I supposed to head me should I escape the first. I turned my horse short about, and rid upon a full gallop for Mistick Road.'[3]

"He continued going as fast as his borrowed horse would gallop and soon crossed the plank bridge that led into Medford. Revere later wrote: 'I awaked the Captain of the minutemen, and after that I alarmed every house till I got to Lexington.'[4]

"In Lexington, Revere went to the Clark parsonage and warned Adams and Hancock that the British were after them. He left the parsonage at one o'clock in the morning. As he continued on his horse, he kept spreading the news. 'The British are marching! Get the warning round!' Just as he was leaving Lexington, he was joined by Samuel Prescott, a young doctor from Concord who had been courting a young lady in Lexington. Here, in the book, Revere tells us what happened:

" 'When we got about halfway from Lexington to Concord,

---

[3]Beecher, op. cit. Revere's own punctuation and spelling.
[4]Ibid.

the other two [he had been joined by Dawes] stopped at a House. . . . I kept along. When I got about 200 yards ahead of them, I saw two officers under a tree. . . . The Doctor jumped his horse over a stone wall and got to Concord. I observed a wood at a small distance and made for that intending when I gained that to jump my Horse & run afoot, just as I reached it out started six officers siesed my bridel, put their pistols to my Breast, ordered me to dismount, which I did. One of them who appeared to have command there, and much of a Gentleman, asked where I came from; I told him."[5]

"Afraid to return to Boston because of the now-aroused citizens, and not knowing what to do with Paul Revere, the British kept his horse and released him. Eventually he got back to his home."

"Did our men in Concord save the ammunition?" asked Harriet.

"Most of it. And it was saved because of Revere and Newman and their friends." The guide then turned and walked away, signaling that his lecture had ended.

As Harriet mounted the buggy, her mother said, "And now we'll go to a clothing store. I know you want to see some of the new fashions."

"Ma," replied Harriet eagerly, "I'm certainly glad you took me to the Old North Church. That's an experience I'll never forget! Both Paul Revere and Robert Newman must have been wonderful men."

"They were."

"Do you think God called them to do what they did?"

"I don't know. God is sovereign. If it hadn't been for them we might not have our freedom."

"I think God must have arranged their lives for a special purpose," Harriet said firmly. "And just think, some unimportant things became extremely useful. If it hadn't been for a petticoat the oars would not have been muffled and the men on the Saratoga might have discovered them. And if it hadn't been for the dog, Revere would not have had his spurs; and without his spurs he could not have made his ride. And if the vestryman had not had the key and opened the door, Newman could not have signaled with his lanterns. And if—"

"Hattie," interrupted her mother, "we've reached the dress

---

[5]Ibid.

shop, and this is the finest in all of Boston. The best dressed women all shop here."

Stepping inside, Harriet was amazed at the many rows of dresses, racks laden with enormous hats, tables overflowing with gloves for all occasions, and still more racks loaded with blouses. "Do you have silk dresses?" asked her mother.

"Certainly. Just step this way," replied the smiling, middle-aged lady dressed in a green blouse topped with a snug, star-shaped white collar. Pointing to a stunning black dress, complete with a wide bustle, she said, "This is the latest." Responding to a bell, she added, "Now excuse me. A lady is being fitted for a dress. I'll be back in a moment. Just look around."

After taking the black dress off the rack, Mrs. Beecher held it up close to Harriet. "You'd look like a queen in this," she announced.

Her mind still on the Revolution, Harriet merely glanced at it and said, "Mama, did you notice that the first person killed in the Revolution was a black man? And did you notice that Paul Revere was guided on his ride by the bones of a slave hanging in an iron cage?"

"I did. But I thought you were interested in the latest fashions. Don't you like these dresses?"

"Yes, I do. But, Mama, I've been thinking that it is about time for some man to climb up a high steeple and tell the world about American slavery. Ma, slavery is a dreadful sin. It's worse than leprosy. No human being has the right to own another human being. All of us, black and white, were made in the image of God." Her voice became intense as she began to pace back and forth.

"Did you know that while we're in this shop thinking about dresses, slave families are being separated on the auction block? Slavers think nothing of tearing a child from the arms of its mother for a few dollars. Those greedy men are more concerned with money than with lives." She blew her nose. "Ma, you should have heard the stories Sam told me. Those stories would freeze your blood. Sometimes I dream about them. And did you know—?"

She was interrupted by the clerk. "Have you found anything you really like? Our sale closes today."

"They're all beautiful. But . . . Well, maybe we'd better return some other time. My daughter seems to have something else on her mind—"

"I can assure you that we have the best and the cheapest—"

"Yes, I know. Your dresses are lovely. But Hattie is more concerned with slavery right now than with fashions."

"Slavery!" balked the lady. "Slavery?" She stared and walked away.

"Yes, slavery," replied Mrs. Beecher, lifting her voice. Looking quizzically at the retreating clerk, she turned to Hattie and led the way outside.

As they were clip-clopping home, Harriet turned toward her mother. "You know, Ma, if I were a man I'd do something about slavery," she said.

"What would you do?"

"I don't know. But I'd do something!"

10
Trapped!

After a breakfast of ham and eggs, Harriet spent extra minutes before a mirror. She fluffed her hair a little higher, made certain her cuff-like collar was snug at her throat; then tightening her belt, she adjusted her curls with pins to frame her face to the best advantage—and again wiped her shoes for the fifth or sixth time.

Although trapped in the body of a girl, it might be that she could use her few feminine charms to influence a talented man to make his life count. Perhaps the Lord could use her in the same way He had used Deborah. . . .

As she and her mother waited for her father to appear with his sermon notes, the church bell began to sound. "Where's Pa?" asked Harriet.

"He's late. He mislaid a commentary. But he'll be here soon. Don't worry."

Boom! Boom! Boom! the bell tolled.

Nervously, Mrs. Beecher went to the staircase. Hands cupped to her mouth, she shouted, "Lyman! We'll be late! Hurry!"

Her only answer was the mocking sound of the bell. *Boom! Boom! Boom!*

"Hattie, you'd better go upstairs and hurry him," ordered her mother.

Harriet bounded up the steps two at a time. As she barged into the study, her father stood up. "I'm ready," he announced. "I just need a pin to bind my notes."

"Ma'll have one," assured Harriet. "We must hurry."

Halfway down the steps, the booms began to slacken.

"We'll be late," moaned Harriet.

The final boom drifted through the window just as they reached the living room.

"Your tie is crooked," wailed Mrs. Beecher. She had just straightened it when she noticed that he had a brown sock on one foot and a blue one on the other. "Dear me," she cried, "you can't go into the pulpit dressed like that! Harriet, get a pin for his notes while I rush upstairs and get another pair of socks; and while I'm doing that, Lyman, take off your shoes."

Unable to find a pin, Harriet removed the one that held a curl in place above her left ear.

One of the black socks her mother produced had a huge hole in the big toe area. "I'll have to go upstairs again," she groaned.

"Oh, no. I'll wear 'em just as they are. The shoe will cover the hole. Besides, my big toe needs some ventilation. It's a hot day."

While the preacher sat on the sofa, Harriet laced one shoe while her mother laced the other. Finally, Mrs. Beecher said, "I guess we're ready. Let's run."

"Oh, but I need my hat," objected Lyman as he rushed around the room with such speed his coattail flew upward. Both Harriet and her mother helped him search. A few seconds later, Harriet exclaimed, "There it is!" She jabbed a finger at the crosspiece under the dining room table. Sinking to her knees, she fished it out.

Lyman dropped the notes in his hat, slapped it on his head, grabbed his wife and daughter, and headed down the street toward the church like a constable rushing a pair of criminals to jail.

With a sigh of relief, Harriet sank into the pew next to her mother. As she relaxed, she wondered if she had smudged her dress when she knelt down. A quick glance indicated that it was all right. Then she thought about the curl above her left ear. Her fingers indicated that it was out of place. While the congregation was standing during the second hymn, she nudged her mother. "I need an extra pin for my curl," she whispered.

"I'm sorry I don't have an extra one," she replied.

"What will I do?"

"Don't worry. It looks all right."

Harriet swept her eyes over the congregation. When she failed to see Garrison she felt better. Nonetheless, she was a little tense. What would people think?

Lyman Beecher's sermon was aimed at the Unitarians. "The newspapers denounce me," he said. "I find that quite encouraging, for whenever I hit the mark the feathers fly. Of course, I have to be careful. Years ago, I threw a book at a skunk and I've learned from experience . . ."

This morning he spoke louder than usual, pounded the pulpit in the manner of a blacksmith, and waved his hands and arms as if he were fighting a cloud of attacking hornets. Spellbound, Harriet moistened her lips. Thoroughly intrigued, she forgot all about the wayward curl until she saw her reflection in the mirror at home.

In the midst of family dinner, Lyman complained, "I wasn't at my best this morning."

"Oh, I thought you did very well," replied Mrs. Beecher. "I've never seen you so animated."

"Humph! Animated? Yes, I was animated." He continued to eat for a while, then said, "Remember: The emptier the wagon, the louder it rattles."

Everyone laughed and Harriet reached for the mashed potatoes.

The next Sunday the meetinghouse was crammed to standing room only. Harriet's curls were in place and her dress was impeccable. But Garrison was not present; nor did he show up the next Sunday nor the next. After he had missed seven Sundays, Harriet approached her father.

"Garrison is a very vigorous young man," replied Lyman. "I also have missed him. I've heard he's been visiting various churches. Let's pray that he doesn't get mixed up with the Unitarians!"

Harriet's "vacation" in Boston soon came to an end and she returned to Hartford. "I don't know what I'd do without you," Catherine confessed as her younger sister stepped off the stage. "We've been having a revival. Many have been converted, and I'm planning a new building. All of us will have to keep our candles burning."

Catherine, Harriet discovered, had an increasing assurance that her calling in life was to promote "female" education. Energized by this absolute confidence, her older sister made use of every second of the day; and she saw to it that her teachers did the same. She never asked anyone to do what she was unwilling to do. Nonetheless, her actions made it apparent that she considered any candle that was not burning simultaneously on both ends an unworthy candle.

Harriet not only taught classes, but was also enrolled. In her book, *True Remedy for the Wrongs of Women,* Catherine described a typical day for her teachers as they taught in the crowded basement room, which was all she could afford in the beginning:

> Upon entering the school they commenced . . . the business of keeping order. . . . To this distracting employment was added the labor of hearing a succession of classes at the rate of one every eight, ten, or fifteen minutes. . . .

> By the time the duties of the day were over, the care of governing, the vexations of irregularities and mischief, and the sickness of heart occasioned by feeling that nothing was done well were sufficient to exhaust the animal strength and spirits, and nothing more could be attempted till the next day rose to witness the same round of duties.

Each night when Harriet prepared for bed she was utterly exhausted. In addition she faced the heart-rending fact that she was not able to ascertain what God wanted her to do with her life. Again and again she prayed, "Dear Lord, I long to do Thy will. Please show me what I'm to do with my life. More than anything, I want to be obedient to Thy will."

But even though she always felt a calm assurance after each session of prayer, she never received any clear-cut direction. Her frustrations continued to deepen. Often, in despair she wished she'd never been born. Sometimes for days she couldn't get to sleep until midnight. After one horrible night of rolling and tossing, she barged into her father's study.

"Papa," she wailed, "I wish the Lord would show me what I'm to do with my life. I'm utterly confused. Catherine has received her assignment and so has Henry Ward, Edward, William H. and Mama. But even though I pray by the hour and search the Bible, I don't receive a hint—not even a hint— as to what God wants me to do." She broke down and wept. "Pa, I'm trapped. Yes, I'm trapped!"

Lyman smiled. Putting an arm around her shoulder, he said, "God loves you. He planted you in His kingdom for a purpose. Flowers take time to grow. And sometimes, as you've noticed, a tree bears more fruit after it's been injured." He pulled her close.

"Do you mean God allows me to be frustrated for a purpose?"

"I don't know. God allowed the Jews to work as slaves in

Egypt; and He allowed them to be exiled in Babylon. He also allowed me to be orphaned when I was born, and for you to lose your mother."

Harriet silently wept for a long moment. Then she asked, "Papa, when the Lord does give me an assignment—if He ever does!—will I be successful?"

"Of course you'll be successful. But you'll only be successful in His way. Isaiah taught us that God's ways are not our ways."

Harriet dabbed at her eyes again and blew her nose. "It's terrible to be unwanted," she groaned. "It's like being in hell."

Lyman removed his spectacles. After moistening them with his breath, he carefully polished each lense. Chin cupped in his hand, he said, "Hattie, God has a plan for you, just as He has a plan for each of my children. Like you, Henry Ward was frustrated. He wanted to go to sea. But now that he's been converted, he has felt God's definite call to the ministry. I'm certain that you're being prepared for something." Putting on his spectacles he continued:

"Both my father and grandfather were blacksmiths. They were experts in fitting horseshoes and beating iron into all sorts of useful shapes. But before they reached for their hammers, they always heated the iron until it was red, and, sometimes, even white hot. I know, for I used to crank the bellows for them."

"Do you mean the Lord allows me to be in such confusion for a reason?" Harriet cried.

"I don't know. He allowed Catherine's fiancé to be drowned; and now Catherine is being acclaimed as a pioneer in female education. Someday books will be written about Catherine. I'm mighty proud of her." He took off his glasses, twirled them around with his fingers, and then put them on again. "It may be, Hattie, that God wants you to be a writer. You have a way with words, and you have a strong memory. If you were a writer, how would you describe a frustrated person if you had never been frustrated?"

Harriet sighed. "I still wish the Lord would speak to me as clearly as He spoke to Isaiah."

Lyman chuckled. "Do you remember when you were a little girl how you and some of the others ate the roots of some of your mother's flowers?"

"We thought they were onions!"

"And what did your mother say?"

"*That* I'll never forget even if I live to be one hundred. She said, 'My dear children, what you have done makes mama very unhappy. Those were roots of beautiful flowers, not onion roots.' "

Lyman Beecher opened his Bible. "Now listen to what Jesus said, 'Except a corn of wheat fall into the ground and die, it abideth alone: but if it die, it bringeth forth much fruit' (John 12:24). Do you believe that?"

"Yes, of course. But it seems to me that I'm like a grain of wheat that fell into the ground upside down."

They both laughed. Becoming serious, Harriet then asked, choosing her words carefully, "Papa, do you think that if God calls a person to a certain task, and he faithfully performs it, he will succeed?"

"Of course." He studied her suspiciously.

"Do you remember when you preached a sermon against dueling?"

"I do. And that sermon was printed and forty thousand copies of it were distributed."

"Yes, I've read it. It was a great sermon. But, Papa, listen to this: Last year when Andrew Jackson was campaigning to be president, his opponent published a pamphlet against him. It was titled 'The Indiscretions of Andrew Jackson.' I read that as well, and it stated that between the age of 23 and 60 he had been engaged in fourteen duels. He even killed a man in a duel. Let me quote what it said: 'This hero of New Orleans has been envolved in 103 hostile encounters as a participant, second, or a member of the dueling party.'[1] And now this man is our president!"

Lyman Beecher chuckled. "Hattie, you've done your research. But you are forgetting one thing. When God assigns a task to a person, that person should respond. But God is sovereign. He never tells us the precise date His assignment will be fulfilled. I have learned that He will fulfill His will when He decides to fulfill His will. Remember, Paul wrote, 'I have planted, Apollos watered; but God gave the increase' (1 Cor. 3:6). God prepared me and inspired me to preach that sermon; and God will put an end to dueling when He decides to put an end to dueling. And He will also end slavery when it is His will to end slavery."

"If that is so, why should we seek to accomplish anything?"

"Because God wants us to obey Him; and, Hattie, the hap-

---

[1]*North American Duels*, p. 190

piest people are those who respond to His commands. Our works and His will must go together. James, the half brother of Jesus, wrote: 'For as the body without the spirit is dead, so faith without works is dead also' (James 2:26). Luther didn't like that passage, and it is not a favorite with Old Light Calvinists. Nevertheless, it's true! Now Hattie, I must get to work on completing my pamphlet, *A Plea for the West*."

Dipping his goose-quill into the ink, he began to write.

Harriet's gloom continued to haunt her. And her feeling of discouragement darkened when she considered the great success her brother Edward was enjoying. He had been the valedictorian of his class at Yale in 1822, attended seminary, was acclaimed as an athlete, and was called to the pastorate of the Park Street Church in Boston when he was only twenty-three. She had a deep affection for her distinguished brother. He had helped solve some of her spiritual problems. She frequently went to hear him at the Park Street Church; and sometimes after the service she would slip over to the nearby Old Granary Burying Ground and pay her respects to Paul Revere, Samuel Adams, the victims of the Boston Massacre, and others who were buried there.

Harriet was proud of Edward. But when she thought of his accomplishments and compared them with her own, she felt very unworthy. In the depths of one of her days of acute hypochondria, she wrote to Catherine and described the despair that had gripped her:

> I don't know as I am fit for anything, and I have thought that I could wish to die young, and let the remembrance of me and my faults perish in the grave, rather than live, as I fear I do, a trouble to everyone. You don't know how perfectly wretched I often feel: so useless, so weak, so destitute of all energy. Mama often tells me that I am a strange, inconsistent being. Sometimes I cannot sleep, and have groaned and cried till midnight, while in the daytime I've tried to appear cheerful, and succeeded so well that papa reproved me for laughing too much. I was so absent sometimes that I made strange mistakes, and then they all laughed at me, and I laughed, too, though I felt I should go distracted. I wrote rules; made out a regular system for dividing my time; but my feelings vary so much that it is almost impossible for me to be regular.[2]

Harriet's despair continued to torment her. Then her father inadvertently altered the trend of her thoughts by relat-

---

[2] *Life and Letters of Harriet Beecher Stowe*, p. 63.

ing an experience he had just had. "William Lloyd Garrison came to see me this morning," he said.

"He did?" Harriet's eyes widened.

"Yes. When he first came to Boston he got a job on the *National Philanthropist*. At first he merely set the type. Then he began to write editorials. He's full of energy. Soon, he began to fight liquor tooth and nail. I still remember one of his poems:

> What is the cause of every ill?
> That does with pain the body fill?
> It is the oft repeated gill
> Of Whiskey. . . .

"That poem was all right, and he did a lot of good fighting the traffic. But now Benjamin Lundy has given him a new cause to fight. He's persuaded him to become an abolitionist!" Lyman scowled.

"Why did he come to see you?" Harriet leaned forward.

"Because he wants me to support abolition."

"And what did you tell him?" Harriet spoke anxiously.

"I told him I had too many irons in the fire. That annoyed him. His eyes burning behind those steel-rimmed spectacles of his, he replied, 'You'd better let all your irons burn rather than to neglect your duty to the slave.'

"I didn't appreciate that. But I do admire his energy. And so I replied, 'Your zeal is commendable, but you are misguided.' Garrison didn't like that very well. He left in a huff."

"How do you think we should stop slavery?"

"We can stop it only by changing people's hearts. And we can change their hearts only by helping them to see that it is wrong. Do you remember how the auctioneer in the story Sam told you wept when he saw the boy torn from his mother's arms. It might be—" He paused in deep thought. "It might be that if someone could dramatize the evils of slavery they might—just might—shake slavers up until they'd be willing to free their slaves. Slavery, Hattie, is the worst problem we are now facing."

"Couldn't a law be passed that would stop it?"

"A law?" her father stared. "No, a law would never do any good. Not a bit of good. It would be easy to get one on the books. But no one would obey it. In 1728 when the British were in Boston, the butchers were annoyed by packs of dogs that bothered them when they slaughtered animals—often in the streets. Those dogs became very skillful in running off with their meat. The result? They passed a law that no one could have a dog more than ten inches high. Did anyone obey it? Of course not. Even Sam Adams had a Newfoundland. He named it Queque. Whenever the monster saw a redcoat, it took after him. He reached for his pen. "I think the real solution to slavery is to send all the present slaves back to Africa."

Deep in thought, Harriet returned to her room. Letting her Bible fall open to any place, it automatically opened to the sixth chapter of Isaiah. There she reread, perhaps for the one hundredth time, the last line of the eighth verse: "Then said I, Here am I; send me." Oh, how she wished she could utter those same words in response to a definite assignment! Pondering over them, she climbed the steps to her father's study.

"Hattie," he said, as he dipped his quill, "I'm absolutely rushed. I can't put off the printer another minute. He's already screaming. I have only about ten more sentences to write."

Harriet watched as his pen skimmed over the paper. As he wrote he mumbled to himself. Again and again he dipped into the ink. Then he crossed out a line, rewrote it, and stacked his papers together. "Well, that's that," he said triumphantly. He dumped the pile in his hat, mistakenly put on another hat, and hurried down the steps.

After he had disappeared, Harriet suddenly noticed that his manuscript was in his other hat, the one he generally wore to church on Sunday. Staring at it, she made up her mind in a fraction of a second. Tucking the hat under her arm, she rushed down the steps.

11

The Lure of the West

Lyman Beecher was searching frantically for his manuscript when Harriet burst into the printing office. "Papa, you put on the wrong hat!" she exclaimed, handing it to him.

Her father grabbed it, fished out the manuscript, and passed it on to the printer. Pulling Harriet close, he declared, "Hattie, you're absolutely indispensable!"

"I'm glad I have *some* talent," she laughed, leading the way down the steps. Once on the street she asked. "Papa, why are you so excited about the West?"

Quickening his pace, he confessed, "The West has everything. Rivers. Fertile soil. Trees. Game. Fish. It's a place of new beginnings. It's a place for pioneers. You know, your uncle, Sam Foote, has been all over the world. He has plenty of money. He can live anywhere he wants to live. And where has he chosen to spend his last years? Cincinnati—the gateway to both the South and Western Territories. And now, Uncle John has joined him.

"The East has been ruined by Unitarians and Catholics. The West is fresh new country. It's like New England was when the Pilgrim Fathers first arrived. If we can get the true gospel planted there, it will spread and save America. Thanks to the Missouri Compromise of Henry Clay, the Western Territories are still free from the curse of slavery."

After striding along in silence for another block, Lyman spoke again, "Hattie, I'm going to let you in on a secret. Some of the leaders at Park Street are unhappy with Edward. They say he's too much like me!" He laughed. "The truth is they don't like our New Light ideas. That door seems to be closing to him. But a much bigger one is opening." Stopping in front of a vacant lot, and glancing about to make certain no one could overhear, he lowered his voice and continued in an extremely confidential manner, "A group of seven Yale students has covenanted to spend their lives in spreading the gospel and education in the West. Their first project is to found a college in Jacksonville, Illinois. They've already secured a large building.

"When they approached Dr. Day [president of Yale Theological Seminary] for his candid advice in securing a president, he suggested your brother Edward."

"Do you think he'll accept?" asked Harriet a little amazed.

"Of course. But that isn't all. Rumors keep coming my way that a wealthy man in New York wants to sponsor a seminary in Cincinnati. And, not only are they going ahead with their plans, they have already secured the land, and they want me to be the first president."

"Are you going to accept their offer?"

"If the terms are right, and the way is clear, and if it's the Lord's will, I'll seriously consider such a call if I receive it in black and white. In the meantime we must pray that the heavenly Father will have His way."

"Do you hope that it will be His will for you to go?" pressed Harriet a little mischievously.

"Well, yes I do." He picked up a stick that had fallen across the sidewalk and tossed it to one side. "Some of the promoters are calling Cincinnati the Athens of the West. If I go, I hope most of the children will go with me. A Beecher invasion of the West could do a lot of good. I'd like to preach some New Light ideas on a new Mars Hill."

"Do you mean you feel like Abraham when he received his call to move to the Promised Land?" teased Harriet.

"In a way, I do."

They both laughed.

During the following summer weeks as Harriet noticed the eagerness with which her father studied the mail, she also prayed for directions. "Oh, Lord," she pleaded every night, "show me how I can make my life useful."

On September 14, 1830, a Tuesday she would never forget, Harriet noticed an article in the *Advertizer* about *Old Ironsides*. Intrigued, she rushed up to her father's study. "Just listen to this, Papa," she said. Standing in the doorway, and holding the newspaper to the light, she read:

It has been affirmed on good authority that the Secretary of the Navy has recommended to the Board Navy Commissioners to dispose of the frigate Constitution. Since it has been understood that such a step was in contemplation we have heard but one opinion expressed, and that in decided approbation of the measure. Such a national pride as Old Ironsides is should never by any act of our government cease to belong to the Navy. . . . In England it was lately determined by the Admiralty to cut the Victory, a one-hundred gun ship (which it will be recollected bore the flag of Lord Nelson at the battle of Trafalgar), down to seventy-four, but so loud were the lamentations of the people upon the proposed measure that the intention was abandoned. We confidently anticipate that the Secretary of the Navy will in like manner consult the general wish in regard to the Constitution, and either let her remain in ordinary or rebuild her whenever the public service may require. (The news item was credited to the *New York Journal of Commerce*.)

Lyman Beecher laid down his goose-quill and stared. "That is just terrible," he said. "I once saw the Constitution in dock and I was so impressed I wept. Old Ironsides is a monument to American gallantry. She got that name in Madison's War (the War of 1812). During a battle with the British ship *Guerrière*, a cannonball struck her side and fell into the sea. Stunned by what he had seen, a seaman shouted, 'Huzza, her sides are made of iron.' "

Thoroughly excited, Lyman got up and paced back and forth. "If the Secretary does away with Old Ironsides," he exploded, "it will be like ripping a star out of Old Glory!"

During the rest of the day whenever Harriet met her father, he had an additional comment about the tragedy of losing Old Ironsides. At lunch, he said, "Old Ironsides showed her stamina in our war with Tripoly. Had it not been for her and her gallant men that war would have dragged on for a long time."

At supper, he added, "Old Ironsides didn't fail us. Her sails were shredded by cannon fire; her decks were reddened by heroes' blood. But now we're failing Old Ironsides! Something must be done about this tragedy. But what, I don't know." He pounded the table with such a thump the knives and forks jumped.

The next day Harriet grabbed the *Advertizer* the moment it arrived. As she studied it, her eyes caught fire. Rushing upstairs she confronted her father. "Listen to this," she all but shouted, "someone else is also disturbed about the fate of Old Ironsides." With a quivering voice, she read:

> Ay, tear her tattered ensign down!
>   Long has it waved on high,
> And many an eye has danced to see
>   That banner in the sky;
> Beneath it rung the battle shout,
>   And burst the cannon's roar;—
> The meteor of the ocean air
>   Shall sweep the clouds no more.
>
> Her deck, once red with heroe's blood,
>   Where knelt the vanquished foe,
> When winds were hurrying o'er the flood,
>   And waves were white below,
> No more shall feel the victor's tread,
>   Or know the conquered knee,—
> The harpies of the shore shall pluck
>   The eagle of the sea!
>
> Oh, better that her shattered hulk
>   Should sink beneath the wave;
> Her thunders shook the mighty deep,
>   And there should be her grave;
> Nail to the mast her holy flag,
>   Set every threadbare sail,
> And give her to the god of storms,
>   The lightning and the gale!

After wiping his eyes and blowing his nose, her father asked, "And who wrote that?"

"I don't know. It's simply signed 'H'."

"Ah, then I know who it is. It's Oliver Wendell Holmes! His father, Dr. Abiel Holmes, and I were good friends. He was a staunch Congregational preacher and we often exchanged pulpits. But Oliver Wendell has become a Unitarian." He sighed. "Even so, he wrote a stirring poem. I hope some other newspapers copy it, and it saves Old Ironsides. But I doubt that it will. Old Ironsides, I'm afraid, is doomed."

Unable to forget the stirring lines, Harriet began to investigate the circumstances under which it was written. To her amazement, she learned that after reading about the proposed fate of Old Ironsides, Oliver Wendell Holmes had been so stirred he had dashed off the poem while standing by a window. She also learned that he had just turned twenty-one and was less than two years older than she.

But Harriet didn't have time to lament that she was merely an accomplished hat-finder, while this young medical student was already a successful poet. She had to pack her things and once again head back to Hartford.

"A couple of weeks ago I had a most interesting visitor," said Catherine one day over a cup of tea. "His name is James G. Birney, from Huntsville, Alabama. He was born in Danville, Kentucky, and is quite wealthy. And—"

"What did he want?" interrupted Harriet, wondering if her sister was on the verge of a new romance.

Catherine thoughtfully stirred her tea. "Birney used to be a slaveholder. Then he freed his slaves. For a time he believed like Father that all slaves should be returned to Africa and colonized. But I think he's given up that idea. He is a brilliant man and has a degree from Princeton. Right now he's establishing the Huntsville Female Academy. He wanted me to recommend some teachers." She poured some tea into Harriet's cup. "I recommended Miss Brown, Miss Southmayd, and Miss Baldwin. I don't know if he'll call them."

"How old is he?"

"He's a little younger than I am—"

"Mmmm. That means he's in his late twenties."

"Hattie, I'm not interested in marriage if that's what you're thinking. My whole heart is wrapped up in one idea: female education! Just think, in our time women never go to college; they're not allowed to vote; and those who do work are confined to the most menial jobs. I'm working eight days a week for the time when there'll be women doctors, women lawyers, women senators. Moreover, I'm prepared to lead the way."

Harriet laughed. "You sound just like Pa and all the other Beechers. All of you are determined to change the world—"

"And why not? If God be for us, who can be against us! We have a big job to do and we all must do our part." Catherine stood up. "Not to change the subject, but, Hattie, I've been wondering if you have seen that poem about Old Ironsides? It seems to have been republished in all the newspapers."

"Yes, I've seen it and I think it's great. Do you think it'll save the old ship?"

"I don't know. It may. Words, Hattie, have power. And when properly put together words have dynamic power. John even wrote, 'In the beginning was the Word' (John 1:1)."

As summer eased into fall and fall hardened into winter,

Harriet kept praying that God would show her what she was
to do with her life. But even though she reminded the Lord
that she was going on twenty, the only response she received
was that she should keep going. In addition to this frustra-
tion, she failed to attract the attention of a single young man.
She changed her hairdos, and even acted as if she were as
dull as everyone else. Nothing worked. Her only joyful companion was Georgiana.

When school let out, Harriet returned to Boston. There,
she learned that her father had endured a seeming-tragedy.
The Hanover meetinghouse had burned to the ground. "It
could have been saved," lamented Lyman, "but the firemen
refused to use any of their equipment. A friend told me they
just stood in front and let her burn. And while she burned,
they mocked me by singing:

> While Beecher's church holds out to burn,
> The vilest sinner may return.

"It was a terrible fire; and one of the things that made it
worse was that without knowing it, a merchant who'd rented
one of the missionary rooms had packed it full of liquor. The
alcohol made the fire so hot the steeple split in two."

"And what happened to the organ?"

"It fell into the flames and is completely gone."

"That's terrible."

"We've been using a rented building. But we have full in-
surance and we'll rebuild." Suddenly he began to laugh. "After
she had burned to the ground, I happened to be in a bookstore. There I remarked, 'Well, my old jug's broke, just been
to see it.' Instead of laughing, the people stared at me as if I
were insane."

Harriet frowned as she studied her father. Finally she
said, "Papa, you used to get the hypos every three or four
months. How could you have been so casual when the meetinghouse was utterly destroyed?"

"Easy. I'm doing the work of the Lord. And, Hattie, I've
learned across the years that if one is doing the work of the
Lord, he need not worry. God is sovereign!"

While Lyman Beecher was awaiting a formal call to Cincinnati, William Lloyd Garrison was hurriedly laying the
foundation for his attack on slavery. With the smell of ink on
his hands and the music of a rumbling press in his heart,
he decided that his best move was to publish a radical newspaper which would unite the abolitionists, inspire the

slaves—and convert the masses to his way of thinking.

Garrison had no money, but that didn't stop him. He persuaded the foreman of the *Christian Examiner* to lend him their type in exchange for a day's work. Since the type had to be returned the next day, he had to compose the copy at night, print the paper, replace the type into their trays, and return them in the morning. But having an oversupply of adrenaline, a twenty-four-hour day on an empty stomach didn't bother him.

With his words formed like a hatchet, Garrison set the type for his first editorial in the *Liberator*. Determining the tone for what was to follow, he wrote:

> On this subject, I do not wish to think, or speak, or write, with moderation. No! no! Tell a man whose house is on fire to give a moderate alarm; tell him to moderately rescue his wife from the hands of the ravisher; tell the mother to gradually extricate her babe from the fire into which it has fallen—but urge me not to use moderation in a cause like the present. I am in earnest—I will not equivocate—I will not excuse—I will not retreat a single inch—AND I WILL BE HEARD.

That first issue was printed on a format that measured fourteen by nine and a quarter inches. There were only 400 copies; and the editorial, appearing on page one, was slightly askew. (By the end of two years it had only attained fifty subscribers.) But the small circulation didn't worry Garrison. He knew that a small flame can start a big fire. And he determined to start a big fire.

With incredible genius for publicity, Garrison mailed copies to those papers he knew disagreed with him—especially to those in the deep south. Many southern editors denounced him with heated invective. Others could use strong language, but few could match Garrison. In answer to one editorial, he replied, "My contempt of it is unutterable. Nothing but my own death, or want of patronage, shall stop the *Liberator*."

Arthur Tappan, a New York City businessman who had earned a fortune with cash-and-carry stores, was attracted to Garrison and supplied him with the necessary funds.

Garrison did not believe in violence; and he denounced those who did. But when on August 31, 1831, a group of from fifty to seventy-five slaves who had been inspired by the black prophet, Nat Turner, went on a rampage in Virginia and killed sixty-one whites, many pointed fingers at Garrison.

Lyman Beecher was aware of all these things, but his heart was set on establishing a seminary in Cincinnati, and that project claimed his full attention. The agent of the projected seminary was satisfied that Lyman Beecher was the only one who could make the school a success. He had written to his superiors:

> After much consultation it appeared to be the common impression . . . that Doctor Beecher of Boston, if he could be obtained, would be the best man. That, as he is the most prominent, popular and powerful preacher in the nation, he would immediately give character elevation and success to our seminary, draw together young men from every part of our country, secure the confidence and cooperation of the ministers and churches both east and west of the Alleghany Mountains, and awaken a general interest in the old state in behalf of the West.

Beecher was excited by the call. Still, persuaded by his congregation that he must remain with them until the building was completed, he declined. The following year he was approached again. This time it was explained that Arthur Tappan, the man who was supporting Garrison's *Liberator*, had offered a large sum for the seminary, provided Beecher could be secured to be president.

Lyman was flattered. Yet he had a problem. "I should exceedingly depreciate the annual drilling of a class one year in biblical literature, the next in theology, and lastly in composition and eloquence—one stratum of knowledge piled on another without any cement between is about as wise as if a man should eat his meat one day, his vegetables the next, and his pies and cake on the third." He then went on to explain that he would like to pastor a congregation while he was also serving as president of the seminary.

All of this was agreeable to the trustees; and so, in due time, it was arranged for Beecher to also be the pastor of the Second Presbyterian Church of Cincinnati. Lyman was excited by his opportunity, but since all arrangements had been by mail, and since his acceptance meant severing all that was dear to him, he decided to take Catherine with him and view the city with his own eyes before he made his ultimate decision. Boarding a stage in Boston, they went to Wheeling, and then from there took a riverboat down the Ohio to Cincinnati.

With both her father and oldest sister gone, Harriet succumbed to an acute state of hypochondria. Almost wishing she were dead, she called on Georgiana. "Everyone is making a success but me," she wailed.

"You're only twenty-two," comforted her friend.

"Yes, I'm twenty-two!" She nodded her head vigorously. "What have I accomplished? Nothing. Absolutely nothing. Zero. I've never even had a date. I'm just an unwanted, good-for-nothing nobody. Oh, yes, I've accomplished one thing. I'm an expert hat-finder."

They both laughed.

"Sarah didn't have her baby until she was ninety."

"Maybe so, but she was beautiful and was married when she was quite young. Mary became the mother of Jesus when she was in her teens and Joan of Arc threw the English out of France before she was eighteen."

Georgiana stood up. "Let me brew you some tea. That'll make you feel better. Then I'll fix your hair. Any suggestions?"

"Yes. Part it in the center, sweep it to the back of my head, and make a lot of ringlets. I'll then put a metal band over the top of my forehead."

"Are you teasing?" Georgiana frowned.

"No, I'm no teasing. I know that'll make me look as if I'm in my thirties." She sighed. "But what's the difference? I'm not even a has-been. I'm a never was!"

Two hours after Georgiana had started, Harriet was the proud possessor of a dozen curls—six on each side. After peering in the mirror, Harriet remarked, "You did a good job, considering what you had to work with."

Catherine was delighted with Cincinnati. In a letter to Harriet she expressed her enthusiasm. "We reached here in three days from Wheeling. The next day father and I with three gentlemen walked out to Walnut Hills. The site of the seminary is very beautiful and picturesque, though I was disappointed to find that both the river and city are hidden by intervening hills. I never saw a place so capable as being rendered a Paradise. The seminary is located on a farm of one hundred and twenty acres of fine land, with groves of trees around it.

"It seems to me that everybody I used to know is here or coming here. Besides our two uncles, there is Ned King, an old Litchfield beau, and Mother's own cousin, now General King; Cousin E. Tuthill; Abraham Chittenden's family from Guilford; Mrs. James Butler, from Litchfield; Mr. and Mrs.

Bingham, with whom we used to board at Dr. Strong's, and diverse others.

"Yesterday Father preached in the morning and evening to crowded houses.

"As to Father, I never saw such a field of usefulness and influences as is offered here. I see no difficulties or objections; everything is ready and everybody gives a welcome except Dr. Wilson's folks, and they are finding that it is wisest and best to be still, and we hope that before a great while they will be *friendly*. Father is determined to get acquainted with Dr. Wilson, and to be *friendly* with him, and I think he will succeed."

As Harriet read and reread that last paragraph she wondered why Catherine had underlined the word "friendly." In her heart, she knew that one of the reasons her father was anxious to leave Boston was to escape the Unitarians. Could it be that he would be stepping from the skillet into the fire? Trying not be pessimistic, she folded the letter and filed it away in her drawer.

12
Cincinnati

With customary skill at generating enthusiasm, Dr. Beecher persuaded all of his available children that Cincinnati was the Jerusalem of the Promised Land, and that they should move there immediately.

Five Beechers found the move impossible. Married to Thomas C. Perkins, a successful lawyer, Mary Foote was firmly established in Hartford. William H. was busy in his first pastorate in Rhode Island. Charles and Henry Ward were completing their schooling in the East, while Edward was already in the West, serving as president of Illinois College in Jacksonville.

Although five could not go, the remaining nine were most eager to be a part of the Beecher invasion of the West. Those nine were Lyman, his wife, Esther (his half sister), Catherine, Harriet and George, together with the second Mrs. Beecher's children: Isabella, Thomas, and James. According to the preacher's plans, they would first travel to New York City where he would set out to raise two twenty-thousand-dollar endowments in order to produce the income to support two additional professors, one of which was to be Calvin Stowe.

The City, sometimes referred to as Babylon on the Hudson, fascinated all the Beechers—especially Harriet. In a letter, she wrote: "Father is all in his own element, dipping into books; consulting authorities for his oration, going round here and there, begging, borrowing and spoiling the Egyptians, delighted with past success and confident of the future."

From New York City, the Beecher "troops" raided Philadelphia. There, Dr. Beecher spoke to packed churches, contacted rich men, and raised more money. Although weary of all the hurry, the clan became more enthusiastic by the day. As their train puffed out of the City of Brotherly Love, twenty-three-year-old George started all the Beechers singing; and a little later he got them distributing tracts. At an inn in Downington, about thirty miles east of Philadelphia, Harriet addressed a letter to Georgiana.

"Here we all are," she wrote. "Noah and his wife and his sons and daughters, with cattle and creeping things, all dropped down in front of this tavern. If today is a fair specimen of our journey, it will be very pleasant: obliging driver, good roads, good spirits, good dinner, fine scenery, and now and then some psalms and hymns and spiritual songs."

Several homes in Wheeling were opened to them and the churches were crowded where Lyman spoke. But all was not tranquility. The newspapers screamed with the story that Cincinnati had been stricken with an epidemic of cholera. "The streets are covered with a pall of smoke," reported a recent escapee. "They are burning bituminous coal so that the smoke will kill the disease. I saw stacks and stacks of coffins."

"What are we to do?" asked Mrs. Beecher, concern written on her face.

"We'll remain in Wheeling until the panic is over," assured Lyman. "The Lord will direct our steps."

The local Congregational and Presbyterian congregations were delighted that the Beechers would remain. Even though Beecher's New Light theology seemed a little strange, the people filled the meetinghouses, made pledges, and enrolled their sons in the new seminary.

While they awaited news that the epidemic had abated, Harriet became excited over a news item in one of the papers. "Listen to this," she cried. "Old Ironsides will be spared!"

Startled, Lyman grabbed the paper. Out loud, he read the item: "Due to pressure brought about by the reprinting of Oliver Wendell Holmes' poem, 'Old Ironsides,' in newspapers all over the country, the Navy has decided to save The Constitution."

After folding the paper and swatting a fly that had settled on Harriet's shoulder, he concluded, "That shows the power of the pen."

"But we still have dueling even though they printed forty thousand copies of your sermon," commented Harriet somewhat mockingly.

Beecher held up his palms. "Ah, but remember the Bible says: 'Cast thy bread upon the waters: for thou shalt find it after many days' (Eccles. 11:1)." A confident smile brightened his face.

"Maybe so, but Andrew Jackson, the man who killed his enemy in a duel, is still president," scoffed Harriet.

"Don't you have faith?"

"I do. I'm just teasing."

Following two weeks of waiting, the news from Cincinnati was that the epidemic was lifting. Encouraged by this, Lyman chartered a stagecoach to complete the journey. Packed with Beechers and their luggage, the coach jolted southward on a rut-filled, pothole-filled, corrugated road that paralleled the Ohio. In one particular stretch where the coach alternately swayed, bounced, shuddered, got stuck in the mud, and slipped into ditches, Mrs. Beecher eventually asked, "Dearest, why could we not have sailed down the river?"

"Because I wanted us to all be alone and together as a single unit," replied Lyman. "Besides, a little shaking is good for us. It's good for our dyspepsia. In addition, it's free and *it'll help shake the devil out of us,*" he laughed.

Each problem of the journey recorded an indelible memory in Harriet's mind. Years later, she used her memory to brighten a story. She described a region in the West "where the mud is of unfathomable and sublime depth, roads are made of round, rough logs, arranged transversely side by side, and then coated with earth, turf, and whatsoever may come to hand." She also wrote about "the interesting process of pulling down rail fences to pry their carriages out of mudholes."

The difficulties of the way, however, did not squelch all the Beecher optimism and joy. George inspired them to sing even in the roughest places, and when occasion arose they continued to hand out tracts.

Finally, the stagecoach reached Cincinnati on Wednesday, November 14, 1832. Uncle Samuel and Uncle John were prepared to receive them, so all of the Beechers had a comfortable place in which to relax after their long, tiring journey from Wheeling. The smell of smoke from the fire that had been kept burning on numerous street corners in order to dissipate the cholera was still pungent in the air as uniformed blacks carried the Beechers' luggage into their assigned rooms.

While waiting for supper, Harriet noticed an advertisement in bold type on an inside page of a newspaper. Her eyes widened as she read:

NOTICE

The undersigned, having an excellent pack of HOUNDS for trailing and catching runaway slaves, informs the public that his prices in the future will be as follows: For each day employed in hunting or trailing . . . 2 dollars and fifty cents.

For catching slaves . . . 10 dollars. For going over ten miles and catching slaves . . . 20 dollars.

If sent for, the above prices will be exacted in cash. The subscriber resides one and a half miles south of Dadeville, Alabama.

Not believing what she read, Harriet said, "Uncle Samuel, is that sort of thing going on *now*?"

"It is. A friend mailed me that paper from Alabama. But even though Alabama is a long way from here, Kentucky is right across the river. Kentucky is a slave state. Let me show you an advertisement that I clipped out of a Kentucky paper." He withdrew a clipping from his billfold. Harriet felt her heart jump as she scanned the notice.

$750 REWARD!

RAN AWAY from my plantation on the 10th of June, a family of five slaves.

Jim is about 22. His wife, Mary, is about 23. Mary's mother is a very black woman about 60. She has white hair and is stooped. Jim and Mary are quadroons and may pretend they are white. Jim has the letter T branded in his left palm. Their twin girls are about 3 and are also nearly white. Jim and Mary are very intelligent. They can even read.

I will give the above award to anyone who will bring the entire family to me. Or I will pay $75 for the securing of any one of them—dead or alive.

Elijah Dent
Nashville, Tenn.

Trying to keep her voice calm, Harriet asked, "Uncle Samuel, what's a quadroon?"

"A quadroon is a slave with three white grandparents."

"How could that be?"

"Don't you remember the story of your aunt, my sister Mary? She married John Hubbard, a Jamaica planter. When she got to Jamaica she learned that he had fathered a houseful of mulatto children, and that he considered these children his slaves. She was so horrified she left him."

"I remember stories about her. But I was only two when she died." Handing the clipping back to her uncle, she asked another question. "Since slavery is so wicked, why isn't it stopped?"

"Oh, but everyone doesn't think it's wicked! There are many kind slaveholders. Freed slaves have even returned to their masters and asked to be slaves again. Also, there are freed blacks who own their own slaves; and some of *them* are hardhearted."

Harriet shook her head. "There may be kind slavers. Still, slavery is a wicked business."

"I agree. And yet many slavers feel that they are doing the work of the Lord—"

"The work of the Lord?"

"Yes, the work of the Lord! The biggest slave ship in the days of Queen Elizabeth was the *Jesus*, and another was the *John the Baptist*. Many slavers had their slaves baptized before they branded them and loaded them in their ships."

"How horrible!"

"Do you like the hymn, *Amazing Grace*?"

"Of course."

"It was written by John Newton, a former slaver."

"Everyone knows that."

"Yes, but everyone does not know that Newton continued to slave for a long time *after* he was converted."

"After he was converted?" Harriet gasped.

"Yes, after. Sometimes he studied his Bible on his knees in the cabin of his ship while the slaves he had just purchased were screaming in terror as they were being branded."

"That's dreadful!"

Their conversation was interrupted by the butler. "Dinner has been served," said the magnificently uniformed black.

All of the Beechers with the exception of Harriet allowed their plates to be refilled. "Harriet, is anything wrong?" asked her stepmother.

"I—I'm afraid I don't feel very well," replied Harriet.

Harriet enjoyed walking around the city, going down to the docks, watching the slaves whose Kentucky masters rented them out to people in the city. Everything seemed so new and interesting. But she didn't like the sight of the pigs that roamed the streets and left their droppings in whatever place they happened to be. While she and the others were still unsettled, awaiting a place to live, she wrote to her sister in Hartford. "I have much solicitude on Jamie's account," she referred to her four-year-old stepbrother, James, "lest he should form improper intimacies, for yesterday we saw him parading by the house with his arm over the neck of a great hog, apparently on the most amicable terms; and the other day he actually got on the back of one, and rode some distance. So much for allowing these animals to promenade the streets, a particular in which Mrs. Cincinnati has imitated the domestic arrangements of some of her elder sisters, and a very disgusting one it is."

Eventually the Beechers moved into a rental while they awaited the completion of their permanent home. Although Mrs. Beecher hated Cincinnati, she delighted that at least her temporary home was not infected with rats as was the house in Litchfield. Nonetheless, the house which they rented from an old bachelor had problems. Harriet expounded on those problems in a letter to Georgiana.

It is the "most inconvenient, ill-arranged, good-for-nothing, and altogether to be execrated affair that was ever put together. The kitchen is so disposed that it cannot be reached from any part of the house without going into the air. Mother is actually obliged to put on a bonnet and cloak every time she goes into it. In the house are two parlors with folding doors between them. The back parlor has but one window and has its lower half painted to keep out what light there is."

The housing didn't bother Lyman. "Cincinnati," he exulted, "wasn't even incorporated until 1802; and, already in its mere thirty years of existence, it has 30,000 inhabitants— and is still growing." The preacher had a right to be proud, for the young city had ten hotels, forty churches, forty-seven doctors, fifty-six lawyers. Also, there were hospitals, medical schools, and sixty-four weekly mails. (Seventeen arrived by steamboat, eleven by post riders, and thirty-six by stage.) Likewise, there was a fire department which was equipped with hand-pump engines, cisterns filled with emergency water, and wooden mains to transport the water. Better yet, the wooden mains belonged to his brothers-in-law, John P. and Samuel Foote!

Cincinnati was proud of the forthcoming Lane Seminary, so named in honor of the man who had donated the land. It was also proud of the new president and his distinguished daughter, Catherine. One paper boasted that other than Ben Franklin, Lyman Beecher was the most quoted man in America.

Beecher enjoyed his celebrity, even though he knew that the Reverend D. Joshua Lacy Wilson, an Old School Calvinist, and pastor of the First Presbyterian Church, had been so opposed to his appointment he had resigned from the seminary board. Still, as uninhibited as ever, he, the Big Gun of Calvinism, was not afraid to express his views whenever and wherever he chose to express them.

Beecher despised Andrew Jackson, and his reelection that November didn't improve his support for him. The fact that he was a duelist and had bullets of antagonists within his body was like a malignancy in Beecher's system. Nonetheless, his loyalty to the Bible meant that he should pray for him. On a certain Sunday morning, Harriet was delighted to hear him pray, "Oh, Lord, grant that we may not despise our rulers—and grant that they may not act *so we can't help it.*"

Somewhat to her dismay, Catherine discovered that the people in Cincinnati were determined that she, according to them, an authority, should launch a female academy in their midst. She also found that a children's book on geography was desperately needed. Physically exhausted from winding up her affairs in Hartford, she realized that she did not have the strength to undertake both projects at the same time. Ah, but she did have a reliable helper!

Approaching Harriet who was busy mending Jamie's pants, she said, "Hattie, how would you like to write a children's book on geography?"

Harriet made a final stitch as she considered the question. Then, after tucking her needle in a spare patch, she replied, "I'd love to, provided I could use my imagination and make it readable."

Catherine explained both the age and page requirements and Harriet got busy. With access to her father's library and other books, she kept her pen flying. The pages piled up. Soon the modest little book was finished. Within weeks it was accepted by a reliable Cincinnati publisher. The publisher paid cash. Harriet's share was $187. This was the first money she had earned as a writer and she was elated. On March 8, 1833, she noticed an advertisement in the Cincinnati papers. It read:

A NEW GEOGRAPHY
For Children

Corey & Fairbank have in the press
and will publish in a few days, a
GEOGRAPHY FOR CHILDREN
with numerous maps, and engravings,
upon an improved plan
BY CATHERINE E. BEECHER

Puzzled that her name was not in the ad, Harriet felt a stab of disappointment. Then she realized that although she had written the book, it had, indeed, been based on Catherine's plan. With great effort, she tried to console herself that she had not been slighted.

But deep inside, she knew it wasn't quite fair.

13
Semi-Colon Club

When Harriet was asked to join the Semi-Colon Club shortly after her arrival in Cincinnati, she had no idea that the club, along with at least three of its members, would completely change her life. The major thing that impressed her was the club's rather odd name.

Among the members was a rising attorney by the name of Salmon P. Chase. Throughout the city, this slightly balding, square-faced young man, a mere three years older than Harriet, was known for his fairness. But since he defended so many runaways, Kentucky slaveholders sneered at him as "the attorney general of fugitive slaves."

Calvin Stowe and his wife Eliza, daughter of the president of Dartmouth, were also members. Harriet was especially attracted to Eliza. In a letter to Georgiana, she wrote: "Let me introduce you to Mrs. Stowe, a delicate pretty, little woman, with hazel eyes, auburn hair, fair complexion, fine color, a pretty little mouth, and a most interesting simplicity and timidity of manner."

Calvin, a short, stocky man, whose wide face seemed even wider because of soft sideburns, was nine years older than Harriet. He had taught at Bowdoin College, his alma mater, and at Dartmouth. He was now Professor of Biblical Literature at Lane and was famous all over America for his scholarship.

Harriet was intrigued by the way he shortened *expect* to *'spect*. In some of his idiosyncrasies, he reminded her of her father.

But perhaps the most prominent member of the Semi-

Colon Club was Judge James Hall, a writer and editor of the new *Western Monthly Magazine.* The group met each Monday night at 7:30 in Samuel Foote's home. During normal routine, a reader was elected at the beginning of the session. This reader then read stories written by the members. Some were signed. Others were anonymous. Then, after a period of discussion, refreshments were served.

Harriet wrote numerous anonymous selections and was flattered to hear the word genius used during the period of comment. Encouraged, she was excited when Judge Hall offered a prize of fifty dollars for the best story submitted by November 10. When that date came and nothing suitable had been turned in, he advanced the deadline to February 1, 1834.

Pondering over her New England days and the stories her father had told her about Uncle Lot, she secured a fresh pen and began to write. The title was easy. She wrote: A NEW ENGLAND SKETCH by Miss Harriet E. Beecher. The opening lines were also easy:

> And I am to write a story—but of what, and where? Shall it be radiant with the sky of Italy? or eloquent with the beau ideal of Greece? Shall it breathe odor languor from the Orient, or chivalry from the Occident? or gayety from France, or vigor from England? No, no; these are too old—too romance-like—too obviously picturesque for me. No; let me turn to my own land—my own New England; the land of bright fires and strong hearts; the land of deeds and not of words. . . .[1]

As she labored on her story, visualizing the prize and imagining what it would be like in the *Western Monthly Magazine,* she hoped that if she were successful, her name would be used. Moreover, she had cause to hope because when Hall reviewed the geography book in his magazine, he had noted that it was by C. & H. Beecher. The sight of that "& H." sent excitement racing down her spine.

Finally, the story finished, she turned it in. She now had to wait until February 1 to learn the result. And that seemed a dozen eternities away. The time, however, flew by quickly as Catherine kept her busy at her new school. In addition, Theodore Weld, an abolitionist enrolled at Lane, was in the

---

[1] When republished in her collection of stories entitled *Mayflower,* it was renamed Uncle Tim. Later, in the Houghton Mifflin edition, it was changed to Uncle Lot.

process of turning the student body of nearly one hundred into fire-eating abolitionists.

Converted under the ministry of lawyer-turned-evangelist Charles G. Finney, thirty-one-year-old Weld was just as dynamic as his spiritual father. In addition, he concentrated his immense talent into one channel: *immediate abolition.* Inspired by the fact that Cincinnati was just across the river from legal slavery, he determined that the seminary was to be both a terminal in the Underground Railroad and a publishing center for all abolitionists.

At the time he enrolled at Lane, he was the only dedicated abolitionist in the school. Most of the students felt that slavery was wrong, but none of them were quite certain how the system could be changed. There was, however, a colonization society, and many of the students were at least moderately active within this organization.

Weld decided that he would change all of this. Having discovered that William T. Allan, a native of Alabama, had been raised by a slaveholder and was scheduled to inherit slaves, he pursued this friendship. After turning Allan into an abolitionist, he and his convert went after the others. Soon, a large portion of the student body was enrolled in their cause. At this point, Weld approached Dr. Beecher. "We'd like to debate this subject," he said.

Beecher thought it was a good idea and the debates were announced. The *Lane Debates,* as history knows them, continued for eighteen nights. Harriet attended most of them and was deeply impressed. James Bradley, a black student, kept the audience in tears as he related how he had been brought to the United States on a slaver when he was a child; how he was sold to a South Carolina planter, and how that planter had allowed him to work out his freedom.

James A. Thome, a native of Kentucky, told how degrading slavery was to the sons of the planters and sought to prove his point with stirring anecdotes. Others, from various parts of the South, made additional statements—all dramatic.

After the abolitionists had dominated the floor for nine days, the colonizers were given the remaining nine days. But their arguments were neither dramatic nor convincing. At the end of the debates, almost all the students were convinced abolitionists. Elated, Weld wrote to Lewis Tappan, brother of Arthur, "We believe that faith without *works* is dead. We have formed a large efficient organization for elevating the colored people of Cincinnati."

Influenced by Finney, Weld believed that action should be preceded by thorough research. After studying the problem, he informed Lewis Tappan: "Of the almost 3000 blacks in Cincinnati more than three-fourths of the adults are emancipated slaves who worked out their own freedom. I visited this week about 30 families, and found that some members of more than half these families are still in bondage, and the father and children struggling to lay up money enough to purchase their freedom. I found one man who had just finished paying for his wife and five children. Another man and wife who bought themselves some years ago, have been working day and night to purchase their children; they had just redeemed the last! and had paid for themselves and children 1400 dollars! But I cannot tell half, and must stop. After spending three or four hours, and getting facts, I was forced to stop from sheer heartache and agony."[2]

Weld's concern about the blacks was so overwhelming, he devoted every moment he could spare to them. He remembered: "If I ate in the city it was at *their* tables. If I slept in the city it was in *their* homes. If I attended parties, it was *theirs*; weddings—*theirs*; funerals—*theirs*; religious meetings—*theirs*. . . . During the 18 months I spent at Lane Seminary I did not attend Doctor Beecher's Church once."[3]

President Beecher had no racial prejudice. Blacks had lived in his home. But he was a realist and was sensitive to the mores of the times. The seminary was in a precarious financial condition and he did not want to jeopardize its success in any way. He summoned Weld into his office.

"You are taking just the course to defeat your own object," he said in his fatherly way. "If you want to teach colored schools, I can fill your pockets with money; but if you visit colored families, and walk with them in the streets, you will be overwhelmed."

Weld listened respectfully. But he did not agree. His differences with Beecher continued to widen. One night they argued until 2 a.m. without coming to agreement or reaching the slightest compromise.

Watching the dissenting fires growing from a distance, Harriet was concerned. But her main focus remained on whether or not she had won that fifty dollar prize. Waiting

[2]Weld-Grimké Letters, 1, 135. As quoted from *Crusader of Freedom*, by Theodore Weld, p. 73.
[3]Ibid. 1, 273. As quoted from *Crusader of Freedom*, p. 74.

for February 1 to arrive was almost as painful as it had been to await July 4 when she was a child. Finally, the great day arrived. After fixing her hair in a manner to increase her height, she dressed in her finest and headed for the Semi-Colon Club.

Uncle Samuel's house was unusually crowded that evening and Harriet felt a tense feeling of anticipation as she awaited the outcome. After what seemed to her an eternity, Judge Hall stood up. Obviously enjoying the suspense, he prolonged it as much as possible by mentioning the past accomplishments of the club and outlining what he hoped the members would be enabled to accomplish in the future. Then, after removing his spectacles and carefully polishing each lense, he coughed, and acknowledged, "Several of the submissions were unusually fine. They showed strong, native ability. The best one, however, was the one submitted by Harriet Elizabeth Beecher. Will the winner kindly step forward."

Harriet was so excited she almost tripped on her long dress. And her hand trembled as she reached for the fifty dollar check. After thanking Judge Hall, she faced the members. "This is one of the happiest days of my life. I now have a request. I wish all of you would pray that the Lord would guide my life and my pen so that I can be useful in His kingdom."

The story, renamed *A New England Tale*, was the lead story in the April issue of the *Western Monthly Magazine*, filling the entire front page. Her name, Harriet Elizabeth Beecher, had been printed at the top in bold type. Skipping from cloud to cloud, she now dreamed of the future. Within minutes she placed on her desk a new sheet of blank paper.

Quickly, she wrote the title *Aunt Mary*, and began to compose. The first paragraph was easy:

> Since sketching character is the mode, I too take up my pencil, not to make you laugh, though peradventure it may be—to get you to sleep.

After the story was completed, she personally handed it to Judge Hall. Then she spent an almost sleepless night. Would it be accepted? It was. Again there was a fresh check in her hand.

Two stories in a row in the West's leading magazine meant that she had talent! As she smiled at her gray-blue eyes in the mirror, a daring thought widened her smile. Could it be that she might, just might, be another Sir Walter Scott?

Harriet's confidence in herself increased by the day. True, the boys continued to shun her; and she remained the runt of the family. Nonetheless, she was a writer—and her words were being read all over America. Yes, God was opening a door for her to step through. Perhaps the time would come when she would even exchange letters and greetings with the great writers of the world. Her ecstasy, however, came to an abrupt end when she opened the May issue of the *Western Monthly Magazine.*

There, before her, was a vicious attack on the student body at Lane. Obviously incensed at the way the students were fraternizing with the blacks, the writer used such colorful words as "embryo clergymen," "precocious undergraduates" and accused them of uttering "sophomoric declamations." When she showed the column to her father, he became very upset.

"Maybe we should not have had those debates," suggested Harriet.

"You may be right," replied her father.

Infuriated, Weld replied to the attack in a column in the *Cincinnati Journal.* Following some strong, defensive words, he asked: "Whom does it behoove to keep his heart in contact with the woes and guilt of a perishing world if not the student who is preparing for the ministry?" He concluded: "Through the grace of God, the history of the next five years will teach this lesson to the most reluctant learner."[4]

Although Ohio was not a slave state, Cincinnati had a large proslavery element; and this group was so stirred by what the students were doing that many of them threatened to march on the school. Alarmed, Lyman Beecher faced the entire student body. Using carefully chosen words, he assured them that they were right, slavery was wrong, the blacks should be helped; but, he insisted, they were ahead of their time. He advised them to go slowly and quoted Ecclesiastes 1:1—"To everything there is a season, and a time to every purpose under the heaven."

The more radical of the student-abolitionists disagreed. Elizur Wright sneered: "The young men . . . were not guilty of doing wrong, but of doing *right* TOO SOON."[5]

Hoping to calm the tempest, Beecher mounted his pulpit

---

[4]*Liberator,* June 14, 1834.
[5]Annual Report of the American Antislavery Society, 1835. Both quotes from *Crusader of Freedom,* p. 77.

in the Second Presbyterian Church and preached on why he believed in the colonization of the slaves. The sermon was impressive, but many of the citizens with slave-owning relatives across the river in Kentucky were not impressed.

When summer came, all of the faculty with the exception of Calvin left in order to rest and raise money for the school. Beecher hoped that during the summer vacation calm would be restored to both the school and the city. His hopes were in vain. Since many of the students could not afford to go home, they remained in Cincinnati and spent most of their time cultivating and aiding the blacks. As they visited in their homes, attended their churches, walked with them down the streets, and were guests at their tables, the flames beneath the proslavery boiler of discontent flamed higher and became more intense. Bystanders looked on awaiting the inevitable explosion.

Dismayed, Harriet knew that she had to get out of Cincinnati for a while in order to retain her sanity. Henry Ward's impending graduation from Amherst that June provided the excuse. After making a new dress, she took the stage to Toledo, crossed Lake Erie by steamboat, transferred to another stage at Buffalo, and continued on to Massachusetts.

Harriet was delighted to learn that although Henry Ward had not graduated at the top of his class, he had overcome his thickness of speech, was very popular—and had become an effective preacher. She was also happy to learn that he would be enrolling at Lane that fall.

While visiting relatives, stopping at Niagara Falls, and viewing other sites, Harriet received a letter filled with disturbing news. Cholera had again broken out in Cincinnati and Eliza Stowe was not well. Remembering the fine times she had had with the little woman with the hazel eyes, Harriet felt impelled to pray for her. A few days later, a letter arrived with the news that Eliza had died. Back in Cincinnati, Harriet called on Calvin to comfort him.

"When I knew that she was stricken, I wept out loud," said Calvin. Removing his spectacles he wiped his eyes. "But Eliza—God bless her!—Eliza murmured, 'Don't weep for me. Just repeat the 14th and 15th chapters of John.' While I was doing that, her eyes followed each movement of my lips. As the end drew near, she exclaimed, 'Oh, joy—joy unspeakable and full of glory—full of glory!' Her final words were, 'I am a lamb.' I believe, Hattie, she must have been thinking about the 23rd psalm. It was one of her favorite psalms."

As they continued to visit, Calvin pointed to a large portrait of Eliza hanging on the wall. "I'll never forget her," he murmured. "She was the angel of my life."

Calvin Stowe had other reasons as well to be discouraged. During the middle of August, some of the extreme abolitionist students had staged a party for black women on the Lane campus. This had so enraged the public; some had threatened to burn the school down. Alarmed, the Board of Trustees had decreed that the Lane Anti-Slavery Society, created by Weld, was no more. They also insisted that the slavery issue should not be discussed in any of the seminary rooms—not even across the table at mealtime. Moreover, to enforce their restrictions, and to let the public know what was being done, they published their restrictions in the *Cincinnati Daily Gazette.*

This hot news item was copied by other papers throughout the nation. Eventually, William Lloyd Garrison denounced the school in *The Liberator.* He wrote: "Lane Seminary is now to be regarded as strictly a Bastile of oppression—a spiritual Inquisition."

Weld's response was to persuade his followers to live in tents in the nearby hills. "We will remain here," he announced, "until we find a school which permits freedom of speech." Aggravated by what was taking place at Lane, Arthur Tappan, now a dedicated abolitionist, provided funds to open a theological department in Oberlin College, a revived school in Oberlin, Ohio, just south of Lake Erie. The new department was to be headed by Charles G. Finney, Weld's spiritual father and the most renowned evangelist in the world. A prominent feature of the new department was that it was open to all "irrespective of color."

Feeling he was on Mt. Pisgah, Weld inspired his followers to enroll at Oberlin for the next term.

Informed about what was taking place in Cincinnati, President Beecher eventually broke away from his money-raising trips and returned to the seminary. He firmly believed that he could cleanse the wound, and that Lane would influence the entire West. He was sadly mistaken. Nonetheless, he continued on as president even though many classrooms were nearly empty.

That October, he approached Harriet. "The Cincinnati Synod is meeting at Ripley," he informed her. "Why don't you come along? John Rankin has invited us to stay in his home—"

"Is he the preacher who keeps a light burning in his home in order to help escaping slaves?" Harriet's eyes widened.

"He is. And other than Levi Coffin, he knows more about the Underground Railroad than anyone. Professor Stowe will be staying with us—"

"But will there be room?" Harriet asked.

"Of course. Rankin may even tell you how he helped Eliza after she crossed the Ohio on the ice. It was a hair-raising experience."

"Then I'm going with you!" exclaimed Harriet. "That material might—just might—give me an idea for an article, or, perhaps, a short story."

14

The Underground Railroad

The sun was nearing the horizon when Harriet, along with her father and Calvin Stowe, stepped into the Rankin house—a small brick building perched on a cliff overlooking the river.[1]

"Welcome! Welcome!" greeted the plump lady of the house. "You're just in time for supper. John and I've been counting the hours until you'd get here. But before we go to the table, let me show you your rooms." She led the way to a tiny chamber just off the kitchen. "This is for Dr. Beecher and Professor Stowe." Then she opened another door next to the porch on the south side. "And this, Harriet, will be your room." She pointed out the window to the river. As Harriet followed her finger, she saw the broad stream just beneath them.

"Is that where Eliza crossed on the ice?" ventured Harriet.

"It is. I'll never forget the day she came. The old river was a-groanin' with huge chunks of ice slammin' into each other. We could hear 'em a-rumblin' even up here."

"How did she cross?"

"She just leaped from one chunk to another."

"Weren't they slippery?" Harriet stared.

"Reckon they were. She fell several times. But Eliza was a determined gal. When she got here her feet and knees were all bloody and she'd lost her shawl. We almost ran out of bandages—"

"Was she alone?"

"Oh, no. She had a young'un. Poor thing. He was shiverin'

---

[1]The Rankin house is still standing.

134

with the cold. Excuse me while I light the lantern. I imagine you're 'bout to starve." She tightened her apron and went out on the porch. Harriet watched as she lit the wick of a heavy lantern. "What's that for?" she asked.

"To show 'em where the house is." She spoke in a matter-of-fact way.

"Will any come tonight?"

"Maybe. We've already had over five hundred.[2] If they come, just ignore 'em. John will know what to do. But we'd better stop talkin' and start eatin'."

Harriet had many more questions, but she forced herself to keep still as she thoughtfully ate her supper.

"You'd better be on your toes tomorrow," said Rankin as he passed the mashed potatoes to Dr. Beecher. "Wilson is fighting mad. He says that you've forsaken the faith."

"In what way?" asked Beecher.

"He says you're not a true Calvinist."

"Mmmm. What's he going to do about it?"

"He thinks you should be tried for heresy."

Beecher cut another slice of ham. "He's that serious?"

"Yes, Dr. Beecher, he's that serious."

"Will any of the ministers agree with him?"

"I'm afraid so. He's going to demand a vote."

"I'm not worried." Beecher stirred his coffee. "John Calvin was a mighty man of God and so was Martin Luther and Jonathan Edwards. Trouble is, some of their followers have not interpreted them correctly. But I've faced the brethren before. I'm not afraid of a trial. It will clear the air."

For the first time on the trip Calvin Stowe chuckled. "If you're tried, I want to be there," he said. "It'll be a circus. Wilson and his friends won't have a chance. The Old School is finished. A few days ago I saw the New England *primer,* which has a poem that pretty well sums up the thinking of Ashbel Green and his Old School theology. It goes like this:

'In Adam's fall
We sinned all;
In Cain's murder,
We sinned furder,
By Dr. Green,
Our sin is seen.'

"The pitiful thing is that we spend time splitting hairs

---

[2]It is estimated that by the end of slavery, 2,000 fugitives passed through the Rankin home.

while we neglect the weightier matters. Slavery, for example."

"Are you against slavery?" asked Harriet.

"Of course I'm against slavery. Still, I don't have the solution." He massaged his sideburns.

"Some of us are for colonization. Others demand immediate abolition," commented Beecher. "But I wouldn't be surprised—" he chuckled. "I wouldn't be surprised that the good Lord will provide another solution."

"Like what?" demanded Rankin.

"I really don't know. When Jesus fed the five thousand, the food was supplied by a little boy—and a miracle. That's the gospel I preach. Good works plus faith enables God to supply miracles—and solutions."

As the conversation drifted into technical theology, Harriet excused herself. "I'm tired," she said, suppressing a yawn with her hand. "I must get some rest."

Harriet had just prayed for guidance and slipped between the cool sheets when she noticed that a full moon was illuminating the land with soft, golden light. From the window she followed the Ohio as it flowed from the east to the west. Remembering the geography book she had written, she knew that the mighty stream began in Pittsburgh where the Allegheny and Monongahela united; and, growing in size, continued in a southwesterly direction to Cairo, Illinois. There it united with the mighty Mississippi and continued on to the Gulf.

As she viewed the dark ribbon below and the shadows of the hills beyond where blacks were owned and sold like cattle, she visualized Eliza crossing the ice. The black woman with a child in her arms had just reached a large chunk of ice in the center of the river when Harriet was startled by a voice.

"Now don't you worry," she heard Mrs. Rankin say. "John and I will take care of you. We'll get you to the next place in the mornin'. But aren't you hungry?"

"Yes, ma'am. We hain't had nothin' to eat fer two days."

"How many of you are there?"

"Just me and Pa."

Soon Harriet could hear the sound of utensils; then the smell of bacon and eggs drifted into her room. A couple of hours later she heard a wagon, and looking out the window, she saw John Rankin driving toward the road with the fugitives crouched on the straw in the back.

At breakfast the next morning, Harriet said, "I think you had some visitors last night."

The Rankins exchanged glances.

"What are you talking about?" asked the preacher.

Harriet related what she had heard, seen, and smelled.

"Yes, we had some visitors," agreed Mrs. Rankin. "It was an old man and his wife. Both were nearly toothless. They escaped from Tennessee and are hoping to get to Canada before winter. John took them to the next stop."

"Where's that?" asked Harriet.

"Oh, it's on the way," replied Rankin evasively.

"Then where will they go?"

"Hattie, you're asking too many questions," cautioned her father.

"That's all right," put in Rankin hurriedly. "We're all friends and we all know how to keep things under our hats. There are all kinds of stations on the Underground Railroad. Many of them are in the Cincinnati area. Most of them are so secretive that no one even knows they exist—"

"Several times when Theodore Weld and his friends were there," interrupted Beecher, "I found my horse was covered with sweat. Do you suppose that one of them might have used it to transport a slave to another station?"

"It's entirely possible," replied Rankin. "But let me tell you more about our section of Underground Railroad. An important station is in Fountain City, Indiana—about six miles north of Richmond.[3] That station is operated by Levi Coffin and his wife Catherine. Both are dedicated Quakers. They're the ones who helped Eliza after she left here.

"Even though the Quakers don't baptize or serve communion, they have done more good things for the human race than almost any denomination. They were a big help to Wilberforce in his struggle against British slavery." As he thoughtfully buttered his toast, his mood changed. Laughingly, he added, "I'll never forget an experience I had with a wonderful Quaker family. While I was visiting them, two of their daughters got into an argument. Since the one thought the other to be a little stuck-up, she shook her finger in her face and cried, 'Thee little thou thee!' "

After the laughter had quieted, he continued. "But now since I'm the moderator, I think we'd better go to the meet-

---

[3]Reconditioned, the Levi Coffin House is open for tourists.

inghouse. Dr. Wilson's probably already there!" Rising from his chair he put on his hat.

Turning to Harriet, Mrs. Rankin said, "While we're gone you can stay here and entertain yourself." She handed her a new book. "This just came last week. It's the latest biography of William Wilberforce. If you get tired of it, you might follow the path down to the river and see what a steep climb Eliza had after she had crossed the ice. I'd stay with you, but I have to help the ladies get the meal for the preachers. As you know, preachers like to eat!" She laughed. Then at the door, she said, "We'll be eating at noon and you've been invited to join us."

Harriet had read several biographies of this apparent hunchback. Most had emphasized his life-long struggle to get the transportation of slaves outlawed in the House of Commons. This book did that, but it also outlined how England got into the business of transporting slaves.

The world, Harriet learned, had been divided by Pope Alexander V1 in 1493. His *Line of Demarcation* bull barred Spain from Africa. Since Spain wanted slaves from Africa for their New World colonies, they issued *asientos* to other nations to transport slaves for them from Africa.

When the British had this license, they were as cold-blooded in supplying slaves as other nations when they had the license. Realizing that a minimum of one-third would die on the way and be tossed to the sharks, they packed their ships with enough victims so that their trip would be financially worthwhile. On a typical transport, a male slave was allotted a space six feet long by sixteen inches wide. Since the women and children were shorter, they were given less space.

Most captains arranged for their slaves to lie on their right sides "to protect their hearts." In this position, they were shackled in pairs. Handcuffs were secured to the right wrist of one and to the left wrist of his partner. Likewise, leg-irons were locked onto the left ankle of one and the right ankle of the other.

Knowing that the British public did not approve of what they were doing, the slavers developed what was known as the *Middle Passage*. This grim deception worked as follows: The public watched as the ships were being loaded with British merchandise: beads, cloth, brandy, guns, iron bars. Thus loaded, the ship sailed for Africa. There, the merchandise was traded for slaves. Then, the captains headed for Jamaica. This was the *Middle Passage*. After the slaves had been sold at auction, the ship was reloaded with sugar, rum, spices. Thus, the man-on-the-street saw British merchandise leave port, and return with products from the New World, and was supposedly unaware of what took place in the Middle Passage.

Year after year, Wilberforce fought the trade in the House of Commons. He lectured, wrote books, was defeated, started over again, continued, prayed. Sometimes his speeches were three hours long. Finally, the transportation of slaves was made illegal in 1807, a mere four years before Harriet was born.

British slaves were not actually freed until 1833. *This was just two years ago*, Harriet mused. Fortunately, Wilberforce was still alive when the final legislation was passed.

It was because of this legislation that slaves were free in Canada, and American slaves sought to get there on the Underground Railroad.

Sick and worn-out from what she had read, Harriet closed the book, put on a shawl and started down the narrow path that led to the Ohio River. Down, down she followed the goat path that twisted and turned around ravines gnawed into the surface by the elements. Once she nearly stumbled on a root that crossed the path, and several times she slipped on gravel that had worn to the surface. By the time she got to the edge of the river she was tired and out of breath.

From where she stood, she estimated the Ohio was about half a mile wide. In an effort to imagine the problems Eliza must have faced when she crossed, Harriet visualized huge chunks of ice bobbing, bumping, swirling as the winds and currents swept them toward Illinois. As a child she had often pondered over the way George Washington had crossed the Delaware that Christmas night in 1776. At the time, Washington had the advantage of a boat. Eliza had no such advantage! Instead, she had been handicapped with a child in her arms.

As Harriet daydreamed the scene and saw the desperate woman leaping, falling, getting up, and leaping and falling again, her eyes suddenly overflowed. Yes, Eliza's desire for freedom must have been overwhelming. Forcefully dismissing Eliza from her mind, she studied an isolated house or two on the opposite bank. Thinking about them, she wondered if the owners might have slaves; or if, perchance, some of them might help slaves escape by pointing them to the lantern in the Rankin house on the cliff.

Knowing that it was getting late, Harriet slowly began to climb the narrow path toward the Rankin house. Utterly exhausted when she finally got back, she faced Mrs. Rankin.

"And where have you been?" asked the lady in the apron.

"Oh, I've just been down to the river. I wanted to experience the difficulties Eliza experienced after she had crossed the ice."

"And what do you think?"

"I think she was a brave woman." Harriet shook her head. "There were so many places where she might have fallen. And she must have been dreadfully tired. Tell me, Mrs. Rankin, why did she want to escape?"

"Her master was very cruel to her. She showed me lash marks on her back that she had received from a recent beating."

"Are all masters cruel?"

"Certainly not. Many of them are very kind. After all, slaves are considered property; and who would want to damage his own property?"

"The river is so wide." Harriet's eyes brightened. "I can hardly believe that she managed to cross it," she muttered as she shook her head.

The moderator's wife tightened her apron. "The Ohio, my dear, is to the slaves what the Jordan was to the Children of Israel when they crossed over into the Promised Land. From the time they're little tots they dream about following the North Star and then crossing over into freedom. They even sing about it; and, Hattie, they're great singers. A while back a family of musical slaves knocked at our door. After we'd fed them and showed them that we'd take them to the next station, they insisted on singing to us one of their songs. I'll never forget the words. They went like this:

> Deep River, my home is over Jordan,
> Deep River, Lord, I want to cross over
>   into the campground.
> Oh, don't you want to go to the Gospel feast
> That promised land, where all is peace?
> Oh, Deep River, Lord, Deep River.

"When they got through singing I was in tears. I do hope they got to Canada. Now, Hattie, my dear, it's time to eat. Let's go."

"I-I don't think I want anything to eat."

"Nonsense. We have ham, mashed potatoes, beans, cabbage, three different kinds of pie, a couple of puddings, fruit."

"N-no. I'd better stay here."

"Are you sick?"

"N-no, I'm not sick. But I can't stop thinking about Eliza and the thousands of other slaves just like her on the other side of the river. I guess my thoughts have ruined my appetite."

"I was hoping you'd go. The preachers are going to vote this afternoon on whether or not Dr. Beecher should be tried for heresy. Dr. Wilson's a very determined man. If you come along you might encourage your father."

Harriet laughed. "Pa doesn't need any encouragement. He can take care of himself. No, I'll stay here and read about Wilberforce. That small man really inspires me."

After considerable debate, it was agreed that Lyman Beecher should be tried for heresy. Undisturbed, he agreed that he would face the ministers at any time they chose, provided it didn't interfere with his schedule.

While they were bouncing back in the stage toward Cincinnati, Harriet suddenly noticed that Calvin had removed the black mourning band that had been so conspicuous just above the rim of his hat.

"What happened to the black band you were wearing?" she asked.

"Oh, I just had a visit with the Lord and He assured me that I had mourned for Eliza long enough—that I have a long life ahead of me and I should use that energy for more constructive purposes. David said, 'Weeping may endure for a night, but joy cometh in the morning' (Ps. 30:5). Notice the word 'night' is singular." A troubled smile shaped his lips.

"Even so," he continued, "I've been thinking how Eliza would have enjoyed being here—and being with you. She thought you, Hattie, were the greatest!"

"Well, I considered her a very dear friend."

"You *were* an inspiration to her. She often mentioned how she loved your writings. She said that you had a great talent for making people come alive on paper."

That evening as they stepped off the stage in Cincinnati, Calvin helped her down. Then he commented, "You remind me of Eliza."

"Which Eliza, the one who crossed the ice or your wife?"

"Both!"

"Both?" Harriet questioned.

"Yes. Your features are those of my Eliza and your determination is that of the Eliza who crossed the ice. Your indomitable determination must come from all those blacksmiths in the Beecher line."

Facing each other, they laughed.

"Incidentally, will you be at the Semi-Colon Club next Monday?" he asked.

"I certainly will," she replied with animation.

"Then I'll see you there?"

"Yes, you'll see me there," agreed Harriet.

15

Romance!

Hours before it was time to leave, Harriet selected her best Sunday dress, the long black one with lace at the collar and fringes of lace at the ends of the arm-length sleeves. After ironing it, she carefully combed and tightened the five curls on each side of her head.

Standing before the mirror, she smiled at herself. As an afterthought she put a touch of perfume behind each ear. Being an hour ahead of time, she tried to outline a story about Eliza crossing on the ice. The words didn't flow. She wrote, rewrote, crossed out. She couldn't even think of a first sentence. And the minutes seemed to merely creep by. She wound the clock to make certain that it was running.

Harriet was the first to arrive at the Semi-Colon Club. "I hear my brother-in-law is about to be tried for heresy," said Uncle Samuel after he had greeted her.

"That's right. It's Dr. Wilson's idea."

"Are you worried?"

"Worried about Pa? Never! He knows more about the ins and outs of theology than anyone in America. He used to practice on us while we were stacking wood. The Five Points of Calvinism and all their problems are as familiar to him as the palm of his hand. And he's a great debater. He loves a church fight."

While they were talking, Calvin Stowe strode in and took a seat behind her. "What's on the program?" he asked.

"Nothing to be excited about," replied Samuel. "Salmon Chase was going to tell us how to look up obscure legal points in the law, but he's tied up with another runaway case."

After Sam Foote had disappeared, Calvin said, "I came early because Dr. Beecher asked me to preach a series of sermons on the origin of the Bible. I'm excited, since that's my field. He assured me that if someone will record excerpts of my sermons, they'll be printed in the Cincinnati paper. Do you know anyone who might help?"

"I'd be glad to help," offered Harriet quickly.

"Great. But it might be a good idea if we could meet together before the services so you'll know better what to write. Some of my material will be a little complicated."

"We could meet in Papa's study."

"Fine. I want to do a good job. Lane has had enough bad publicity. Maybe we could help turn things around."

Neither Harriet nor Calvin paid much attention to the program that followed nor did they stay for refreshments. Calvin walked her home, taking the longest route.

Several weeks after the series was completed, a teacher friend invited Harriet to go with her to Kentucky. Traveling eastward on the Ohio, they stopped at Maysville and then continued a dozen miles south to Washington where they visited a plantation. There, they were received as guests in the comfortable "Big House." Harriet was fascinated. Here was slavery at its best. She saw the little cabins where the slaves stayed, noticed their private gardens, heard them singing and laughing as they worked. She also visited nearby plantations. At one of them she watched a little boy dance, do imitations, sing, make faces and entertain the whites who came to watch. On a Sunday, she visited a church in a small town. In her book, *A Key to Uncle Tom's Cabin*, Harriet described the occasion:

My "attention was called to a beautiful quadroon girl, who sat in one of the slips of the church, and appeared to have charge of some young children. . . . When [I] returned from the church [I] enquired about the girl, and was told that she was as good and amiable as she was beautiful; that she was a pious girl, and a member of the church; and finally that she was *owned* by Mr. So-and-so. The idea that this girl was a slave struck a chill to [my] heart, and [I] said earnestly, 'Oh, I hope they treat her kindly!' "

"Oh, certainly!" was the reply; "they think as much of her as their own children."

"I hope they will never sell her," said a person in the company.

"Certainly they will not; a southern gentleman, not long ago, offered her master a thousand dollars for her; but he told him that she was too good to be his wife, and he certainly should not have her for his mistress."[1]

Her mind filled with scenes she would never forget, Harriet returned to Cincinnati. Soon she learned that her father would be tried for heresy within a few weeks. The trial, she knew, could have severe consequences. If he were found guilty, he would have to resign from Lane; and, being nearly penniless, that would mean he would be destitute. But he seemed unconcerned, although he frequently brought up the problem at mealtime.

"If a man," he often said, "cannot obey the law of God, why should he try? It is fatalism to say, 'If God chooses to save me, I'll be saved—if He doesn't, I'll be lost. One way or another, I can do nothing about it.' " This state of mind, he contended while thumping the table with his fist, is letting "the bottom fall out of accountability."

It was his feeling that part of his task in life was to restore the doctrine of man's accountability. He believed in the possibility of immediate repentance and that man could repent of his own free will and then, by God's grace, be saved. Jesus, he insisted, died for all.

On the day of the trial, Harriet sat in the back of the church. As she was praying, Henry Ward joined her. Calvin Stowe took a seat in front. In his autobiography, Lyman Beecher described the occasion.

> When the trial came on, I took all my books and sat down on the second stair of the pulpit. It was my church. I looked so quiet and meek my students were almost afraid I shouldn't come up to the mark. I had everything just then to weigh me down. My wife was lying at home on her dying bed. She did not live a fortnight after that. Then there was all the wear and tear of the seminary and of my congregation. But when I had all my references and had nothing to do but extemporize, I felt easy. I had as much lawyer about me as Wilson and more. I never got into a corner and he never got out, though the fact is he made as good a case as could be made on the wrong side. . . .[2]

As the trial droned on with an occasional flurry of sparks, Harriet was proud of her father. He proved that he was correct

---

[1] *A Key to Uncle Tom's Cabin*, p. 41.
[2] *Autobiography*, Vol. 2, pp. 351–352.

when he boasted, "I know to a hair's-breadth every point be-tween the Old School and the New School." But even though he was acquitted by a vote of twenty-three to twelve, Dr. Wilson announced that he was appealing the case to the Synod, which was scheduled to meet in Dayton that October.

The moment the meeting was dismissed, Calvin Stowe rushed up to Harriet. "I knew your father would win!" he exclaimed, taking both her hands in his. "He has a great mind—and he knows the facts."

"But what about the appeal?" asked Harriet nervously.

"That's nothing to worry about. He'll win again." He patted her shoulder. "Yes, he'll win again."

Harriet visited her stepmother as frequently as possible. But her illness, which had started several months before, took a turn for the worse immediately after the trial. On a Thursday afternoon, after she had had a visit with her, Harriet had a long talk with Henry Ward.

"What do you think of Professor Stowe?" she asked.

"He's the best professor in the entire seminary; and he knows more about the origin of the books of the Bible than anyone alive. He was the valedictorian of all his classes. Franklin Pierce [President of the United States, 1853—1857] says that the only reason he made good grades at Bowdoin was because he always sat next to Calvin Stowe when examinations were given." He laughed. "But why do you ask?"

"We've been together a lot lately, and I don't want to make a mistake—"

"It wouldn't be a mistake to marry him. He's a great and good man. But like Pa he's a hypochondriac and when he gets the blues he gets the blues. Sometimes he even has to go to bed because of the blues. He also loses his hat and he's completely impracticable about ordinary things. And he likes to eat. In fact, he'll eat anything in sight."

Harriet Porter Beecher died on July 7. She was buried next to Eliza Stowe on the seminary campus. After Harriet had placed flowers on her stepmother's grave, she left her father and accompanied Calvin to Eliza's grave. She had been dead for nearly a year. Harriet's heart especially went out to the now motherless children of her stepmother. James was seven, Thomas thirteen, and Isabella fifteen.

A bright glow softened the sorrow in the Beecher home a month later. All of the eleven Beecher children decided to have a grand get-together in Cincinnati. It was a great time for Lyman Beecher since his children had never been together before; and Mary had never even seen little Jamie.

Each of the children had glowing reports about what they were doing. Edward was colorfully articulate, for he had just succeeded in getting a charter for his Illinois college from the state legislature. "One member who fought me," he said, "liked to boast that he was 'born in a briar thicket, rocked in a hog trough, and had never had his genius cramped by the pestilential air of a college.'[3] That fellow was as tough as Old Hickory himself. But there was another member I really liked. He was a tall, thin man by the name of Abraham Lincoln. Abe was always full of stories."

"I knew you'd succeed," beamed Lyman. "I've never forgotten how when you were going to Yale, you used to spend Saturday night in Litchfield, sing in the choir, have Sunday dinner with us, and then, packing a knapsack, walk all the way back to New Haven and recite in a class on Monday morning." He shook his head. "I never knew how you managed it."

"The night air was good for me," replied Edward.

"It must have been. You were the valedictorian of your class."

The Beecher clan had a great time. They teased. Laughed. Boasted. Henry Ward, with the help of Samuel P. Chase, had founded the Young Men's Temperance Society; Catherine's geography book (with ghost writer Harriet!) had sold 100,000 copies; and Harriet was writing and selling numerous articles.

On Sunday Lyman Beecher was proud to have his sons take the Sunday services in the Second Presbyterian Church. Edward preached in the morning, William H. in the afternoon, and George in the evening. And during each service the Beecher clan filled the first three rows.

The newspaper had a glowing report of the three-day session:

> Monday morning they assembled, and, after reading and prayers, in which all joined, they formed a circle. The doctor stood in the middle and gave them a thrilling speech. He then went round and gave them each a kiss. They had a happy dinner.
>
> Presents flowed in from all quarters. During the afternoon the house was filled with company, each bringing an

---

[3]Saints, Sinners and Beechers, p. 147.

offering. When left alone at evening, they had a general examination of their characters. The shafts of wit flew. The doctor being struck in several places; he was, however, expert enough to hit most of them in turn. From the uproar of the general battle, all must have been wounded.

Tuesday morning saw them together again, drawn up in a straight line for the inspection of the king of happy men. After receiving particular instructions, they formed into a circle. The doctor made a long and affecting speech. He felt that he stood for the last time in the midst of all his children, and each word fell with the weight of a patriarch's. He embraced them once more in the tenderness of his big heart. Each took of all a farewell kiss. With hands joined, they sang a hymn. A prayer was offered, and, finally, a parting blessing was spoken. Thus ended a meeting which can only be rivaled in that blessed home where the ransomed of the Lord, after weary pilgrimage, shall join in the praise of the Lamb.[4]

From his stand on top of Mt. Pisgah, Lyman Beecher viewed the future. He was profoundly satisfied with the progress of his children; but he was disturbed by darkening clouds moving in from the east. He wondered about the future of Lane, of his children—and of himself. He knew he would soon be heading for his heresy trial in Dayton; and he also knew that his fellow pastor, Joshua Lacy Wilson, encouraged by voices from Princeton, was determined to nail him to the wall.

The time of the trial arrived and, accompanied by Henry Ward and Charles, Lyman took his seat in a canal boat and headed for Dayton. Letters from Henry Ward to the family in Cincinnati provide a glimpse of what took place. Being young and caustic, he wrote: "I never saw so many faces of clergymen—and so few of them intelligent."

During the trial, which lasted nearly a week, Lyman Beecher knew he faced a packed jury. This was because none of the ministers from the Cincinnati Presbytery were allowed to vote. But remembering that Paganini had moved an audience with merely a G string, and convinced that he was right, this son and grandson of blacksmiths was not unduly worried.

Beecher listened with great patience as Wilson denounced him. Then Lyman stood to his feet. Again he was "old man eloquent." Still the Big Gun of Calvinism, he fired, reloaded, and kept firing until he could see by the faces of his former

[4]*Crusader in Crinoline*, p. 159.

opposition that he had won them over.

The vote was ten to one in Beecher's favor. When the verdict was announced, Dr. Wilson turned pale. This was because, according to the Book of Discipline, if an accuser failed to prove his accusation, he himself could be subjected to trial as a slanderer of a fellow minister.

After Calvin had explained to Harriet some of the more subtle points in the hair-splitting that had taken place in her dad's trial in Dayton, he drew her close. "Hattie," he said soberly, "I have something I want to share with you tonight. It's extremely important and I think we ought to be alone. Do you think we could go somewhere for dinner at around seven o'clock."

"I was planning to write an article. But, yes, I think I can make it," she replied.

That afternoon as she ironed her dress and refashioned her curls, she wondered what he had in mind. In recent weeks their meetings together had increased in length and in number. And once he had accidentally used the word 'dear.' *Was he going to bare his heart? And if he did, what would be her response?*

Sitting opposite from Calvin in a private cove in a moderately expensive restaurant was a new experience. Across the candle-lit table, tastefully set with costly silver, he began. "I have something important to share with you. Do you remember when I gave those lectures on the origin of the Bible?"

"How could I ever forget? I learned more from you and in writing up the lectures for the paper than I had ever learned about the Bible. You really opened my eyes." She leaned forward.

"The Bible *is* a most fascinating library, and you were a big help. I couldn't have—" Calvin smiled with satisfaction.

He was interrupted by the appearance of the waiter, a tall black man in a blue coat featuring two rows of brass buttons. "Our specialty today is catfish," he said, flashing two rows of sparkling white teeth.

"Sounds good to me," responded Calvin.

"I've never eaten catfish, but I'll try it," agreed Harriet.

After they had chosen between soup and salad and had selected their vegetables, Calvin asked, "Do you have religious scruples against catfish?"

"Oh no. I've just never eaten catfish. Are there those who have religious scruples against it?"

"Of course."

"Why?"

"Because in the eleventh chapter of Leviticus Moses taught the people that they should eat nothing from the seas or the rivers that didn't have scales and fins. Catfish have fins, but they don't have scales."

"Then why are we eating catfish?"

"Because in the eleventh chapter of Acts our friend Simon Peter revealed that he had had a vision from the Lord in which he was instructed not to call such things unclean."

"That means that we have scriptural support for eating catfish?"

"Yes, we can eat catfish and shrimp and even lobster without being heretics, and lobsters have neither fins nor scales!"

They both laughed.

As they proceeded with the meal, Harriet kept wondering when Calvin was going to bring up the "important subject." Finally, as they were eating apple pie topped with ice cream, Calvin withdrew a thick envelope from his pocket. Opening it, he said, "Hattie, you did such a good job reporting my lectures, Corey, Fairbank & Webster are going to bring them out in a book. This is the contract. The book will be titled *Introduction to the Criticism and Interpretation of the Bible*."

"Congratulations," replied Harriet, forcing a smile. "I hope you follow it with many other books. Your knowledge should be spread on paper."

"Actually, Hattie, you're a much better writer then I am. You think in pictures. I think in facts."

"An ideal writer should think in both facts and pictures."

Calvin stirred his coffee. "True, but we're all different. However, there is a way that such a person might be made."

"How?" Harriet asked.

"It's a biblical way." A tiny smile tugged at his lips.

"Explain."

"Jesus said, 'For this cause shall a man leave his father and mother, and cleave to his wife; and they twain shall be one flesh" (Mark 10:7-8).

"What do you mean?"

"You think in pictures. I think in facts—"

"And when shall we go about making such a person?"

"How about the first week of January?"

"The first week of January will be fine even though there will be snowdrifts, icicles, slippery roads, and cakes of ice in the Ohio."

"What do you mean?" asked Calvin.

"Oh, I'm just thinking in pictures!" Harriet smiled.

"The date, then, will be January 6. I've checked the calendar and Hattie, my dear, that is the most convenient date. I always consider the facts!"

They both burst out laughing. As he took her hands in his, Harriet could hardly believe that at last she had found someone who loved her and thought she was special. After finishing the meal, they continued to discuss the future—their writing, his children and her new responsibility. She was confident about her future role since she herself had had a stepmother and enjoyed a warm relationship.

Harriet's engagement was kept secret for a long time, even from the family. But both Harriet and Calvin counted the days, then the hours, and then the minutes when the one who was dominated by facts would be united with the one who was dominated by pictures—a union forming a unique person.

The wedding day arrived, with some trepidation on Harriet's part. Dressed in her finest, and with her curls freshly formed, Harriet stepped into her father's home. Upon her arrival, she learned that Calvin had not yet appeared. Still, it was early, and Harriet knew that he, the fact-loving man, never did anything until the last split second. While hoping he would appear on time, she trusted that he would not faint during the ceremony as did Salmon P. Chase.

While she waited, Harriet scribbled a note to Georgiana:

Well, my dear G., about half an hour more and your old friend, companion, schoolmate, etc., will cease to be Hattie Beecher and change to nobody knows who. Since you are engaged and pledge in a year or two to encounter a similar fate, do you wish to know how you shall feel? Well, I have been dreading and dreading the time. I lay awake all last week wondering how I should live through this overwhelming crisis, and lo! it has come, and I feel *nothing at all*.

The wedding is to be altogether domestic—nobody present but my own brothers and sisters, and my old colleague, Mary Dutton; and as there is sufficiency of the ministry in our family we do not have to call in the foreign aid of a minister. . . .

Well, here comes Mr. S., so farewell, and for the last time I subscribe,

Your own
H.E.B.

Curiously, Harriet did not immediately mail that note. Was it because of the expensive postage—25¢ a sheet? Or was it because she was upset by an ad that appeared in a Cincinnati paper a few weeks before? That ad in the *Republican* read:

$1000 REWARD

RAN AWAY from the Subscriber, on Saturday the 12th instant, December, 1835

ELEVEN SLAVES

First, DANIEL, aged about 55; ABBE, his wife, about 50; and their children: Daniel, about 25; Adam, about 22; Jonathan, about 21; Anthony, about 20; Judy, about 19; William, about 16; James, about 11; Ruben, about 10; Moses, about 9.

The above Slaves are all remarkably likely Negroes—light complexioned, tall, and of fine appearance, and no doubt well-dressed and independent in their appearance, having been much indulged by me. I will give the above reward of One Thousand dollars for the delivery of the above family of Slaves to me, or the securing of them in any jail, either in or out of the state, so that I can get them. Or I will give One Hundred dollars for the securing and delivery of each one of them, and pay all reasonable expenses incurred in the delivery of them.

JAMES TAYLOR
Newport, Ky.

In spite of that disturbing news, Harriet set her mind on new ventures. She and Calvin had a good and loving relationship.

Toward the end of January, after Harriet had settled in her new home—probably the one in which Calvin and Eliza had lived—Harriet picked up her unmailed note and added several pages. This is the opening paragraph:

Three weeks have passed since writing the above, and my husband and self are now quietly settled by our fireside; as domestic as any pair of tame fowl. . . . Two days after our marriage we took a wedding excursion, though we would have most gladly been excused this conformity had not necessity required Mr. Stowe to visit Columbus. . . .

The reason Stowe was "required" to go to Columbus was

to address the Western College of Teachers on *Prussian Education*. It so happened that General William Harrison, hero of the Battle of Tippecanoe, was in the audience. He—elected President of the United States in 1840—was so impressed by Stowe's thesis, he helped fulfill one of Lyman's fondest dreams.

Lane Seminary needed books—thousands of books. Since many of the needed books originated in Europe, Calvin, fluent in several European languages, was the ideal person to select them. But where would the struggling school get the money to send him? Harrison helped arrange for the state legislature to supply part of that need.

Plans having been made for Calvin to go on a book-buying tour, Harriet picked up her pen to add a few more lines to the first double spurts of writing which had not been mailed. She wrote:

> Dear Georgy, naughty girl that I am, it is a month that I have let the above lie by, because I got into a strain of emotion in it that I dreaded to return to. Well, it shall be no longer. In about five weeks Mr. Stowe and myself start for New England. He sails the first of May. I am going with him to Boston, New York, and other places, and shall stop finally at Hartford, whence, as soon as he is gone, it is my intention to turn westward.

Why didn't Harriet sail with him? London, Vienna, Florence, Venice, Rome were cities she longed to visit. She couldn't go, for she had learned that in due time she would become a mother.

On their final day together, neither realized the troubles that they, Lane Seminary, and the city of Cincinnati would soon be facing. Had they known about those troubles, he would not have sailed.

16
Trail of Tears

S truggling with tears, Harriet began the long journey back to Cincinnati alone. Her nearly four months of marriage had been a continuing and ever-increasing ecstasy. And now *he* was gone!

Parallels between Calvin Stowe and Alexander Fisher kept wedging into her mind. Both were brilliant. Both were dominated by worthy purpose. Both had sailed to Europe in the spring. Alas, Fisher had gone down with the ship off the coast of Ireland. Harriet still remembered the day her father had received the sad news and relayed it to Catherine. For months afterward Catherine had been so broken-hearted she had longed to die.

Again and again Harriet prayed, "Oh, Lord, protect Calvin in every way. Help him fulfill the purpose of this trip. Shield him from every temptation. And, dear Lord, help me carry this child that is growing beneath my heart. May it, whether it is a boy or girl, grow up to serve Thee and Thy purpose."

Since the home she and Calvin were building was far from completion, Harriet moved in with her father and the children by his second wife along with her other relatives. She kept busy making and repairing clothes for the children, helping them with their lessons, writing an occasional article or story—and keeping a stream of letters flowing to Calvin. Calvin liked news; and since Cincinnati was brimming with news, she kept him well informed.

That April, about a month before Calvin sailed, a white boy and a black boy got into a fight. A riot developed and several blacks were killed. Then while Cincinnati seethed with rumors, James G. Birney, the rich abolitionist from Alabama who called on Catherine in Hartford for advice in starting a school for women in Huntsville, moved into the city. There, he set up his abolitionist paper, the *Philanthropist*. Soon his presses were turning out copy that was sent all across the country. Confident that few would object, Birney hired Dr. Gamaliel Bailey, a young surgeon in the Cincinnati Hospital, to be his assistant editor.

Bailey, a devout Methodist, worked hard. The paper denounced slavery in every issue. Harriet watched—and wondered; and as the days passed the modest grumblings of opposition became a roar. Soon, Jacob Burnet, a deacon in Beecher's church and a judge on the Ohio Supreme Court, led a committee that called on James Birney.

"The people in Cincinnati don't like your paper," said the judge. "Take my advice and close down."

"What if I refuse?" asked Birney.

"There will be a riot. Houses will be burned. People will be killed."

"But isn't Ohio a free state?"

"It is free. But every July southern planters come to Cincinnati on their semiannual buying trip. Their business is our mainstay. Free or not, our merchants need business. The south loathes your paper. . . . You're sitting on a keg of dynamite. The fuse, Mr. Birney, is extremely short; and there are many radicals anxious to touch it with a flame."

Both Birney and Bailey merely smiled.

On July 12 a mob broke into the printing shop of Achilles Pugh—the antislavery Quaker who was brave enough to print the *Philanthropist*. While substantial citizens looked on without saying a word, they damaged both the press and the type that was all set ready to print.

Undaunted, the editors repaired the damage and the *Philanthropist* appeared on schedule.

Swollen with child, Harriet wondered what would happen next. Her father was in Pittsburgh facing his third heresy trial. Fortunately for her morale, Henry Ward was near. Better yet, Henry Ward had access to a brace of pistols.

Samuel Davis, the newly elected mayor who had campaigned on a law-and-order ticket, printed a notice and posted it in almost every public place. His notice offered $100 to anyone who could secure the arrest and conviction of any member of the mob. The next day startled citizens noticed that the mayor's bulletin had been replaced by another which offered $100 for the arrest of James G. Birney. The fine print declared that he was a fugitive from Kentucky. Equally dismayed merchants when opening their shops discovered a bulletin which ordered them to post their slavery sentiments in the window or "face the consequence." It was signed "Anti-Abolition."

Seventeen radicals who boarded at the Franklin House told their landlord that if he didn't throw Birney out, they would leave. The landlord ignored their threats and a dozen of them left.

On Sunday, July 31, the mob descended on Pugh's printing establishment, wrecked his presses, and threw them in the river. Then they headed toward the Franklin house to get Birney. Armed, angry, and shouting hate, each was prepared to kill anyone who got in their way. But when they reached the Franklin house they faced a defiant man.

"No one will pass here," said the man at the door.

"Who are you?"

"I'm Salmon P. Chase."

It required incredible courage for Chase to confront that mob because he was the counsel for two of the city's banks; and Lawrence, president of the Lafayette Bank, had been on the committee that demanded that Birney extricate himself from the city.

As Chase withstood the hysterical men, tensions increased. While fingers itched to press triggers, Mayor Davies faced them. "James G. Birney is not here," he said. "Take my advice and go home."

The mob left the Franklin house, but they did not go home. Instead, they returned to Pugh's office, smashed his furniture, threw it into the river—and "invaded" the black section. There, they contented themselves by burning the row of negro shacks.

As Cincinnati trembled on the verge of a bloody massacre, Harriet approached Henry Ward as he was working in the kitchen. "What are you doing?" she demanded.

"Making bullets," he replied, as he poured molten lead into a series of molds.

Loathing physical violence, Birney turned the *Philanthropist* over to Dr. Bailey and continued his antislavery activity by lecturing. While Harriet eagerly awaited the return of her husband, the pro and antislavery groups in Cincinnati continued to threaten each other. Even the churches became divided. Harriet watched the growing flames of distrust, read the papers, kept Calvin informed—and continued to produce copy for several periodicals.

Lyman Beecher was duly exonerated of heresy in Pittsburgh. But several censored him because he, in turn, did not accuse Dr. Wilson of slander. Beecher refused to censor his "enemy" because he believed in turning the other cheek. Also, he had, at the time an unusual interest in Boston. This city of memories and twisting streets was where he had courted and won his second wife.

That summer, the President of Lane married Mrs. Lydia Jackson of Boston, a widow with several grown children. He, along with her two younger children, Joseph and Margaret, returned with his new bride to Cincinnati for the fall term.

The Beecher house on Walnut Hills was now uncomfortably crowded. In late September as the leaves began to curl, Harriet went into labor. On the 29th, twin girls were placed in her arms. When asked to name them, she said, "This one is Eliza Tyler Stowe, and this one is Isabella." Four months later, Calvin, accompanied by five thousand books, arrived in Cincinnati.

Following a glorious reunion, Calvin said: "It was nice of you to name one of the girls after my first wife. But I think the other one should be named after my second wife. Her name, Hattie, is Harriet Beecher Stowe!"

Harriet did not object. She realized that her Calvin was a man of facts; and one of the facts that dominated his life was that he loved both her and his deceased wife with a sublime intensity. Moreover, he was experienced in changing names. While in college, he had changed his own from Stow to Stowe.

Two months after Calvin's return, the eyes of Cincinnati were focused on a new drama. A slaveholder from Virginia had decided to move to Kentucky. While the steamboat on which he and his slaves were traveling was docked at Cincinnati, his slave Matilda had escaped into the city where she was hidden by some blacks. In time, she got a job working for James G. Birney, who did not know that she was a fugitive slave.

Always available to those in need, Salmon P. Chase agreed to defend Matilda. His argument was that since Matilda's owner had *voluntarily* taken her to Cincinnati, a free city, Matilda was a free person.

As Chase was leaving the courtroom, a man was heard to remark: "There goes a fine young fellow who has just ruined himself." There was another listener, however, who had a different opinion. This man, a medical student, was deeply impressed by the line of reasoning Chase had employed, and he promised himself to follow, and if possible, help his career.

Chase lost. The case then developed into another phase. Birney was now accused of harboring a fugitive. Again Chase took over as the defense attorney. Again, he lost and Birney was fined fifty dollars. Chase appealed to the Supreme Court of Ohio. This time he won on a mere technicality. But even though the court rejected his argument that in reality Matilda was *not* a slave, the court ordered that his argument be published.

Chase's published argument was read by judges and lawyers across America. Among those who found it interesting was an Illinois lawyer by the name of Abraham Lincoln.

The entire Beecher clan held its breath when Martin Van Buren, Andrew Jackson's Secretary of State, was elected President in 1836. Known by many as "the Little Magician," it was believed that he would maintain prosperity. Instead, two months after he was sworn into office on March 4, 1837, the nation was plunged into a severe financial depression.

Unable to collect his salary because the House of Tappan had failed, Lyman Beecher had to rely on the income he received from the Second Presbyterian Church; and there, the elders generously raised his income by two hundred dollars. Calvin Stowe had no such cushion, and he was in dire need. Harriet's third child, Henry Ellis, had been born on January 14. That year he was able to collect only one half of his twelve hundred dollar annual salary. Moreover, the future seemed bleak. Only fifteen new students had enrolled for the fall semester.

The panic deepened. Samuel Foote lost his palatial home. This meant the end of the Semi-Colon Club. Harriet tried to remain cheerful. Other disasters followed.

Immediately after the arrival of Henry Ellis, a black woman had called seeking employment. "Are you a free person?" asked Harriet.

"Yes, ma'am, I'se free," she replied.

Assured that the eager black woman was telling the truth, Calvin hired her. She was a hard worker. Harriet was thus enabled to spend more time at her writing desk. But one afternoon the slender woman faced Harriet. Trembling from head to foot, she cried, "Ma'am, I told you a lie. I's not free. I's a runaway. Dis afternoon I heered dat my owner is in Cincinnati lookin' for me. What is I to do?" She bit her lip and wept.

Henry Ward and Calvin who had been standing nearby exchanged glances. "Get all of your belongings together and we'll take care of you," promised Henry.

About midnight Henry and Calvin led the fugitive to a wagon and covered her with straw. After warning her to keep quiet, they drove the wagon over some back roads to the farm of John Van Zandt, a man who was known to cooperate with the Underground Railway.

Van Zandt received them kindly, pointed the woman to a hiding place, and assured them that she would soon be on her way to Canada. That night the candles burned late as Harriet listened to the stories related by both her husband and favorite brother. As Harriet listened, she made mental notes about all that had taken place—especially the details. Something within prompted her that she might be able to use the drama in a story later on.

After some time and much discussion of this escapee, the Beechers as well as all Cincinnati were jolted by the news of an explosion. The *Moselle*, a steamboat built in Cincinnati, had blown up just as she was backing into the center of the river. Altogether, 136 people were killed and bodies or portions of bodies were found on the roofs of houses more than a block away.

Investigation revealed that several companies had employed unqualified engineers. Owners worked hard to attain a cover-up. But Chase, along with several substantial citizens, finally got the story printed. Their exposure led to a congressional investigation and the installation of an examining service.

While verbal war, explosions, and other calamites burst around her, Harriet kept busy with her writing and domestic chores. In a letter to Georgiana she described a typical day:

> Bless me, how light it is! I must get out of bed and rap to wake up Mina [one of the servants], for breakfast must be had at six o'clock. . . . So out of bed I jump and seize the tongs, and pound, pound, pound over poor Mina's sleepy head, charitably allowing her about half an hour to wake up. . . . Then the baby wakes—*qua, qua, qua*—so I give him his breakfast, dozing and soliloquizing as follows: "Now I must not forget to tell Mr. Stowe about the starch and dried apples." Doze—"ah, um—I wonder if Mina has soap enough! I think there were two bars left on Saturday." Doze again. I wake again. "Dear me, broad daylight! I must get up and go

down and see if Mina is getting breakfast." Up I jump, and up wakes baby. "Now, little boy, be good and let mother dress, because she is in a hurry." I get my frock half on, and baby by that time has kicked himself down off his pillow, and is crying and fisting the bed clothes in great order. . . . I apply myself vigorously to sweeping and dusting. . . .

The meal being cleared away, Mr. Stowe dispatched to market with various memoranda of provisions, etc., and baby being washed and dressed, I begin to think what next must be done. I start to cut out some little dresses, have just calculated the length and got one breadth torn off, when Master Henry falls to crying with might and main. I catch him up and, turning around, see one of his sisters flourishing the things of my work box in fine style. Moving it away and looking the other side, I see the second little mischief seated by the hearth chewing coals and scraping up ashes with great apparent relish. Grandmother lays hold upon her. . . . I set at it again, pick up a dozen pieces, measure them once more to see which is the right one. . . . Number one pushed number two over. Number two screams; that frightens baby, and he joins in. I call number one a naughty girl, and take the persecuted one in my arms. . . . Meanwhile, number one makes her way to the slop-jar and forthwith proceeds to wash her apron in it. Grandmother catches her by one shoulder, drags her away, and sets the jar out of her reach. . . .

Well, Georgy, this marriage is—yes, I will speak well of it, after all; for when I can stop and think long enough to discriminate my head from my heels, I must say that I think myself fortunate in both husband and children. My children I would not change for all the ease, leisure, and pleasure that I could have without them. They are money on interest whose value will be constantly increasing.

Caught in the increasing spin of activity, time seemed to pass with ever-increasing speed. A bright spot in 1839 was that dueling was prohibited in the District of Columbia and several other states. When Harriet showed a newspaper clipping headlining this information to her father, he beamed. "I first preached my sermon against dueling in 1806," he said. "That's thirty-three years ago—"

"Did you ever think you had wasted your time?" asked Harriet.

"Never! God's Word is true. Planters inspired by God will always have a harvest. Perhaps the harvest will not come during the planter's life. Moses never set foot in the Promised

Land. But it will come.[1] God desperately needs faithful planters."

"Do you think the slaves will ever be freed?"

"Of course. That is, they'll be freed if His children continue to plant the proper seed."

1840 was a rare year of accomplishment. The first regular transatlantic steamship service was established; Samuel Morse, the artist who painted the portrait of Catherine's boyfriend, Alexander Fisher, patented the magnetic telegraph; and the National Treasury was established in Washington, D.C.

In May of that year, Harriet gave birth to her second son. Calvin named him Frederick William, in honor of the king of Prussia, a man he deeply admired. Mysteriously, shortly after Frederick's birth, Harriet recovered from a siege of near-blindness that had been growing progressively worse for nearly a year. She explained her problem in a letter to a friend:

> For a year I have held the pen only to write an occasional business letter. . . . This was primarily owing to a severe neuralgic complaint that settled in my eyes, and for two months not only made it impossible for me to use them in writing, but to fix them with attention on anything. I could not even bear the least light of day in my room. Then my dear little Frederick was born, and for two months more I was confined to my bed.

In the spring of 1842, Harriet selected a sheaf of stories, and with six-year-old Hattie in tow, set out for the East. Harper and Brothers liked her material and issued a contract. (The 393-page book of New England stories, entitled The MayFlower, went to press the next year.)

Encouraged, Harriet visited editors and dispatched glowing reports to Calvin. He replied with excellent advice:

> My dear, you must be a literary woman. It is so written in the book of fate. . . . Make all of your calculations accordingly. Get a good stock of health and brush up your mind. Drop the E out of your name. It only incumbers . . . with the flow and euphony. Write yourself fully and always Harriet Beecher Stowe, which is a name euphonious, flowing, and full of meaning. Then, my word for it, your husband will lift up his head in the gate, and your children will rise up and call you blessed. . . .

---

[1] In 1958 a duel was fought between two Peruvian congressmen. But since both missed, it was bloodless. Duels are now against the law everywhere.

And now, my dear wife, I want you to come home quick as you can. The fact is I cannot live without you, and if we were not so prodigiously poor I would come for you at once. There is no woman like you in this wide world. Who else has so much talent with so little self-conceit; so much reputation with so little affectation; so much literature with so little nonsense; so much enterprise with so little extravagance; so much tongue with so little scold; so much sweetness with so little softness; so much of so many things and so little of so many other things?

Harriet boarded a train bound for Cincinnati. As it click-clacked westward, she could hardly wait until she was back with Calvin and the children. Her chin was high, and her mind overflowed with good reports—and future plans.

17
Purgatory

Harriet quivered with joy as she melted into Calvin's arms. It had been so long! Then she greeted her children. It was wonderful to be home, to be with Calvin, and to be with her children. It was also wonderful to have unbelievable literary news to share.

Harper and Brothers was enthusiastic about her new book. Robertson, a publisher in Hartford, had assured her that the book would sell. Royalties would be due. Johnson of the *Evangelist* was begging for copy, and the *Boston Miscellany* had offered twenty dollars for three pages of "Not very close print."

In response to Calvin's letter, which had assured her that she was a literary woman, Harriet had replied:

> There is one thing I must suggest. If I am to write, I must have a room to myself, which shall be *my* room. . . . I have bought a cheap carpet for it, and I have furniture enough at home to furnish it comfortably, and I only beg in addition that you will let me change the glass door from the nursery into that room and keep my plants there, and then I shall be quite happy.

Calvin was enthusiastic about all of these ideas; and soon Harriet was busy with a series of articles. In spite of a thousand duties, she arranged devious schemes to keep manuscripts going to the editors. A friend remembered and years later produced this sketch:

> "Now this is the place you left off," said a helper. ". . . the last sentence was, 'Borne down by the tide of agony, she leaned her head on his hands, the tears streamed through

his eyes, and her whole frame shook with convulsive sobs.'
What shall I write next?"

"Mina, pour a little milk into this pearlash," said Harriet.

"Come," the helper says, ". . . What next?"

Harriet paused and looked musingly out the window, as she turned her mind to her story . . . and she dictated as follows:

"Her lover wept with her, nor dared he again to touch the point so sacredly guarded"—"Mina, roll that crust a little thinner." "He spoke in soothing tones."—"Mina, poke the coals in the oven."[1]

Soon checks and then magazines with her stories in them started to arrive. But about the time people began to say, "I just read your story," an epidemic of typhoid descended on the city. So many students succumbed that the Beecher house was transformed into a hospital. A little after the epidemic started to lessen, Harriet went into labor. Her third daughter was born in August.

Harriet named the rather sickly child Georgiana May in honor of her old friend. Not well herself, Harriet complained to her half brother Thomas a year or two after the event: I was "haunted and pursued by care that seemed to drink my life-blood. A feeble, sickly child, irritable nurse, with whom I feared to leave it, from whom I feared to withdraw it—slowly withering in my arms . . . harassed, anxious, I often wondered why God should press my soul . . . with a weight of cares."[2]

Harriet's troubles were made more unbearable by the accidental death of her brother George—the "brilliant one"—a few weeks before, on July 6. While pastoring a church where he was deeply loved, he went out into the orchard to frighten the birds. Unused to guns, he accidentally shot himself. Shocked, Harriet was deeply shaken.

These troubles were merely a prelude. While Calvin was in the East attempting to raise money for the seminary, Harriet dragged herself to her desk and wrote to him: "I am already half sick with confinement to the house and overwork. If I should sew every day for a month to come I should not be able to accomplish a half of what is to be done, and should only be more unfit for my other duties."

Her problems continued. On June 16, 1845, she poured

---

[1]*The Beechers* by Milton Rugoff, p. 236.
[2]Ibid., p. 241.

out her heartbreak in a letter addressed to Calvin in Detroit where he was attending a minister's meeting. This letter was probably the most despondent letter she ever composed. "My dear husband," she began, "It is a dark, sloppy, rainy, disagreeable day, and I have been working hard (for me) all day in the kitchen, washing dishes, looking into closets, and seeing a great deal of that dark side of domestic life. . . .

"I am sick of the smell of sour milk, and sour meat, and sour everything. . . . The clothes *will* not dry, and no wet thing does, and everything smells mouldy; and altogether I feel as if I never want to eat again.

"Your letter, which was neither sour nor mouldy, formed a very agreeable contrast to all these things. . . . I am much obliged to you for it. As to my health, it gives me very little solicitude, although it is bad enough and daily grows worse. I feel no life, no energy, no appetite. . . . Upon reflection I perceive that it pleases my Father to keep me in the fire, for my whole situation is excessively harassing and painful. I suffer with sensible distress in the brain as I have done more or less since my sickness last winter, a distress which some days takes from me all power of planning or executing anything. . . .

"Georgiana is so excessively weak, nervous, cross, and fretful night and day that she takes all Anna's strength and time with her; and then the children are, like other little sons and daughters of Adam, full of all kinds of absurdity and folly.

"When the brain gives out, as mine often does, and one cannot think or remember anything, then what is to be done? All common fatigue, sickness, and exhaustion is nothing to this distress. Yet I do rejoice in my God, and I know in whom I believe, and only pray that the fire may consume the dross. . . . No real evil can happen to me, so I fear nothing for the future, and only suffer in the present tense.

"God, the mighty God, is mine, of that I am sure, and I know that He knows that though the flesh and heart fail, I am all the while desiring and trying for His will alone. As to a journey, I need not ask a physician to see that it is needful to me as far as health is concerned, that is to say, all human appearances are that way, but I feel no particular choice about it. If God wills I go, He can easily find the means. Money, I suppose, is as plenty with Him now as it always has been, and if He sees it is really best, He will doubtless help me."

The idea of a journey was like the glow of a distant firefly on a dark night. Perhaps if she could get away from the dampness of Cincinnati, she *might* feel better. But how could she finance such a journey? The seminary was months behind in Calvin's salary, and each time she approached the treasurer, the shadows on his face deepened.

Still she was convinced that if the Lord wanted her to get away, the money would be provided. Mysteriously, extra money did arrive and she was enabled to spend the summer of 1845 in Hartford, Boston, and Matick. The change helped. But she remained an invalid. Back in Cincinnati, she prayed that the Lord would help her to know what she should do. The desire to make her life count still dominated her. And she was still secure in the conviction that the Lord wanted her to be a writer. But how could she put words on paper if she barely had enough energy to get out of bed?

After consulting with doctors and friends, she was convinced that she should go to Brattleboro, Vermont, and take Dr. Wesselhoeft's water cure. "It will work miracles," assured a friend.

"I think you should go," said Calvin.

"But where will we get the money?" asked Harriet.

"God will supply it," assured Calvin.

Since Calvin knew that he would need lessons in housekeeping before she left, he submitted to her instruction. He was such a good apprentice, Harriet informed Georgiana: "My husband has developed wonderfully as housekeeper and nurse. You would laugh to see him in his spectacles gravely marching the little troop in their nightgowns up to bed, tagging after them, as he says, like an old hen after a flock of ducks. The money for my journey has been sent in from an unknown hand in a wonderful manner. All of this shows the care of our Father, and encourages me to rejoice and hope in Him."

Harriet left for Brattleboro in March and began the prescribed system of hydrotherapy. It included taking cold baths, needle-showers, and internal irrigations. She also took long walks, played games, spent hours in complete relaxation, drank milk, and ate brown bread. Likewise, she endured what seemed to her interminable sitz baths.

Feeling better, she left the sanitarium the following March. Then, after a two-month visit with various friends, she returned to Cincinnati. She had been gone for fourteen months. Calvin and the children were delighted to have her back. Soon she was expecting her sixth child. But again her health began to fall apart.

Samuel Charles was born in January 1848. Her experience while carrying him was quite similar to the one she had had while carrying Frederick William. She explained this to Georgiana:

"For six months after my return from Brattleboro, my eyes were so affected that I wrote scarcely any, and my health was in so strange a state that I felt no disposition to write. After the birth of little Charley my health improved, but my husband was sick, and I have been so loaded and burdened with cares as to drain me dry of all capacity of thought, feeling, memory, or emotion.

"Well, Georgy, I am thirty-seven years old! I am glad of it. I like to grow old and have six children and cares endless."

With recovered sight and a new son in her arms, Harriet felt certain that she would have both the time and energy to write the stories and articles that had been brewing in her mind. But this was not to be. Calvin now succumbed to a prolonged illness. That June he took off for Brattleboro and the course in hydrotherapy.

Alone with six children and the care of their new house on Walnut Hills, Harriet was forced to take in boarders to meet the expenses. Even so, she managed to do some writing. Then, in the early summer of 1849, cholera broke out in Cincinnati. Alarmed, Calvin wanted to return. Harriet sympathized with his longing to be with her and the family, but she felt that his return would be a mistake. On June 29, 1849, she wrote:

"My dear Husband: This week has been unusually fatal. The disease in the city has been malignant and virulent. Hearse drivers have scarce been allowed to unharness their horses, while furniture carts and common vehicles are often employed for the removal of the dead. . . .

"On Tuesday one hundred and sixteen deaths from cholera were reported, and that night the air was of that peculiarly oppressive, deathly kind that seems to lie like lead on the brain and soul.

"As regards your coming home, I am decidedly opposed to it. First, because the chance of your being taken ill is just as great as the chance of your being able to render us any help. . . . Second, none of us are sick, and it is uncertain whether we shall be.

"July 4. All is well. There is more or less sickness about us, but no very dangerous cases. One hundred and twenty burials from cholera alone yesterday, yet today we see parties bent on pleasure or senseless carousing, while tomorrow and the next day will witness a fresh harvest of death from them. . . . A while ago ten a day dying of cholera struck terror to all hearts; but now the tide has surged up gradually until the deaths average over a hundred daily, and everybody is getting accustomed to it. Gentlemen make themselves agreeable by reciting the number of deaths in this house or that. This together with talk of funerals, cholera medicines, cholera dietetics, and chloride of lime form the ordinary staple of conversation. . . .

"July 10. Yesterday little Charley was taken ill, not seriously, and at any other season I should not be alarmed. Now, however, a slight illness seems like a death sentence. . . . I still think it best for you not to return. . . .

"July 12. Yesterday I carried Charley to Dr. Pulte, who spoke in such a manner as discouraged and frightened me. He mentioned dropsy on the brain as a possible result. I came home with a heavy heart. . . .

"July 15. Since I wrote our house has been a perfect hospital. Charley apparently recovering. . . . Sunday Anna and I were fairly stricken down. . . . I lay on the bed all day reading my hymnbook and thinking over passages of Scripture.

"July 17. Today we have been attending poor old Aunt Frankie's funeral. She died yesterday morning, taken sick the day before while washing. . . .

"Yesterday morning our poor little dog, Daisy, who had been ailing the day before, was suddenly seized with frightful spasms and died in half an hour. Poor little affectionate thing! . . . While we were all mourning over her, the news came that Aunt Frankie was breathing her last. Hatty, Eliza, Anna, and I made up the shroud yesterday, and this morning I made her cap. We have just come from her grave.

"July 23. At last, my dear, the hand of the Lord hath touched us. We have been watching all day by the dying bed of little Charley, who is gradually sinking. . . . I dare not trust myself to say more but shall write again soon.

"July 26. My dear Husband: At last it is over and our dear little one is gone from us. He is now among the blessed. My Charley—my beautiful loving, gladsome baby, so loving, so sweet, so full of life and hope and strength—now lies shrouded, pale and cold in the room below. Never was he anything to me but a comfort. He has been my pride and joy. Many a heartache has he cured for me. Many an anxious night have I held him to my bosom and felt the sorrow and loneliness pass out of me with the touch of his little warm hands."

After an absence of fifteen months, Calvin Stowe returned to Lane Seminary. With Harriet by his side, he went to the graveyard and visited Charley's grave together with that of Eliza. It was a time of sorrow. But amidst his tears, he had good news for Harriet. "Bowdoin College in Brunswick has offered me a position on the faculty," he said.

"Will you accept it?"

"They've only offered me $1,000 a year. But I'm ready to leave. This climate and the cholera are not for me."

"When will we leave?"

"I don't know. I would be less than Christian if I did not get an official release from Lane before I sign a contract with Bowdoin."

When Calvin approached the trustees, they shocked him by offering to increase his salary to $1,500. (They were enabled to do this because of two almost unbelievable events: The panic of 1837, which wiped out the House of Tappan and closed many banks, had inspired thousands to go West. The population of Cincinnati had increased to 100,000. This immigration had skyrocketed the value of land. In addition, it had been discovered that the land in Walnut Hills was ideal for raising an especially valuable type of grapes.)

With their acres worth a thousand dollars each, Lane Seminary had suddenly become quite adequately endowed.

After Calvin had explained the situation, Harriet had one question: "What shall we do?"

"Pray," he replied.

When Bowdoin learned about Lane's offer, they agreed to give Calvin a $500 bonus.

During the weeks of negotiation, Harriet discovered that she was again to become a mother in July. What should they do? It was finally decided that they would accept the offer from Bowdoin, and since they did not provide a home, Harriet would leave in the spring and rent a house and get it prepared in time for Calvin's arrival for the next semester.

Ignoring her usual morning sickness, Harriet prepared to move. She carefully packed Charlie's things, made clothes for the children who would accompany her, and put together a dress or two for herself. A visitor noticing her kneeling on the floor and cutting out a dress was curious. "Don't you have a pattern?" she asked in a tone of amazement.

"I don't need a pattern," replied Harriet as she continued to snip. "Patterns are a waste of money. I know my own shape."

Standing with fourteen-year-old Hattie, one of the twins, together with Freddie William and young Georgiana May at Cincinnati's Public Landing, Harriet bid farewell to Calvin and her other two children who were remaining with him in Cincinnati.

As time for departure drew near, she herded the family up the gangplank and lingered at the rail for a final glimpse of those who were being left behind. Soon the whistle's melancholy announcement filled the air and the huge sidewheels began to turn. Harriet and her children waved until those who were being left behind were out of sight. While heading toward their cabin, Harriet noticed a handbill on the deck. What she read stirred her deep within.

$1200 TO 1250 DOLLARS
FOR NEGROES!!

The undersigned wishes to purchase a large lot of NEGROES for the New Orleans market. I will pay $1200 to $1250 for No. 1 young men and $850 to $1000 for No. 1 young women. In fact, I will pay more for likely NEGROES than any other trader in Kentucky. My office is adjoining the Broadway Hotel, on Broadway in Lexington, Ky., where I or my agent can always be found.

WM. F. Talbott

The sun was near the horizon when the ship began to ease by Ripley, Ohio. Hurrying her children to the rail, Harriet spoke excitedly. "This is the place where Eliza crossed on the ice." Then pointing to the house on the cliff, she added with even more excitement, "That's the home of Brother John Rankin. He's the one who helped Eliza after she'd crossed. He gave her and her little boy food and clothes and got them started on the Underground Railway. Rankin's a real man of God. Your father and I began our courtship in his house."

Suddenly Harriet bubbled over with even more excitement. "Look! Look!" she all but shouted. "They've just lit their lantern!"

"And why did they do that?" asked Hattie, straining to see it.

"To guide other runaways."

Following a long silence, Freddie peered into his mother's face. "Mama," he asked, "why don't you write a story about Eliza crossing the ice? I can almost see her as she falls and slips; and I can even hear the cakes of ice as they slam into each other."

"Yes, Mama," added Hattie, "why don't you write a story about her? Such a story could show the evils of slavery."

"Maybe I will," replied Harriet thoughtfully. "Yes, maybe I will."

The boat reached Pittsburgh between three and five on Wednesday morning. Harriet described the event in a letter to Calvin: "The agent for the Pennsylvania Canal came on board and soon filled out our tickets, calling my three chicks one and a half."

Passing through the locks was a unique experience. As the inflowing water lifted the ship higher in the first lock, the children were fascinated. Then, when it entered the next lock for additional lift, their eyes widened. It was an occasion none of them would forget. But the next morning their joy was quenched by a surly agent who confronted them at a depot where they were scheduled to change trains at between two and three in the morning. Noticing Harriet's swollen abdomen—she was six months along—the shawl over her head, and the sleepy children in their hand-me-downs, he made up his mind quickly.

"I'm sorry," he snapped, "we don't allow no immigrants in the waiting room. You and your children will have to wait outside."

Fortunately, the weather was rather mild. But not wanting her children to form a bad opinion of the agent, Harriet focused their attention on the exceptionally clear sky. "Look at the stars," she said. "When runaway slaves are heading toward Canada, they don't have maps to follow. Ah, but the Lord has provided them a map in the stars."

Pointing to the North Star just above the Big Dipper, she continued, "The escaping slaves follow that star, and it leads them to Canada. They even have a song they sing about it. It goes like this:

> 'When the sun comes back,
>   and the first quail calls,
> Follow the drinkin' gourd,
> For the old man is a-waitin'
> For to carry you to freedom
> If you follow the drinkin' gourd.' "

At three o'clock in the afternoon their train rolled to a stop in Philadelphia. At Lancaster, Harriet sent a telegram to Henry Ward in Brooklyn and he arranged for their cousin Augustus to meet them at the ferry in New York.

18

The Vision

After a day of rest, Harriet felt a fresh glow of health. Inspired by what her brother was doing, she immediately wrote to Calvin. "Henry's people are more than ever in love with him, and have raised his salary to $3300, and given him a beautiful horse and carriage. . . . My plan is to spend a week in Brooklyn, one in Hartford, one in Boston, and then go on to Brunswick sometime in May or June."

While in Brooklyn, Harriet called on several publishers. "Yes, we like your work and we want to see more of it," they said. Inspired, she began to think about writing some stories about slavery. One evening she approached the subject of slavery to Henry. "I read about how you raised some money to buy and free a pair of mulattoes," she began.

Henry Ward smiled. "That happened in the Broadway Tabernacle," he replied. "I'll never forget the occasion. It was on Thursday, December 7, 1848. I, along with several others, had been asked to speak on slavery. When I learned that those two beautiful runaways were about to be returned to New Orleans, I decided to raise the money to pay for them."

"And so what did you do?" Harriet moistened her lips and leaned forward.

"I stood with the girls on the platform; and then, pretending I was an auctioneer, I began to sell them in order to raise enough money to buy their freedom from their owner.

" 'Who'll give a thousand?' I cried. Several hands went up. 'Who'll raise it to fifteen hundred?' When they hesitated, I said, 'I'm sure you know what will happen to these girls. Since they are beautiful they will be sold for evil purposes.

Come, let's pay fifteen hundred. After that had prompted more hands to be lifted, I raised the challenge to twenty-five hundred. That seemed to be too much and so I urged them to dig deep by saying, 'These girls can be trusted. They were converted at a camp meeting. If we don't buy their freedom they will be bred by their owners and their children will be torn from them and sold. Twenty-five hundred dollars is just a pittance in comparison to their worth. Remember Jesus Christ died for these girls.'

"Soon the twenty-five hundred was offered and I was able to cry, 'Sold.'

"Hattie, you should have been there. People emptied their pockets. They put their rings and watches in the offering plates. There wasn't a dry eye in the building."

"I'm so proud of you," Harriet said softly. "I only wish that I, too, could do something."

"You can."

"How?"

"Write a book. Hattie, you have great talent."

Pondering this suggestion, Harriet outlined quickly in her mind the book she had dimly considered writing. "It's main thrust," she explained, "would be to show people through the use of fiction the utter inhumanity of slavery. While in Cincinnati and on my trips into Kentucky, I saw things I'll never forget—"

"Write it!" encouraged Henry Ward. "Write it and I'll scatter it like the leaves of Vallambrosa."

Thoroughly excited, Harriet was unable to get to sleep until early the next morning. She had been dazzled by her younger brother. He was rapidly becoming the most popular preacher in America. Reporters shadowed him. He had access to editorial offices. His lectures were in demand. Usually when he spoke the crowds filled the buildings to standing-room-only. And now he had pledged to use his influence to make *her* book known!

Yes, it was God's timing for her to be in Brooklyn.

According to plan, Harriet next visited Hartford, where she stayed with her sister Mary and her lawyer husband. She then journeyed to Boston and spent time with Edward. No longer a college president, Edward—now a Doctor of Divinity—had returned to Boston in 1844 as the pastor of the Salem Street Church. It was on this trip or another—the data is confusing—that Harriet either met Josiah Henson or read an early version of his autobiography that had been published in 1849.

Henson, claimed by many to have been Harriet's model for Uncle Tom, was unusual. This man, with a high forehead and expressive lips, had lectured in England, met the Archbishop of Canterbury—and had even exchanged nods with Queen Victoria. He was born in Maryland on June 15, 1789. Both parents were slaves. They worked for Francis Newman on a farm about a mile from Port Tobacco.

Josiah's only memory of his childhood was bitter. It seemed that the white overseer had taken his mother to a lonely place in order to rape her. Attracted by her screams, his father struck the man. Realizing the consequences of this act, he fled to the woods. Eventually starved out, he was bound, and led to a public place to be punished in the presence of other slaves.

Hewes, a strong-armed blacksmith, was assigned the task of applying fifty lashes. While the whip was cutting furrows in the man's back, it was feared that he might be killed. This would never do, for he was a hard worker and was worth a substantial amount of money. But after his pulse was taken, it was decided that he could stand the entire prescription, and the fiftieth lash was duly applied. He was then assisted to a post where his right ear was securely nailed with a tack. Then, while every eye watched, the ear was severed close to his head and left on the post as a warning to other slaves that "a nigger should never strike a white man."

While growing up, Josiah kept hearing about John McKenny, a baker who preached. McKenny despised slavery, and Josiah longed to hear him. But each time he approached his master for permission, he was beaten. Eventually, however, the master relented.

Josiah was spellbound as he listened to the man who refused to own slaves expound the text: "That he, by the grace of God, should taste of death for every man" (Heb. 2:9).

Overwhelmed by the unbelievable news that Almighty God loved everyone—even black slaves—Josiah's tears streamed down his face. Eventually he was converted and became a Methodist preacher. After a lot of hard work he managed to buy his freedom. But, tricked out of his manumission papers, he was resold into slavery. And since his new owner could not buy his wife and children, Josiah was separated from them. Even so, he kept the faith.

Through prayer, God's providence, and a few miracles,

Josiah crossed the Ohio, was reunited with his family, and after numerous hair-raising episodes, escaped with them to Canada. There he became financially prosperous.

With Josiah's story burning within her heart, Harriet bade Edward and his wife farewell and headed for Brunswick. The new baby was due in July, so there was no time to waste.

Harriet arrived in Brunswick on May 25. Almost immediately she rented the Titcomb house. It was ideally located—only a fifteen-minute walk from the Bowdoin campus. Better yet, Calvin, along with Henry Wadsworth Longfellow and his brother Samuel, had roomed there while the three of them were attending Bowdoin.

In spite of her condition, Harriet hired and managed workers in order to make the place livable. Also, they helped her set up the furniture she had bought and shipped from Boston. While she was rushing from one task to another, the postman handed her a letter from Calvin. No one has a copy of that letter, but we do have Harriet's comments about it: "Then comes a letter from my husband, saying he is sick abed, and all but dead don't [sic] ever expect to see his family again; wants to know how I shall manage, in case I am left a widow; knows we shall get in debt and never get out; wonders at my courage; thinks I am very sanguine; warns me to be prudent, as there won't be much to live on in case of his death, etc., etc., etc."

How did this affect Harriet? From the beginning of her marriage she knew that Calvin, like her father, was afflicted with the hypos. But since Calvin's pessimism was much deeper and lasted longer than that of her father's, she dubbed his: the *indigoes*. Paying no attention to his indigoes, she continued: "I read the letter and poke it into the stove, and proceed. . . ."

Harriet was too busy to enjoy a seige of pessimism just then. One of her problems was the sink. "In all my moving and fussing, Mr. Titcomb has been my right-hand man. Whenever a screw was loose, a nail to be driven, a lock mended, a pane of glass set—and these cases were manifold—he was always on hand. But my sink was no fancy job, and I believe nothing but a very particular friendship would have moved him to undertake it. So this sink lingered in a precarious state for some weeks, and when I had *nothing else to do*, I used to call and do what I could in the way of enlisting the good man's sympathies in its behalf.

"How many times I have been in and seated myself in one of the old rocking chairs, and talked first of the news of the day, the railroad, the last proceedings of Congress, the probabilities about the millenium, and thus brought the conversation little by little round to my sink—because, till the sink was done, the pump could not be put up, and we couldn't have any rainwater. Sometimes my courage would quite fail me to introduce the subject, and I would talk about everything else, turn and get out of the shop, and then turn back as if a thought had just struck my mind, and say, 'Oh, Mr. Titcomb—about that sink?'

" 'Yes, ma'am, I was thinking about going down the street this afternoon to look for parts for it.'

" 'Yes, sir, if you would be good enough to get it done as soon as possible; we are in great need of it.'

" 'I think there's no hurry. I believe we're going to have a dry time now, so that you could not catch any water, and you won't need a pump at present.'

"These negotiations extended from the first of June to the first of July, and at last my sink was completed. . . . Also during this time good Mrs. Mitchell and I made two sofas, or lounges, a barrel chair, divers bedspreads, pillow cases, pillows, bolsters, mattresses; we painted rooms; we revarnished furniture; we—what *didn't* we do?"

On July 8 Harriet faced another task. She went into labor and produced another son. She named him Charles Edward.

Calvin had arrived just before the baby was born and kept busy helping Harriet, who took two weeks off to remain in bed and gather her strength. She did not however, spend her time sleeping. Instead, she kept a pile of Sir Walter Scott's novels nearby and thought of a series of articles she could write at the end of those two weeks. In the meantime, Calvin approached the Bowdoin trustees. Now that he had a new baby he needed more money. *How about a one hundred dollar raise?*

Secretly, Calvin was not concerned about how the trustees would respond because he had a more lucrative offer from Andover. Remembering that Calvin had been one of Bowdoin's most brilliant students, the trustees agreed to the raise without a question. When Calvin met again with the trustees, this time they exchanged glances.

"Lane has been unable to secure my replacement. I don't want to leave without help. Would it be possible for me to give them the next semester?"

After a private meeting, the chairman summoned Calvin. "Since we want you and need you, we'll spare you for the next semester. Then we'll expect you to be with us."

They shook hands in agreement.

Because their expenses had been unusually high, Harriet got out of bed as soon as possible and began to write. Every minute of her time was valuable; for, in addition to her writing and the care of the new baby along with the children, she had opened a school. Also, the nurse had left. The following letter indicates a typical day:

"I have written more than anybody . . . would have thought. I have taught an hour a day in our school, and I have read two hours every evening to the children. . . . Since I began this note I have been called off at least a dozen times—once to buy codfish from the fisherman; once to see a man who had brought me some barrels of apples; once to see a bookman; then to Mrs. Upman to see about a drawing I promised to make for her; then to nurse the baby; then into the kitchen to make chowder for dinner; and now I'm at it again, for nothing but deadly determination enables me ever to write; it is rowing against wind and tide."

Early in her writing career, Harriet discovered that people like to read about characters with whom they can identify. This in mind, she wrote about Christmas in Brunswick and sold the article to the *Evangelist*. After that she wrote a hilarious account about how Calvin had tried to raise a vegetable garden in Cincinnati. She titled it *A Scholar's Adventures in the Country*. But to whom should she send it?

As she considered various editors and their needs, her mind settled on Dr. Gamaliel Bailey. This former Cincinnati surgeon had been an assitant to J. G. Birney, founder and editor of *The Philanthropist*. After the rioters had silenced this paper, he had moved his headquarters to Washington, D.C. There, he started the *National Era*—another paper dedicated to the elimination of slavery.

Bailey was an expert at luring top authors. Among these, was the famous Quaker poet J. G. Whittier, Mrs. E.D.E.N. Southwick, and Grace Greenwood. Impressed by these big names, Harriet wondered if she would even be considered. Nonetheless, she decided to take a chance. Placing both this article and another on the economic woes of liberated slaves in one envelope, she mailed them to Dr. Bailey. Harriet's response came sooner than she expected. Bailey accepted both articles, asked for more—and enclosed a check for $100. With a substantial house renting for only one hundred dollars a year, ham priced at ten and three-quarters of a cent per pound, and butter at twenty-five cents a pound, one hundred dollars could last a long time—especially in the home of the Stowes.

One afternoon the mail brought her a letter from Isabella, wife of her brother Edward. Included in her note was an idea: "Hattie, if I could write as well as you, I would write something that will make this whole nation feel what an accursed thing slavery is."

Harriet studied that line for a moment. Then, her face sparked with a blend of wonder and determination, she read the challenging line to her children. Glowing with a new fire, she stood up, crumpled the letter in one hand and solemnly vowed: "I will write something." Then she thoughtfully added: "I will if I live."

That moment was electric. Each of the older children knew that something had happened to their mother.

For the rest of the day Harriet's mind was preoccupied. Toward evening she found herself slipping from the high pinnacle of inspiration into a deep, waterless valley of despair. *Who was she to think that she could write something that would stir an entire nation?* The idea was preposterous, utterly absurd! In her family, all ten of her brothers and sisters had made their lives count. She was the only one who had accomplished almost nothing. Here she was, nearly forty, and yet all she had accomplished was to give birth to seven children and publish two not so popular books. And one of those had Catherine's name on it!

That February, headlines brought the issue of slavery into every home—especially in such free states as Ohio and Maine. President Fillmore had signed into law the Compromise of 1850. This bill, also known as the Fugitive Slave Law, was to stop runaway slaves from escaping to the North. It stated that *anyone* could accuse *any* black of being a fugitive and take him to *any* court. If the one in charge agreed that the accused was a fugitive, he was paid $10. But if he freed the accused, he received only $5.

Under no circumstance was the accused allowed to testify in his own behalf. He was also denied trial by jury or habeus corpus. A warrant was not required for his arrest, and anyone who aided a fugitive was subject to a fine of $1,000 and six months in jail.

With these facts in the background, Harriet followed the sensational story of Shadrach, a black who had escaped from Virginia. While employed as a waiter, he was arrested at work and taken to a magistrate. Outraged, five Boston attorneys agreed to defend him.

The commissioner decided that they could have until Tuesday to prepare their defense. In the meantime, where was the accused to be kept? Massachusetts' law forbade the use of jails for holding fugitives. While the commissioner was pondering over a way to solve this problem, the court gradually emptied. At that point, a crowd of blacks suddenly rushed in, surrounded Shadrach, and whisked him away.

Eventually Shadrach escaped to freedom in Montreal.

Thoroughly aroused, Harriet went to her bedroom, closed the door, and knelt by her bed. "Dear Lord, if it is Thy will that I should do something to help end this terrible slavery," she prayed, "show me how and what to do. If I am to use my pen, guide it." On Saturday night, while alone with her Bible, she turned to her favorite passage in Isaiah. Once again she reread the record of the prophet's vision in the sixth chapter. As always, the opening verse seemed sublime:

> In the year that king Uzziah died I saw also the Lord sitting upon a throne, high and lifted up, and his train filled the temple.

As she read the first nine verses, she remembered how she had studied them in her grandmother's home. Then she went back to the eighth and ninth verses. Eyes glistening, she read them out loud:

> Also I heard the voice of the Lord, saying, Whom shall I send, and who will go for us? Then said I, Here *am* I; send me. And he said, Go, and tell this people, Hear ye indeed, but understand not; and see ye indeed, but perceive not.

Head bowed, cheeks drenched, Harriet prayed: "I am ready to do Thy will Lord. But, if it is in Thy will, assure me dear Lord, that I have been assigned to this task."

On Communion Sunday that same month Harriet listened carefully to the sermon. While the choir softly repeated the first verse of the communion hymn over and over again, she slipped into the aisle and knelt at the communion rail. While meditating after taking the bread and the wine, she became aware that she was having a vision.

With considerable effort, for her eyes were blinded with

tears, she groped back to her pew. While resting with bowed head, the vision became more real than life. But her vision was not a duplicate of the one experienced by Isaiah. Instead of a seraphim, she saw a saintly old black man crowned with cotton hair kneeling on the ground. And immediately in back of him, she saw two black youths beating him with cattle whips.

And while the whips tore into his flesh, she heard the brutal white slaveholder repeat again and again, "Beat him harder. Beat him harder. Kill him! Kill him!"

Back at home, Harriet sat with the family at the table. Then she excused herself and went to her study. With a pencil, she described the scene on a bit of wrapping paper. The names of the characters were easy. The old man was Uncle Tom. The youths were Sambo and Quimbo. The hard-faced white man was Simon Legree.

The scene duly recorded, Harriet placed it in a drawer. Then she returned to the table but instead of eating, she merely stared into space and wept.

19
Uncle Tom

As vivid as her vision had been, Harriet left the sketch in the drawer and turned to other projects. The wolf was still near and she needed to produce copy.

Having finished his term at Lane in early March, Calvin returned to Brunswick. While rummaging through the drawers to find a lost item, he came upon Harriet's sketch. The idea inflamed his heart.

Facing his wife, voice quivering, he urged, "Hattie, you must go on with it. You must make a story, with this as a climax. The Lord intends it so."

Deeply inspired, for Calvin's approval was of utmost importance, Harriet composed a query letter—perhaps the most important query letter ever to be written. In carefully worded sentences she wrote:

Brunswick, March 9

Mr. Bailey, Dear Sir:

I am at present occupied with a story that will be much longer than any I have ever written, embracing a series of sketches that give the lights and shadows of the "patriarchal institution," written from either observation, incidents which have occurred in the sphere of my personal knowledge, or in the knowledge of my friends. I shall show the *best side* of the thing, and something *faintly approaching the worst.*

Up to this year I have always felt that I had no particular call to meddle with the subject, and I dreaded to expose even my own mind to the full force of its exciting power. . . .

My vocation is simply that of a *painter*, and my object will be to hold up in the most lifelike and graphic manner

possible slavery—its reverses, changes, and the negro character, which I have had ample opportunities for studying.
There is no arguing with *pictures*, and everybody is impressed by them whether they mean to be or not.
. . . The thing may extend through three or four numbers. It will be ready in two or three weeks.

> Yours with sincere esteem,
> H. Stowe

Having mailed her query, Harriet continued with the
story. It had started with an eye-catching picture amply laced
with action, and sharpened with characterization that was
equal to Charles Dickens at his best.

"Late in the afternoon of a chilly day in February, two
gentlemen were sitting alone over their wine, in a well-furnished dining parlor, in the town of P—, in Kentucky. There
were no servants present, and the gentlemen, deeply en-
grossed, seemed to be discussing some subject with great
earnestness.

"For convenience' sake, we have said, hitherto, two gentlemen. One of the parties, however, when critically examined, did not seem, strictly speaking, to come under the spec-
ies. He was a short, thickset man, with coarse, commonplace
features, and that swaggering air of pretention which marks
a low man who is trying to elbow upward in the world. He
was much over-dressed, in a gaudy vest of many colors, a
blue neckerchief, bedropped gayly with yellow spots, and arranged with a flaunting tie, quite in keeping with the general
air of the man. His hands, large and coarse, were plentifully
bedecked with rings, and he wore a heavy gold watch, with
a bundle of seals of portentious size."

As Harriet kept dipping her pen, she continued to pray
that her story would not only be gripping, but it would be
appreciated in *both* the North and the South. This in mind,
she pictured the slave-owning Shelbys as cultured people.
Indeed, Mrs. Shelby was an earnest Christian who taught
Eliza the ways of the Lord, and treated her as a member of
the family. Likewise, she did not confine the crude dialect she
often used to the blacks. The slave-trader Haley himself
twisted English into all sorts of shapes. In arguing that Eliza
would recover from having her little Harry taken away from
her and sold, Harriet had him respond:

"Lor' bless ye, yes! These critters ain't like white folks, you
know; they gets over things, only manage right. Now they say
that this kind o' trade is hardening to the feelings; but I never

found it so. Fact is, I never could do things up the way some fellers manage the business. I've seen 'em as would pull a woman's child out of her arms, and set him up to sell, and she screechin' like mad all the time; very bad policy—damages the article—makes 'em quite unfit for service sometimes. I knew a real handsome gal once, in Orleans, as was entirely ruined by this sort o' handling. The fellow that was trading for her didn't want her baby; and she was one of your real high sort, when her blood was up. I tell you she squeezed up her child in her arms, and talked and went on real awful. It kinder makes my blood run cold to think on't; and when they carried off the child and locked her up, she just went ravin' mad, and died in a week. Clear waste, sir, of a thousand dollars, just for want of management—there's where 'tis. It's always best to do the humane thing, sir; that's been my experience."

Bailey replied almost immediately to Harriet's query with an offer of $300. This was a lot of money for the impoverished Stowes. Harriet accepted the offer immediately. After all, she believed her work would be done in about three weeks; and then she could begin writing some other stories and articles that had been fermenting in her mind.

On May 8, Editor Bailey alerted his readers about a fresh story he was about to offer to them. His insertion in the *Era* reveals his opinion of Harriet.

A New Story by Mrs. Stowe—
Week after next we propose to commence in the *Era* the publication of a new story by Mrs. H. B. Stowe, the title of which will be, *Uncle Tom's Cabin* or *The Man That Was a Thing*. It will probably be of the length of the Tale by Mrs. Southworth, entitled *Retribution*.
Mrs. Stowe is one of the most gifted and popular of American writers. We announce her story in advance, that none of our subscribers, through neglect to renew their subscriptions, may lose the beginning of it.

In the middle of June, Harriet received by mail the author's copies of the first issue of THE NATIONAL ERA to carry her story. The four-page paper, printed on coarse stock, was 26½ inches high and 18¾ inches wide. The subscription price was "two dollars per annum, payable in advance." Ads "Not exceeding 10 lines and inserted three times" could be run for one dollar, and "afterward 25¢ an insertion."
Eagerly, Harriet scanned the front page of that June 5,

1851, issue, which, by coincidence, had been dated nine days before her fortieth birthday. Yes, her story was the featured one! It began at the best place—the top of the left-hand column. Eyes glowing, she read the notice just above the title.

(Copyright secured by the Author)
For the National Era
UNCLE TOM'S CABIN:
or
LIFE AMONG THE LOWLY
By Mrs. H. B. Stowe

The first installment of her story occupied more than half of the front page. The next installment appeared in the June 12 issue. This installment had shrunk to a mere column; and it came *after* Grace Greenwood's short story, which began in the choice place at the top of the left-hand column.

Harriet was concerned. But her concern ended when Bailey published a "fan" letter in the first July issue. Summoning Calvin, she said, "Listen to this." Holding the paper to the light, she read: "Sir: 'Uncle Tom's Cabin' increases in interest and pathos with each successive number. None of thy various contributions, rich and varied as they have been, have so deeply interested thy female readers of this vicinity as this story of Mrs. Stowe . . ."

Harriet folded the paper. "Well, Professor Stowe," she demanded, "what do you think of that?"

"I think it's wonderful," he replied, wrapping his arms around her. "It proves that *I* was right when *I* told you that *I* knew that God wanted *my* little wife to be a writer." He kissed her soundly and they both laughed.

Encouraged by the steady stream of fan mail, Bailey restored Uncle Tom to the number one spot in most issues. On July 10, chapter 7—Harriet was still calling each section an article—appeared. Harriet had found it difficult to contain her excitement as her pen rushed over the pages while she was writing about Eliza crossing the ice. Having twice been to that spot just below Ripley, and having lost her own little Charley to the cholera, she identified with Eliza as she clutched little Harry to her bosom, fled the dogs—and faced the ice-jammed Ohio.

One can imagine the tenseness of the Quaker woman who wrote the published fan letter as she pursued Harriet's lines:

"The trader caught a full glimpse of her, just as she was disappearing down the bank; and throwing himself from the horse, and calling loudly to Sam and Andy, he was after her like a hound after a deer. In that dizzy moment her feet—to her—scarce seemed to touch the ground, and a moment brought her to the water's edge. Right on behind they came; and, nerved with such strength as God gives only to the desperate, with one wild cry and flying leap, she vaulted sheer over the turbid current by the shore, onto the raft of ice beyond. It was a desperate leap—impossible to anything but madness and despair; and Haley, Sam, and Andy, instinctively cried out, and lifted up their hands as she did it.

"The huge green fragment of ice on which she alighted pitched and creaked as her weight came on it, but she stayed there not a moment. With wild cries and desperate energy, she leaped to another and still another cake—stumbling—leaping—slipping—springing upwards again! Her shoes were gone—her stockings cut from her feet—while blood marked every step; but she saw nothing, felt nothing, till dimly, as in a dream, she saw the Ohio side, and a man helping her up the bank.

" 'Yer a brave gal, now, whoever ye ar!' said the man, with an oath."

In the back of Harriet's mind when she finished writing that seventh "article" was the conversation she had had years before with the freed-slave Sam in the back of the Wolcott home. They had been discussing how the women in Litchfield had melted the statue of George III and turned it into 42,088 bullets for the benefit of the Continental Army when he said, "Miss Hattie, I wish we had some statues which could be turned into bullets."

At the time, she didn't know what he meant. But during their discussion about the horrors he had experienced as a slave, she realized that he meant that past experiences were like statues—statues that could be melted just as George III was melted. And that evening she had promised herself that someday she would transform some of her own experiences into word-bullets and fire them at the institution of slavery. That time had come! *The National Era* was now hurling her 30,000 word-bullets at the public.

But Harriet faced a new problem. The story had merely started! By the time she was finished, it would be over 100,000 words long. Bailey had agreed to pay $300 for the *complete* work. Her query had stated: "The thing may extend through three or four numbers." If she continued with an additional 70,000 words, she would be writing them for nothing. She was not greedy. Still, the bills had to be paid. Perplexed, she went to her room, closed the door, reread the first nine verses of the sixth chapter of Isaiah, sank down on her knees, and prayed for direction.

Her answer was not audible. Nonetheless, it was categorical. *I have given you talent. I've prepared you to identify with the slaves by allowing you to be poor, nearly blind on two occasions, to be unwanted, made to stand outside at a train depot, to hold a lifeless son in your arms; to have a famous father, an angel-mother, and to be married to a brilliant husband. I will take care of your financial needs. I provided the names for your main characters. Write "Uncle Tom's Cabin"!*

Getting up, Harriet washed her face, went down to the kitchen, and began to prepare a large kettle of chowder. As she chopped the clams, cubed the potatoes, added milk and seasoning, new ideas and characters leaped fully developed into her mind. Needing a comic to relieve the more intense drama, she allowed the "goblin-like" Topsy to step onto the stage.

    " 'Have you ever heard anything about God, Topsy?' "
    "The child looked bewildered, but grinned as usual.
    " 'Do you know who made you?' "
    " 'Nobody, as I knows on,' " said the child with a short laugh.
    "The idea appeared to amuse her considerably; for her eyes twinkled, and she added, 'I spect I grow'd. Don't think nobody never made me.' "

Where was the fictional Topsy born? Undoubtedly she was a composite of several black children Harriet had met in Kentucky. As to her frequently used word "spect" it may have come right out of the mouth of Calvin himself who often used it.

Uncle Tom was undoubtedly inspired by Josiah Henson and many other kind blacks Harriet had known. The portly black woman Candace had been a special comfort to Harriet when her mother died. She remembered how the freed woman had drawn her close and how her tears had dropped on her hand. Candace had that same type of Christlike compassion which Harriet placed in the character of her black hero.

There were numerous blacks in both the North and the South who had at least some of the attributes of Uncle Tom.

Likewise, there were many brutes in both sections of the nation who resembled Simon Legree. On his trip back from New Orleans, Charles Beecher met an overseer on the boat. Explaining the occasion to Harriet, he said, "The man's fist was as solid as a burl of oak. After I had complied by feeling it, he boasted, 'I got that from knockin' down niggers.' " With this key, Harriet had no difficulty in describing the monster.

"After purchasing Tom, Legree noticed the black man's Methodist hymnbook. Incensed, he sneered, 'Humph! pious to be sure. So, what's yer name—you belong to the church, eh?'

" 'Yes, Mas'r,' said Tom firmly.

" 'Well, I'll soon have *that* out of you. I have none o' yer bawling, praying, singing niggers on my place; so remember. Now, mind yourself,' he said with a stamp and fierce glance of his gray eye, directed at Tom, '*I'm* your church now! You understand—you've got to be as I say.' "

The more Harriet wrote, the more she needed to write in order to keep up with the ideas that kept flooding her heart demanding to be expressed. Soon the story was one hundred thousand words long. But in her heart she knew that she would have to write at least that many more. The writing was easy. It flowed like a stream. In love with the dash, she often ignored other types of punctuation. After all, correcting copy was the way editors earned their livings. Harriet's writing had its peculiarities. Where letters were repeated, the first letter was by far the largest; and when she used the symbol for *and* it resembled the first cousin of the symbol for the figure two.

But the mere mechanical effort of putting words on paper was not her major problem. Her major problem was that as she melted portions of her memory-statue, she so identified with the character or scene that she became emotionally exhausted. This is what happened when she wrote chapter 26—the story of Eva's death. When she finished writing it, she was so drained she had to remain in bed for two days. This meant that on Thursday, December 18, *The National Era* appeared without an Uncle Tom installment. Embarrassed, Bailey apologized:

> We regret as much as any of our readers can regret that Mrs. Stowe has no chapter in this week's *Era*. It is not our fault, for up to this hour we have nothing from her. As she is generally so punctual, we fear that sickness may have prevented. . . .

Sometimes Harriet became weary as she continued on in the second one hundred thousand words. Not only were her fingers and mind exhausted, but the cupboard, too, began to look bare. She hoped that Bailey would send her an additional check. He did not. A frugal man, he reasoned that a deal was a deal.

Straining at the exhausting task before her, Harriet kept filling her inkwell and reaching for more sheets of paper. Then Bailey published a reader's suggestion that she might shorten the story and bring things to a rapid conclusion. That idea seemed to Harriet to be an excellent one. But as she wrestled with temptation, Bailey published another suggestion. This one was like a whiplash. She reread it several times, gulped, smiled, and reached for a fresh stack of paper. The writer whose name was signed J.D.L. had written:

> Please signify to Mrs. Stowe that it will be quite agreeable to the wishes of very many of the readers of the *Era* for her *not to hurry through* "Uncle Tom." We don't get sleepy reading it . . .

Soon after Harriet received her second wind, her father and his stepdaughter moved in. "Now that I've resigned from Lane," explained Beecher, "Jewett & Co. want to bring out six volumes of my sermons. Since this is a quiet place, I'll work on them here."

"Yes, Pa," replied Harriet, making a strong effort to hide her exasperation.

As Harriet feared, her father and stepsister appropriated her writing table. It never occurred to him that he was inconveniencing Harriet. After all, he was giving the world his exposition of *New Light* theology, while she was merely writing fiction!

In November Harriet received a new type of letter. This one was from Mrs. Hale, the editor of *Godey's Lady's Book*. This editor from Philadelphia, Harriet learned, was publishing a book about distinguished American female writers, and wanted to do a chapter about her. And, in order to properly do this, she needed a sketch of Harriet's life—and a daguerreotype.

Harriet read the letter out loud to the family, and then she replied:

> Dear Madam:
> I am quite amused, I must say, at your letter to me, wholly innocent as I am of any pretentions to rank among 'distinguished women.'

The idea of the daguerreotype especially was quite droll, and I diverted myself somewhat with figuring the astonishment of the children, should the well-known visage of their mother loom out of the pages of a book before their astonished eyes.

Harriet then scribbled a short two-paragraph outline of her life. It included a P.S. "In answer to one of your queries, I would say that I have published but one book, *The Mayflowers*, by the Harpers." She didn't mention the requested daguerreotype for the practical reason that such a chemical picture cost from $15 to $25 each—the price of a silk dress. And since Harriet had never owned a silk dress, the purchase of one in the future had top priority.

Harriet was practically scraping the bottom of the barrel for money when Calvin received an offer to teach a course in Andover for the winter semester. This supplied fresh income and provided Harriet the use of his study. *Yes*, she agreed, *the Lord was supplying their need*!

The martyrdom of Uncle Tom in chapter forty totally exhausted Harriet. As she spread her thin line of ink on the paper, she saw, felt, and heard each detail of the event. Emmeline and Cassy had fled, and since Uncle Tom alone knew where they were, Simon Legree confronted him.

" 'Well, Tom!' said Legree, walking up and seizing him grimly by the collar of his coat, and speaking through his teeth in a paroxysm of determined rage, 'do you know I've made up my mind to kill you?'

" 'It's very likely, Mas'r,' said Tom calmly.

" 'I *have*,' said Legree, with grim, terrible calmness, '*done—just—that—thing*, Tom, unless you'll tell me what you know about these yer gals!'

"Tom stood silent.

" 'D'ye hear?' said Legree, stamping, with a roar like that of an incensed lion. 'Speak!'

" '*I han't got nothing to tell*, Mas'r,' said Tom, with a slow, firm, deliberate utterance.

" 'Do you dare to tell me, ye old black Christian, ye don't *know*?' said Legree.

"Tom stood silent.

" 'Speak!' thundered Legree, striking him furiously. 'Do you know anything?'

" 'I know, Mas'r; but I can't tell anything. I *can die*!'

"Legree drew in a long breath; and, suppressing his rage, took Tom by the arm, and, approaching his face almost to his, said, in a terrible voice, 'Hark'e, Tom!—ye think, 'cause

I've let you off before, I don't mean what I say; but this time, I've *made up my mind*, and counted the cost. You've always stood it out agin' me: now I'll *conquer ye*, or *kill ye*—one or t'other. I'll count every drop of blood there is in you, and take 'em, one by one, till ye give up!'

"Tom looked up to his master, and answered, 'Mas'r, if you was sick or in trouble, or dying, and I could save ye, I'd give ye my heart's blood; and, if taking every drop of blood in this poor old body would save your precious soul, I'd give 'em freely, as the Lord gave His for me. Oh, Mas'r! don't bring this great sin on your soul! It will hurt you more than 'twill me! Do the worst you can, my troubles'll be over soon; but if you don't repent, yours won't *never* end.' "

As these words streamed from Harriet's pen, she again became acutely conscious that she was being used by God. *Could it be that "Uncle Tom's Cabin" might be used to strike a mortal blow against slavery?* Tingling with inspiration, her mind returned to Oliver Wendell Holmes. His few lines of poetry had saved Old Ironsides from oblivion.

Canvassing her mind for a way to bring an unforgettable conclusion to Tom's martyrdom, Harriet recalled the occasion when her mother took her to the Old North Church in Boston. She remembered as if it had happened a few minutes before the way the guide had related how Robert Newman had climbed the tower with the lanterns. "They were," he said, "to alert the Minute Men whether the British were coming by land or by sea." As she pondered her problem, she remembered the words of Jesus: "No man, when he hath lighted a candle, putteth it in a secret place, neither under a bushel, but on a candlestick, that they which come in may see the light" (Luke 11:33).

But *what kind of lanterns should she use, and where should she have them waved?* The answer came immediately. Tom's actions could become the lantern that would not only solve the problem of slavery, but all other human problems as well. Feeling a divine inspiration, Harriet dipped her pen and started to write.

"After Tom had fainted, Sambo and Quimbo put him on a bed and gently washed his wounds. When he opened his eyes, he saw the men who had beaten him hovering about.

" 'Oh, Tom!' said Quimbo, 'we's been awful wicked to ye!'
" 'I forgive ye, with all my heart!' said Tom, faintly.
" 'Oh, Tom! do tell us who is *Jesus*, anyhow?' said

Sambo—'Jesus, that's been a-standin' by you so, all this night!—Who is he?'

"The word roused the failing, fainting spirit. He poured forth a few energetic sentences of that wondrous One—His life, His death, His everlasting presence and power to save.

"They wept—both the savage men.

" 'Why didn't I never hear this before?' said Sambo, 'but I do believe—I can't help it; Lord Jesus, have mercy on us!'

" 'Poor critters!' said Tom, 'I'd be willing to bar all I have, if it'll only bring ye to Christ! O Lord! give me these two more souls, I pray.'

"That prayer was answered!"

As the serial continued, Harriet asked Calvin to call on the John P. Jewett in Boston and arrange for book publication. Jewett was not enthusiastic. "It's a long book," he said, "It will have to come out in two volumes." He paused and rubbed his chin. "Tell you what, Professor Stowe, if you'll put up half the cost, I'll share half the profits."

Calvin winced and scratched his side-whiskers. He barely had enough money to last through the end of the month.

"Or," continued Jewett thoughtfully, "I'll pay ten percent royalty. The decision is yours."

An advance was not even mentioned.

After discussing the proposition with his friend, Congressman Philip Greeley, Calvin decided to take the ten percent royalty. When Harriet saw the agreement signed by her husband, she remarked, "I hope it will make enough so that I may have a silk dress." (She was often embarrassed at church because she was the only professor's wife who couldn't dress in silk.)

Although the contract had been signed, Harriet added an additional fourteen thousand words. She also combed the script for errors and made numerous changes. Perhaps because she remembered the name Aaron Burr with horror, she changed the Ohio Senator Burr to Bird. She also improved the dialect. Yer oughter became ye oughter; just was changed into jist; der Lord was altered to de Lord.

Since Jewett had been setting each installment in type as it appeared in the *Era*, Harriet did not have to wait long before the book came off the presses. The March 4 issue of the paper promised that it would be ready on March 20.

When Harriet read that announcement, together with the descriptive line which followed, she began to wish that she could speed the calendar.

20

Grapes of Wrath

By March 13, Jewett had printed 5,000 copies of the two-volume book. He described the set as having "six elegant designs by Billings, engraved by Baker." The price was reasonable: "Paper cover for $1, cloth $1.50, cloth full gilt $2."

Having finished his term at Andover, Calvin secured several sets for Harriet, and he also presented one set to Congressman Greeley. Greeley had not read any of it as it was published in the *Era*, but he thanked Calvin, and told him that he would read it on the train during his trip to Washington. Halfway expecting to be bored, he opened the first volume and started at the very beginning.

The first line, "Late in the afternoon of a chilly day in February, two gentlemen were sitting alone over their wine in a well-furnished dining-parlor in the town of P—, in Kentucky," sank claws into his heart and refused to let go. With the Fugitive Slave Law on his mind, the book became a living thing. The click-clack of the carriage wheels faded into silence as the characters came to life. The pages shuffled beneath his fingers. Then he became conscious of tears fighting their way down his cheeks and of people staring at him. But in spite of the scene he was creating, he could not lay the book down. In desperation he broke his journey at Springfield, checked into a hotel, and sobbed his way through both volumes.

Uncle Tom's Cabin was on its way!

Secretly, Calvin had been calculating what the royalties might be if the 5,000 sets were sold in a year. All his figuring was a waste of time. On the morning of publication, Jewett faced 3,000 orders, and the next day 2,000 additional orders thumped into his box. He ordered another printing and then another and another. By the end of three weeks twenty thousand copies had been gobbled up.

Harriet was wide-eyed as she read the news. The Portland, Maine *Inquirer* unashamedly printed an apology: "Our readers will please excuse any omissions this week, for we are reading *Uncle Tom*."[1] The Boston *Traveller* was also excited. It reported that one hundred book-binders could not keep up with the orders, that "the publisher is still thousands of copies behind."[2]

As the orders streamed in, so did the fan letters. Henry Wadsworth Longfellow declared, "It is one of the greatest triumphs recorded in literary history, to say nothing of the higher triumph of its moral effect." And Whittier wrote, "Ten thousand thanks for thy immortal book."

Toward the end of July, Harriet received a letter from Jewett, which she surmised was her first royalty check. Her fingers trembled as she slit it open. Then she gasped, "Calvin, look at this. It is for $10,300! And it earned that much in only three months. . . . The orders are still pouring in!"

Calvin picked up the check and stared. Then he held it to the light and studied the signature. Finally, he said, "Please remember Hattie that *I* am the one who told you to be a writer."

Harriet smiled and threw her arms around his neck. Then, recovering herself and standing before a mirror, she said, "Now I'm going to have a silk dress together with a bustle even if they cost twenty-five dollars!"

In answer to the constant praise that crossed her desk, Harriet kept insisting in various ways that she didn't write the book, that she had been merely a tool in the hand of the Almighty. To a British Lord she wrote: "I am utterly incredulous of all that is said—it passes me by like a dream. I can only see, that when a Higher Being has purposes to accomplish, He can make even 'a grain of mustard seed' the means."

In answer to a lady who inquired about her, Harriet replied with a descriptive, much-quoted letter:

> So you want to know something about what sort of woman I am! Well, if this is any object, you shall have sta-

---

[1]*Crusade in Crinoline*, p. 281.
[2]Ibid.

tistics free of charge. To begin, then, I am a little bit of a woman—somewhat more than forty, about as thin and dry as a pinch of snuff; never much to look at in my best days, and looking like a used-up article now.

Everyone, however, was not happy about *Uncle Tom*. The *Alabama Planter* sneered: "The woman who wrote it must be either a very bad or a very fanatical person. For her own domestic peace we trust no enemy will ever penetrate into her household to pervert the scenes he may find there with as little logic or kindness as she has used in 'Uncle Tom's Cabin.' "

Some northern papers also disliked it. The *New York Observer* was blunt: "We have read the book and regard it as anti-Christian. . . . We have marked numerous passages in which religion is spoken of in terms of contempt."

Many southern bookstores refused to stock the book. When Henry Pillow, just out of Cambridge, was asked by a young lady in Charleston, South Carolina, to get her a copy, he went to a Charleston bookstore.

"We don't carry no such book in our house!" exclaimed the clerk, not believing what he had heard.

Finally, Pillow found a copy by ringing the back doorbell of a house in the slums. He had to pay five dollars for the used paperback. When the story got around, some young planters threatened to challenge him to a duel. He escaped by fleeing to South America. Years later, he inherited the title Earl of Exmouth.

The book became a sensation in England, where it sold one and a half million copies, but because the international copyrights did not come into effect until four years later, Harriet received only voluntary renumeration.

Uncle Tom's Cabin went into many European translations. Without permission, it was made into a play and filled the house night after night on Broadway.

Queen Victoria and Prince Albert both read it. *Uncle Tom's Cabin* was reviewed by the literary greats: Charles Dickens, George Sand, Heinrich Heine. Presses all over the world worked night and day thumping out either authorized or unauthorized versions. Then the musicians entered the tumult. As the leaves were turning brown, throngs in the music halls were wiping their eyes as they sang F. Howard's *Uncle Tom's Glimpse of Glory*, or Miss Collier's *Eliza's Flight*, and many, many others.

Counter-propaganda also fanned the flames. Soon the

bookstores were displaying such volumes as *Uncle Tom's Cabin As It Is; Proof That Black's White*; and many others.

Harriet was swamped with requests from magazines and book publishers. Soon she began a novel to be titled *The Pearl of Orr's Island*. But this work was interrupted by the storm that was brewing in the South and the attacks on *Uncle Tom's Cabin*. With a new stack of paper nearby, she began *A KEY TO UNCLE TOM'S CABIN*. She explained the purpose of this new volume to the Duchess of Sutherland:

> It is made up of the facts, the documents, the things which my own eyes have looked upon and my hands have handled that attest this awful indictment upon my country. I write it in the anguish of my soul, with tears and prayers, with sleepless nights and weary days. I bear testimony with a heavy heart as one who in court is forced by an awful oath to disclose the sins of those dearest.

In April of 1853, Harriet, along with her husband and brother, Charles, sailed to England. She had been invited by the Anti-Slavery Society of Glasgow to speak throughout Great Britain against slavery. Everywhere she traveled she was lionized.

At Edinburgh she was presented with a thousand gold sovereigns on a silver platter. "This money," said the master of ceremonies, "is to help the cause of the slaves." In London she was invited to the Lord Mayor's dinner. There, she was seated next to Lord Chief Baron Pollock and across from Charles Dickens.

Days later, she was guest of honor at a reception given by the Duke and Duchess of Sutherland at Stafford House. Among the celebrities were numerous lords, William Gladstone, Archbishop Whately, and the famous historian, Lord Macauley. With due ceremony she was presented with a gold-chain bracelet fashioned in the shape of a slave shackle. Engraved upon it was the statement: "We trust it is a memorial chain soon to be broken."

Back in America, the Stowes found another problem. Calvin had been made Professor of Sacred Literature at Andover; but neither of them liked the house to which they had been assigned. After viewing the campus, Harriet had an idea. For years the seminary had supplied work to the young theologues by operating a coffin factory. Now, the former coffin shop was empty. "Let's remodel it into a home," she suggested.

When the trustees objected, she used a little pressure: "We'll supply the money, and accept a note for the cost when the remodeling has been completed." Reluctantly, they agreed. Having money, Harriet learned, was quite agreeable. It enabled one to turn a coffin house into a home!

While Harriet was enjoying her silk dress, traveling and writing, the tensions between the North and South continued to accelerate. There were many reasons. One was *Uncle Tom's Cabin*. It had so shocked the North that it was becoming increasingly difficult to enforce the Fugitive Slave Law. Thousands of slaves for whom masters had paid large sums of money were being aided by abolitionists to escape to freedom in Canada.

In South Carolina the word *secession* had wedged into daily conversation; and the subject of state rights became the heated object of discussion on many a park bench. One radical refused to use *Webster's Dictionary*. He dubbed it "Yankee trash." Many boasted that they preferred to be "statriots" rather than patriots. Union Street in Charleston was renamed State Street. The younger brother of governor-to-be William Henry Gist was christened "State Rights Gist."

But all radicals did not live in the South. One notorious fire-breathing abolitionist named John Brown lived in the North, with his twenty children.

Born in Torrington, Connecticut, he attended school for a time in Litchfield; and, being a Congregationalist, probably sat spellbound as Lyman Beecher thundered on the glories of *New Light* Calvinism. Extremely religious, John Brown was a convinced reformer. When his three-year-old son Jason insisted that his dream was reality, John Brown whipped him until his own eyes swam with tears. Having assumed that he was a prophet, Brown reasoned that he had no other choice.

John Brown Jr. was composed of the same genes as his father. When he refused to toe the line, his father forced him to keep an account book that indicated the amount of punishment due. One week the current balance was grim. It indicated that nineteen lashes were due for the following itemized transgressions:

Disobeying mother........................ 8 lashes
Unfaithfulness at work .... 3 lashes
Telling a lie .... 8 lashes

Prepared to settle his account, Junior stripped to the waist and held his breath. His father applied about one-third of the lashes due. Then he stripped, knelt before his son, handed him the blue-beech switch, and ordered him to apply the balance due to him.

Junior recalled: "I dared not refuse to obey, but at first I did not strike hard. 'Harder!' he said; 'harder, harder!' until he *received the balance of the account*."[3]

This was John Brown's way of illustrating the doctrine of the atonement.

Brown had a burning obsession to free the slaves; and, feeling that he was above the law, he was quite willing to both steal and kill. This obsession had dominated him since, as a boy, he had seen a slave beaten with a fire shovel.

After he was involved in the Osawatomie massacre in eastern Kansas, he was referred to as "Old Brown of Osawatomie." From then on he was a hated man—especially in the South.

A Key to Uncle Tom's Cabin began to be displayed on the bookstore shelves in 1853. Before the book came off the press 58,000 copies were ordered, and within one month after publication, the sales had zoomed to 90,000 copies. In addition, tens of thousands of additional copies were placed in England and across Europe. Harriet had protected her English copyright by filing an application while she was in Canada.

Phillips, Samson & Company now approached Harriet with a request for a new antislavery novel. Since a vague idea had been stirring within her, she was ready. As the plot formed in her subconscious, an event in Washington, D.C., moved her with purpose.

Senator Charles Sumner of Massachusetts had stood in the Senate and flayed South Carolina together with its Senator Butler in a speech titled "Crime Against Kansas." That May while Sumner was bent over his desk writing a letter, Representative Preston Brooks of South Carolina, a relative of Senator Butler, crept up behind him, and beat him over the head with his gutta-percha cane.

Then, while Sumner was bleeding on the floor, Brooks strode defiantly out of the chamber. No one moved a finger to stop him. As Sumner lingered between life and death, both the North and the South hurled invectives at each other. Headline writers kept busy trying to outdo one another. Pa-

---

[3]*To Purge This Land with Blood*, p. 24.

pers in the North claimed that civil war was becoming more and more inevitable. The South gloated over the deed and mailed Brooks dozens of new canes. Puffed by this sudden fame, he boasted, "I wore out my cane completely, but saved the gold head."

The theme for Harriet's new book concerned the dreadful effect slavery had upon the owners of the slaves. While pacing back and forth, she dictated the story as it flamed within. Her usual quota was twenty pages of script per day. The emotional drain became so intense, she said, "It leaves me in as weak and helpless state as when my babies were born."

Her thankful publishers arranged for her to vacation in England. Even though the novel was not quite finished, she boarded the *Niagara* and sailed on July 30, 1856. With calm seas and invigorating breezes ruffling her curls, Harriet continued to work on her manuscript. By the time she reached London, she had wrapped the final pages and mailed them together with a letter. The letter concluded: "I am worn to a rag, but shall now mend rapidly."

The book was titled *Dred*—a sensational title for the period. It was sensational because the minds of the North and the South were concentrated on Dred Scott. His case had started to darken newspapers in 1846. The case was both unusual and dramatic.

Dred Scott had been the slave of army surgeon, Dr. John Emerson of Missouri. Emerson had taken Scott to the *free* state of Illinois, and then to the part of the Wisconsin territory that became the free state of Minnesota. He was then returned to Missouri, a *slave* state. Here, he was sold to John Sanford. On being told that since he had lived in a *free* state he was free, he sued in 1846.

The circuit court in St. Louis County agreed with Scott. But its decision was reversed by the State Supreme Court. Scott appealed. His case was then argued in the Federal courts. Eventually it went to the United States Supreme Court. At this time the Supreme Court had within it seven Democrats and five southerners. The decision, announced by Chief Justice Roger B. Taney of Maryland, was that it had no jurisdiction in the matter, that Scott was still a slave. It then went on to state that the *Missouri Compromise* was unconstitutional. This decision, announced on March 6, 1857, was like an exploding bomb. It shook both the North and the South.

With the name *Dred Scott* constantly appearing in the

headlines, Harriet's *Dred* became a popular book, even though it was not equal to *Uncle Tom's Cabin.*

Upon her return to America with a large royalty check waiting, Harriet was supremely happy. Then on July 9 she received a heart-breaking telegram. Her son Henry, who had been studying at Dartmouth, had drowned in the Connecticut River at Hanover. She immediately left for Hanover. She wondered how she could bear this grief. She was devastated. In this condition, she heard a knock at the door. As she opened the door she saw a poor black woman standing before her. In the same manner in which their washerwoman Candace had comforted her when her mother died, this rather thin and extremely deaf former slave sympathized with her. They wept together. After she had gone, Harriet poured out her grief in a letter to the Duchess of Sutherland:

> While I was visiting in Hanover, where Henry died, a poor deaf old slave woman, who still has five children in bondage, came to comfort me. "Bear up, dear soul," she said; "you must bear it, for the Lord loves ye." She said further, "Sunday is a heavy day to me, 'cause I can't work and can't hear preaching and can't read so I can't keep my mind off my poor children. Some of 'em the blessed Master's got and they's safe; but, oh, there are five that I don't know where they are."
>
> What are mother-sorrows to this! I shall try to search out and redeem these children; though, from the ill success of efforts already made, I fear it will be hopeless.
>
> H. B. Stowe

Harriet sought to calm her grief by starting her third novel, *The Minister's Wooing.* Overwhelmed by travail of spirit, it was hard to concentrate. She tried to relieve her mind by writing to her youngest daughter, Georgiana:

> I am cold, weary, dead; everything is a burden to me.
>
> I let my plants die by inches before my eyes and do not water them. I dread everything I do, and wish it was not to be done and so when I get a letter from my little girl I smile and say, "Dear little puss, I will answer it." But I sit hour after hour with folded hands, looking at the inkstand and dreading to begin. The fact is, pussy, Mama is tired. . . . Henry's fair, sweet face looks down upon me now and then from out of a cloud, and I feel all the bitterness of the eternal "No" that says I must never, never in this life see that face, lean on that arm, hear that voice. . . . Weak, weary as I am, I trust on Jesus in the innermost depths of my soul, and I am quite sure there is coming an inconceivable hour of beauty and glory when I shall regain Jesus, and He will give

me back my beloved one, whom He is educating in a far higher sphere than I proposed. So do not mistake me, only know that Mama is sitting weary by the wayside, feeling weak and worn, but in no sense discouraged.

Your affectionate mother, H.B.S.

Weary and brokenhearted though she was, the events of the day kept her writing. The morning hours of October 16, 1859, seemed normal to almost everyone. But that evening a daring move by one man and about two handfuls of followers placed the North and South on a collison course.

After weeks of preparation, long-bearded, fire-eyed John Brown and his men seized the Federal arsenal at Harpers Ferry, Virginia, and imprisoned several hostages. This determined man from Kansas believed that his move would inspire a general slave uprising throughout the South. But the slaves did not respond. John Brown was easily defeated by United States troops under the command of Colonel Robert E. Lee.

The jury only required forty-five minutes to pronounce him guilty. But sentencing had to await a later session of the court. During this month of waiting, newspapers throughout the world argued the case. Few were neutral. And since Brown was allowed to receive visitors and send out mail, his defiant, often mystical words provided tools for writers to stir the public. To the son of a business friend, he wrote: "Men cannot *imprison*, or *chain*; or *hang the soul*. I go joyfully in behalf of Millions that 'have no rights' that this 'great & glorious'; 'this Christian Republic,' 'is bound to respect.' "[4]

On the day he was to be hanged, he stood in front of the wagon that was to transport him to the gallows and handed a note to one of his attendants:

Charleston, Va, 2nd, December, 1859.

I John Brown am quite *certain* that the crimes of this *guilty, land: will* never be purged away; but with Blood. I had *as I now think: vainly* flattered myself that without *very much* bloodshed; it might be done.[5]

Perched on his coffin, Brown was taken to the special gallows that had been erected. In addition to the 1,500 cavalry and militia, the area was crowded with spectators. Many had come from the deep South. Among the guards was a young actor by the name of John Wilkes Booth.

After the sheriff had sprung the trap by severing the rope

---

[4]*To Purge This Land with Blood*, p. 351. Original punctuation retained.
[5]Ibid.

with his hatchet, there was intense silence. Then Colonel J.T.L. Preston of the Virginia Military Institute lifted his voice: "So perish all such enemies of Virginia! All such enemies of the Union! All such foes of the human race!"

Having been pronounced dead, Brown's corpse was placed in a black walnut coffin and shipped to the North. Unknown to those in Charleston, during the very hour that Brown was being hanged, the city officials in Albany, New York, were firing a one hundred gun salute in honor of the "martyr." In addition, church bells from New England to Kansas began to toll for him. Cleveland, Ohio, marked the event by stretching a banner across the street on which was written in large letters, "I cannot better serve the cause I love than to die for it."

When Brown's coffin reached New York, his corpse was taken out of the "southern" coffin and placed in a "northern" coffin. (His friends did this in spite of the fact that the southern coffin was made of black walnut.)

Soon after the funeral services were conducted at the Brown farm in North Elba, New York, on December 8, a catchy song was revived. Using a lively camp meeting tune, the song had dramatic new meaning:

> John Brown's body lies a-mouldering in the grave,
> His soul goes marching on.

The reaction to the execution was diametrically different to those who lived in slave states. The Savannah *Daily Morning News* trumpeted their thoughts:

> . . . the notorious horse thief, murderer, insurrectionist and traitor expiated his guilt. Would that his might be the fate of the craven-hearted necks in New England and the Northern states today that are deserving of John Brown's hempen tie as well as his own.

Edmund Ruffin made a special trip to gloat at the hanging. He secured a number of pikes, a type of spear, Brown had planned to give the rebelling slaves. The one he carried was labeled: SAMPLE OF THE FAVORS DESIGNED FOR US BY OUR NORTHERN BRETHREN. He sent a pike to each southern governor with the suggestion that it be displayed in a prominent place as a warning of northern intentions.

While war clouds darkened, lightning flashed, and headlines widened, Harriet and Calvin watched the changing political situation with alarm. Not only did they loathe war, but their son Frederick, now a medical student, was of draft age.

As the Republican National Convention was arranging to meet in Chicago in May 1860 to nominate its candidate, the Stowes kept praying that the right man would head the ticket. Both were pleased that all three of the favored candidates were antislavery. Their esteemed friend, Salmon P. Chase of Cincinnati, especially remembered for his part in the Matilda case, was an honest man. Also, he had been twice elected governor of Ohio. They knew him better than the other two and hoped that he would have a chance. But they also were impressed by Senator Seward of New York. He had been so enthusiastic about *Uncle Tom's Cabin* he had declared it "the greatest book of the times."

Neither had had contact with the rail-splitter, Abraham Lincoln of Illinois; but they had read his speeches and were impressed by both his views and ability. Calvin especially liked his remark at Cooper Union: "Let us have faith that right makes might; and in that faith let us to the end dare to do our duty as we understand it." And Harriet often found herself pondering over his statement at the Republican State Convention in Springfield: "I believe this government cannot endure permanently half slave and half free."

As May 16, the date the Republican Convention was scheduled to open, approached, both Harriet and Calvin were deeply concerned. Both prayed that God would have His way.

21

Emancipation Proclamation

While Republican delegates were pushing into Chicago's Wigwam, all of them were rejoicing that the Democrats were hopelessly deadlocked. At their convention in Charleston, South Carolina, they had failed to nominate a candidate. Instead, they had split; and the two separate wings were planning separate conventions in June.

Straw votes indicated that Seward was the overwhelming favorite. Chase was respected, but he lacked the support of the entire Ohio delegation. It seemed the tall man from Illinois didn't have a chance.

On the first ballot Seward received 173½ votes, while Lincoln trailed with a mere 102. Lincoln gained on the second ballot. He now had 181 votes in comparison to Seward's 184½. The third ballot boosted Lincoln to 231½ votes and lowered Seward to 180. Lincoln was two votes short of victory. In the midst of this stalemate, black-haired, heavily pocked David Cartter from Ohio leaped on a chair. "O-ohio," he stammered, "h-h-has s-s-s switched four votes from Chase to Lincoln."

Cartter's announcement turned the hall into pandemonium. Supporters of Lincoln screeched with enthusiasm while some of Seward's wept. When quiet was restored, other delegates switched to Lincoln. Soon the vote was unanimous.

When asked what it cost to nominate him, Judge David Davis replied. "The entire expense of Lincoln's nomination, including headquarters, telegraphing, music, fare of delegations, and other incidentals, was less than $700."[1]

---

[1] *The Prairie Years*, Vol. 2, p. 349.

During the campaign, Lincoln spent most of his time in Springfield, leaving the traveling and speaking to his followers. Even so, his opponents denounced him in colorful terms. They claimed that he could not speak correct English, that he was merely a third-rate country lawyer, that his stories were coarse and clumsy, and that he was a descendant of a gorilla. They also attacked his running mate from Maine, Hannibal Hamlin.

Since four of Hamlin's uncles were named Europe, Asia, America, and Africa, it was claimed that he, Hannibal—an African name!—was a mulatto. To any doubters, it was pointed out that Hamlin had a swarthy face.

But after the votes were counted in November, it was learned that the Lincoln-Hamlin ticket had received 180 electoral votes, while Breckinridge received only 72, Bell 39, and Douglas a scant 12. Still, Lincoln's popular vote was only 1,866,452, while the combined votes of his opponents totaled 2,815,617—949,165 more. It was a stunning majority and indicated that problems lay ahead.

Some problems showed up immediately. On December 20, South Carolina seceded, and by March 4, another six states severed their ties with the Union. More alarming yet, South Carolina voted to raise an army of 10,000 volunteers.

Lincoln made his farewell speech in Springfield on February 11, 1861, and departed for Washington. His route had been arranged so that he could speak to the masses in many eastern cities. But when his train chugged into Harrisburg, it was learned that an assassination plot had been discovered. He was then whisked secretly into Washington.

As Harriet followed the events, she prayed that Lincoln would free the slaves as soon as possible. But when she read his first inaugural speech, she felt a little apprehensive at his statement: "I have no purpose, directly or indirectly, to interfere with the institution of slavery in the states where it exists. I believe that I have no lawful right to do so, and I have no inclination to do so."

While staring at the newspaper, Harriet thought of the deaf, black woman who had comforted her when Henry drowned. That poor woman and five children in "bondage." *What would happen to them?*

The Confederate States had started to organize on February 4 when six of the seceding states had met in Montgomery, Alabama, and elected Jefferson Davis of Mississippi to be the president of the Confederacy. Tensions increased during the following weeks. Then on April 12, General Beauregard fired on Fort Sumter—the Federal stronghold on an island just outside Charleston, South Carolina.

The fort surrendered the next day.

Lincoln responded by calling for 75,000 men to put down the rebellion. This call inspired North Carolina, Virginia, Arkansas, and Tennessee to join the Confederacy, swelling it now to eleven states.

War became inevitable. When Robert E. Lee was asked to take command of the Union forces, he replied, "If I owned the four million slaves of the South, I would sacrifice them all to the Union. But how can I draw my sword against Virginia?" He then donned the gray uniform of the Confederacy and became their commanding general.

The North was confident the rebellion would be crushed within three months—the time it would take to subdue Richmond. But when Union forces were decisively defeated at Bull Run—less than thirty miles west of Washington, it was recognized that the Civil War or the War between the States would be a long and bloody one.

As Harriet was trying to complete two novels at the same time, her son Frederick came to see her. "Mama," he said, "I've decided to volunteer."

"What about your courses in medical school?"

"They can wait. My country needs me. I'm not a coward."

Harriet's eyes brimmed as she watched her undersized son head for an enlistment station. Not fearing danger, he selected Company A of the Massachusetts Volunteer Infantry. The next time she saw him, he was carrying a rifle and wearing a blue uniform. From then on she lingered a little longer on her knees, for she knew that his company was headed for the front lines.

Following Bull Run, Julia Ward Howe left Baltimore by train for Washington. On the way she noticed bands of armed pickets and groups of soldiers sitting around open fires. The District of Columbia by then had become an armed camp.

On November 18, she and her husband were asked to watch a review of some Union troops. While viewing these men in blue, the Confederates attacked. Julia, along with her friends, was forced to flee. Bogged in the mud, they passed the time by singing army songs—especially *John Brown's Body*. That night as she retired in the Willard Hotel with her

little baby, she prayed that the Lord would enable her to write
a useful poem, perhaps one that could be sung to the tune
that was used for *John's Brown's Body.*

Just as dawn was breaking, the words of a new poem
began to "twine" themselves in her mind. "Having thought
out all the stanzas, I said to myself, 'I must write these verses
down, lest I fall asleep again and forget them.' "

Afraid to awaken the baby by turning on a light, she found
the stub of a pen. "I scrawled the verses almost without looking at the paper. . . . Having completed my writing, I returned to bed and fell asleep, saying to myself, 'I like this
better than most things I have written.' "

In the morning, while the sun was streaming through the
window, Julia Ward Howe picked up the scrap of paper she
had used and read:

> Mine eyes have seen the glory of the coming of the Lord:
> He is trampling out the vintage where the grapes of wrath
> are stored;
> He hath loosed the fateful lightning of His terrible swift
> sword;
> His truth is marching on.

Liking the five verses she had written, she mailed them
to the Atlantic Monthly where they were published in February 1862. Julia Ward Howe received $5 for her poem.

Almost immediately after its publication, regiments all
over the North began to sing it to the tune of John Brown's
Body. Eventually, it was named the *Battle Hymn.*[2]

When asked the meaning of the words *grapes of wrath,*
the author replied that she was inspired by Isa. 63:3 where
the prophet wrote: "I have trodden the winepress alone; and
of the people there was none with me: for I will tread them in
mine anger, and trample them in my fury; and their blood
shall be sprinkled upon my garments, and I will stain all my
raiment."

Julia Ward Howe was convinced, as were many others,
that the Lord had inspired her hymn just as He had inspired
Uncle Tom's Cabin.

As the war intensified, both the Union and Confederate
armies increased in size. Neither army was completely sec-
tional. The Union army had volunteers from every Confederate state. Likewise, the Confederate army had volunteers

---

[2]See *Mine Eyes Have Seen the Glory,* A biography of Julia Ward Howe, by
Deborah Pickman Clifford.

from every northern state. Often families were divided, brothers fighting brothers. In fact, Lincoln's wife, Mary lost three brothers who fought for the Confederacy. A former Mississippi senator was a Union agent in Europe; and a man from Massachusetts was a purchasing agent in Europe for the Confederacy.

The fatalities on both sides were staggering. During the second day of the Battle of Antietam (September 17–18, 1862), the Federal Army lost 12,400, while the Confederates had nearly 10,000 killed. By the end of the conflict, nearly 525,000 had been killed in action.

While the war continued and the casualty lists mounted, Harriet became more and more concerned about the ultimate fate of the slaves. This concern was whetted by a letter Lincoln wrote to Horace Greeley on August 22, 1862.

Holding the newspaper that quoted the letter, Harriet said to Calvin, "Listen to this." Her voice tinged with sarcasm, she read:

> "My paramount object in this struggle is to save the Union, and is not either to save or destroy slavery. If I could save the Union without freeing any slave, I would do it; if I could save it by freeing some and leaving others alone, I would also do that. What I do about slavery and the colored race, I do because I believe it helps to save the Union."

When she had finished, she folded the paper and tossed it on the table. Then she asked, "What do you think of that?" Before Calvin could answer, she struck the table with her fist and said, "I'm going to Washington and tell Lincoln a thing or two."

Calvin, amazed, pointed out, "He's a busy man. Do you think you can really get to see him?"

"Of course! Don't you know my old friend Salmon P. Chase is the Secretary of the Treasury? And don't you know that Seward is the Secretary of State? Seward said that *Uncle Tom's Cabin* put Lincoln in the White House! He also said that my book was the greatest book of the time."

"But Hattie! . . ." Lines of dismay deepened in his face.

"Don't worry. I *am* going. And I'm going to take Charley with me."

"But, Hattie, Charles is only twelve! Washington's an armed camp." He bit his lips and massaged his side-whiskers.

"Calvin, I'm barely five feet tall. I'm over fifty and I'm not even equal to a tiny pinch of snuff. But the Lord gave me a vision of Uncle Tom." She dabbed at her eyes. "Yes, Calvin, the Lord gave me a vision of Uncle Tom. I watched as he was beaten to death. The Lord wrote that book, and I cannot forsake the slaves. Isaiah was not afraid, neither is Harriet Beecher Stowe!" She looked in the mirror and made a face at herself. Then she laughed.

Senator Henry Wilson of Massachusetts escorted Harriet and Charles to the White House and introduced them to the President. Lincoln walked over from the fire where he was warming his hands. "So this is the little lady who made this big war," he greeted as her little hand disappeared into his big one. After a few pleasantries he led her to a window-seat.

Sitting there, Lincoln visited with her for nearly an hour. Carefully, he explained that after Lee's defeat at Antietam, he had issued a preliminary proclamation in which he had said that if the Confederates did not lay down their arms and return to the Union by January 1, 1863, he would announce that all their slaves were "forever free."

That statement, he emphasized, was issued on September 22.

As Harriet listened to the man who had grown a beard at the request of a little girl, she realized that she was listening to an extremely loving, thoughtful, and yet troubled person.

"I have to be very careful not to antagonize the border states," explained Lincoln. "As it is, they are divided and their loyalty is not too secure." After he had explained his position, he led the way back to the fire. While warming his palms and the backs of his hands, he commented, "I do love an open fire! I s'pose it's because we always had one to home."

After they had left the White House, Charley turned to his mother. "Ma," he asked, "why does the President say 'to home' instead of 'at home'?"

"He speaks that way because that's the way they spoke in Kentucky where he was born."

Back at home, Harriet was more confident. "I do believe Lincoln will free the slaves," she said. "But I do hope he does it soon. While I was in Washington, a lot of people wanted to shake my hand because of *Uncle Tom's Cabin*. They said that when the slaves *are* freed, I should receive the credit. I don't look at it that way." She stood up and put an arm around Calvin.

"When I was a little girl," she continued, "we had an unusual Fourth of July celebration. As was the custom, Colonel Tallmadge stood up to read the Declaration of Independence. But instead of reading the one written by Jefferson, which was issued on July 4, 1776, he began with the one put out by Jonathan Trumbull on June 18, 1776—"

"So?" interrupted Calvin.

"Well, that's the way I feel about *Uncle Tom's Cabin*. It was merely a *preliminary* document. The *Emancipation Proclamation*, if Lincoln ever signs it, will be *the* important one."

On January 1, 1863, Harriet, together with thousands, crowded Boston's Tremont Temple. This was the day Lincoln had promised to free the slaves. But would he? Harriet took a seat in the balcony.

As the masses waited, Ralph Waldo Emerson read a poem. Then Zerrahn's orchestra played a Beethoven overture. As the time passed, the audience became restless. Each one realized that Lincoln was on a tightrope between two high buildings in the midst of a storm. Pressures pushed from all sides. While tensions became almost unbearable, a chorus sang Mendelssohn's *Hymn of Praise*.

Intermission had just started; and while the masses were getting up, stretching, visiting, a man in formal attire stepped onto the nearly empty platform. Lifting his hands, he demanded quiet. During the hush, he said, "President Lincoln has just signed. The Emancipation Proclamation is now coming over the wire."

The word *signed* was like a flame touching gunpowder. The building exploded with cheers. Many embraced; others tossed their hats in the air, jumped, shouted, waved. When it became known that Harriet was in the building, there was another explosion.

"Mrs. Stowe! Mrs. Stowe! Mrs. Stowe!" they shouted.

Slightly bewildered, Harriet squeezed the balcony rail. In doing so her hat and silk dress twisted awry. When she waved, there was such an ovation the windows shook. Still puzzled, she finally returned to her seat. Then she closed her eyes and thanked God that the slaves were free.

22
Epilogue

After the Emancipation Proclamation was published, the masses in the North celebrated as if the event were the Fourth of July, Thanksgiving, and Christmas all being celebrated at once. Salvos from one hundred guns were heard in Buffalo, Pittsburgh, and Boston.

But when Harriet read the document, she learned, as she had suspected, that the only slaves who were freed were those in areas which were in "rebellion against the United States." The *New York Herald* was candid: "While the Proclamation leaves slavery untouched where his decree can be enforced, he emancipates slaves where his decree cannot be enforced . . ."

Having studied the document several times, Harriet realized that the slaves who were freed would not gain their actual freedom until the war was won; and the slaves in the sections that supported the Federal Government would not be freed until the Constitution could be amended. Nonetheless, there was great rejoicing among the blacks. Some even noted that the actor who portrayed Uncle Tom in the play on Broadway spoke with additional fervor when he said, "Mah body belongs to you, Massa, but mah soul belongs to God!"

Knowing that total freedom was still not a reality, Harriet knew that she had to continue writing. While her thin lines of ink filled page after page, the war continued—as did her personal sorrows. Ten days after she had been cheered in Tremont Temple, her father died at the age of 87. Memories of searching for his hat, awakening him in the morning, and hearing him say, "Then a new flower has blossomed in the

212

kingdom today," stirred within her. His last words were: "I am left alone . . . alone . . ."

The war did not abate, but increased in violence. Tens of thousands were killed. At Chancellorsville (May 2–4) the Federals lost 17,300; the Confederates 12,460. On July 1 Meade's Army of 100,000 clashed with Lee's Army of 70,000 at a little shoe-manufacturing town in Pennsylvania, now remembered as Gettysburg. The slaughter continued for three days. Every minute shrapnel and minnie balls exacted their toll. The violence climaxed when long-haired General George Pickett led 15,000 Confederates up the valley to Cemetery Ridge.

The Federals waited until the Confederates were close; then they attacked in full force. Even so, Pickett's determined men broke through the Federal lines. Bayonet met bayonet, and for twenty minutes both sides engaged each other in a bloody hand-to-hand battle. Overwhelmed, the Confederates began their retreat. Lee had been defeated, but Meade did not follow him.

On the following day, July 4, the great Confederate stronghold in Vicksburg, Mississippi, fell to the Federals, led by U.S. Grant. The war had peaked, and the Confederates were facing defeat.

A week after Lee's defeat, Calvin Stowe received a letter in the post office with a Gettysburg cancellation stamp. Alarmed because the address was not in their son's handwriting, his knees suddenly weakened. Early reports indicated that Lee had lost 26,451 and Meade 23,003. He knew Fred had been fighting under Meade. The letter said:

Dear Madam,

Among the thousands of wounded and dying men on this war-scarred field, I have just met with your son, Captain Stowe. . . . He was struck by a fragment of a shell, which entered his right ear. He is quiet and cheerful.

Yours with sincere sympathy,
J. M. Crowell

Harriet and Calvin wrote to and visited Fred. When his ear refused to heal, he requested his mother to try to get him out of the army. She wrote to Stanton who arranged his discharge. Unfortunately, as he fought for health, someone gave him a drink. He became addicted.

When Lee stopped the Federals at Cold Harbor, Grant shifted to Petersburg, Virginia—the key to Richmond. His siege of this rail terminal started in June 1864 and continued for months. The city fell the following year when Lee ordered a retreat on April 2, 1865. Seven days later, Grant and Lee met at Appomattox Court House.

The War Between the States was over.

But although the hostilities had stopped, the slaves in the areas that had sided with the Union were still slaves. Still, their freedom was on the way. In his Annual Message of December 1862, Lincoln had proposed a Constitutional amendment that would compensate all slaveholders for their slaves to be paid in United States bonds. Two year later at the Republican Convention of 1864, which nominated Lincoln for a second term, a plank in their platform was that such an amendment be considered. When Lincoln spoke to Congress that year, he made a strong plea for such legislation.

Alas, President Lincoln was shot by John Wilkes Booth on April 14, and died the next day. But Andrew Johnson, the new president, had not forgotten. The Thirteenth Amendment was proposed on February 1, 1865, and duly proclaimed on December 18 of that same year. It stated:

> Neither slavery nor involuntary servitude, except as a punishment for crime whereof the party shall have been duly convicted, shall exist within the United States, or any place subject to their jurisdiction.

Harriet's vision had finally been fulfilled! *Uncle Tom's Cabin* had exerted its influence. American slavery had come to an end. All the slaves were free, including the children of the deaf woman who had sympathized with her when Henry was drowned.

Yes, insignificant though she was, Harriet had been used by the mighty hand of the Lord!

With all of her books selling well and orders for articles coming in, Harriet remembered some of her dreams from the past—and began to fulfill them. As a girl, while visiting with Georgiana, she had noticed a magnificent grove of trees in Hartford. Since both of them had agreed that when they were famous they would build homes in the grove, Harriet had said, "And my house will be a large one. It will be surrounded by flowers and trees. It will have a garden and gables. There will be an enormous parlor where I can entertain famous authors and editors. There will be paintings on the walls. The shelves will be packed with the latest books. All the servants will wear bright uniforms . . ."

With success smiling, Harriet moved into just such a house. In addition, she had a winter home in Florida with orange groves. Their lives began to blossom in other areas. With a little nagging, Harriet persuaded Calvin to write his long-planned masterpiece—*The Origin and History of the Books of the Bible.* It was hard to coax him away from the table. She never gave up though, and eventually the book was published. It became a minor classic and earned them ten thousand dollars, not to mention the satisfaction of seeing a project to its completion.

Calvin continued to gain weight. In time he became so fat he could barely walk, and when seen by some neighborhood children, they reported that "Santa Claus had escaped."

In the spring of 1885, Harriet wrote to her old friend, Dr. Oliver Wendell Holmes, "My dear husband is slowly and gradually sinking under Bright's disease. . . . He is longing to depart to a higher rest; or, as you said, to have inscribed on his grave 'Not Finis, but End of Vol. 1.' "

On August 6, 1886, after murmuring "Peace with God! Peace with God!" he passed away. He was buried in the Andover Chapel cemetery next to his son Henry.

Though the loss of Calvin was severe, Harriet continued on. She kept hoping that Frederick would eventually show up. Her mind began to slip. Sometimes she was certain that Frederick would return the next day, and she would prepare the house with fresh flowers for his welcome. But Frederick had disappeared and no one ever learned his fate.

A glimpse of Harriet at this time has come to us from the temperance leader, Francis Willard, who had arranged an interview: "The bell was promptly answered by a plump colored maid who evinced uncertainty as to the whereabouts of her mistress. A voice from upstairs called out, 'I am home—I *am* home,' and we were shown into a pleasant study with bookcases, easy chairs, writing table, and many photographs, the largest being of Henry Ward Beecher, evidently taken just before his last illness, his hair snow white.

"A little woman entered, seventy-five years old, decidedly undersized, and weighing less than a hundred pounds. She was very simply attired in a dress of black and white check, with linen collar and small broach; her hair which had once been brown hung fluffily upon a broad brow and was bound by a black ribbon. This is what time has left of the immortal Harriet Beecher Stowe."

Though Harriet was forgotten, *Uncle Tom's Cabin* was still in demand. During the last half of 1887, its American sales alone were 12,225 copies, even though it was then thirty-five years old. Harriet's mind dwelt in the past. Her collection of nearly all its thirty-seven translations kept reminding her of the long, long ago.

The next year, her daughter Georgiana May, who had married George Allen and had become a victim of morphine as the result of an illness, passed away. As Harriet mourned her loss, she remembered how she had often paced the floor with Georgiana when she was an infant.

Harriet's memories continued to fade. By 1896, she found it increasingly difficult to remember anyone. On July 1 of that year, while the nurse was sitting by her bed, she struggled to open her eyes. At about midnight she managed to say, "I love you." Then she was gone. She was eighty-five.

Standing at the grave on Friday, July 3, were her three surviving children: the unmarried twins, Harriet and Eliza; and her son, the Reverend Charles E. Stowe. After the people sang *Nearer My God to Thee*, the Episcopal service was read. The casket was then lowered into the grave that had been prepared between her son Henry and her husband.

Of the many wreaths, one of the most beautiful had been sent by the blacks in Boston. Attached to it was a card bearing the inscription:

THE CHILDREN OF
UNCLE TOM

Appendix

LYMAN BEECHER'S CHILDREN

By Roxana Foote

BIRTH		OCCUPATION	DEATH
Catherine	1800	Educator	1878
William H.	1802	Minister	1889
Edward	1803	Minister	1895
Mary F.	1805	Housewife	1900
Harriet	1808		1808
George	1809	Minister	1843
Harriet E.	1811	Writer	1896
Henry Ward	1813	Minister	1887
Charles	1815	Minister	1900

By Harriet Porter

Frederick	1818		1820
Isabella	1822	Suffragist	1907
Thomas K.	1824	Minister	1900
James C.	1828	Minister	1886

Chronology

1775		Birth of Lyman Beecher and Roxana Foote.
1776	July 4	Declaration of Independence.
1799		Lyman Beecher married Roxana Foote.
1800		Birth of Catherine Beecher.
1802		Birth of William H. Beecher.
1803		Birth of Edward Beecher.
1805		Birth of Mary F. Beecher.
1808		Birth and death of the first Harriet Beecher.
1809		Birth of George Beecher.
1811	June 14	Birth of Harriet Elizabeth Beecher.
1813		Birth of Henry Ward Beecher.
1815		Birth of Charles Beecher.
1816		Death of Roxana Foote Beecher.
1817		Lyman Beecher married Harriet Porter.
1818		Birth of Frederick Beecher.
1822		Birth of Isabella H. Beecher.
1824		Harriet wrote "Can the Immortality of the Soul Be Proved by the Light of Nature." Went to school at Hartford and taught in the same school.
1824		Birth of Thomas K. Beecher.
1825		Harriet attempted to write a play in verse.
1826		Lyman Beecher accepted the Hanover Street Church in Boston.
1828		Birth of James C. Beecher.
1832		Lyman Beecher elected president of Lane Seminary in Cincinnati, Ohio—and moved there.
1833		Harriet published her first writings in *Western Monthly Magazine*.

1835		Death of Harriet Porter Beecher.
1836	Jan. 6	Harriet married Calvin Stowe.
	Sep. 22	Harriet gave birth to Eliza and Harriet Stowe.
1838		Birth of Henry Ellis Stowe.
1840	May	Birth of Frederick William Stowe.
1843	Aug.	Birth of Georgiana May Stowe.
1848	Jan.	Birth of Samuel Charles Stowe.
1849		Samuel Charles died in cholera epidemic.
1850		Calvin received appointment to Bowdoin in Brunswick, Maine. Harriet preceded him to Burnswick, arriving on May 22, 1850. Charles Edward, her last child, was born on July 8.
1851	June 5	First installment of *Uncle Tom's Cabin* published in the *National Era*.
1852		*Uncle Tom's Cabin* was published in book form. Calvin received appointment to Andover Theological Seminary. The family moved to Andover, Massachusetts, the same year.
1853		Harriet was lionized in Europe.
1856		*Dred*, Harriet's second novel, was published.
1857	July	Henry Ellis, Harriet's first son, was drowned.
1859		Publication in book form of Harriet's third novel—*The Minister's Wooing*.
1862		Book publication of *The Pearl of Orr's Island*.
1863	Jan. 1	Emancipation Proclamation.
	Jan. 10	Death of Lyman Beecher.
	July 1–3	Battle of Gettysburg. Frederick wounded.
1864		Calvin retired. With Harriet, he moved to Hartford.
1865	April 9	Lee surrendered at Appomattox Court House.
	April 15	Lincoln assassinated by John Wilkes Booth.
	Dec. 18	13th Amendment which abolished slavery went into effect.
1886	Aug. 6	Death of Calvin Stowe.
1896	July 1	Death of Harriet Beecher Stowe.

Bibliography

Adams, John R. *Harriet Beecher Stowe.* Twayne Publishers, 1963.

Beecher, Charles, (ed.). *Autobiography of Lyman Beecher.* Harper and Brothers, 1865. 2 Vol.

Bishop, Jim. *The Day Lincoln was Shot.* Harper and Brothers, 1955.

Bradford, Gamaliel. *Union Portraits.* Books for Libraries Press, 1968.

Caskey, Marie. *Chariot of Fire.* Yale University Press, 1978.

Chamberland, Samuel. *Six New English Villages.* Hastings House (undated).

Chambrun, de Clara Longsworth. *Cincinnati, Story of the Queen City.* Charles Scribner's Sons, 1939.

Charnwood, Lord. *Abraham Lincoln.* Henry Holt, 1917.

Chase, Salmon P. *Diary and Correspondence of Salmon P. Chase, Vol. 2.* De Capo Press, 1971.

Clark, Clifford E. Jr. *Henry Ward Beecher.* University of Illinois Press, 1941.

Clifford, Deborah Pickman. *Mine Eyes Have Seen the Glory.* Little Brown and Co. 1978, 1979.

Cochran, Hamilton. *Noted American Duels and Hostile Encounters.* Cilton Books, 1963.

Coffin, Levi. *Reminiscenses of Levi Coffin.* Arno Press, 1968.

Committee on Historical Publications. *Connecticut Tercentenary Commission.* Yale University Press, 1933.

Dixon, Archibald. *The History of the Missouri Compro-*

mise. The Robert Clarke Co., 1898.

Donald, David. *Charles Sumner and the Rights of Men*. Knopf, 1970.

Edgcumbe, Richard. *Byron, the Last Phase*. Charles Scribner's Sons, 1919.

Fast, Howard. *The Crossing*. Morrow, 1971.

Fields, Annie. *Life and Letters of Harriet Beecher Stowe*. Houghton Mifflin, 1897.

Forbes, Esther. *Paul Revere & The World He Lived In*. Houghton Mifflin, 1942.

Gossett, Thomas F. *Uncle Tom's Cabin and American Culture*. Southern Methodist University Press, 1985.

Grant, Bruce. *Issac Hull, Captain of Old Ironsides*. Pellegrini and Cudahy, 1947.

Hensen, Josiah. *Father Hensen's Story*. John P. Jewett and Co., 1858.

Holbrook, Stewart H. *Ethan Allan*. Binford & Mort, 1940.

Holmes, Oliver Wendell. *Poetical Works*. Houghton Mifflin, 1975.

Hunt, H. Draper. *Hannibal Hamlin of Main*. Syracuse University Press, 1968.

Hyman, Harold M. (ed.) *The Fugitive Slave and Anthony Burns, A Problem of Law Enforcement*. Lippincott, 1975.

Jennings, John. *Boston, Cradle of Liberty, 1630–1776*. Doubleday, 1947.

Johnston, Johanna. *Runaway to Heaven*. Doubleday, 1963.

Kirkham, E. Bruce. *The Building of Uncle Tom's Cabin*. University of Tennessee Press, 1977.

Lomask, Milton. *Aaron Burr*. Farr Strauss Giroux, 1982.

Ludwig, Charles. *Levi Coffin and the Underground Railroad*. Herald Press, 1975.

Ludwig, Charles. *He Freed Britain's Slaves*. Herald Press, 1977.

Mansfield, E. D. *Mansfield's Personal Memories*. Robert Clarke, 1879.

McDowell, Bart. *The Revolutionary War*. National Geographic Society, 1967.

Myers, William Starr. *The Battle of Monmouth*. Kennitkat Press, 1927.

Nolan, Jeannette Covert. *The Shot Heard Round the World*. Messner, 1967.

Oates, Stephen B. *The Fires of Jubilee, Nat Turner's Fierce Rebellion*. Harper and Row, 1975.

Oates, Stephen B. *To Purge This Land with Blood*. University of Massachusetts Press, 1984.

Pillsbury, Parker. *Acts of Anti-Slavery Apostles*. Arno Press, 1969.

Purcell, Richard. *Connecticut in Transition*. University of Massachusetts Press, 1984.

Ross, Marjorie Drake Ross. *The Book of Boston, The Colonial Period*. Hastings House, 1960.

Rugoff, Milton. *The Beechers*. Harper and Row, 1981.

Saussine, Renée de. *Paganini*. Hutchinson & Co., 1953.

Sandburg, Carl. *Abraham Lincoln: The Prairie Years and the War Years*, 6 Vol. Harcourt Brace, 1926, 1939.

Schuckers, J. W. *The Life and Public Service of Salmon P. Chase*. D. Appleton, 1874.

Silverman, Kenneth. *The Life and Times of Cotton Mather*. Harper and Row, 1984.

Sklar, Catherine Kish. *Catherine Beecher, a Study in American Domesticity*. Yale University Press, 1973.

Smola, Hedwig, (ed.) *Tales From the Arabian Knights*. Duel Sloan and Duel, Sloan and Pearce.

Stevens, William Oliver. *Pistols at Ten Paces*. Houghton Mifflin, 1940.

Stowe, Charles Edward. *Harriet Beecher Stowe*. Houghton Mifflin, 1889.

Stowe, Harriet Beecher. *The May-Flower*. Harper, 1843.

Stowe, Harriet Beecher. *Uncle Tom's Cabin*. John P. Jewett, 1852.

Stowe, Harriet Beecher. *Dred*. Charles R. Osgood, 1856.

Stowe, Harriet Beecher. *A Key to Uncle Tom's Cabin*. John P. Jewett, 1854.

Stowe, Harriet Beecher. *The Minister's Wooing*. Derby & Jackson, 1859.

Stowe, Lyman Beecher. *Saints, Sinners and Beechers*. Bobbs-Merrill, 1934.

Swanberg, W. A. *The Story of Fort Sumter*. Charles Scribner's Sons, 1957.

Stryker, William. *Battles of Trenton and Princeton*. Houghton Mifflin, 1898.

Thomas, Benjamin P. *Theodore Weld, Crusader of Freedom*. Rutgers, University Press, 1950.

Thomas, John L. *The Liberator*. Little Brown, 1963.

Tilton, Eleanor M. *Amiable Autocrat*. Henry Schuman. 1947.

Todd, Charles Burr. *In Olde Connecticut.* Grafton Press, 1906.

Wagenknecht, Edward. *Harriet Beecher Stowe.* Oxford University Press, 1965.

Wilson, Forrest. *Crusader in Crinoline.* J. B. Lippincott, 1941.

Wilson, Francis. *John Wilkes Booth.* Houghton Mifflin, 1929.

CHRISTIAN HERALD
People Making A Difference

Christian Herald is a family of dedicated, Christ-centered ministries that reaches out to deprived children in need, and to homeless men who are lost in alcoholism and drug addiction. Christian Herald also offers the finest in family and evangelical literature through its book clubs and publishes a popular, dynamic magazine for today's Christians.

Our Ministries

Family Bookshelf and **Christian Bookshelf** provide a wide selection of inspirational reading and Christian literature written by best-selling authors. All books are recommended by an Advisory Board of distinguished writers and editors.

Christian Herald magazine is contemporary, a dynamic publication that addresses the vital concerns of today's Christian. Each monthly issue contains a sharing of true personal stories written by people who have found in Christ the strength to make a difference in the world around them.

Christian Herald Children. The door of God's grace opens wide to give impoverished youngsters a breath of fresh air, away from the evils of the streets. Every summer, hundreds of youngsters are welcomed at the Christian Herald Mont Lawn Camp located in the Poconos at Bushkill, Pennsylvania. Year-round assistance is also provided, including teen programs, tutoring in reading and writing, family counseling, career guidance and college scholarship programs.

The Bowery Mission. Located in New York City, the Bowery Mission offers hope and Gospel strength to the downtrodden and homeless. Here, the men of Skid Row are fed, clothed, ministered to. Many voluntarily enter a 6-month discipleship program of spiritual guidance, nutrition therapy and Bible study.

Our Father's House. Located in rural Pennsylvania, Our Father's House is a discipleship and job training center. Alcoholics and drug addicts are given an opportunity to recover, away from the temptations of city streets.

Christian Herald ministries, founded in 1878, are supported by the voluntary contributions of individuals and by legacies and bequests. Contributions are tax deductible. Checks should be made out to Christian Herald Children, The Bowery Mission, or to Christian Herald Association.

Administrative Office: 40 Overlook Drive, Chappaqua, New York 10514
Telephone: (914) 769-9000

 Fully accredited Member
of the Evangelical Council
for Financial Accountability